PLEASURE AND PAIN
MY LIFE

PLEASURE
AND PAIN
MY LIFE

CHRISSY AMPHLETT WITH LARRY WRITER

hachette
AUSTRALIA

hachette
AUSTRALIA

First published in Australia and New Zealand in 2005
by Hodder Australia
(An imprint of Hachette Australia Pty Limited)
Level 17, 207 Kent Street, Sydney NSW 2000
www.hachette.com.au

Second edition published by Hachette Australia in 2007

This updated edition published in 2009

Copyright © Chrissy Amphlett 2005, 2009

National Library of Australia
Cataloguing-in-Publication data:

Amphlett, Chrissy.
Pleasure and pain / Chrissy Amphlett, Larry Writer.

978 0 7336 2474 2 (pbk.)

Amphlett, Chrissy.
Divinyls (Musical group)
Rock musicians--Australia--Biography.
Women rock musicians--Australia--Biography.
Multiple sclerosis--Australia--Patients--Biography.

Other Authors/Contributors:
Writer, Larry.

782.42166092

Cover design by Nada Backovic Design
Main cover image by Sandrine Lee
Other cover images by Tony Mott
Digital production by Bookhouse, Sydney
Printed and bound in Australia by McPherson's Printing Group

For my mother, Mary,
for her unconditional love and support

CONTENTS

A BRAT FROM BELMONT

Gathering memories for this book, long-forgotten events, sights and sounds came vividly rushing back to my mind. Some have caused me deep pain, others abiding sadness, and a few anger. We'll get to those. Yet many recollections have made me smile. Like that of the clatter of my pusher as Mum wheeled two-year-old me along the gum tree and paling-fence-lined paths and nature strips of Belmont, the Victorian suburb where I grew up, and how my cheeks and mouth would vibrate as we bounced and jerked. I'd like to say I hummed along to the beat of the pusher's wheels on the gravelly pathways, but, as you'll see, I'm about honesty, and the noises I made were more likely the gurgles, mumbles and yelps most babies make.

Before Belmont, we lived at Barwon Heads, but all I can recall of that place is heavy rains flooding us out, and soon after my family—me, my big sister Leigh, my mother Mary and my father Jim—moved into the weatherboard bungalow in Eton Road, Belmont, that became my childhood stage.

Belmont is near Geelong, an industrial working-class city. There is a Shell oil refinery there, shopping malls, lots of crime, and many of its citizens are obsessive about cars and Australian Rules football. It has some remarkable Victorian architecture and big and gorgeous trees, but, to me, its saving grace is that, like many an industrial city with a bit of an inferiority complex, such as Newcastle in New South Wales, Manchester and Chicago, it has a strong cultural tradition. The performing arts have long flourished in Geelong, never allowing the cheers of rabid football fans or the squeal of souped-up shaggin' wagons doing wheelies in the main street to drown them out.

Mum came from a well-to-do Hawthorn family, and attended Church of England Girls' Grammar. The only girl in the family, she was spoiled rotten by Nanna and Poppa Banbrook and her brothers. Nanna's grandmother was a countess who fled the Prussian War, married the captain of the boat that took her to safety, one Captain Bolton, and finally ended up in Victoria. So I have a skerrick of royal blood somewhere in my DNA. Poppa was a postmaster in Melbourne, and when he was transferred to Geelong, the family made the short move there.

Today, music is as vital to my existence as oxygen, and, looking back, it's always been in my life. Nanna and Poppa held singalongs around the piano at their home. Mum herself was an enthusiastic comedian, pianist and performer and a pillar of the Geelong Musical Comedy Company. What choice did the daughter of such a trouper have? I was scarcely out of nappies when I was singing and dancing for family and friends.

My great-uncle was Ernest Sage, opera star and renowned singer of choral hymns, a grand and imposing gentleman who had a way of sitting with his arm raised and finger imperiously crooked. He sang when I was christened at the beautiful Baptist church with its big white columns in Collins Street, Melbourne. Photos of the great event portray me as the centre of attention, flanked by Ernest, my parents, grandparents and their families. Seems it was quite the occasion. The name on my birth certificate is Christine, which became 'Christina' when Mum and Dad were cross with me. Usually, though, people called me 'Chrissy'.

When I was very young, Great-uncle Ernest would take me with him on his trips through rural Victoria when he judged eisteddfods. Sometimes I'd recite in the drama division, other times perform song and dance, but I'd never sing for Ernest because he had no tolerance for untrained vibratos or any singing but opera and hymns. We'd stay in country pubs, which I'm sure gave me a feel for being on the road that came in very handy in my rock'n'roll life.

We were staying at a big bush pub in Ballarat when I peeked through the door of Ernest's bedroom and saw him fastening his toupee to his head with sticky tape. The wig was dark with streaks of grey and resembled a small, furry animal. First chance I got, I stole it.

My father's family, the Amphletts, was much more down to earth, a left-wing, beer-and-potatoes bunch. Dad's mother, Wilhemina, was a German immigrant and his father, Robert, a Melbourne chef who specialised in French cuisine. Dad didn't get on with his mum, but he loved his father. His one sister, Rose, and a brother, Wally, are still alive. Two of his brothers, Bill and Joe, like Dad, have now passed on.

Dad's brother Joe, a colourful knockabout who reminded me of Edward G Robinson, moved to Sydney, married and had a daughter, Patricia, and a son, Little Joe. Patricia grew up to be pop star Little Pattie, who had a number of hits in the early 1960s, including 'He's My Blond-Headed Stompie Wompie Real Gone Surfer Boy' and 'Stompin' At Maroubra'. Tricia Amphlett is a friend and inspiration to me to this day.

Dad went into the army in 1941, when World War II was in full swing. He was only just seventeen, and lied about his age to get posted overseas. He left Australia with all the brave optimism of his fellow diggers, but returned a damaged man, having spent the entire war as a captive of the Germans. His first posting was to Greece, where he fought in the Battle of Crete only to be taken prisoner almost immediately and interred in a POW camp. As the son of a German, he spoke the language, so it was his job to negotiate with his captors for better food and conditions on behalf of the other prisoners. He was savagely beaten for his trouble.

Dad escaped three times. The first two he was recaptured, but his third attempt was successful. Amazingly, considering his ordeal in that brutal camp and his long and dangerous flight across war-torn Europe, he arrived in London fit and healthy. To celebrate his good fortune, he got drunk, fell, and broke his leg.

Dad and Mum met on his return to Melbourne after the war. As manager of a company called Business Equipment, Dad travelled around Victoria selling Royal typewriters and called on Mum when she was working in her father's post office in Geelong. She was beguiled. They fell in love and married in 1949. Dad by then had reinvented himself, smoothing out his rough edges. He had taken elocution lessons, learned to dance like Fred Astaire, was charming, suave and a snappy dresser. But behind his breezy and dapper façade, he was a troubled soul. Mum said that they first argued on their wedding night, and never really stopped. When she told her parents of her fears about spending the rest of her life with him, they said, as people did in those days, 'Mary, you've married him. You have to stay with him.' There were good times in the years that followed, and a lot of love and laughter, but Mum and Dad's marriage could never be mistaken for one made in heaven.

My father's wartime experiences left deep emotional scars. It would have been a miracle if they had not. Every Friday night, virtually for the rest of his life, Dad would meet up with his old army mates at the local RSL and they'd talk about the war and drink. Dad loved beer. VB. Melbourne Bitter. So long as it was *Victorian* beer. At the end of the night he'd come home and cry. Sometimes, too, he'd get angry, other times he'd drift off to sleep as he played his favourite musical comedies, *The Merry Widow*, anything by Puccini or Verdi, on the radiogram.

Today, we are more enlightened about rehabilitating returned servicemen. In Dad's day, men who were little more than kids who'd seen and done the most horrendous things in war were simply set adrift into society when the fighting stopped. Many, like my father, were deeply traumatised, and he used alcohol to heal his emotional wounds and calm his shattered nerves. At least Dad survived.

Dad tuned in each week to *The Perry Como Show* on TV. Como was a smooth American crooner who wore a cardigan and sang 'Catch A Falling Star'. And Dean Martin was a real favourite. Dad identified with his boozy swaggering. Dean was funny, suave, and he was cool, everything Dad aspired to be. Frank Sinatra didn't get a look-in. My father would sit on the lounge, a bit tipsy, and conduct as the music of Dean, Perry and the Black and White Minstrels blared. Other times he nodded off to the sound of politicians berating each other on the ABC parliamentary broadcasts. 'Point of *order*, Mr Speaker!'

We always had lots of pets. Dogs, cats, mice, tortoises, guinea pigs, possums, bantams. Dad, being of German stock, was especially fond of dachshunds and he had a little army of them named Fritz, Otto, Heinz... Otto was a bit savage and once bit me on the head, but that was all right. I loved animals, too, and do to this day. Throughout everything that's happened in my life, my dogs and cats, axolotls and horses have always been true, and better friends than many humans.

Leigh and I were brought up by Mum to be well mannered and unfailingly polite. Our table manners had to be perfect. Of course, I rebelled by mucking up at the table and crunching my carrots and apples noisily. I escaped all that domestic decorum at the beach. I'd run up and down the sand screaming to get rid of all my pent-up energy. Then there was the day I tried to poison my grandfather by putting fly spray in his tea. He didn't speak to me for weeks. I can't remember why I did it, or even if I realised what I was doing.

I attended Sunday school with Leigh when we were little, then once I was older I went to church with Mum, who, after her mother died, would bawl through the service, overwhelmed by the hymns and the ceremony because they reminded her of the funeral. We tried different churches—first Church of England and then Church of Christ... Mum gave me money to put in the collection plate, and I always took two shillings change and bought lollies.

When I was three and Leigh was seven, Mum took us shopping at Myer in Geelong for hats to wear to Sunday school. A woman named June Saunders asked Mum if Leigh and I could model in her fashion parades at the store. Mum gave her blessing. She had compered many charity mannequin parades in aid of the local orphanage and other worthy causes and thought we'd find it fun. My recollection of flouncing around on the catwalk in toddlers' dresses is pretty scanty, but I was a modest little thing and I do remember being embarrassed in the dressing-room when I had to take my clothes off and change into my outfits in front of the other models. I forgive anyone who saw me in the notorious nude musical *Let My People Come* years later for being a little surprised to hear that.

Mary Amphlett

Chrissy was a dear little girl, but very active. Leigh, when she was a baby, she was so good. Perfect. Put her down and that would be it. Shut the door, she'd sleep all night. But not Chrissy. She was a night owl. And she's still a night owl. Yet she had her quiet moments when she'd go away from everybody down to her bedroom or sit alone on the beach and write little stories and poems.

Chrissy was interested in everything. And loved music right from the word go. She was up on her feet when she was two, and she had a dear little voice and lived to dance. She was always dancing. My mother was musical and Dad had a gorgeous baritone voice. When Chrissy was around six, she, Leigh, Jim and I would have lovely evenings when we stayed with my parents at the beach during school holidays. Chrissy used to sing in her way and my mother said to me, 'You'll have to have this child taught singing and dancing.' I said, 'Mum, I couldn't stand it! I don't want her to be like Shirley Temple! That's not us!' My mother protested, 'No, you *must* have her taught. She has a talent.' In my heart I knew Chrissy had potential, so I enrolled her to learn classical ballet. And that's how it all started.

By age seven, I was learning ballet. My first teacher was Kath Gill, a woman in her seventies who, coincidentally, was the mother of June

Saunders from Myer. Kath saw something in me and drove me to work hard at this most graceful, but gruelling, art. She'd stand there in her Geelong studio grasping her cane and making eyes at me that signalled approval or admonition. When Kath died, I found a new teacher in Miss Hannah, who taught me to dance *en pointe*, or on the point of your toes. That was excruciating, the contorted feet, the blisters, the tight binding, but it was deeply gratifying when I finally mastered it. Today my feet are misshapen by ballet.

In seven years I never missed a ballet class, not even when Dad tried to punish me by locking me in my bedroom. I simply climbed out of the window, clutching my bag with pumps and tutu inside, and caught the bus into Geelong, never for a moment considering the inevitable and painful consequences of my defiance.

My ballet teachers were also involved in Geelong's Musical Comedy Company, where Mum was a stalwart, and they encouraged me to learn song and dance. It was here that I was taught how to put on a show. I soon found that people got a kick out of my rendition of 'When The Red Red Robin Comes Bob Bob Bobbin' Along', and I appeared in productions of the great popular musicals of the day, such as *The Sound Of Music, Song Of Norway, Oklahoma!* and *Annie Get Your Gun.* Great-uncle Ernest did not approve.

Mary Amphlett

The Geelong Musical Comedy Company needed kids for their productions and always asked if Chrissy could take part. The producers knew she had something special. They were only small parts, but . . . I'm biased . . . with her blonde hair and big brown eyes, you couldn't take your eyes off her when she was on stage.

At an end-of-year concert when she was six, she recited from AA Milne wearing a little halo and she was so beautiful, and people were crying.

Chrissy made her debut at the old Plaza Theatre in Geelong, where the Geelong Musical Comedy Company put on our productions. It used to be called the Flea Pit, and was falling apart. Bits of the ceiling would come loose and land on the stage. It was a darling old theatre. The technicians and other backstage helpers who handled the audio and the lights and all the props had *noooo* experience whatsoever, but they gave up their evenings and weekends to help us stage our shows, and everything was on an amateur basis. Today it's the Geelong Performing Arts Centre.

The Company usually staged two productions a year and because comedy was my forte I was inevitably cast in a funny role. I've always loved theatre—seeing Chrissy in *Blood Brothers* and *The Boy From Oz* were two of the proudest moments in my life—and film. I adore *Casablanca* and anything starring Katharine Hepburn or Joan Crawford.

At about age ten I came under the wing of Mary Walker, a great friend of my mother's from the Musical Comedy Company, who, every Tuesday at 5 p.m., taught me speech and drama, which included elocution and voice projection, recitation, good manners and how to move on stage. Speaking well had its advantages when I performed, but as I grew into a teenager in ferociously working-class Geelong my well-rounded vowels saw me picked on for 'talkin' posh'.

Mary Walker

From the very first, Chrissy was a little pro and a perfectionist. She was determined and had a belief in what she could do. In our lessons, she'd work hard to overcome whatever was tripping her up. 'Let's do it again, let's do it again till we get it right,' she'd say, and she'd repeat it over and over until she had it perfect.

Chrissy was doing an exam and she had to recite a piece with the word 'chrysanthemum' in it. About 10 minutes before the exam she came up to me terribly upset and wailed, 'I can't say chrysan . . . chrysan . . .' and I said very calmly, 'Chrissy, yes you *can*—chrys-an-the-mum. You *can* do it. Now stop worrying.' Sure enough, she went into the exam, said 'chrysanthemum' without any worries and came out saying it over and over at the top of her voice.

On stage, Chrissy had no ego. She was completely unselfconscious. That's rare. Most children are naturally shy and self-effacing and getting up on stage is an ordeal. It never was for Chrissy. She performed as naturally as other kids might shoot a shanghai.

What *did* delight me was when *The Boy From Oz* came to Melbourne in 1999 and Chrissy, playing Judy Garland, received a thunderous ovation. I saw that she had never forgotten what I'd taught her as a child about posture and commanding the stage and that, quite literally, thrilled me to tears. And I was proud because she told me that [up to that point] she had never had another acting teacher.

It wasn't that I thought I was an especially talented kid. I was a realist even then and knew that while I could entertain an audience, if I was ever to be a great performer I would have to work damned hard at it. That suited me, too, for there was nothing else I wanted to do.

When I was ten, Miss Hannah, who did a lot for charity, took me and a group of other pre-teen entertainers to Geelong Gaol to perform for the prisoners. The Aboriginal artist Albert Namatjira had been locked up there in the late 1950s and I saw his drawings on the wall. There I was, a sweet little girl with braids vamping up 'Big Spender' for the delectation of a hundred hardened criminals who were *freaking out* at the sight, whistling and yelling what they'd do to us if only they could. I wasn't fazed, but a woman sitting next to Mum in the front row was definitely unsettled. 'Oh dear, Mary,' she said, 'we might get raped...' and Mum replied with her wicked sense of humour, 'Good!' I escaped unscathed. That was my first prison experience, but it wasn't my last.

From those faraway days to the present it has taken a lot to faze me on stage. I've been pelted with coins and razor-sharp beer can tops, had firecrackers hurled at me, had my foot smashed by an infuriated roadie, and once, only once, did a performance of *Blood Brothers* still hungover. The show has always gone on. As a child, however, apart from the time one jealous mother of another eisteddfod contestant pulled out the power cord from my tape recorder right in the middle of my pièce de résistance, 'Big Spender', my disasters were usually to do with falling scenery and hats that refused to stay on my head. I always ploughed on oblivious.

I had no nerves or stage fright as a child (this would come later), and I thank my speech and drama teacher for that. Mary Walker gave me speaking exercises to perform, designed to help me project and enunciate and conquer more complex passages, such as the Shakespeare I was reciting then, and to move and gesture in front of an audience.

As well as acting with the Geelong Musical Comedy Company, Mum staged charity dances at church halls and while she was fussing around collecting money and organising the records or the performers, Dad handed out soft drinks and manned the door in case some of the wilder locals got out of hand. Years later I loved to terrorise bouncers at Divinyls shows. If I thought they were mistreating the fans, I'd swear at them, hit and kick them, leap onto their backs. Was I transferring my anger at Dad onto the steroid-soaked baboons who threw their weight around at my gigs? Perhaps.

Mum was a performer at heart. She was really very funny, had excellent comic timing and a nice voice. She cherished the theatrical world and the larger-than-life people attached to it. I think Dad resented her being such an extrovert. Everyone was attracted to her. Dad may have been a bit jealous. Though we never had much money, he refused to allow her to get a job.

So Mum threw herself into charity work. She was a member of the Aboriginal Advancement League. The League would be considered paternalistic today, but in those less politically correct times it was highly regarded by the community, a well-meaning organisation that really wanted to help indigenous Australians. In school holidays Aboriginal children from the Victorian outback stayed at our house. One girl, Heather, spent a couple of weeks with us when I was seven or eight. She arrived with very few clothes and her hair infested with lice. Mum had to spray her hair and comb them out before we could play. Heather was a nice kid, and together we'd ride our bikes around Belmont. I don't know what became of her. I've always wondered.

I like to think that deep down I'm a kind person, and if that's so, I've inherited it from Mum. God knows, with Dad being so autocratic and not having a lot of money, she didn't have it easy, but she was always trying to help those she thought were less fortunate. She would organise to have people down on their luck appear on the popular tear-jerking TV show *It Could Be You*. Mum would write to the show's producers telling of such-and-such's plight, and often they'd be invited onto the program to tell their story and be showered with gifts by the host Tommy Hanlon Jr.

And of course, Mum's good works got her out of the house and away from Dad.

Dad was a crack salesman who usually exceeded all his sales targets, but no matter how successful he was, he was always racked by anxiety. The responsibility of being a husband, father and provider weighed upon him heavily, possibly exacerbated by his wartime ordeal. I have a photo of him walking down a Melbourne street. He could pass for a movie star with his beautiful clothes and Joseph Cotten hair, but he looks worried, as if he has just received terrible news. The only time he seemed able to relax was when he was on the boat Great-uncle Ernest had given him, fishing from it and lavishing care on the old tub. Leigh and I would go out on the *Selly Oak* with Dad and he'd be happy when the seas got rough because he believed the experience was toughening us up.

I confess. I was a little horror when it suited me. Mum adored me so much she couldn't discipline me. She never hit me, although once she chased me with a brush but I was too fast for her. Dad tried to control me but I defied him, which made him go nuts.

Dad could be weird. For an animal lover, he happily strangled—with what I thought was excessive violence—the chooks in our backyard when it was time for a roast. And he'd get nasty when we left food on our plates at dinner. He'd yell, 'During the war the only food we had was scraps!' The war was always with him, and so with us. To scare us, or shock visitors at Christmas lunch, he would yell, 'Heil Hitler!' often accompanied by a Nazi salute, then fall about laughing. Sometimes, when he'd been drinking, he'd rant at us in a high-pitched voice, like I imagined Hitler had at a Nuremberg rally. That could be frightening.

Perhaps even weirder was the fact that Dad got a buzz from nicking things from people, then returning them. One morning I woke up and running around in the backyard was a goose he'd stolen. And sometimes he'd make me a promise, then renege. Since then I've been uncomfortable asking people for things. He unwittingly taught me to rely on myself.

It couldn't have been easy for Dad having to contend with a petticoat government. I think he probably would have liked a son. He was always having mock fights with me, wrestling and punching. Sometimes they got a bit willing. He toughened me up by making me work with tools and chunks of wood. If I did something wrong he'd bark at me, and I would seize up and cry. He taught me to stick up for myself and to not be a victim. Since then I've never shied from a rumble. In fact, many who know me say I welcome them.

While Mum loved us to stand out and perform, Dad couldn't bear Leigh or me being the centre of attention. When my sister was chosen to appear in a TV commercial for Smarties, Dad broke her heart by point-blank refusing to let her do it.

You never knew with Dad. When his car pulled into the driveway he could be in a good mood or spoiling for trouble. When we'd fight, Dad's face would contort with rage; and it was the scariest face I have ever seen. When I was with Divinyls and being intimidating on stage I'd glower ferociously at the audience and the band. That face was my father's.

Yet for all his strictness and the angry outbursts that increased in frequency and intensity when I became a teenager, Dad adored us and wanted us to have a wonderful life. He insisted on cutting my hair because it was too precious for any hairdresser to get their hands on. Once he hacked my locks so badly Mum bought me a wig to wear till my hair grew out. I remember him lovingly applying lotion to my measles, and right up until he died, he'd say, 'Come on, Bub,'—he always called me 'Bub'—and hold my hand as we crossed the road together.

Mum's love was unconditional. Every time I looked at her I saw affection shining from her eyes. I was spoiled and given anything I wanted that my parents could afford. My desires were gratified instantly, and I wonder sometimes now if I'd been made to wait for treats whether I'd have turned out differently.

I always felt very special, and never for a moment have I lacked self-confidence, not even when I grew up and my world fell apart.

Only one other person has ever offered me such unconditional love. My husband, Charley.

After Dad had behaved badly, which was often, he'd trip over himself trying to make amends. He'd spoil me with breakfast in bed and if I didn't want to go to school he'd let me stay at home.

I was not a good student. Instead of doing my homework, I preferred to read the books of Enid Blyton and AA Milne or watch TV. I was mesmerised by the pop music shows where bands like The Loved Ones would lip-sync their latest hit, and *Young Talent Time*, *Peter's Fun Fair*, *Pick-A-Box*, *Video Village*, Happy Hammond, Panda, ventriloquist Ron Blaskett and his dummy, Gerry Gee. Leigh and I loved *Mr Ed*, the talking horse, and we created our own *Video Village* set in the backyard. How could homework hope to compete with these treasures?

Mum let us come home from school at noon each day to watch the midday movie and have a home-cooked lunch. Dad would drop in to join us. He, Leigh and I would take up our time-honoured positions in the lounge room, each sitting at one of our trio of nestle tables. Dad had the largest one, Leigh the middle one, and me the smallest. We were just like the three bears. Mum would shuffle in and out of the kitchen, waiting on us while trying not to obscure our view of the TV screen.

And there was always the distraction of wars with the boys from the neighbourhood. We'd pelt each other with rocks in vacant blocks and on the dirt street—in spite of its grand name, Eton Road wasn't paved then. The tarring of Eton Road was a memorable occasion, for all the wrong reasons. The day they laid the tar, Leigh and I, returning from the beach, walked over the still-warm, gooey substance and tramped black footprints all over our brand-new mushroom-hued carpet. Dad was so angry that Mum, Leigh and I moved into a motel for a few days until he calmed down.

For a time Mum and I shared a bedroom—Dad and Leigh each had their own—so I was with my mother through many of her asthma attacks when she'd gasp and fight for air, hanging out of the bedroom window because she couldn't breathe.

Another problem with being my mother's roommate was her habit of waking up screaming. All her life she has had a recurring dream in which a man is standing at the end of her bed. As recently as a year ago, when I stayed with Mum for a week, she woke up yelling the house down. This time it wasn't a strange man who had invaded her sleep but two small boys, standing at the end of her bed, gazing at her.

I was a little diva in my Belmont days. I changed my clothes, costumes and ballet tutus sometimes three or four times a day and was always fussing with my hair. Mum indulged my sister and me by entering us in beauty competitions. Leigh, tall and attractive, usually won. Dad said to me only a few years ago, 'You know, Chrissy, Leigh used to win those competitions and you were always so happy for her. You were never jealous. You would never win, but you'd come in skipping and singing, so proud of Leigh.' I was. I really looked up to my sister. Which didn't stop her terrorising me. Once she tied me to the bed and practised plucking my eyebrows, and when I screamed she stuffed Castlemaine Rock toffees in my mouth to muffle the racket. Maybe I deserved it. I drove Leigh crazy. I was always putting on her make-up and clothes (even today I have a thing about trying on friends' clothes).

I was a climber, too. Mum could never hide Christmas presents, she couldn't hide her make-up. Leigh couldn't hide her clothes. I simply climbed up into whatever cupboard they'd been hidden in and got them.

Not content with pillaging Leigh's clothes and make-up, I used to put lobsters and fish in her bed. I'd lie awake waiting for her to go to bed so I could hear the scream.

Leigh was sophisticated. She wore Valentino at fifteen and had a spectacular German boyfriend who drove an even more spectacular white E-Type Jag. Dad never warmed to him, despite the German link. Leigh and this guy used to dye their hair white. Dad hated that, of course, and when my sister's platinum locks fell out he found yet another reason to go ballistic.

My first dreams of being a rock singer were inspired by the TV music shows, all the records I played and the Top 40 on the radio—'Rock Around The Clock' by Bill Haley and the Comets, anything Elvis did, novelty songs such as 'The Purple People-Eater' and 'Does Your Chewing Gum Lose Its Flavour (On The Bedpost Overnight)?' by Lonnie Donegan . . . all those lovely songs. Then a little later 'Good Vibrations' by the Beach Boys, 'You've Really Got Me' by the Kinks and anything by the Beatles.

My cousin Little Pattie was always an icon. With her blonde fringe, gingham dresses and happy surfie songs, she was a regular on TV's *Bandstand*. A true star and a complete professional, Tricia has been achieving all her life. She still sings, teaches performance to kids, and, how's this, she is the national president of the Media, Entertainment & Arts Alliance (MEAA), the entertainers' union. Recently, she was elected unopposed for about the fifteenth time. As a child, I followed her career closely on TV and saw her live when she toured Geelong. Dad came too, and in giving his niece a good-luck hug backstage just before her gig, typically managed to burn a hole in her frock with his cigarette. He was mortified.

Tricia was proof that an Amphlett could make it. In those years I saw more of her on the television than I did at family gatherings. Our fathers weren't particularly close, and, besides, she lived in faraway Sydney.

I wish I could say my cousin's glory made life easier for me at Roslyn Primary School and then at Belmont High, but, if anything, Little Pattie's fame caused me grief. It seemed to me that the teachers and children resented me for the connection and my ability to sing and dance made it worse. I was always overlooked for concerts and shows. I didn't even make the school choir.

Belmont High was a bad school. There's no other way I can say it. There was no encouragement for anyone who, like me, was into the arts. The basic curriculum of maths, English, science, history and geography was all the teachers wanted to know about. That and sport. To many of these people, had I not been the sister of the beautiful, popular and clever Leigh Amphlett, or able to swim and run fast, which I could, I would have been a total waste of space. So, like most kids who feel alienated, I mucked up. This, naturally, made the teachers try to control me. As Dad had discovered, and as a succession of band members, managers and promoters would find out soon enough, being controlled is something I resist with all my heart. I threw the teachers' attempts to rein me in right back in their faces. I was rude and rebellious, and always being hauled out in front of the assembly because my uniform was too short, I was wearing green mascara, or I'd been a holy terror in class. I developed a bad attitude. Business as usual.

My schoolday memories don't include too many good ones. I was ridiculed for sucking my two middle fingers, a neurotic habit I'd had since a baby when Mum refused to let me have a dummy, which she thought would be a germ trap if it fell on the floor, and which may have contributed to my top front teeth being buck.

In class, in primary school, aged four, I wet my pants, and my wee spread all over the carpet square I was sitting on and soaked the carpet squares of my schoolmates. This horrified all the other kids, especially one prim classmate who squealed, 'Oh yuck!' The teacher,

Miss Nimon, sent me home, my wet dress clinging to my legs. I was so ashamed. That teacher was never nice to me again.

The kids were merciless about my cultured speaking tones and jealous that I'd been in the local paper for my ballet and performances with the Musical Comedy Company. They called me Donald Duck and I'd hear the name being shouted or whispered often. 'Donald Duck! Donald Duck!' Tall poppies were quickly cut down at Belmont High. Not me though. The more people picked on me, the more I rebelled.

My classmates' mothers seemed to dislike me even more than their kids. There was the one who unplugged my tape recorder at the eisteddfod, and when I entered freestyle sprint races at the local pool I was unfairly handicapped. One freezing day I was made to stand on the blocks long after all the other swimmers had dived in. Some girls had finished the race before I even got into the water. I left that club and went to another, much more competitive, club and that was better for me because it made me try even harder. I took up the sport when Mum insisted. Because she suffered from asthma and the girl next door had suffered a fatal attack, my mother thought swimming would strengthen my lungs and ward off any asthma attacks I may have been prone to. I enjoyed it and turned up at school from the pool with my hair wet and eyes stained red by chlorine.

Mum was protective of me, but to her credit she was never a stage mother, one of those pushy women who inflict their own thwarted dreams on their children. Others' cruelty to me upset her deeply, and we both wept when I poured out my frustrations to her. All she could do was assure me that the problem wasn't mine, but my persecutors'. I loved her for that, and developed a bulletproof self-confidence in the face of adversity and criticism that has served me well my whole life.

My mother was my organiser and support system. She arranged everything for me, my ballet, singing, dancing, modelling and swimming. She had my costumes and the sets for my stage acts made. She was endlessly on the telephone planning my curriculum.

I can still see her wearing holes in the carpet with her feet as she sat for hours by the phone.

While Mum was focused on me and Leigh, each day Dad set off to sell his typewriters. His suit would be immaculate, his shirt ironed, his shoes shined, his tie just so. The nails on his long, graceful fingers would be perfectly trimmed, his thick, dark hair sprayed and precisely combed. If I concentrate hard, I can summon up the smell of his aftershave lotion all these years later. He would lay siege to the bathroom in the morning to make sure he looked and smelled his best when he was selling his wares. To him, how you looked was how you were. His dream for me was that one day I would marry a television newsreader (any newsreader would do as long as he was conservative, neat, older than his years and holding down a well-paid job). 'But Dad,' I'd yell, 'he looks like a paedophile!' Mum, on the other hand, while glamorous, cared more about substance than style.

Mum didn't really care how our house looked. Never could she be accused of being a great housekeeper. She hated housework and I often saw her sweep the dust under the carpet. Other mothers I knew kept a pristine house, but that didn't impress me. Mum always had more important things to do, like loving me and living the theatre.

She couldn't bear to show Dad bills as he would flare up and she would hide them from him. Of course, he'd find out when the men came to cut off the gas or electricity and then he'd lose his temper with all of us anyway. Once I was sitting in the yard with a schoolfriend and Dad was shouting at Mum inside the house. 'What's that?' said my alarmed friend.

'Oh,' I replied, 'just Dad beating the cat again!'

Mum wasn't always Dad's victim. Once she fed him dog food. He enjoyed a good lamb or beef stew for dinner but such choice meat was expensive and he was a skinflint when doling out the housekeeping money. By the end of the week she'd run out of cash and the cupboards would be bare. (To this day, I know of few things so wonderful as a full shopping trolley.) When Dad demanded stew Mum knew there'd be an explosion if he didn't get it, so she went to the butcher and bought a pound of fresh dog meat, cooked it, and served it to him. He gulped it down with gusto. That was one time when the tyrant got his just desserts.

I love Mum's wicked sense of humour. Dad could never break her. She endured everything he put her through with a smile, and on a good day, she could make *him* laugh. 'Aw, go and have some Phenyle,' she'd mutter at him, referring to a particularly unpleasant household sanitiser we used to rid our dogs of fleas and clean toilets, drains, grease traps and animal pens.

As I grew older my relationship with Dad, which had always been edgy, deteriorated. He was constantly trying to control me, and I would never, *will never*, be controlled. Sometimes he would grill me about whether I'd lost my virginity, long before I'd given a thought to sex. He insisted that I must have 'done it' with boys, and that made me feel ashamed to be female. I think my father was really afraid that I'd be a slut, and this was his way of dealing with his fears.

Our frustrations with each other boiled over into terrible arguments. Once, I sat on the back doorstep and screamed obscenities at him, knowing the whole neighbourhood could hear. He was a man who cared deeply what others thought, and I enjoyed his humiliation. There were times when Dad went out on his boat and I wished he'd never come back. That was cruel. He was doing his best in his own way.

In time I did start going out with boys. None of these 'relationships' lasted. Mum and Dad set high standards for my young suitors, and many were dismissed as not being good enough. I didn't care. To me, boys were fun, and that was all. Mum had instilled in me from an early age a horror of growing up and getting married to some local bloke and then having to walk around Belmont wheeling a pram, all of my performing dreams dashed by responsibility. Mum said, 'Don't have children. Don't have children.' For Dad, no one less than that TV newsreader was good enough for his little girl.

Unlike his brother Joe, Patricia's dad, who swore like a trooper, Dad affected airs and graces. The dapper demeanour he'd adopted when he returned from the war and the dashing appearance he perfected, not forgetting his impressive dancing, won him many female admirers, but as far as I know he was never unfaithful to my mother.

Even when he was frothing at the mouth with rage he watched his language. The only time I ever heard Dad say 'fuck' was once when we were in the car, running late for an appointment, and Mum was taking her time leaving the house. To my parents' generation, the F-word was the ultimate obscenity and Dad didn't use it lightly. In our home the worst word he would come up with was 'Shite!' which I figured was some German version of 'Shit!' (The first time I ever heard anyone else say 'fuck' was when I was ten and a man blurted it out at the local swimming pool. I felt violated, and it took me days to recover.)

Only rarely did my father let the old Jim Amphlett out of the bag, and when he did I loved him for it—his 'Heil Hitlers' that were guaranteed to shock, and stealing that neighbour's goose. After Leigh got married, Mum, Dad and I visited her and her AFL-player husband and mother-in-law at Berwick. Throughout dinner, Dad drank heavily and continued after we all left the table to get ready for bed. We all heard what he did next. He got up from the table, went to his room, switched off the light, and let go of the most tremendous fart. This was his way of saying the festivities were over. I giggled myself to sleep.

My childhood years were always interesting. I'd have died in an emotionally frigid household. For all our faults as a family, there was passion in our house, and noise and chaos and love. Plus music, lots of music. Mum would tinkle her piano, Dad and Leigh would play their records, and, of course, when I wasn't stirring up trouble I'd sing.

SURFER GIRL

In the early seventies, Torquay Beach was a heady scene, a world of waves, boards, drugs, music, parties, gorgeous guys and, as surely as a thunderstorm follows a blazing summer day, sex. For a young teenager determined to bust free of convention and control, school, home and the Geelong Musical Comedy Company were no competition. Every weekend, winter and summer, I made a beeline for the surfing mecca, 21 kilometres south of Geelong, at the start of the Great Ocean Road. This prim little ballerina was now a surfie chick. My friends, Janice Middleton, Anne Newton, Gail Vogel, and I would tell our parents we were off to each other's houses, to the movies in Geelong or a record night at St Bernard's Church and we'd hitch to the beach.

Janice Smith (nee Middleton)

We hated school and we made sure everyone knew it. We were smart, physically well developed and had attitude. Thirteen-going-on-twenty-one. To Chrissy, Gail, Anne and me, anyone who wasn't us was a dag. We had a lot of fun and played up a lot. I don't know what it was about

Geelong or about our families, but we started hitchhiking to Torquay one weekend, for excitement. And we found this whole new world. We thought it was fabulous because it was totally away from our homes and our school. It was such a free thing to be doing. We found older boys, and after that there was no turning back.

Torquay, where we were very small fish, was so different to Geelong—where we strutted around and the revheads and sharpies would cruise by us in McCann Street in their hotted-up yellow Toranas whistling and calling out to us. They always got the same response: a withering glare and a smart-arse putdown.

No, surfers were our thing. They rented cheap shacks on the beach and we'd sit there with them on cushions, listen to records, smoke pot and pash.

We had no fears about hitchhiking, or anything else. We stood on the Geelong Road with our thumbs stuck out till a car stopped and picked us up. We became quite well known, and some boys would hang around waiting for us to appear on the highway. One guy in particular was always lurking. He never tried anything, but none of us wanted to sit in the front seat with him because he wore tiny King Gee work shorts and everything he had hung loose. He kept a box of condoms in the glovebox in case he got lucky, but he never did with any of us.

Torquay, with its wide, white-sand beaches, big waves and youth culture, was at the epicentre of the Australian surfquake. It was there, in ramshackle garages and tool sheds, where enterprising young surfers, such as Rip Curl founders Doug 'Claw' Warbrick and Brian 'Sing Ding' Singer and Quiksilver creator Alan Green, first fashioned their surfboards, wetsuits and clothing lines that made them millionaires and are now sold all over the world.

Gail and I used one of these wood and corrugated iron garages as our hangout, and we shacked up there with friends who dropped by. In our coloured corduroys, baggy shirts, ugg boots and holey mohair jumpers, partying, sleeping over, we experimented with life.

We'd sit on the beach among the Norfolk Island pines and watch the surfers ride the waves. We created our own soundtrack to their graceful slashes, cutbacks and carves: the Beatles, the Rolling Stones, Cream, the Doors, Aretha Franklin, the Rascals, Dylan, and Sly and the Family Stone blaring on our transistors. When the boys returned to the shore we pounced. They were tanned, had long, sun-bleached hair and smelled clean and fresh, unlike the revheads in Geelong who reeked of sump oil and fried chicken. To the impressionable kid I was then, there was something coolly spiritual about the surfers of Torquay. They seemed always to be searching for something, the perfect wave, something to believe in, a new thrill, and that appealed to me. They were wild, and as cool as rock stars.

We didn't know it then, of course, but many of these Adonises were doomed. Drugs were rampant in Torquay at that time and took their toll on the surfer boys. A roll call of the surfers I knew who overdosed or committed suicide as a result of addiction is enough to make me cry.

For most of these guys, girls came a distant fifth behind surf, drugs, each other's company and the latest Eastern religion, and their indifference attracted me all the more. Like many young girls, I only liked guys who didn't like me. Those who did, I just wasn't interested in. Did this make me miserable? No, just confused.

The surfer boys of Torquay could be as cruel as they were beautiful. Some said and did terrible things to me. Calling me 'Jail-bait' made me feel like shit. I happily put up with their heartlessness when I was young, but I would have my revenge. Years later, the Divinyls played Geelong and during the gig I looked down into the audience and there was a group of blokes I recognised from the beach, the very ones who had given me a hard time. Their names were Fledge, Boong and Brew and they couldn't believe that the crazy little person from the beach had transformed into this rock star in a school uniform going berserk up on stage. I could see I scared them. After a blistering set, I stood there sweating, triumphant, as the crowd went wild, and I looked down at them and yelled, '*Now go and get fucked!*' A sweet moment, but any satisfaction I felt didn't last long. Within a year or so, Fledge, Boong and Brew were dead, all drug victims.

I lost my virginity and smoked dope for the first time on the same night. I was fifteen and I went to a house at nearby Anglesea with a group of kids and there was a guy there in his early twenties named Garry Bryant. I slept with him and it was horrible. I arrived wearing a long wig and false eyelashes to make myself look older and more sophisticated and when Garry and I went into the bedroom I said, 'Oh, excuse me for a minute, I have to do something,' and I went to the bathroom and took off my accessories. When Garry saw me the way I really was he nearly had a fit. The next day I was at Gail's parents' place and there was a knock at the door. Standing there was Garry Bryant holding my false hair and eyelashes. He handed them to Gail's mother, said, 'Here, give these to Christine,' and left. I was devastated. Garry, too, who had a drug habit, has since passed away.

As far as I was concerned it was no big deal to lose my virginity, just something that had to be done. After years of my father insisting I must have 'done it' I fulfilled his prophecy. I had a girlfriend who was *really* precious and neurotic about her virginity and she hung onto it and hung onto it and I'd go, 'Just get *rid* of it!' I was so vulnerable and had no idea of where I was at sexually. I wasn't aware there were boundaries or of what was right or wrong. All this while I was going through puberty and my hormones were racing. My friends were useless as sounding-boards because we were all as ignorant about sex as each other, and if I'd tried to raise the topic with Dad he'd have blown a fuse. My behaviour was just another way to rebel against him. Anne and Janice fell in love with surfers and married them. I didn't have a steady boyfriend, just some forgettable flings. Craig Dickenson, who wasn't a surfie, but a sharpie, small, with snappy clothes and rooster-cut hair, said he was in love with me. Naturally, because he fancied me, I turned him away. But Craig's problem wasn't me, it was smack, and, like all the others, it killed him.

Boys confused me. Perhaps Dad's unpredictability and moods were to blame. Perhaps I thought all males were like him.

I got very smashed on some sweet and sticky alcoholic drink—sherry, vermouth?—when I was fifteen, but generally speaking alcohol wasn't a big thing at the beach. Booze was for the revheads and footy blokes, and definitely not cool, and, to us, being cool was important. Drugs, however, were everywhere, and I smoked marijuana and hash. Dope made me feel awful, paranoid, unable to speak, but I indulged because everyone else did.

Most nights after the beach, Janice, Anne, Gail and I hitchhiked back to Belmont, pretending to our parents that we'd been somewhere we hadn't and blithely denying the existence of our telltale sunburn, salty hair and lovebites. But one night after a long day of fun and sun it was suddenly too late to hitchhike home, and I decided to spend the night in a big tent with a large group of boys and girls. I didn't sleep with anyone, but one guy kept grabbing my hand and trying to get me to touch him. To my horror, in the middle of the night Dad and Mum turned up and dragged me out of the tent, put me into the car and drove me home, doing my cool chick cred no good at all.

Through all this, singing was my rock. This was something I could do better than anyone else at the beach. It gave me power and direction, and an escape. Singing was how I communicated, my lifeline. I was known as the girl who sang. People thought, 'Oh, it's Chrissy singing again, she's nuts.' No matter where I was or what was happening, whether I was happy or sad, I was always breaking into rock songs. My voice in those days was nothing like it would become. I was in transition, still forming my musical taste and singing style, leaving the Plaza Theatre and eisteddfods of my youth far behind. When the surfers lit a fire on the beach and some guy pulled out a guitar, I'd accompany him, and I began singing with some local kids in a Geelong band called Steamhammer.

Torquay, like just about everywhere on earth, had gone hippie. Flower Power ruled. Psychedelia, tie-dyed T-shirts, peace, love, Indian jewellery, Eastern religions such as Meher Baba and Hare Krishna (whose philosophies, though I scarcely understood them, I happily spouted) were all encompassing. Neil Young, Creedence Clearwater Revival, Jefferson Airplane, Jimi Hendrix, Led Zeppelin and George Harrison's 'My Sweet Lord' blasted out across the sand. I got my first whiff of patchouli oil and my life changed. It was heavy and cloying and *so* exotic and made me feel incredibly daring, as though none of life's experiences would be denied me. Even now when I smell patchouli I'm transported back to those days.

But below the surface I wasn't so daring or buoyant. I felt abandoned. Abandoned by Dad, when he tried to control me; by Anne and Janice, who were spending more time with their steady guys; and by my own boyfriends. I always felt the odd one out in any group. Consequently, I did some irrational things, like putting clothes on lay-by in a Geelong store with no way of ever paying for them. Once, when I was feeling especially alone, I tried to commit suicide by swallowing an entire bottle of Bex tablets. Bex was a bitter-tasting, over-the-counter concoction to relieve headaches and stress. Dad took one look at me woozy and distressed and lovingly walked me up and down till I felt better. Then, always one for keeping up appearances, he warned me, 'Now make sure you don't mention this to anyone!'

Janice Smith

Part of Chrissy's problem was that she wasn't like other girls. She was an enigma. She was beautiful, very poised and a law unto herself. She drank sarsaparilla and smoked coloured Russian Sobranie cigarettes. She spoke beautifully, which was rare. When she wasn't wearing surf gear she had tremendous dress style and was great at putting different looks together. One outfit I'll never forget was a purple minidress with a big keyhole cut in the front that showed off her gi-normous boobs. She had a fantastic body. And she was so wild. Anne and I met our future husbands at the beach. When we started getting serious with Tom and Greg, Chrissy felt a bit lost and drifted away. She started hanging out with older fellows who were a bit all over the place. Some weren't too kind to her. She went off the rails for a while, hanging out with all sorts of characters and taking a lot of risks. People said nasty things about her. We all met up at Anne's place years later and she played us her new record 'Boys In Town', and said it was about the Torquay boys.

Chrissy was intimidating and self-possessed and the boys couldn't cope so they lashed out at her. Girls, too. At a dance one night Chrissy annoyed most of the girls by looking fabulous in a red, white and blue dress, false eyelashes, full make-up. Then she really put some noses out of joint. She had a way of gazing disconcertingly at people, looking them up and down. Didn't even realise she was doing it. She did this to a group of very tough chicks, some of whom had just been released from prison, and they took offence. One came up to Chrissy and went *whack*!

To us, Chrissy was very, very brave and very, very adventurous. Even though we were out there, we wished we had half her guts! We idolised her. It didn't surprise me when Chrissy became a rock star. I knew she had extreme determination. And she really wanted to get out of Geelong and make something of herself. She was fighting her past. Geelong can be a nasty little country town and she was just too big for it.

Good old, long-suffering Dad was there for me another time, when I *could* have, should have, died. I was with the doomed Craig Dickenson in a house in Geelong and we were dropping acid. By then heroin was in his heart and soul, but he put it aside this night for the hot new psychedelic drug LSD, and I was happy to join him. But the acid was too strong and for someone like me with an inherent low tolerance for drugs it had a disastrous effect. I couldn't handle it. I started hallucinating and became distressed. Craig fled. Abandoned again. In my mind I was still sitting in the house but, in reality, I had stumbled outside and then lay down in the middle of the highway. Before a car or truck could turn me into roadkill, the police saw me and hustled me into a patrol car.

Mum and Dad were there when they dropped me off in Eton Road. Because I'd spent the past few days either at the beach or at Janice's place I hadn't seen them for a while. Dad looked at the police, looked at his wreck of a daughter, realised I was off my face . . . and gathered me up in the biggest hug. Later, he tucked me into bed, and wasn't even angry the next day after I'd recovered. He was simply glad I was alive.

For all his faults and all our clashes I am the first to admit my father had his hands full.

When Janice and Anne moved out of home and into an apartment in Geelong I was always dropping in and staying. We'd all left school and were enjoying the freedom. I remember one night at a dance the band was the Valentines, who wore brightly coloured jumpsuits. The Valentines featured the now late and legendary Bon Scott of AC/DC fame, and a singer by the name of Vince Lovegrove, who would come back into my life a few years later with cataclysmic results.

Janice Smith

After we all left home, Anne and I were living in an apartment in Geelong. Chrissy used to come and go. We had parties and smoked pot and carried on. One night, the police came and hauled Anne and me into the Geelong Police Station. We soon found out why. Chrissy had been picked up by the police as she walked down the street tripping on acid. They also found a matchbox of pot on her. When the police asked her for her address, she gave them ours so they wouldn't go around to Eton Road. So they figured we were all druggies and came and took us away. All our parents were notified. I was belligerent as all hell because I'd been dragged into the cop shop for no reason, so I stood there, hands on hips, giving the police a mouthful. I didn't give a shit about authority. We were not intimidated by police what-so-ever! And there was Chrissy standing there looking so innocent, as if none of this fiasco was her fault. An officer gave Anne and me a warning and let us go.

The police gave me a much harder time. In front of my deeply ashamed father, they said I was hanging around with grievously bad people and at risk of getting into serious trouble. I was told it would be in my, and Geelong's, best interests if I left town.

Not normally one to listen to the voice of authority, this time I did what I was told.

INTO THE MUSIC

Melbourne's Sunbury Festival was Australia's early-seventies version of Woodstock. With my love of music there was no way I wasn't going. Anne Newton and I hitchhiked the 30 kilometres to join the 35 000 other fans, but we were soon separated in the throng and didn't see each other again till we were safely home. I wore only a bikini and a skimpy short top. I had no change of clothes, no food or money. Horribly sunburned and sucking on ice because I had nothing else to eat or drink, I sat at the front of the crowd and watched all the bands. I was determined to become a rock singer even though not one of the bands had a girl up front—such a thing was virtually unheard of in Australia then—I wanted to know how Billy Thorpe and the Aztecs, Chain, and my great favourites Lobby Lloyd and the Coloured Balls pulled it off.

I had followed the Geelong cops' advice and moved into a flat in Auburn Road, Hawthorn. I would often see Gerry Humphreys from The Loved Ones, the band I used to watch on TV at Eton Road, shopping with his girlfriend, who had bright hennaed hair. They lived only one block away on the same street. I thought they were the coolest couple and the way Gerry looked and performed reminded me of Keith Moon from the Who. I would go to the music clubs Bertie's and Sebastian's to see him and The Loved Ones which made me even more determined to become a rock singer. One day, I met Gerry's girlfriend on the street. She invited me back to their flat and hennaed my hair. But I was to learn that talent doesn't guarantee success or longevity: in time Gerry returned to his hometown of London and became a hospital orderly. What a loss to Australian music.

Alison Baker, a girl I knew from Geelong, had also moved to Melbourne and we became great friends. Her cousin, David Flint, owned the Thumping Tum which, with its red-velvet curtains and antique furniture, vied with Bertie's and Sebastian's to be the best Melbourne nightclub of the time. Alison was just as enamoured of the music scene as I was and we'd visit the clubs together. After the confines of Geelong I couldn't believe the vibrancy of Melbourne. The very hip clothing store, Merivale and Mr John, had just opened at the top of Collins Street and sold green leather jackets, tight velvet flares with a 'V' cut into the knees, tight small jumpers with buttons and holes all down the sleeves, and T-shirts with flared arms. My style exactly, and I topped off the look with false eyelashes top and bottom. There was a group of girls who worked at Merivale and hung out at Bertie's and Sebastian's. They all had pop-star boyfriends. One was Fleur Thiemeyer, who always dressed head to toe in Merivale and later married Darryl Cotton from the band Zoot. Fleur was too cool for school and I would watch her and her Merivale friends from afar and admire their style.

Alison Baker

It doesn't surprise me at all that Chrissy became a rock star, and led such a life. She was a girl with a destiny. I can picture her now at Bertie's or Sebastian's, smoking Courtleigh cigarettes with their little gold band, wearing velvet jeans and a vest cut in strips. Everyone who met Chrissy was overwhelmed by her talent and energy. There were cooler

girls, such as Fleur Thiemeyer and the Merivale chicks, but Chrissy
Amphlett was the real thing.

When my idol Wendy Saddington, a blues singer with a voluminous
afro who wore lots of bangles, sang with the band Chain at these clubs,
Alison and I would go and marvel. Sitting there gazing at the stage,
we looked so 'in', as they said in the seventies. We both sported Miss
Lynne brand dark maroon nail polish, Merivale pants, ugg boots, and
trailed thick wafts of patchouli oil. I also flaunted a gorgeous Navajo
jacket. There I'd be, looking just like that, whenever the bands I
admired played. Lobby Lloyd and the Coloured Balls were a big
event for me. Lobby seemed very dangerous and over the edge, and
he played *loud*. They never played Bertie's (as far as I know!). I was
also into the British bands T.Rex with Marc Bolan, and the Faces and
I don't think they ever played Bertie's either. Once, at a very sixties
venue with a black-and-white tiled dance floor, I saw my sister Leigh,
oh so glamorous in Louis Feraud, with her gorgeous, this time French,
boyfriend. I felt so different I couldn't bear to say hello.

One day, Alison and I met a fellow who was a complete music
fanatic. He was so enthusiastic and weird and lived in his parents'
garage. We were friends with a band called Highway and this guy was
really into their music and got off on carrying their amps and other
gear. The night we bumped into him we sat for hours talking music
and playing records. His name was Michael Gudinski, and he went
on to found Mushroom Records and the Frontier Touring Company
and become one of the biggest names in Australian music.

A guitarist in Highway was very keen on Alison. He saw her walking
with another bandmember and the jealous bastard beat her up. Alison
still has a scar on her face. The guy was sacked from the band.

During this time, I got to know the Payne brothers, who played
in a bluesy rock group called Daisy Clover. They did cover versions
of songs like 'I Put a Spell On You', and they needed a singer. 'How
about me?' I asked and, at fifteen years of age, I got the job. We gigged
around Melbourne for a few months and then signed on to support

Darryl Cotton and Zoot at Chequers, a spivvy Sydney nightclub. But if I thought I'd have respect I was wrong. It amused Darryl to creep up on me at the little flat both bands shared and rub a large plastic penis in my face. I was so intimidated by these people that I just sat there, unprotesting, as he denigrated me. Not too many years later, any man attacking me with a plastic penis would have lost his own.

Midway through a song at Chequers one night I looked over to the door and saw the most incredible-looking guy I'd ever seen in my life standing there watching me. He had long red hair, a top hat and a cane. I learned he was a musician with the exotic name of Ray Rivamonte, and standing with him was an American who wore one long earring, which was unheard of for a man then unless he was a pirate. Ray returned to Chequers night after night checking me out. Finally he approached me. 'Why don't you come and join our band, One Ton Gypsy? We need a back-up singer. We're based in Melbourne and our leader is Ray Brown,' he said. I didn't hesitate to say yes. Ray Rivamonte was an exciting guy, and in comparison the blokes in Daisy Clover seemed boring. Besides, I was miserable in that band. Some of my fellow bandmembers, perhaps egged-on by Darryl Cotton and his plastic penis, were treating me vilely. Even before Ray made his offer I'd psychologically left Daisy Clover. I walked out on them without a qualm and caught the train back to Melbourne.

Everyone in One Ton Gypsy, an eight-piece rock band with pretensions to emulating Joe Cocker and Leon Russell's Mad Dogs and Englishmen outfit, was well into his or her twenties. Of course I knew of Ray Brown. He was one of Australia's biggest pop stars of the sixties and with his band the Whispers had had a string of top ten records—'20 Miles', 'Fool Fool Fool', 'Pride', 'In The Midnight Hour'. A handsome guy with a light voice, Ray would die of a heart attack in 1996.

Apart from the Rays, Brown and Rivamonte, others in the group were Rockwell T James, Margaret and Tim Piper and a mad American drummer with a long ball and chain earring (the guy with Ray Rivamonte at Chequers) who would every so often catch the earring with his drumstick as he pounded away and end up bleeding on his drum kit. But that didn't put us off. One night we were all sitting around high on vodka after a gig and decided to be like our drummer and get our ears pierced.

One Ton Gypsy's base was an old hotel in St Kilda. I moved in and slept in a cupboard. Almost immediately I developed a crush on Rockwell T James, who was a very attractive man; and then his girlfriend arrived and that was that.

Of course, there were drugs. A couple of the bandmembers were doing heroin. I was smoking pot and taking LSD. It was a heavy scene. I'd started drinking, too, and one night after a binge I didn't make it on stage for a gig in the town of Rosebud. I was vomiting my heart up in the toilet and then I passed out on the floor. My absence really made a difference to the band because of all of the girls I was the only one who could really sing. Another of the female singers, whose name was Denny, whom I really looked up to because she was cool, was having an affair with Ray Brown. Denny didn't wear underwear, which I thought was just terrible so, feeling sorry for her, I went out and bought her some paper knickers. I still had my mother's sense of decorum—at least for some things.

About this time, a Melbourne guy named Ray Evans, who became my first manager, asked me to record Rita Coolidge's song 'Superstar'— about a groupie. At the same time, Colleen Hewett recorded what I thought was a dreadful version and had a hit. I wasn't too disappointed because I didn't think I could really handle fame at that stage; I was too young. Ray also organised me to be Girl of the Week in *Australasian Post* magazine. I posed for their photographer in my trademark ugg boots, corduroy jeans and Navajo top.

Inevitably, One Ton Gypsy broke up before we got to the studio, so there's no record existing of this interesting and ambitious group. We were too unwieldy, undisciplined and there were just too many of us to make any money. The pittance we earned playing small gigs around Melbourne was hardly enough to sustain eight performers and all the hangers-on.

After One Ton Gypsy's demise, I drifted into yet another Melbourne band, whose name I've forgotten. John Payne from Daisy Clover was in it and we played things like 'Season of the Witch'. One day at rehearsal I fell asleep, a combination of my boredom and staying up all night smoking pot and dropping acid. I'm not sure if that was the only reason but I was sacked by a bandmember named Danny Bourne. Years later, I came across Danny playing piano in a bar. He approached me with a delighted grin and said, 'Remember me, Chrissy? I fired you!' He gave me the impression sacking me was a highlight of his life.

When I was sixteen, Alison and I moved in together into a house in Greville Street, Prahran, home to a bunch of funky shops, including some exquisite vintage clothing stores where I bought old furs and gorgeous beaded dresses. The Station Hotel, a bastion of pub rock run by a guy called Mark Barnes and his girfriend Manag (they had a dog named Jeffrey, the first dog I knew with a person's name), was down the road and on Saturday afternoons Alison and I would go there to listen to Captain Matchbox. I first saw AC/DC at the Station, as well as Carson with Broderick Smith and Chris Stockley and the Dingoes. I'd get up and sing if whatever band was playing would let me.

Chris Stockley

It's a long time ago now, but Chrissy made an unforgettable impression. She was part of the Station Hotel crowd and when we played she would come up and ask if she could sing with us. We loved her, and so did the crowd; she was so pretty—and that *voice*! She had a song called 'Captain Bobby Stout' that she'd belt out. She didn't have the confidence then that she developed later in Divinyls. She was shy, but very special.

Every Friday Alison and I bought a matchbox of grass each for ten dollars and then we'd go out and party. Sometimes we'd crawl home. We didn't drink that much but one particular night, Alison's birthday, we went to the Greyhound Hotel and knocked back a number of tequila slammers. We ended up passed out on our front lawn. I have been told that a friend's mum who saw us was disgusted and I'm sure it didn't look pretty. Plenty went on at that house in Greville Street, but we both drew the line at intravenous drugs. One night, some guy tried to get into the house to shoot up but we got rid of him and went back to dropping acid and listening to Cream and Emerson, Lake & Palmer.

For me music was magic. I listened to music all the time in my room at Greville Street, with its panelled wood walls, huge fireplace and four-poster bed. I'd associate songs with good times, bad times, boys, dreams, ambitions. I know I'm not the only one who thinks songs and the people who sing and play them have incredible power. It is not surprising that sometimes people impose their own fantasies on what they hear and who they listen to. I heard only recently about a woman who had been unable to hear my name or my music without having a fit, and the reason was she had caught her brother masturbating over a photograph of me years before. The Greville Street house is still there and looks exactly the same, but I'd say it has a more genteel life these days.

Alison Baker

Those times in Greville Street . . . it was party central. We had jam sessions with various muso friends in our lounge room. The wild schoolgirl from Divinyls was still way in the future, but Chrissy would sing and be so much better than anyone else who was taking part. You'd have had to be an idiot not to realise, even at sixteen, that she was a major talent just waiting for an opportunity to whisk her off to realise her potential.

If you were into live music at that time, Melbourne was the place to be. There were so many bands gigging all over town and Alison and I followed them around. Our social life revolved around rock'n'roll. I can't remember having a steady boyfriend throughout that period. I was friends with boys, but, like at the beach, there was nobody special in my life. I was still pining after unattainable guys and giving the bum's rush to anyone who liked me. The only real affection and encouragement I got at this time was from Mum. She always welcomed me with a cuddle and a hearty meal, and assured me that singing stardom was just over the horizon. My dream was to sing in a band better than any of those I'd performed with to date, and I was always on the lookout for a gig.

To pay the rent at Greville Street and buy clothes and other essentials, I got a job in a Melbourne private hospital, assisting the matron and reading to the patients. This was the perfect role for someone like me who had become so self-absorbed, and, just like Mum, I discovered that I was fulfilled somewhere deep in my soul by helping others. This, I realised even at my young age, was true spirituality, far removed from the fakery of Torquay Beach-style Meher Baba. There was an old man at the hospital who had cancer of the mouth and I would read to him from his precious copy of *The Rubáiyát* by Omar Khayyám. He was a difficult guy and, understandably, because he knew he was dying, a bit cranky. I was very fond of him. I've always been drawn to difficult people, unconventional people. I was with him when he died, and was incredibly touched when he left me his copy of *The Rubáiyát*.

I grew up a lot in that hospital. I became close to people, like the old man, who were sick and who then died. Most of the patients were suffering from terminal cancer. It was physically and emotionally demanding for me, but far worse for the doctors and nurses who, I noticed, often raided the drug cupboards. Some drank heavily. After what I saw them go through, who would blame them? Certainly not me.

My world till then had been confined to Belmont, Torquay, Geelong and Melbourne, with short excursions to rural Victoria with Great-uncle Ernest and Sydney to sing at Chequers. Working in the hospital had made me think a little more seriously about my life. Yes, I still wanted to sing, but I was also desperate for new experiences, new adventures, and even as a teenager I realised that these would mature me and help my creativity. Occasionally I had thought of travelling overseas, but then I would get distracted by an exciting new band playing in some pub or another offer to sing or some unattainable guy. And Europe and America seemed too far away. Then came an unlikely catalyst for change. A friend named Jan McIntyre, who lived across the road from me in Greville Street, asked me if I'd go to London with her. Her father's new baby was having an operation and he wanted Jan to be there. Why not? I thought. I'd saved some money from working at the hospital and could afford to go if I was frugal. I didn't ponder too long and Jan and I went to a travel agent and booked passage on the *Fairstar Princess* bound for London. It was time to see new places and meet new people, taste a different life—but I didn't have any idea just how different it would be.

DRIFTER

On the voyage to London, the *Fairstar Princess* dropped anchor in Durban, South Africa, and Jan and I set off to see the sights. Many things we saw on that short visit were deeply shocking. I watched black people being beaten by the police for jaywalking, and shops run by blacks where whites were not allowed to go. Of course I went straight in. No one, and especially not the bigots and racists of South Africa, was going to tell me where I could and couldn't shop. When, at a street market, Jan and I saw a black man selling Durban poison, the notoriously strong South African marijuana, we bought some. Deal done, I gave him a big kiss and he freaked out, terrified that the authorities would see him being kissed by a white woman and punish him.

To our horror, Jan and I found ourselves sharing a cabin with the most uncool passenger onboard, a particularly stitched-up 70-year-old woman. We had to wait till she fell asleep before we could smoke our bullets of Durban poison. Of course she busted us and reported what we had done to the captain. 'You're gonna get it!' she cackled at me. 'You are in *so much* trouble. You're going to end up in prison!' She was right, but not on this particular occasion. We were terrified that the skipper would report us to the police and unload us from the ship, but he turned out to be a sweetie. He and the first mate gave us biscuits and brandy . . . and our very own cabin.

Jan and I smoked that potent Durban poison all the way to London and when we docked at Southampton we were tripping. I was so off my face I strolled through customs carrying a bag of Durban poison bullets in my suitcase, too stoned to appreciate what would happen to me if I was caught. Somehow I made it through. Jan, however, was in bad shape. She freaked out and arranged to head straight back to Australia.

I teamed up with two acquaintances from the ship, a girl named Carol and an older guy who played piano, and we spent my first night in London in Baron's Court in a tourist hotel, one of those places with creaky stairs and scuzzy carpet and a breakfast room downstairs. Carol and I had some more dope. I sat in a shabby little room imagining neon lights shooting all over the London sky, while my friend began to dance and cry hysterically. Then she began screaming so loudly I was afraid the police would hear her and burst in. Durban poison was well named.

Next morning we hired a car and drove to Dover on England's south-east coast. There we loaded ourselves and the car onto the Channel ferry and then, with the piano player at the wheel, drove down through France and across Switzerland to the northern Italian city of Milan. The signs had been building but when the piano player finally tried to have his way with us, we gave him the slip in Milan. It wasn't hard to do, because the beautiful Italian fashion centre was in chaos. At the time, Black September terrorists were setting off blasts all over Europe, and the day we arrived it was Milan's turn. Every street was jammed with cars trying to negotiate roadblocks, there was a cacophony of sirens as police hunted the bombers, and people were frantic and afraid. Soon after, I left Carol and caught a train to

Florence. I have no real memory of being excited by my first weeks in Europe. It was a crazy blur.

In Florence I saw a man handing out advertising flyers for a local disco and bar named Space Electronique. I followed the guy, whose name was Tony, back to the establishment, which was one of Florence's finest, and talked the manager into giving me a job behind the bar. I'd never done this kind of work before but he was impressed that I knew that the Italian word for 'dry' was 'sec'. How hard could it be to pour drinks, preferably dry white wine, dry vermouth or dry martinis, and keep smiling? And if I had trouble I could seek help from my fellow barmaid Katy Bevan, a lovely girl from Scotland who befriended me. While we served drinks together we filled each other in about who we were and where we'd come from. It turned out Katy's parents owned a castle. Very different from Eton Road, that's for sure.

I fancied Tony, who was the DJ at Space Electronique. He was adorable in that very Italian way. He gesticulated attractively, wore denim, and looked like a Mediterranean Mick Jagger. But Tony had another agenda. Like many a young Italian guy, his dream was to live in the United States and join the mafia and to do that he needed an American girlfriend. Being Australian, I wasn't any use to him. So he hooked up with an American girl who came into the bar. She was big and she was fat and she served his purpose perfectly. He got his ticket to the States and I got another rejection.

Eventually I started singing with Space Electronique's band, who needed an English-speaking singer. The leader of the band was the organist, Ricardo Toni, a genuine Italian count, who was the son of Florence's best-known furriers. Ricardo had a girlfriend named Lilly who became a friend.

Things were working out well, but new horizons are often more attractive ones, and soon a better offer, or what seemed like one, came along. Lilly and I became entranced by, respectively, the guitarist and the bass player in a Swiss band, Tea, that was gigging in Florence. When Tea returned to Zurich we were with them. My guy, whose name was Thoreau, turned out not to be as keen on me as I was on him, so we parted and I lodged in a nunnery. To pay my board I found a street corner and started singing for money. It was nice to know I had a talent that could keep me, if not rolling in money, then at least alive. I sang Irish songs, sea shanties, and the blues, which made me some money and some new friends as well. Even though Thoreau and I were no longer together he suggested I stay with his mother at her home. I walked into my bedroom and there on the bed was a big fluffy doona. I'd never seen a doona before and I slept on top of it. Thoreau's mum was aghast. 'No, no, you don't sleep on top of it. You sleep *underneath* it!' I knew travelling would add to my education!

One day I was struck down by an attack of gallstones. I was literally paralysed by pain. I'm sure my change of diet since arriving in Europe was to blame. After a lifetime eating bland Aussie food, I was gulping down rich Italian fare and spicy Swiss sausages. With treatment I recovered, and I returned to London and found a tiny bed-sit to live in. Lilly followed hard on my heels and moved in with me, but our friendship didn't survive. She was about ten years older than me, and I'm sure I was selfish and difficult, as teenage girls are. She left the flat one morning and never returned. I got by. Even without Lilly's contribution I could always rake up four pounds and sixty pence a week to pay my rent and fill the electricity meter. And though sometimes it meant I ate poorly, I always had enough money to go out and see some of the wonderful bands in London at that time. I saw Golden Earring and Phil Lynott and Thin Lizzy. After one gig, I was at a pub in Hammersmith and met a cute guy. I took him home and we slept together. He was long gone when I looked in my bag and discovered he'd stolen all my money.

Hungry and broke, I went to the local supermarket and got caught stealing a steak and some butter. The manager called the police, and I was taken away in a van and ended up in court, at the Old Bailey. I was devastated. I stood in the dock where murderers and thieves, including the notorious East End gangsters the Kray Brothers, had stood before me, not forgetting the convicts who were sent to Australia centuries before. In fact, I thought as I stood there trembling, didn't they transport people for stealing butter? Thankfully, the arresting officer was my saviour and asked the judge, a woman, for understanding. 'Your Honour,' he said, 'she's had her money stolen, and is used to eating meat. After all, she *is* from Australia.' Said the judge, 'Christina Amphlett, I hereby fine you twenty pounds and give you six months to pay it off.' Even I could manage that. They felt sorry for me, and I was grateful.

My money wasn't the only thing that guy from Hammersmith stole. He also took my good health. A week or so later, when I stepped off a bus in Scotland, I was yellow with jaundice.

I had come to Airlie, Scotland, near St Andrews, to stay with Katy Bevan's parents. They really *did* live in a castle. They put me up in a room at the top of this magnificent building and, while they all swapped Easter eggs downstairs, I was having the most serious health crisis of my life to date. A doctor diagnosed hepatitis and sent me to an isolation ward in the local hospital, where I stayed for three months until I'd recovered. I was seriously ill. Mum flew over from Melbourne and lavished me with her usual boundless loving comfort throughout my illness.

Mary Amphlett

When Chrissy got out of hospital we both returned to London and spent a fortnight together before I had to come home. Saying goodbye was awful. We had a farewell coffee and cried and cried. Oh, the tears! And Chrissy said, 'Mum, I'm so sorry for all the sadness I've caused you in my life.' I was so exhausted by the prospect of leaving her behind that when I got on the plane I slept all the way to Singapore.

As soon as I was stronger Mum went home and not long after I received some excellent news. Because I was eligible to work in Britain, the National Health Service had paid me sickness benefits for every week I was in hospital, and because I hadn't spent a penny of it, there was quite a windfall waiting for me. I used the money to travel alone to Crete, one of the cradles of civilisation, where Dad had fought in World War II. I slept on the beach where Dad had been captured. I telephoned to tell him a few days later and he asked me exactly what night. I told him and he was stunned. He swore to me on that very night he had dreamed of the terrible fighting on the beach all those years ago and had vividly seen, again, his mates lying dead.

From Crete I headed to Spain where I ended up renting an apartment in the picturesque south coast town of Torremolinos, renowned for its clean, sandy beaches, fresh fish bars and buzzy nightlife, about 100 kilometres east of Gibraltar. I was inspired by a book I'd read called *The Drifters* by James A Michener, about six young runaways adrift in Spain, living a life they'd created from dreams, drugs and the pursuit of pleasure. I wanted to be just like them. What made it extra special was that parts of the book were set in Torremolinos. As I roamed around the port I met up with a group of kids who, it turned out, had also read *The Drifters* and we all pretended we were characters in the book. There was a French couple, Maurice and Benedicte; Billy, an English-Chinese guy determined to buy Spanish property with a sizable chunk of his mother's fortune; and Clara, a Portuguese woman. They were all naughty, but Maurice was a real rogue, the kind of person who'd steal a motorbike, ride it to another country and abandon it. To say he was not exactly imbued with any great sense of responsibility to his fellow humans is an understatement, but he was great fun. I joined him busking in the streets, his girlfriend Benedicte whirling around us collecting the money.

In Torremolinos, I had a romance with an American named John Thomas, who crafted pornographic cutlery handles. I also met a Canadian Antarctic explorer, whose name I've now forgotten, who asked me to sail with him on his boat to Tangiers in Morocco, North Africa, and, having no good reason not to, I said, 'Sure.' Bad move. The voyage was a fiasco. First, there was no wind. We sat becalmed in the middle of the Gibraltar Straits for five days. Initially I didn't care, because in the mornings whales would surround the boat diving and swishing their flukes. Beautiful creatures though they are, the novelty soon wore off.

The wind picked up. *Really* picked up. Soon we were being battered by a violent storm. The tiller broke and the boom hurtled around dangerously in the howling wind. The Canadian locked me in the cabin so I wouldn't get hurt. My life passed before my eyes. I truly thought I was going to die. When the storm at last subsided, the guy said we'd been blown way off course and he had no idea where we were. Then, as if on cue, a thick fog enshrouded us. All that horrendous voyage, the Canadian drove me nuts trying to get me into bed, or bunk. I was badly sun- and windburned and my hair was sticking out all over my head due to being constantly doused in salt water, but that didn't bother him. He chased me all around the boat, and the more amorous he became the more I couldn't bear him to come near me.

Finally, we saw land and some harbour lights and limped into port. We'd missed Morocco completely and were in the port of Algiers in Algeria, of all places! The Canadian told me to go into the hold where he kept all the flags and hoist one that signified we wanted to tie up at the dock, but of course I flew the wrong flag. The Arabs saw it and shook their heads, 'Nuh!' So I pulled out another flag, 'Nuh!', until I came up with the right one and we were able to enter. I'd had enough of the Canadian explorer so caught the first boat to Torremolinos.

I went back to living a James A Michener novel and played around there with my fellow drifters, busking, hanging out, doing dope, in exotic Spain. One day I heard a knock on the door of my little room and there was Alison Baker, my old friend from Greville Street.

Alison Baker

It was good to see Chrissy and hear her adventures. I reckoned if I was after some fun and memorable experiences I couldn't have a better guide. We soaked up Spanish culture, the music, the food, the art, tapas bars. We enjoyed the Spanish custom of a siesta in the middle of the day and then partied all night long. Chrissy had a heavy wooden pencil case. She used it to carry odds and ends from her travels, but it proved more useful as a weapon. Many a Spaniard taking liberties with her felt that wooden box slam down on his groping hand. The worst were Moroccan men who came to the town to live it up. These guys had no respect for Western women, and the T-shirts and shorts we wore made them think we were fair game. They grabbed our bums and boobs and laughed. That is, until Chrissy whacked them with her secret weapon.

When Alison arrived I was supplementing the money I made busking with a job as a bar girl in a flamenco dive, chatting up patrons and persuading them to buy champagne for themselves and me at a huge mark-up. As soon as the fellow wasn't looking I would pour my drink into a pot plant so I could remain sober while he got more and more pissed. The idea was the more drunk he got the more money he'd spend, which of course was management's plan. I wasn't expected to sleep with these men, just dance with them, talk to them, maybe give them a hug, and encourage them to empty their wallets. If they thought their big night out was going to lead to something more, it wasn't my problem. Usually the guys were pretty disgusting. One night a group of farmers in town for an agricultural show rocked in at 3 a.m. and their pigs would have smelled better. It wasn't a wonderful way to make a living, but a girl had to do what a girl had to do.

The bar was a surreal place. While I chatted to the drinkers, flamenco dancers, guitarists and gypsies performed on stage. There was a fat black stripper named Rose Rolls-Royce who took her clothes off in a huge champagne flute. When Alison turned up she must have thought she'd fallen through the looking-glass.

Today when I hear 'Killing Me Softly' I time-travel back to my Spanish days. The song, so beautifully sung by Roberta Flack, was everywhere in the hot, fragrant air. I'd walk around singing, 'Strumming my pain with his fingers/Singing my life with his words . . .' It was music to fall in love to, and while I was in Spain I always seemed to be getting a crush on someone—but it never seemed to come to much.

Even though I was living the life of a free young Aussie I wasn't oblivious to the shadow of the right-wing Spanish dictator Francisco Franco upon the landscape. You weren't allowed to protest or be left wing, irreligious or gay. You weren't allowed to sing in the street for money, and you certainly couldn't smoke pot. That didn't stop me or the little gang of people who had become my friends from busking, doing drugs and staying up all night. It was a heady time.

It was inevitable that the *policía* would take notice of the wild gaggle of tourists but we were having too much fun to realise, so it was a huge shock one morning when they raided the place I had crashed at, put us in a van and herded us into the *comisaría*, the police station. There we stayed under lock and key for three days. All without laying a single charge. (True, we'd had a huge acid trip the night before but the officers had no proof of that.) The cell was filthy, with urine and faeces all over, and there were no beds so we had to sleep on the concrete floor. The guards derived deep pleasure from watching us pee.

On the fourth day we were sent to the *penitenciaro* in nearby Malaga. Maurice and Billy went to the men's wing on the ground floor and Benedicte, Clara and me to the women's on the next floor up. Luckily for Alison, she'd left Spain not long before. None of us had anything resembling a trial, let alone charges levelled against us, so our imprisonment was illegal. We were just easy marks for the police, who were under orders to clean up the streets. They also got their hands on Billy's money, which, like all of our possessions, they confiscated.

Benedicte, Clara and Maurice were soon freed because their countries, France and Portugal, had treaties with Spain. I was stuck, because Australia had no such deal. I told the police to contact the Australian Embassy but they said the Embassy couldn't help because my crime, taking drugs, was illegal. I seriously doubt the people at the Australian Embassy were ever notified of my predicament, but if they were they did nothing to help.

My eighteenth birthday fell soon after I was transferred to the *penitenciaro* and I spent it in my cell weeping. Singing 'For She's a Jolly Good Fellow' and blowing out the candles with Mum, Dad and Leigh seemed so long ago and so far away. But I didn't cry for long. I never do. I knew I was in trouble, and I was often frightened and lonely, yet a part of me was revelling in this incredible experience.

Wasn't this the grand adventure I left Australia to find? Anyway, I was confident I wouldn't be there forever. I worked hard at my job scrubbing toilets and would finish by seven each morning.

The first time I drank the prison coffee I vomited. I had no choice but to get used to it, and I did. The food was as disgusting as the coffee. The male prisoners took all the vegetables and sold them before they could be delivered upstairs to our mess. Soup was just oily water. Sunday was paella day, but there was no seafood, chicken or vegetables in the prison paella, only grungy burned rice with a slick of oil and a few unidentifiable objects strewn about. I bought tubes of condensed milk and sucked them to try to get some nutrition into my body. I smoked cheap black tobacco and drank Spanish beer, both of which were eked out to us by the guards, all of whom were women.

When girls were released I would sew a letter into the hem of their coat to Mum or Dad, saying what a splendid time I was having in Spain, and they posted it for me from an outside location. This way my parents would never know I was behind bars.

My cellmate was a gypsy named Dolores. She was a formidable-looking woman, in spite of having had an arm shot off in a hot-blooded argument. She wore a polka-dotted apron and shoes and sang amazingly. She was also a fine flamenco dancer, and taught me some of the steps. Dolores lay in her bunk at night, cajoling me to have sex with her. 'Ven aquí, chica,' she'd say breathlessly. 'Ven aquí.' To distract her and avoid the advances I asked her to pose while I drew her picture. I found I had the talent to sketch excellent likenesses. My Dad and Leigh both drew well, but I had never been a drawer, until then. My efforts weren't too bad, except for the ears. I could never draw ears. Drawing saved me from Dolores and also made me popular in our wing.

The prison was full of Moroccan girls who'd been locked up for drinking, it being a crime for a Muslim woman to imbibe alcohol. At night, they'd wail in their cells as they put curses on their enemies. Prisoners who'd been cursed believed punishment was inevitable, so would mutilate their own faces to fulfill the spells. There was a

Moroccan girl named Seleka, and all the others had it in for her. The poor girl's face constantly bore new self-inflicted scratches and cuts.

Most of the Moroccan inmates were very butch. They left me alone because I drew them. I had a power. Time passed slowly and each day was much the same. In the quadrangle, I'd do my sketches, Dolores would wash with her one arm and sing. I wrote a really tragic song called 'The End' on the back of a prison art book—more to keep busy than to make a statement. Brawls were everyday occurrences. The French prostitutes would clean the other girls' skin, a bit like monkeys, pricking blackheads, for which service I found myself grateful because the greasy prison food had made my skin a mess.

If the prisoners behaved like animals, the women guards were worse. I couldn't pass them without being denigrated or having my breasts grabbed. I'd swear at them and knock their hands away. One thing I learned in that Spanish prison was that I was tough, physically and mentally, and that I was self-reliant and a survivor. So long as I believed in myself, nothing could hurt me.

The prisoners came from many different lands, and had been busted for a variety of crimes. There were drug offenders (Spain then was awash with hash), prostitutes, murderers, thieves, left-wing protesters, abortionists, beggars and lesbians. I got on well with most, but my great friend was an Englishwoman named Helen, a lesbian who wore a man's suit, which fitted her perfectly. Dolores was moved from my cell and Helen moved in. Dolores was furious and paid me back by stealing all but three of my drawings. Helen had restaurants in Fuengirola, down the coast. She and I bonded; she protected me and never once made a pass at me.

While the other women were squabbling, drinking beer and picking blackheads in their pen, I would crawl upstairs with some of the other girls and look down at the men's prison on the lower level. Down in their yard they were always playing 'I Shot The Sheriff', the Bob Marley version, not Eric Clapton's. I've loved that song ever since. Like Roberta Flack's 'Killing Me Softly' it is part of the soundtrack to my life.

Helen and I often dreamed of escaping. It's a common human failing that we take freedom for granted and only miss it when it's taken from us, and we were missing it terribly. One day we were doing a job in the laundry and a door flew open, revealing the outside world beyond. We made a run for it, never really expecting to escape but unable to resist having a go. Suddenly we were surrounded by men with guns and they were pointing them at us and shouting furiously in Spanish. We tried to explain we were only joking. Eventually they cooled down and threw us back inside.

All the time I had been frantically trying through local officials to persuade the Australian Embassy to help me, to no avail. Helen, however, had friends in high places. She knew the local archbishop, who agreed to pressure the prison authorities. After two months of illegal incarceration in Malaga prison, an officer approached me and said, 'You're being released tomorrow.' Helen's archbishop had been busy on my behalf, and the night before I was released all my belongings and money materialised. Of course I threw a farewell party, which everyone seemed to enjoy—with the exception of Dolores, who sneaked into my cell and ripped up a number of my drawings. She was still beside herself with rage that I had chosen Helen as my friend.

Next morning, my belongings and I were bundled onto a prison bus bound for Barcelona, further up the coast. I would be locked up there for a short while, then bussed to the Spanish–French border and released some time after that. I was the only female onboard. All the guys were criminals being sent from Malaga to continue their prison terms in Barcelona. There was a cage at the front of the bus and I was locked in it, away from the clutches of the male prisoners who were handcuffed to each other in the regular seats. I was just glad that my imprisonment seemed to be nearing an end and went with the flow.

The bus trip took a week or so as we bounced over rough roads, stopping at small and ancient towns that probably hadn't changed much since the Middle Ages, to pick up other prisoners. Fellow passengers included black-eyed, ferocious-looking gypsies about to start 60-year sentences for killing someone who murdered or raped their sister or mother. (Years later I was asked in an interview whether I was intimidated being a woman in the male-dominated world of rock. I remembered being in that bus with those feral guys and smiled.) The gypsy women stood on the road wailing and handing out fruit as their men were loaded onto the bus. In spite of the terrible future awaiting them, the prisoners were in good spirits and danced the flamenco and sang all the way. At toilet and meal stops on our journey people took pity on us and spiked our coffee with cognac. We all got smashed. I made friends with the guards by sketching rude figures inside the crowns of their hats. Ever since a childhood friend of my mother's gave me a wooden donkey, I'd dreamed of travelling in Spain, but I'd never envisaged seeing it this way.

When the bus reached Barcelona I was escorted to the most beautiful modern jail. This was where I would spend the final two weeks of my prison time before another bus came and took me to Portbou just south of the Spanish–French border where I'd be released and sent on my way. The prison had parquetry floors and lattice windows that overlooked historic Barcelona and the Mediterranean Sea to the east. I was locked up in a long dormitory with forty French prostitutes. My job was to make plastic flowers, and although my fingers bled from twisting and pulling the wire and the plastic petals and leaves, I was feeling little pain.

Unlike at Malaga, where doing so would have been a red rag to the bulls who were guarding us, in Barcelona we were allowed to shower a couple of times a week, and stretch and exercise. The prostitutes were young and beautiful and had the most graceful posture. We had lessons—all in Spanish, which I still couldn't understand—in craft and cooking. One cook was serving a long sentence for putting her baby in an oven, and we all thought, 'Oh gawd, what's she cooking for *us*?'

After two weeks in this place, which was more like a hotel than a prison, I was once more on a bus, travelling north to a world without bars. Again, I was the only woman onboard, but this time my fellow passengers weren't murderers and rapists bound for prison, but others, like me, who'd done their time and were being booted out of Spain. They were an interesting bunch—artists, adventurers and wild kids. I was reunited with Billy, my friend from Torremolinos, on the bus. He was distraught because his mother's money, which the *policía* had taken from him, had not been returned. It totalled hundreds of thousands of pounds. He had no way to retrieve it and now he was literally penniless.

At Portbou, Billy and I left the bus and caught the first train into France. We spent a few days in a hotel somewhere in Provence to recover from our prison ordeal. I counted my blessings that I had my freedom back; Billy only counted the pounds he had lost. The poor guy worried me, for he was growing more and more upset at the thought of having to tell his mother about her money. He was often in tears of despair. I was afraid he'd try to end it all. I knew he had a major issue to contend with, but, frankly, he was miserable company. In spite of my paying his hotel and meal bills, he shunned my friendship because I reminded him of prison and the terrible things that had happened to him. I'd had enough. I left him there, travelled to the north coast of France and caught a hovercraft to England.

London in the mid-seventies was an extraordinary hotbed of musical creativity. Traffic, Blind Faith, the Faces, the Rolling Stones, Queen, Elton John. I met someone who had a squat in High Street, Kensington, opposite Olympia, and I moved in. This place was *palatial*. As with most squats, a bunch of homeless young people with nowhere to live had simply occupied the premises one day when the owners had vacated it and the law had no way of evicting them quickly. My room had velvet curtains and a beautiful little glass balcony. I liked to think Marianne Faithfull was just down the road tripping out on something—which was probably true.

One room in the squat was occupied by a group of African dancers. You'd walk into the kitchen and there'd be a woman squatting on the floor cooking fish African-style and *fou fou*, a water, salt and cornmeal concoction. When the Africans left, their room was taken by my old busking and prison mates Maurice and Benedicte who had come over from Torremolinos. I was glad to see them, for there were weird people in every nook and cranny of that mansion, and it got just a bit spooky. There was a touch of the Charles Mansons about it (there was even a guy named Ian who reminded me of Manson), but happily nothing bad happened to me apart from when one squatter, a tall, black man crazily addicted to Purple Hearts who wanted to take over my room, tried to attack me with a radiator. Maurice and Benedicte called the police who subdued the berserk guy, speeding out of his mind.

True to my desire for adventure, I didn't stay around London too long. Next stop: Belgium. In Antwerp I made friends with a group of people who hung out in an ancient square ringed by coffee houses and bars. I took a flat above a bar called the Pannonhouse. The gang would make their way to the square every day to listen to music and play pool. I landed a job cleaning the Pannonhouse bar, but got sacked because, like Mum I guess, I'm not a very good cleaner.

I soon noticed a handsome blond guy named Jan Verkammen who kept turning up in the square. He was married with two children and had a band comprising some Flemish fellows playing bass and drums, and an English lead guitarist. Jan, who was the singer, said he needed an English-speaking back-up singer and offered me the gig. Soon after I joined, Jan and I became romantically involved. Retribution was swift. I was ostracised by all the others from the square because I'd snatched Jan from his family.

Our little band moved on, leaving the square-dwellers and Jan's wife and children behind, to Gerardsbergen. There, the band lived together in a small private hotel owned by the bass player's wife's father. Jan and I had a room out the back. We all helped run the hotel in the mornings and practised in the afternoons. Jan wrote the songs for this very free-form experimental band, a Led Zeppelin-like jam band, or so Jan hoped. I began experimenting with new singing styles—like wailing. We played dance halls throughout Belgium and in Holland, where the fans, entranced by our psychedelic jams, danced *very* slowly.

But things were not rosy. I grew disenchanted. I considered myself a lead singer, and I was unhappy being in Jan's shadow, both as his back-up singer and as his girlfriend. When we moved back to Antwerp and rented a flat his kids could come to visit, I didn't like that at all. Domesticity was not what I had travelled so far to experience—I could have stayed in Geelong for that.

To qualify for the dole in Belgium Jan had to do a couple of days' work a week and he toiled away as a cartoonist and at the local shipyards, coming home late and encased in grease. I was left at home—waiting. To make matters worse, there were noisy Moroccans living on the floor below, and then, to top things off, the English lead guitarist moved in with us. After three months of this hell, I was planning ways of escape.

The English guitarist hastened my exit. One night, Jan and I heard him crying and moaning in his room. Jan insisted he was okay and just wanting attention. Against my better judgment I didn't investigate. Next morning I knocked on the Englishman's door. No answer. I pushed it open and blood was everywhere, on the floor, on his bed, all up the walls. He'd slashed his wrists. His moans were cries for help and I'd ignored them. I was deeply ashamed of my subservience to Jan and unthinking selfishness. The Englishman was barely breathing and was turning blue because he'd lost so much blood, yet somehow he managed to whisper that he'd tried to kill himself because he was having an affair with the bass player's wife and she wanted to call it off. We phoned for an ambulance and he was taken to hospital where I hope he recovered. I have no way of knowing for sure if he did because I walked straight out of the flat that morning and caught a train back to London.

There, I moved in with a woman I knew, an antique dealer, with a lovely, antique-filled but lived-in home in Chiswick. There was an intense young Irish poet staying there too, named Finbar Breen Omarku, and a charismatic forty-something American sculptor,

Lindsay Decker, living next door. I went out with both of them. I simply couldn't decide who I liked best.

Finbar was a gorgeous man. I found a job as a dresser at the Mermaid Theatre, then one of the jewels of London's West End, and he would meet me afterwards at the train station and we'd go home together, both of us dressed in the rich velvet that was so in vogue in those romantic times. The Mermaid Theatre paid me the princely sum of ten pounds a week so I had to sing in the streets, accompanying myself with a vintage autoharp I'd been given, to make ends meet. They were wonderful days, singing sweet old Irish songs, walking through Hyde Park among the fallen golden leaves, Finbar...and Lindsay.

Finbar and I were regulars at the fabled Troubadour Club on the Old Brompton Road where Monday night was poetry night. There, in the dark and smoky room where Dylan, Hendrix and Joni Mitchell had performed, I sang between the readings.

Finbar also comforted me after rough nights at the Mermaid Theatre helping the temperamental actors whip their costumes on and off between acts. The biggest backstage pest was a venerable and much-respected thespian who worked himself up into a tizz and slapped me if he thought I was too slow.

I can't say I was in love with Finbar, but he was in love with me. He went around to Island Records and tried to blarney them into giving me a record deal.

At the height of this little love triangle, Jan turned up. I was not pleased to see him and told him to go away. At one point all three guys were in my room at the same time, pulling me every which way. Lindsay had a boat and was insisting I join his crew and sail away with him on the high seas. I was tempted, for a minute or two.

My father, of all people, helped me chart my own course. He called me and said simply, 'Chrissy, come home. It's time.' So I went. Right after I kissed Finbar goodbye, he shaved his head as a sign of mourning. I have never seen him or Lindsay again. Guys, if you read this, get in touch.

This incredible period in my life ended on a happy note. When I checked in at the airline desk at Heathrow Airport I was upgraded from economy to first class. Maybe the clerk was impressed by what I was wearing, a 1910 schoolgirl's hat and a velvet poncho I'd made from discarded curtains from the Mermaid Theatre. Whatever the reason for my good fortune, I reclined my seat and for the rest of that long haul down through Europe and Asia, I wallowed in luxury, my mind racing over the events that had transformed me from a girl to a woman. I'd left home a young teenager and now I was twenty and eager for new experiences, new music, new romance. I would not be disappointed.

BARING IT

All I wanted was to be a rock star. Everything else in my life, relationships, family, friends, came second. After three years in Europe busking in city after city, flitting like a moth from band to band, it was time to make my dream of being a professional rock singer in a band that really mattered come true. My time away had matured me. It had focused my ambition and made me less inclined than ever to accept anything other than what I'd set my heart on.

When I arrived at Tullamarine airport my family was there to meet me with tears and hugs and to whisk me off for a party. I entertained them with some songs and autoharp. Everyone professed themselves proud of me for surviving so long overseas on my own. I guess they were just glad to have me back in one piece. Mum's brother Ern and his wife Peg, of prominent Melbourne stock, were especially pleased to see me and wondered what I'd do next. If they thought I'd settle down, get a guy, a baby and a mortgage they were mistaken.

I moved into a flat in Hawthorn then hit the usual Melbourne haunts. But I was now out of the loop. Most of the bands and musicians I knew had moved on, and the music scene had changed. Even the groupies I'd known had forsaken their dreams of bedding rock royalty and had settled for the boy next door. I found myself a virtual unknown starting from scratch. With nothing else on offer, I joined a loose-knit group of musos who played around Melbourne in pizza bars or wherever there was a stage and a socket to plug an amp into. I had no choice. My heart sank. These guys had no idea what kind of music they wanted to play and were not organised enough to even have a name. Their unprofessionalism was staggering. They agreed I should be lead singer, but when I took the microphone I could sense these journeymen, with, to be brutally honest, nothing like my talent or experience, felt the spotlight should be firmly fixed upon them. And when I dressed up in my glam black-satin suit and sang with my long hair out these dags grumbled and whined. I was simply on a different planet. An outsider again. Story of my life. Surely, I felt, I could do a whole lot better than this.

One day while meandering along Collins Street, preoccupied trying to figure out a way to get a real gig, I passed by Merivale and Mr John and applied for a position as a part-time sales assistant. Much as music was my life, it wasn't paying my board or putting food in my mouth, and I needed money. Merivale and John Hemmes' shop was still Melbourne's most out-there fashion emporium, a place for the most fashionable girls to shop and work. I got the job. As vogueish as it was to work at Merivale, it was bloody hard. We were paid no wage, only a commission on the clothes we sold, so competition among the sales staff was brutal. A customer would stroll in and be set upon by a pack of ravenous she-wolves in designer clothes and stilettos.

In the mornings we had to line up while Mr John, like a sergeant-major, inspected us, making sure we had the Merivale 'look' which, basically, was that you had to appear pretty amazing. I passed muster, thanks to my *femme fatale* dress with its very low back and little black shoes (that I called my 'fuck me' shoes because that's the sound they made as I stalked about in them). The icing on the cake was my spectacular hairstyle: long fringe, long from the top and at the back, and shaved sides. This, remember, was pre-punk. I was into glam and romance, trying to look the way the music I loved then sounded: Fleetwood Mac's 'Rhiannon', David Bowie's 'Changes', Peter Frampton's 'Frampton Comes Alive' and the steamy disco soul of Donna Summer and Hot Chocolate. Already, though, the 'look' was changing. Punk rock was only months away. When Blondie, the Sex Pistols, Ian Dury and the Blockheads, and Elvis Costello and the Attractions really made it worldwide, around 1977 and '78, I forgot about looking dreamily romantic as my outfits got edgier and my attitude hardened.

At night, I'd still follow the bands, always conniving to sing with them. Sometimes they said yes. At a gig in Geelong I supported Jo Jo Zep and the Falcons and Hush. How nice it would be to say that they were knocked out by me and offered me work, but that wasn't so. In fact, these slick and arrogant guys put me down. They laughed and told me I was too *different* to make it as a rock singer. They said that with my quirky voice and dress and my buck teeth I didn't sing or look like a lead singer should. They were saying success and acceptance comes with conformity. That was crap. Rock'n'roll is for rebels.

As much to annoy my critics as anything else, when I did get the chance to sing I reverted to my Belgian free-form jam band wailing. I created my own songs, sometimes on the spot, and just wailed them, regardless of what anyone thought. Even Mum, for once, found it impossible to give me her unstinting support. 'Darling, *why* are you singing like this?' she'd say with a puzzled expression.

I could only answer, 'To piss people off and find my style.'

Whatever my contrariness achieved, it wasn't a gig in a band. No one wanted to know about weird, wailing Chrissy.

Time to try another tack. When I was fifteen I'd auditioned for the rock musical *Hair* only to be told I was too young. Five years on I again began trying out for stage roles. I auditioned for every show in Melbourne, but couldn't get a part. Then I struck paydirt. Some may just call it dirt. I cracked a role in *Let My People Come*, the Australian version of a musical being staged in New York's Greenwich

Village. The US show was a sensation, although not because of its great songs, script, costumes or message. No, *Let My People Come* was famous, or *in*famous, because the singers and actors at one point in the show performed in the nude.

Let My People Come was hyped as a 'sexual musical, a theatrical emancipation and a milestone for freedom of expression [which] touches upon all forms of human sexuality in the guise of a thought-provoking, suggestive, bitingly satirical, outrageously refreshing, innocent and entertaining childish romp'. The message: 'people are sexual if only because they are human and mortal and if they understand and deal with that fact they will be able to move on to something else.' The publicist forgot to add that *Let My People Come* was also horrible, tacky, cheap and salacious.

Yet it was the right gig at the right time for me. It was regular work, eight shows a week for nine months at the Total Theatre in Exhibition Street then a three-month season at the Bijou Theatre in Sydney's Balmain. As Linda Lips the Porn Queen, I was one of an ensemble cast who performed vignettes and songs whose common denominator was sex. A bunch of talented people who should have been doing better things also got their gear off.

Let My People Come outraged Melbourne. The media, the church and morality groups demanded it be closed down and the theatre fumigated, which, of course, guaranteed queues at the box office.

We rehearsed for a few weeks, and then came the day we were all fearing, when we had to take our clothes off. This was a huge step for me as I'd never been naked in public before. My co-stars were freaking out too. Finally, when we could put it off no longer, the director gave it to us straight: 'Okay, this is it. Get it over and done with. Off with your clothes.' We disrobed, and that was that. Once naked, I felt quite liberated. From then on it was no big deal to be undressed in front of the audience. In one scene I wore only a corset and large rollers in my pubic hair. (The rollers were attached each night with loving care by a sweet gay guy named Danny.) At interval and after the performance the cast blithely strolled about backstage in various stages of undress and thought little of it. Sometimes we'd indulge in some dope smoking in the theatre stairwell. In spite of the producers' blurb, there was nothing sexual about *Come*.

I can't imagine any of us listing the show among the highpoints of our theatrical careers, yet we were a talented bunch and I found I had to fight hard for a solo song to sing. After much cajoling, the director let me perform 'Give It To Me', which was not hard to learn, since its lyrics consisted mainly of declaring I wanted a man to fuck and requesting him to give it to me... Having proved myself, I was allowed to understudy the actress who sang 'Come In My Mouth', another song that passed for a showstopper in this curious little production.

My father was appalled when he learned I was in *Come* and never darkened the theatre door. But Mum came a lot, and Uncle Ern and Aunty Peg turned up too. I'd be halfway through 'Come In My Mouth' and I would look down into the audience and see Mum laughing hysterically. Oddly enough, she had a harder time coping with me singing free form than prancing around nude in front of a packed house. When *Come* moved to Sydney, Dad's brother Joe and his daughter Patricia—Little Pattie—came to see me and, like my mother, they both loved it.

Patricia Amphlett

I took my father to see Chrissy on the opening night of *Let My People Come*'s short Sydney run. Out she came with her huge breasts on show. It was hysterical, but Dad didn't utter a word. He must have been taken aback at the sight of his niece standing there in front of everyone topless. Then, afterwards, backstage, he hugged her and said, 'You were the best in the show, love. No one was as good as you.' That was the difference, by the way, between Dad and his brother, Chrissy's father, Jim. Jim would've been absolutely horrified and would never have gone to that show. Joe was a larrikin and Jim was very conservative.

I never missed a show, not even after I'd had some corns burnt off my feet and could hardly walk. *Come* wasn't much, but it was my first regular gig and I made the most of it. I'd never missed a ballet lesson growing up, and now in *Come*, as I showed up night after night while some co-stars were dropping like flies, I realised that I'd been blessed with a formidable work ethic. And I also learned that I enjoyed shocking audiences. Their stunned faces were proof that I had forced a reaction from them and taken them out of their comfort zone, and as a performer that's an achievement. After *Come* I would never again take my clothes off on stage, but it was a crash course in laying myself bare emotionally. I would put my talent to shock to good use later in Divinyls. After wearing rollers in my pubes how could I ever be inhibited again?

A casting agent working on *Dawn!*, the movie biography of swimming legend Dawn Fraser, came to *Come* and obviously liked what she saw. She offered me a plum role in the film on the strength of my performance. 'We're shooting a nude scene,' she explained, 'and Bronwyn Mackay-Payne, the actress playing Dawn, has a problem with nudity. We were wondering if we could use your bottom as a body double.' I turned her down flat. 'You could never pay me enough,' I explained, 'to play Dawn Fraser's arse.'

Backstage at *Come* was quite a scene, and the Total Theatre's bar became one of the top hangs in Melbourne. Seeing the nude girls and having a drink afterwards was the thing to do for visiting international rock and pop acts, like the Jeff Beck Group who really enjoyed their visit. I met lots of actors and musicians who would become friends, like actors Kris McQuade, Lisa Peers, Tracy Mann, Michael Caton and the amazing Candy Raymond.

As one of the TV soap *No. 96*'s resident sex symbols and a star of the movie *Don's Party*, Candy was one of Australia's best-known actresses, and in 1978 she was in Melbourne filming Bruce Beresford's *The Getting of Wisdom*. A formidable actress, a formidable woman, and a person, when I saw her in the theatre bar one evening, I wanted to get to know. It was clear to all that she was an actress and I loved her diva ways. Candy would go on to become a respected character actress in such prestigious films as *Monkey Grip* and *The Money Movers* and in 1986 she won an AFI Best Actress Award for her performance in the telemovie *Breaking Up*. Later, in The Company of Players she performed the work of the masters, Shakespeare, Shaw and Chekhov.

Candy always had a thing for younger guys and she was besotted by my *Come* castmate Henk Johannes. Henk was not as rapt in Candy, and besides, he had a girlfriend, actress Lisa Peers. Henk toyed with Candy and broke her heart. When she needed a shoulder to cry on and a friend to hang out with, I was there.

In those days there was an old blues song I loved to sing, accompanying myself on my autoharp from Europe, 'St James Infirmary'...

> I went down to the St James infirmary,
> To see my baby there,
> He was stretched out on a long white table,
> So young, so cold, so fair ...
> Let him go, let him go, God bless him,
> Wherever he may be,
> He may search this whole world over
> He'll never find another girlie like me ...
> Sixteen coal-black horses
> Tied to a rubber-tyred hack
> Sixteen miles to the graveyard
> And I'm never going back

Even today if I'm asked to get up and sing something there's a chance it will be this sad and gorgeous dirge that somehow typified that time in my life.

Candy Raymond

I was immediately entranced by Chrissy. We were both into op-shop clothes of the forties and fifties, and her sense of style outweighed mine—no question. I was also drawn to her strength. I was deeply, neurotically, emotional. I was a mess. Chrissy is stronger than me, and she was fearless. A lot of what I was doing on TV and in movies was brave, and I'm sure that appealed to her. It's possible, too, that there was, initially, anyway, an element on her part of wanting to befriend me because I was quite famous. Chrissy does have that streak of ambition, and she is capable of being very ruthless with it but, hey, you don't get to be Australia's first woman leader of a top-billing band without those qualities. That was at first, then our friendship developed and has lasted all our lives, notwithstanding some rocky patches.

Chrissy had something I never did, and that was the support of her mum. She could snap her fingers and her mother would be there doing whatever she needed. Once a month she would go to bed with magazines and have her mum bring her food and cups of tea. She'd have an R and R day and her mum would look after her. It was a damn good idea.

She used to play the autoharp and, as far as I know, that's the only instrument she's ever played. She was no virtuoso on it, it was just to accompany her singing. And she used to sing for me! 'St James Infirmary' and 'My Love Is In Chains': 'My love is in chains/Chained to his whisky . . .' as Chrissy herself was later. I'd say, 'Sing for me, sing for me!' I worshipped the talent of my singing friends, and I worshipped Chrissy long before Divinyls.

A bunch of us moved into a huge mansion in Kew, rented by a countess, Anna Krysinski, who was, of all things, the publicist for *Let My People Come*. Fabulous people came and went. I can recall Candy and Paul Johnstone there, Henk, too, and the exquisitely beautiful Daina, and Kris McQuade, Tracy Mann and Michael Caton (who loved a party more than most and would star in TV's *The Sullivans* and the hit movie *The Castle*). Michael's wife, Vicki, was a gifted photographer and took some beautiful photos of me. I had black cats that slunk languorously through the rooms, casually dropping in on the parties that always seemed to be going on somewhere in that huge house. At Anna Krysinski's people made love, listened to music, smoked dope. Visiting bands heard about the scene and came to hang out.

The residents had a ritual. Every Sunday at 6 p.m. when *Countdown* came on we'd stop whatever we were doing and watch Molly Meldrum introduce his acts. As awful as some of those performers were, seeing them reinforced to me that I could never be satisfied appearing in shows like *Come* while my ambition to sing rock'n'roll still burned.

For the first time, among these professional actors and musicians, I was feeling less of an outsider. I don't think they respected me for my singing or acting at that time, but they accepted me as a feisty, genuinely eccentric young woman with a look and a mind all her own who sang and was fun to be around. I had boyfriends here and there, some flings, but I was never in love. That was an emotion I reserved for singing.

When *Let My People Come* moved to Sydney for its run at the Bijou Theatre, I moved into Candy's flat at Darling Point, overlooking Sydney Harbour. By now I was dating an older guy, a pretentious Canadian wannabe thriller author who had never written anything but was always about to. I'd met him at a party at the Point Piper home of the TV and movie stuntman Grant Page. Grant was co-ordinating the stunts for the first *Mad Max* movie, and his home, a sprawling mansion by the water, was a boarding house for the cast and crew who slept on the floor or any horizontal surface. When there wasn't enough room at Grant's the *Mad Max* crew would come and doss at my place. At Grant's I saw Mel Gibson, Candy's now ex, Paul Johnstone, who played the outlaw Cundalini in the film, and a bunch of actors and stuntmen who, with their biker clothes, tattoos, eye patches and huge biceps, could have stepped right off a pirate ship. Of course no one knew then how successful *Mad Max* would be, or that it would inspire a string of sequels and establish Mel as an international star.

I'm grateful for those times. The late seventies in Melbourne and Sydney were pivotal years for me. I was driven; evolving; adopting and discarding styles, friends, points of view; and slowly but surely realising my ambitions. Luckily, punk, a movement that encouraged outrageousness and attitude, happened along. Punk made a lot of things possible. I was a free spirit, answering only to myself, rebelling against convention. I refused to be dominated or controlled. If Darryl Cotton had tried his plastic penis routine with me then my reaction would have been very different. For me this was a time of experimentation. *Anything* for a new experience. I was a sensual person who liked sexy things, including men, but I would never again fling myself submissively at the feet of my lovers.

I was sexual without having numerous or deep relationships. I simply enjoyed touching and sleeping with people. I was like a cat. I liked to be physically close to people. I'd end up in somebody's bed, and then I'd leave. You couldn't tie me down. Sexuality and creativity live in the same place. Singing was my aphrodisiac.

I was seeing a side of Sydney I missed on my first visit when I briefly sang at Chequers with Daisy Clover. The clubs, pubs and cafés of Kings Cross, Darlinghurst, Paddington and Bondi, atmospheric and very rock'n'roll, became my beat. Lisa Peers, Tracy Mann and I used to hang out at the 21 Café in Double Bay. It was run by Hungarians and had superb matzo ball soup, crisp golden Vienna schnitzel, runny creamed spinach spiced with garlic and the best coffee in Sydney. A tall, noisy comedian named Sandy Gutman (he would become better known as Austen Tayshus) was always muscling in on our afternoon teas and, in spite of our more-than-obvious yawns and eye-rolling, he relentlessly road-tested his jokes on us. We'd see him coming and dive under the table.

Sydney, in its way, was just as vibrant a music city as Melbourne, not that I was getting gigs. Kris took me to see her boyfriend, Barry Leef, and his band play at the Musician's Club. I had always considered myself a wild dancer, but I had nothing on Kris, who took dancing to another level. Kris McQuade was, and is, a fine actress with a beautiful speaking voice that somehow reflects her wisdom and salt-of-the-earth spirit.

Either with my friends or alone I saw all the local and visiting singers and groups. There was an explosion of punk bands in Sydney then. Martha Davis and the Motels and Blondie with Deborah Harry at the State Theatre were especially memorable. The mesmeric Deborah had changed my life when I saw her in a video singing 'In The Flesh' in a bathing costume. She was strong, commanding and, a rarity then fronting a band, she was a woman. I thought if she could do it...Deborah Harry's video was the closest thing to an epiphany I've ever had.

Seeing this amazing, talented singer, so in control of herself, her band and the audience, made me want to sing in a band so badly I could taste it. But along with this desire came a selfish focus on myself. I was driven, raw and never satisfied. In my rush to be a singer I left a number of people in my emotional wake.

Candy and I were still in her little caretaker flat and her friendship and experience had an immense influence on me. She turned me on to reading, literature and biographies like that of Sir Richard and Lady Burton (he was a British explorer who searched for the source of the Nile, translated the *Kama Sutra* and was one of Europe's finest swordsmen). Candy was a great friend when I needed one. But as I was starting to find my wings, I think she felt a little threatened by all the changes that were taking place in me. She liked to consider herself the intellectual and me the compliant follower. Suddenly I was coming into my own as a creative artist, I was growing stronger, and was learning to set my boundaries. My other great friend of that era, Shayna Stewart, on the other hand, revelled in my personal growth and always encouraged my free thinking and excesses.

Candy and I were not cut out to be flatmates. She was emotionally all over the place, very dramatic, delicate and fragile, revelling in her books and long, deep conversations. I was aggressive, loud, with a short attention span, constantly starting arguments and singing at the top of my voice. I was always in a hurry, always running from control and from my middle-class background. I didn't like the guys she went out with, especially a young boyfriend who moved in with us. He was way too affected for me, and I just knew he was another who would treat Candy poorly. In my opinion, he wasn't especially talented and thought it enough to simply be in the acting and music scene. The scene per se meant nothing to me. What I worshipped was talent and creativity and being a great performer. That was an end

in itself, the glitz and the magazine profiles were immaterial, a waste
of time, and I was intolerant of anyone who didn't share my hardline
point of view.

Candy Raymond

We'd been flatting together for about a year in my very small apartment.
Chrissy slept on a futon bed in the lounge room. Early on, for four months
while I was away, she had the place to herself but then I returned and
we squeezed in together. I found her in an absolute myopically
ambitious mood about her career. She was manic, exercising the
divine right of the diva.

We had such fun, and plenty of bummers and heartbreak and
depression. We knew we were alive. We were always swapping clothes:
'Can I wear your black thing with a collar?' Dressing up to go out was
a very serious business. Usually we'd decide we didn't want to cook
so we'd catch a gig and then go to the Piccolo Bar in Kings Cross
until six in the morning.

Then I fell in love with a guitarist and singer nine years younger
than me. He was talented and gorgeous. I had no intention of asking
Chrissy to move out because I believe that you don't treat good women
friends as if they're just there for when you haven't got a lover.

For a time it was beautiful having them both in the house. They'd
sing and I'd be transfixed. Then it became clear that Chrissy didn't
like my lover and didn't want him there. She became bossy with him.
She was also totally preoccupied by making it in rock, to the exclusion
of everyone and everything and that got a bit difficult to put up with.
It got to the point where I had to say, 'Chrissy, I love you but I want to
live with my boyfriend . . . it might be best if you found somewhere else
to live.'

When Candy asked me to leave her flat, I moved in with Shayna and
we became deeply involved. She was a free spirit, a left-wing firebrand
who could sing like an angel. This remarkable woman had so many
interesting friends from the worlds of music, acting, politics and the

arts. Ten years older than me and a single mother, Shayna was naughty, into drugs and general wildness, and I followed her happily.

Shayna was strong and quiet. She had the soul of a hippy, and was always behind the beat. She had sung in two of the country's best bands, Extradition and Tully, but was never especially fussed about her singing career; all she wanted to do was to sing well.

I, on the other hand, was desperately ambitious, and would have *killed* to become the best rock singer Australia had ever seen. All I needed was a chance.

Shayna Stewart

Chrissy was like no one else I'd ever met. She had a huge imagination and a great way of seeing the world. I loved that, and could relate to it.

Chrissy and Candy were both real performers. They were on all the time. And they still are, aren't they? I think neither of them quite know when they're on and when they're not. They get a bit confused about it.

In the early days of their friendship, Chrissy idolised Candy because Candy was a star and Chrissy was desperate to become one. Of course, that situation changed and Chrissy became internationally famous. Chrissy's unbelievably self-centred. She just is, and she is incredibly independent and has survived all sorts of things.

Shayna taught me things about singing I never knew, and when *Come*'s Sydney run ended, she invited me to join her in the various vocal groups she graced with her solo and harmony singing. One of these was the Radio 2CH eight-piece choir and while it was hardly rock'n'roll, singing demanding songs such as 'Just Walking In The Rain' developed the top part of my voice and my range.

As beneficial as it was, singing in that choir alongside largely straight-laced older people was anathema to my punky heart. I'd rehearse at the Sydney Opera House wearing pyjamas, or ripped T-shirts and jeans and bare feet. The outraged glares I drew made my day.

Punk was the look and the mindset of the era. All the actors I knew were into it, especially Tracy Mann. The local bands we hung with were punk rockers, such as the Ferrets, friends of Shayna's who'd supported Blondie at the State Theatre; the Reptiles; and Simon and the Diamonds. The music on our stereos and boom boxes was Sex Pistols, Ian Dury and the Blockheads, Elvis Costello, the Motels, the Specials... the 2CH Choir was not high on our playlists.

Shayna Stewart

The 2CH Choir was very, very straight. The singing was demanding with difficult parts. We sang hymns, old standards and traditional songs and performed with the Sydney Symphony Orchestra. There'd be singers in suits and conservative frocks and Chrissy, who had discovered punk before anyone else in Australia, would turn up to rehearsals at Sydney Opera House in boys' pyjamas from Kmart and a black T-shirt with holes in it. Being Chrissy, she got away with it.

She had a real eye for pop culture and was always way ahead of the trends. I didn't know where the punk thing came from. She got her influences from everywhere, like a bowerbird. She could read a book and all of a sudden that book would be her guiding light until something new came along. She buried herself in each new enthusiasm with a manic glee.

The hard work with the 2CH Choir paid dividends and I started getting singing jobs around Sydney. Nothing permanent or particularly memorable, but part of the process of paying my dues. Shayna and I got a gig singing back-up in a St George Leagues Club production of *Jesus Christ Superstar* that starred Marcia Hines as Mary Magdalene. I was also Marcia's understudy, to sing Mary if Marcia was sick or otherwise unable to appear. I was champing to have a shot at the part. I knew I'd make a great fist of it. Marcia, however, was a trouper who rarely missed a performance, so my chances of playing Mary Magdalene would be minuscule. Or so I thought.

One night, Shayna and I were zapping down the highway in her Morris Mini to sing in *Superstar* at the club when suddenly we saw Marcia's Jaguar roar past us, take off into the air and plunge into a ditch. Shayna looked at me. I looked at Shayna. She said, 'Chrissy, you're on!' and without, I'm sorry to confess, checking on Marcia's condition she floored the accelerator. Nothing was going to get in the way of my big chance.

At the club, word had spread that Marcia had smashed her car. She hadn't been hurt but she was too shaken to appear that night. I *was* on. It's an old showbiz cliché (remember *42nd Street* and *A Star Is Born*?) when the star gets hurt and the understudy performs triumphantly in her place. Well, a star wasn't born at the St George Leagues Club that particular night. All the arrangements had been placed in Marcia's key, which was much higher than mine, and I sounded terrible... 'I don't know how to *laarrrvvve* him...' Making a bad situation worse, if that was possible, I had borrowed Marcia's body stocking for the performance and when she showed up the next night and found out she tore strips off me.

My ruthless drive to perform was in overdrive. One evening around the time of the Marcia Hines fiasco, I was off to a singing gig in North Sydney in the Mini. Shayna should have been with me but for some reason couldn't make it. I was going down a hill towards Neutral Bay when a tyre blew out. I lost control and the car rolled over and over down an embankment and ploughed through a fence. Part of the fence smashed through the front windscreen and ended up beside me in the passenger seat. Had Shayna been in the car she would have been impaled. I landed upside down, suspended in the wreckage by my seatbelt. Somehow I undid it and crawled out onto the grass, cut and with small shards of windscreen-glass embedded in my head. A group of people rushed up to see if I was okay. I was short with them. 'Look,' I explained, 'I've got to be at a gig. Would you people mind taking care of my car for me?' and I left the scene. Not for a moment did I consider that these kind bystanders could have had lives and commitments of their own.

Backstage somewhere, Shayna and I met a singer and bass player named Jeremy Paul. Jeremy had been in an early configuration of Air Supply. We were putting together a group we called Baton Rouge comprising some of the musicians we'd played and sung with around the choir and session work traps and asked Jeremy to join us. Baton Rouge was Shayna, me, drummer John Swanton, Jeremy Paul and others who came and went. We were basically a covers band and performed six times a week in pubs, wine bars, leagues clubs and coffee lounges. Our *modus operandi* was to find songs we liked and then Shayna rearranged them to suit our strength which, to be honest, was her and my singing. She was a wizard at devising interesting vocal arrangements. We shared the singing and, after she showed me how, harmonised.

Baton Rouge operated on a shoestring because bands like us were paid a pittance. We couldn't afford a roadie and carried all our microphones, amps and instruments. Being in Baton Rouge wasn't musically creative enough for me, but it improved my singing. I was building a reputation as a proficient singer and record companies were beginning to notice. One night some friends of John Swanton turned up to see me perform. Mark Opitz, Roger Langford and Phil Mortlock, executives with the WEA label, said nothing; they just stood at the back of the club and watched.

Shayna Stewart

Chrissy began to develop her own style and she'd do this sort of overtly sexual thing, you know, the way she held the microphone, and I could also see elements of AC/DC's Angus Young in her performances. She soon got bigger than the band, and we had some terrible fights on stage, usually over silly things such as one of us arriving late or not wanting to do a particular song. These arguments were part of the rocky territory of our friendship. Sometimes we weren't nice to each other.

It didn't help my frame of mind that I was struggling financially. Unlike Chrissy I had responsibilities. I had a daughter. I'd left her father. I was trying to make a living, singing. So when I was in Baton Rouge I had to have a babysitter living in the house who would care for my daughter because I was working every night. I was often my own worst enemy. We'd do a show then stay out all night, partying and taking drugs, then I'd arrive home at 6 a.m. in time to help the babysitter get my daughter off to school. That done, I'd try to get some sleep before heading off to rehearse for that night's gig. We all had our own private demons and were living in a dog-eat-dog world, a very self-indulgent world. I basically needed support and I needed other women who understood the fact that I had a kid.

Chrissy understood, but she was moving on. She had enormous self-esteem and was becoming a sex symbol on stage, the focal point of the band, whereas I was at the back, just doing my singing and beating myself up because I didn't think I was a good mother.

I was completely focused on singing, on the rock'n'roll dream—and that included the partying, drugs and lack of sleep synonymous with that life. I hadn't touched heroin until this point. Why did I get into it? After all those surfer boys died, I knew it was dangerous, but I was in a dangerous frame of mind then and I thought I was invulnerable. I was quietly frantic that I still hadn't made it as a rock singer, and I was dispirited by what I considered the square world of choirs, musical theatre and the safe mediocrity of Baton Rouge. Smack, I see with hindsight, was a way to give the finger to everything I thought was holding me down. Then, when someone told me heroin was Deborah Harry's drug of choice, the drug, for me, was ordained.

I didn't shoot up. We smoked brown rocks of smack through plastic biros with the ink cartridge taken out. As ever, I'd get violently ill when I was stoned, but I thought it was worth it. Getting singing gigs and scoring drugs was my quest. There was not much sex in my life, but drugs and rock'n'roll were in plentiful supply.

There were the inevitable sordid scenes. My car being stolen one night after I'd scored some smack, me finding the car and trying to drive it while vomiting. Next day having to sing in the choir and with Baton Rouge while feeling like death.

What is it about bands? I've never known one that wasn't a passion pit. Maybe the talent, the ambition, the magic of the music casts a spell over those who play in them and dooms them to labyrinthine romantic entanglements. Baton Rouge was no different. I was mad about John Swanton, at best a fair drummer but a good organiser and quite brilliant when it came to appreciating fine art, his real passion. We had a relationship, but John was a hard man to pin down and it was short-lived. Then Jeremy joined and seemed fascinated by me because I was uninhibited and he was very square and it was a challenge to a man like him to control a girl like me, much like a rodeo rider tames a wild brumby. Naturally, he failed. Shayna was in love with another bandmember, Terry Willis, and had a baby with him.

To make a little money, I sang some radio commercials, one for *Cleo* magazine. Then Shauna Jensen, who had been in the cast of *Let My People Come*, persuaded me to go to a studio with her and cut some vocals for a Kelloggs ad. I flunked badly. Shauna is a fine session singer, technically skilled and at home in a studio. I was different. I was not a technically adept singer. Then, as now, I could only sing one way, from the heart. My voice has rough edges, idiosyncratic colour, unusual tones, and this was the case even back in those early years. It was too individual to be flogging cornflakes. In the ad game, safe is best. And recording was a skill I hadn't learned yet. When you record you work in a rigid time frame and have to be able to stop and start at the advertising agency's whim. It was a pressure situation, not enjoyable or creative. I clammed up, and Shauna was angry with me. Outside in the street she told me off. 'You were disgraceful,' she said. 'You'll never get another commercial as long as you live!' I saw Shauna again recently, for the first time in decades, and she said, 'Remember when I told you that you had no future singing commercials? Aren't you glad I was right.'

While men came and went in my life at this time, it was my friendships with women that influenced me most. Like Candy and Shayna, there was another woman who made a lasting impression on me. A mentor of sorts, I met her at the home of a friend. Tall, blonde, boyish and dressed in velvet, she walked into the living room, our eyes met, and we were instantly drawn to each other. Not sexually, in my case, anyway, but emotionally and intellectually. I was deeply impressed by her sense of fun and her eccentricity—she was a very unusual woman with original attitudes about most subjects under the sun and the weirdest way of dancing—and she saw something in me that she needed. I moved into her home in Mosman and stayed for nearly two years. My passion to sing still raged, but suddenly, thanks to her, there was more in my life. We talked for hours about every conceivable subject while reggae, Radio Birdman and the Rolling Stones played on her stereo. It was like we'd been friends forever. She hated me smoking heroin so I stopped and never did smack again.

What's the saying? If something is too good to be true it's too good to be true. In time our wonderful friendship was corrupted by this woman's jealousy and possessiveness. She wanted to own me. That old control thing reared its head again, and as usual, just like when Dad had tried it, I bucked. She began to resent my having interests outside our own. She was dismissive of my friendships with others, such as Shayna, and she really disliked Candy because she couldn't abide actresses. It annoyed her when I spoke of Mum with affection and of her unconditional love and support. She got testy when I talked of singing rock'n'roll which, of course, was something that could not involve her. I lashed out.

She began seeing a man whom she said was an ASIO spy at about the same time that I had a romance with my old friend the stuntman Grant Page. Grant, of course, wouldn't use the door when he visited me at my friend's apartment, he'd simply scale the wall and climb in my window. One evening, the man from ASIO saw him clinging to the outside of the building like Spider-Man and, convinced that Grant was an enemy agent, caused a fuss. I moved out.

Some months later I was at a film screening when I had a strange sensation. Something was telling me that my estranged friend was in trouble. I left the film and caught a taxi to her home, by now a lovely worker's cottage in Woollahra. I ran through the front door without knocking and there she was on the floor, dressed in a white gown, a tube from the gas oven in her mouth. It was clear she was near death. I pulled the tube out of her mouth and called the emergency number. Within minutes, medics arrived and whisked her off to the hospital.

When she was feeling better I paid her a visit. She looked at me and snapped, 'I saved *you* from heroin. You saved *me*. We're even. Goodbye!'

It seemed all my intense friendships were doomed to fail—but this wouldn't stop me from connecting with people who inspired, stimulated or fascinated me. Looking back, it seemed all roads were leading to my most intense friendship of all.

A BAND IS BORN

Mark McEntee simply materialised in my life. I can't remember the first time I laid eyes on him. Perhaps it was at a Baton Rouge gig— I'm told he lurked around in the shadows checking me out. Perhaps I saw him in the crowd at a 2CH Choir recital, though I have no memory of this if so. He would tell me he was there at the Sydney Opera House the day I got a stool tangled in my microphone cord and carried on singing, oblivious to the furniture I was dragging back and forth across the stage.

When we *did* meet and speak with each other, sometime in 1980 at the old Elephant and Castle pub in Surry Hills, sparks flew. Not romantic sparks at first. That came after two years of touring and playing together. But creative electricity. We were a gang of two. Here at last was someone who was as manic about music as me. Someone who dreamed of a rock'n'roll destiny and thought he knew how to achieve it. The only difference between us was that I sang and he played guitar, blisteringly, eloquently and like nobody else. As I did, Mark affected a bad attitude, and when he was preoccupied people learned to approach him at their own risk. This was possibly a consequence of his shyness. His weapons were cutting words, vicious wit or a disconcerting silence.

Mark also had a quirky sense of humour. Early on, a rock journalist trying to piece together his musical history asked him what was his background. 'Oh, a black curtain and an amp,' Mark replied, straight-faced. Later, on video shoots, he'd tell the director he wanted to be photographed by a camera lens smeared with Vaseline 'to make me look glamorous, like Doris Day!' The director never knew if he was serious. He wasn't.

Mark, who grew up in Perth, lived in Manly with his wife, Linda. He was a skinny little blond guy in a long leather coat with his long hair crowning a prominent forehead, deep-set eyes, slightly sinister chiselled cheekbones and a spivvy moustache. He was a Germanophile and made advanced-level model aeroplanes. He also talked music with an intensity I'd never known and we both realised that our musical lives were entwined; we were creatively bound.

I was blown away by this odd man-child, and looked forward to his visits. He would turn up at my door with his guitar and amp and we'd write songs together, define our tastes and devise our style. We talked endlessly about songs and how to perform them.

We decided we would play full-on rock and embody the anger and refusal to compromise that typified the punk ethos. Our music and our performances would be *real*, honest, raw and straight from the heart. Sometimes I didn't know where Mark started and I ended. We remained on each other's creative wavelength even when, in the years to come, our discussions turned to slanging matches.

When Mark and I got together, we threw almost everything we'd learned out of the window and crafted music that was dynamic and fresh. We eliminated all the frills. I dropped the vibrato I usually used and became a *non*-singer, accentuating my vocal peculiarities, the idiosyncrasies that made me different. In my career, my singing has been described by critics in various ways: it's reminded people of sobs, hiccups, yodelling and guttural screaming, it's been called sweetly affecting, breathy and good-humoured, a rasp, a coo, a shout, a harridan's yowl, a snarl, bruised but defiant. Some have likened my voice variously to that of Buddy Holly, Iggy Pop, Otis Redding... and the Bride of Frankenstein. Screw all that. What I do know is that I try to convey emotion as honestly as I can with the talent I have. I summon that emotion from my heart and my gut. A singer has to be a performer and be able to be emotional. I'm not interested in people who can sing and hit notes and be technical without *feeling* the song. That's not singing to me. Your spirit and soul must come through.

Mark, who was a fine guitarist both emotionally and, as a trained jazz guitarist, technically, vowed to cut out showboat guitar solos, and drive and complement my singing with chords all his own and breathtaking melody lines. He played beautiful parts, as opposed to solos.

After working together every day for weeks, he and I had six original songs that would become career-defining in 'Science Fiction', 'Don't You Go Walking', 'Elsie', 'Only Lonely', 'Girlfriends' (which was about my friend who'd tried to end it all) and a song that had buzzed around my brain since the end of 1979. I couldn't get it out of my head. I'd sing it in the bath. It may or may not have been inspired by the surfer boys of Torquay, by John Swanton or even Mark Opitz, Roger Langford and Phil Mortlock, the smooth executives from WEA who were lurking around Baton Rouge. The song was 'Boys In Town'. Mark devised all those thunderous chopping guitar parts that underpin and propel my melody and words...

I am through with hanging round
With the boys in town
Now I want a man around
Get me out of here
I am just a red brassiere
To all the boys in town
Get this bus in top gear
Get me out of here

I must have been desperate

I must have been pretty low
I must have been desperate
I must have been pretty low

I was always driving home
All the boys in town
But they never telephoned
Get me out of here
I think they're pretty phoney
You're not like the rest
You've heard of matrimony
They've all flunked the test

I must have been desperate
I must of been pretty low
I must have been desperate
I must have been pretty slow

Oh I'm tired
Oh I'm wired
Oh I'm tired
Oh I'm wired ahhhhhhhh
GET ME OUT OF HERE

While Mark and I were writing, Jeremy and I, along with Henk Johannes from *Let My People Come* brought in a tall, dark and handsome young actor and sometime guitarist named Bjarne Ohlin and someone I've forgotten who thought he could play the drums, with the idea of forming a band. To my horror, Henk was making it clear he wanted to be lead singer. Inevitably Mark, who was a better musician than Jeremy, Bjarne, Henk and the forgotten drummer combined, became involved. We continued to audition players to try to get the right combination. Our standards were high and few could reach them. Mark had a Valiant S car, and when we sacked someone or had to tell them they'd failed an audition, Mark and the rest of the guys would put them in the back of the Valiant and drive them around the block to let them know the bad news. Word got around about our little ritual, and any poor guy who thought he'd blown the try-out would say, 'Oh no, not the Valiant!'

Mark introduced us to his friend and former bandmate Richard Harvey, a rascal and a genuinely funny lad, who definitely made the cut. Harve could play ferociously, but also keep regular time and was consistent, and he had great *feel*. He started playing the drums at age eleven and has never stopped. He played cruises, pubs, country and western gigs and rock'n'roll show band concerts and met Mark along the way. He was our resident yobbo. When a journalist asked him, 'Where do you sit in the spectrum of Divinyls personalities?', Harve replied, 'Principally in the bar.'

Richard Harvey

Long before Divinyls, Mark and I played in bands together. Mark was more normal then than when he was in Divinyls. He was a bit aloof, a bit eccentric, not a mate's mate, but he was okay. True, he could be a bit whiney, like, 'Awww, stop it,' if I was getting on his nerves or trying to throw him into a pool fully clothed, but he wasn't as hard work as he became. I used to wear bellbottoms and polka-dot shirts, and Mark was worse. I'd also wear a pink shirt and red pants and red sneakers and a big mo. Mark had the mo, a V-neck shirt, white pants and Hush Puppies. We were such dags.

Chrissy took us both in hand. The day before Divinyls' first live gig, she told me my moustache and long mullet hairdo had to go. She brought a hairdresser in to spruce me up. She didn't even consult me. The hairdresser asked me how I wanted my hair and I showed him an early Police album cover with Sting wearing his hair short and spiky. Of course, I ended up looking nothing like Sting—and he charged me $15.

Each day at ten we all met in the attic of Jeremy Paul's home in Neutral Bay to rehearse the original material Mark and I had written. We sent a demo tape to Mark Opitz from WEA, who by then had produced Cold Chisel and the Angels. I learned later that Mark liked to park his car in a service station next door to Jeremy's and listen to us practise.

I was always Early Shirley at rehearsal, keen to go right on time despite having already been working for hours. To pay my rent and buy food I slaved away in a private hotel across the park from my Mosman flat. From 6 a.m. until 9.30 a.m. I served breakfast and scrubbed toilets and kitchen and bedroom floors. The hotel was full of paraphernalia from ships and a dear old sailor helped me serve bacon and eggs to the clientele. It was at the hotel, while vacuuming, to be precise, where I came up with the words and melody to 'Science Fiction', which the Australian Performing Rights Association (APRA) in 2001 announced had been selected by a group of writers, musicians, critics and broadcasters as the 19th of 'the 30 best and most significant Australian works of the past 75 years'.

At that stage our band still didn't have a name, and the credit for 'Divinyls' must go to Tracy Mann. She and I had remained great friends since our Melbourne days. We had lots in common, including our love of entertaining, punk and shopping. One day we were in Oxford Street, Paddington, with our spiky hair and ripped T-shirts, dipping in and out of the fashion boutiques. As we examined one garment or another we'd exclaim, 'Oh, that's divine! That's *divine!*' and for no particular reason Tracy started saying 'divinyl', just a play on words. 'That's simply *divinyl!*' she'd say, and I yelled, '*Divinyl!* That's the name of the band!'

I channelled all my energy into Divinyls, singing and writing as if possessed, and was in no mood to humour Henk's ludicrous ambitions to be lead singer. He kept nagging away that he thought he should be centre-stage with the mike. Unable to bear his pretensions any longer, I brought matters to a head and Henk was ousted.

The hard work we put in with Mark Opitz from WEA paid off and the label signed us up, a fairly meagre deal as I remember, but we were grateful for anything. Meanwhile, we were getting abysmally paid dates in pubs around Kings Cross and established a regular

Friday-night gig at the Piccadilly Hotel, a rock'n'roll bloodhouse in Victoria Street, Potts Point.

At that time, Michael Gudinski, my strange and rock-obsessed friend from Melbourne days who'd become a major player in the industry, was weighing up whether to sign our little-known but promising band to a tour as a support act. At the time he was promoting the Pretenders, and he invited us to a post-gig function in their honour at the Macleay Street Hotel in Kings Cross. This was before the Pretenders lost Jim Honeyman-Scott and Pete Farndon to drugs, and those guys and Chrissie Hynde were all there in an upstairs room, drunk and stoned. We'd been to their gig and it had been explosive. Bandmembers kept walking offstage during songs—Chrissie *stormed* off at one point—and there was a lot of drama.

The drama continued at the party. Arguments, wild behaviour. I thought, 'This is *so* rock'n'roll.'

Film director Ken Cameron, who was making a movie of Helen Garner's novel *Monkey Grip*, arrived at the Piccadilly one night. He plonked a chair right in front of the stage, sat down and just stared at me. Later Ken came to my flat in Womerah Avenue, Darlinghurst, and said he wanted me to play Angela, a spirited rock chick, in the movie. I said, 'Sure,' and then he cast the rest of the band to play... my band. No great leaps there for any of us. The songs we would perform on screen, our own songs, would be the soundtrack to the film. *Monkey Grip* starred a young Noni Hazelhurst, Colin Friels and Harold Hopkins and the supporting roles included my old Melbourne mates Candy Raymond, Michael Caton and Lisa Peers.

Candy Raymond

We were all slightly enchanted when the Melbourne matrix regrouped in *Monkey Grip*. I don't know if I was instrumental in Chrissy getting a part in the film. I know I told Ken Cameron, 'That girl can act. There's no question.' But whether that made any difference, I have no idea.

Monkey Grip was made in 1981. Set in Melbourne, but shot in Sydney, it was about a group of young people coming to terms with life and love in a world of drugs, infidelity and rock'n'roll. I could relate. There was a bit of tension between Lisa Peers and me. I had been going out with an awful guy, a journalist who dumped me for Lisa as soon as he met her. No great loss, but in the movie my character also loses a man to Lisa's character, Rita. Art imitates life. Candy was a bit funny on that set. She kicked up a fuss because she wanted to wear a pair of over-the-knee boots as nice as the ones I wore. I think because she saw herself as the actress and me as the singer, and was a little threatened by my invading her territory, there was tension between us.

I had never acted in a film, and found daunting the process of sitting around all day and then having to perform suddenly when the director and crew decide they're ready. In a film, of course you have to turn your emotions on and off when the director says, 'Action' and 'Cut'. It seemed awkward, like recording commercials. It was such a different medium to rock, which, the way I performed it, was *all* about spontaneity. My co-stars had earned their acting chops, and I felt alienated. I didn't enjoy the filming. I was nominated for an AFI Best Supporting Actress award in 1982 for playing Angela, and that was a shock because when I was filming I didn't think my performance was anything special. Obviously something was working.

On the strength of *Monkey Grip*, I wasn't remotely tempted to swap my music career for movie acting. To me, it was rock'n'roll first and nothing second. If I was serious about rock, and I was, I couldn't dissipate my energy and creativity acting.

I felt for Richard Harvey. Harve was the only Divinyl who didn't play in *Monkey Grip*. Harold Hopkins' character was the drummer in our band so Harve had to swallow his pride, teach Harold to play, and then watch him from the wrong side of the camera. He did make it onto the screen—if you look closely you can see him slumped drunkenly against a wall in a party scene. Typically, he was good-natured about it all, and told a reporter, 'I had to show Harold Hopkins how to play drums—God, it was horrible. I'd hate to think what it'd be like to be a drum teacher full-time. Harold was all right though. He came over to my place a few times before shooting started, and always bought a half-dozen cans with him. So I'd get pissed while he did all the work, which was pretty okay, really.'

For someone who had dreamed of being a singer and living that life—performing, recording and making good music—it was starting to come together. Our first record was the single 'Boys In Town', produced by Mark Opitz at Paradise Studios in Woolloomooloo and released by WEA in September 1981. The critics loved it and so did the kids. *Countdown*'s compere, the influential Molly Meldrum, was a fan and petitioned radio stations to give it high-rotation airplay. 'Boys In Town', the song I couldn't get out of my mind, was now kicking around in heads all over the country. It shot to No. 8 on the national charts and launched Divinyls as a musical force. 'Boys' was included on our first album—an EP of the seven songs we sang on screen and on the soundtrack of *Monkey Grip*—released in October 1981, and again produced by Mark Opitz.

Opitz taught us how to record and feel at home in a studio. I learned how to double, which is basically singing a duet with yourself against a recorded voice track, and that was hard. When we were recording 'Science Fiction' I started singing it: 'I thought that love was science fic-shhhhh-shun,' and it wasn't happening. Then I tried it another way: 'I thought that love was science fick-shu-hun.' I put a little vocal twist in it. Opitz stopped the tape and said, 'Christine, you are going to be around for a very long time.' I was finding I could be creative in the moment and could experiment with words and sounds and it would work.

We were cutting the tracks at Paradise Studios when Jeremy Paul introduced Mark and me to a guy from Castle Music who said he wanted us to sign a publishing deal for the songs. We were wary and in hindsight should have had a lawyer vet the arrangement, but Jeremy persuaded us to sign it. So we did. We signed all our copyrights away for our first songs, for a ridiculously low split, with no advance and no legal advice, to Castle Music. It was a dumb, dumb thing to do, and it made us wary, maybe *too* wary, about signing anything forever after. I suspect we fell into the trap because we were excited and chuffed that a big publisher wanted our songs. I know we hadn't a clue about the legal or financial ramifications. Castle Music, which would be incorporated into EMI, and Jeremy continue to make money from our early songs to this day. I've never forgiven Jeremy Paul for his part in that terrible and costly deal. There would come a time when Divinyls owed a fortune and could have used the money in Castle Music's coffers.

Smarting from that nasty lesson, Mark and I decided that would never happen again. We became extremely difficult to deal with. Our attitude was initially always one of suspicion: how is this person or that company trying to take advantage of us? Not that our hardball attitude saved us from being ripped off and making more dumb decisions in the future.

It was obvious that we were babes in the dark and labyrinthine woods of the music business. We needed a manager, someone astute and tough who could protect us from the sharks and help us reach our potential. I set my sights on Vince Lovegrove, the bloke in the coloured jumpsuit I'd seen playing with Bon Scott in the Valentines in Geelong all those years ago. Since then, Vince had written for the rock magazine *Go-Set*, compered *Move*, an Adelaide TV music show, released some solo singles in 1971 and 1972, been a booking agent in Adelaide and managed some of Australia's premier bands. In 1974, he introduced his mate Bon Scott to AC/DC with historic results, worked as a rock and youth issues reporter on TV's *A Current Affair* and produced *The Don Lane Show*. He had a reputation as a formidable operator with an abiding love of rock'n'roll. He sounded like our kind of guy.

Talking Vince into taking the job as manager was one hurdle out of the way. With his energy and vision combined with Mark's and my creative spark it seemed that Divinyls could be really successful. But there was no doubt the stage was set for a bumpy ride.

After I'd got Henk out of the band, I found *myself* the victim of a coup, orchestrated by Jeremy Paul. Just before Christmas 1981, at a band meeting, he told me I was too disruptive, demanding and driven. And besides, I'd dyed my hair jet black, which he hated. I was out, Jeremy announced, and would be replaced by an actress named Kim Deacon who had been in *The Getting of Wisdom* with Candy and TV's *The Young Doctors*. Bjarne burst into tears. Mark, who cannot bear unpleasant scenes unless he's caused them, sat there in silence looking uncomfortable. I stormed home to the scuzzy flat in Darlinghurst that I called home and considered my predicament. As the rats performed their daily ritual of crawling up through the floorboards and using my bath as a velodrome, I decided I wasn't going to cop it.

I phoned Mark and said, 'Look who you're sitting with right now in that room! Are they the people you want to make music with? What about us! What about all the wonderful music we're creating together? Are you going to just let it go? What about *us*, Mark!' Silence, then, 'Ohhh, yeah . . .' and he caught a cab to my flat. Soon Vince, Harve and the red-eyed Bjarne joined us. They'd defected to me. Now it was Jeremy who was history. We'd miss Jeremy's organisational skills, though not his bass playing, which I found laboured.

For two years, Mark's and my relationship was based solely on music. We'd never even think to say, 'Hey, let's go out for coffee,' or go to a movie. Yet there was definitely something going on between us. We felt so comfortable together. Once we filled a hotel room with steam from the shower and played atmospheric music; it had been ages since I'd had as much fun. And he would come over to my flat and curl up like a little pussy cat on the end of my bed and fall asleep. We'd be talking, talking, talking, talking about a song or a riff and then he would doze off. Then, when we started touring, he would always come into my room because I would have two single beds and he'd sleep in one. We were just like brother and sister. We didn't want to be alone—either of us—in these soulless hotels, like Macy's in Melbourne, a five-dollar-a-night hotel where rock bands traditionally stayed, with the world's most uncomfortable beds.

We were touring in Coolangatta, Queensland, when I got off the tour bus carrying my teddy bear, as I did in those days, and I noticed Mark staring at me, staring really hard and with longing. I found it quite weird. I had never had any intention of becoming romantically involved with him because he was married, and besides I had truly never considered him as a lover. He was my friend and collaborator. Nothing more. Nothing less. But something in our relationship was shifting.

Then, back in Sydney, everything changed. One night at my flat we made love. It felt right. It was a natural extension of our close, exclude-the-world friendship and musical partnership. We chose not to tell a soul. Apart from the hurt it would cause Mark's wife, Linda, it was really important to us that people didn't see us as a husband-and-wife-style team—and even after the guys in the band learned about us, the general public had no idea Mark and I were lovers.

Our band was now me as lead singer, Mark on lead guitar, Bjarne on rhythm guitar and keyboards, Harve on drums. All we needed was a bass player. We hired a quiet guy named Ken Firth, a former Ferret, who lasted a short time. Then we got lucky and in early 1982 snapped up the best bass player in the business.

Rick Grossman says he was stoned the day he came to play with us. He was already using heroin at that point. But we couldn't tell, and we were so glad to have him it wouldn't have mattered. He was a natural. Like Mark, Rick was a musician's musician. He gave us the hard and gritty rock edge I wanted, and combined almost telepathically with drummer Richard Harvey. Rick and Harve set Mark and I free. Divinyls were ready to rock.

Rick Grossman

I grew up in Sydney, near Bondi. I went to Scots College, then left for Sydney High, which saved my life. With its obsessions with rugby and cadets, Scots was like a gladiators' academy. If you were a little bit different, a little bit 'arty', you were a poof. I played violin and cello, so naturally got a hard time. I went to Sydney High and I couldn't believe it. The place was full of long-haired freaks just like me! A schoolmate who played guitar said to me, 'Oh, you play cello, you could play bass guitar. We could form a band. You meet a lot of girls that way.' And that was why I got into music. If they were honest, 99 per cent of all musos would say they were originally motivated by the same happy prospect. But if meeting girls is your only motivation you don't last long.

I've had a couple of epiphanies in my life and one was going to see Led Zeppelin in Sydney in 1972 when I was fifteen. It sounds corny, but it was like a spiritual experience. I walked out a completely different person. It was like something had opened up for me. No matter what I may have achieved in my life, I have always suffered from low-self esteem, and that was certainly so when I was a teenager. I thought, 'Where Led Zeppelin are, up on stage in front of this huge crowd, playing great music, not a worry in the world, happy, making a fortune . . . that's where I'm gonna go!' I saw playing guitar as a way of escape to a wonderful new existence and I became obsessed.

Soon after I saw Led Zeppelin, I met Mark Kingsmill, who is the drummer in Hoodoo Gurus, the band I play in today, and he and I and Deniz Tek, who was studying to be a doctor and would co-found Radio Birdman, and Anthony Vitale, who looked like Keith Richards and was as obsessed with punk rock as me, formed a band. We practised at nights in a school in Paddington and made a horrendous noise.

I was still learning to play bass. I never copied anyone, even though I had heroes. I tried to find my own style from the beginning. My godmother is an actress who gave me good advice. 'There are many technical geniuses out there,' she said, 'but what will make you a great player is originality.'

My mother worked for a theatre and let us use her rehearsal room in Oxford Street, Paddington, so we moved from the school. A scene developed there. A lot of musicians, such as the guys who would be in Radio Birdman with Deniz, and people who were simply into music, started hanging around the rehearsal room, which was decrepit and a total fire hazard. We'd sit around smoking pot, talking about how we'd become famous and, yes, meeting girls. Of all those people with rock'n'roll stars in their eyes, the blokes from Radio Birdman, Mark Kingsmill and I are the only ones who went on with it.

A family friend called and asked me to pay her a visit in Melbourne. As an afterthought, she added, 'Oh, and bring your guitar because there's a band down here called Bleeding Hearts and they need a bass player.' I'd never heard of Bleeding Hearts, then at the airport I bought *RAM* magazine and there was a huge article about the band, who were legendary in inner-city Melbourne. I played a show with them and was a Bleeding Heart for a year, then I gigged around Melbourne for another two years, learning so much. The late '70s was such an exciting period in the Melbourne music scene. I joined up with a band from Adelaide and then Eric Gradman, who was a violinist and a real force in Australian music then, and I played together in Man & Machine.

I was a chance of linking up with Joe Camilleri's Jo Jo Zep and the Falcons. Rob Hirst of Midnight Oil told me that they were thinking of getting rid of their bass player so I, as I'm wont to do sometimes, jumped the gun, packed up my stuff and came back to Sydney, certain I'd get the gig. Then Rob told me, 'Er, Rick, there's no job yet. It might take us a few months to change the line-up so best you do something else for a while.' I was staying with Iva Davies and he told me about a Sydney band, Matt Finish, who needed a bass player for four weeks because their regular guy was sick. I was into punk and Matt Finish, founded by the doomed Matt Moffitt, were a funk outfit, but we hit it off and I stayed with them from 1979–81, until amphetamines, heroin and fisticuffs took their toll.

In early 1982 I got a call from Vince Lovegrove, who was managing Divinyls. He said producer Mark Opitz had recommended me as someone who would fit in with the band and wondered if I was interested in meeting them. I knew Divinyls. I'd seen them at the Manzil Room in Kings Cross and I'd found Chrissy truly hypnotic. That voice, that attitude, and this was before she developed her stage act. I couldn't take my eyes off her. I thought their songs were different from anything else being played. Hard-driving but with memorable hooks, they stayed in your head. Mark McEntee was an amazing guitar player. I was certainly interested. Vince invited me to have a play and I thought it went well. After, we all went out to eat at a restaurant in the Cross, but it was me, not the food, who got grilled. Chrissy, Mark and Vince bombarded me with a series of loaded questions and each time I responded they'd communicate with each other via surreptitious nods and hand signals. It was farcical. They played their little game of charades as if I wasn't there, and it was bloody unsettling. I felt like I was on trial, and I was. Chrissy wasn't particularly friendly. She seemed suspicious of my motives, as if I was trying to worm my way into their coterie, even though I hadn't approached them, Vince had approached me. In spite of everything, I believed in the band and was in awe of Chrissy and Mark's talent, so I said yes, and when Chrissy trusted me, she became a lifelong friend despite things we did to each other that may have made saner people enemies for life.

Divinyls music was Stones-y and kind of sleazy. I hear influences from Easybeats and AC/DC. Loose, but somehow tight. We were probably more punk than most of the punk bands on the scene. 'Elsie' was one of my favourite songs. Chrissy would do her monster act when she sang it, and I loved to watch the awe and fear on the faces of the audience. If people listen to our early songs, 'Boys In Town', 'Elsie', 'Science Fiction', 'Siren', 'Don't You Go Walking', 'Only Lonely', they'll hear a bloody good band at their best. Forget 'I Touch Myself'. To me, that's not Divinyls.

With Vince onboard, he led us to sign on with Dirty Pool. I remember John Woodruff coming around to a band rehearsal and telling us the only way we were allowed to miss a gig that they had booked was if we were dead. My work ethic to this day!

We were told that they were going to raise Divinyls' profile by booking the band to support their big-name bands, Icehouse, Cold Chisel, the Angels. We went on a national tour with Icehouse and the British group Simple Minds. (Jim Kerr made it clear he was interested in me one night and sat his chair outside my hotel-room door. I wouldn't come out.)

The idea was that the fans would see how good we were and within six months we would be headlining ourselves. We would be exposed to the fans in such places as Sydney's Capitol Theatre, Festival Hall in Melbourne, Adelaide's Apollo Stadium and The Canberra Theatre. There was a great gig I loved at the Cloudlands Ballroom in Brisbane, where the floor bounced up and down as if it was on springs from the weight of the crowd. Another time, Divinyls and Simple Minds had a huge ice fight while Icehouse was on stage.

It was all meticulously planned by Vince and Dirty Pool. There was marketing with handbills and posters on lightposts and building sites. They also would have us play at a venue that held fewer than the number of fans they estimated would turn up. We'd arrive at a gig and be amazed to see queues halfway down the street and people being turned away. Those same people would show up the next night to see this hot new band. All this, combined with positive word of mouth, would, it was hoped, see Divinyls established as one of the top outfits in the country.

We had to be brilliant—fast—and the only way to do this was to play often. When we started out we were okay, but there was a lot of work to be done.

Vince was a great motivator and a frustrated front-man himself, he would have much preferred to be up there onstage. I think of him now as a kind of Jack Black character from *School Of Rock*. He told us we had to make every gig special and he would always say before we went on, 'Be loose as a goose but aggro'. He suggested we play an introduction tape before we went on to create an atmosphere. We started playing Judy Garland's 'Over The Rainbow'. Then the band would play a fixed set for an hour.

I started calling Vince 'Coach', as he was always there to discuss the band's performance and give feedback. He was much more into the creative side than the organisational side and handling the finances, although he was good at getting money out of the record company.

Like all things, the mix has to be right for magic to happen. Vince Lovegrove was definitely part of getting the mix right and taking Divinyls to another level.

THE COACH'S VOICE

Vince Lovegrove

I was living in Underwood Street, Paddington. After playing in bands and managing acts such as Cold Chisel and being an agent and promoter for such groups as AC/DC, I made a television documentary in the late seventies called *Australian Music to the World*, which was directed by Paul Drane. Peter Faiman, the Melbourne-based director of TV's *The Don Lane Show*, saw it and hired me as producer. My main role was to attract younger viewers by making the music more contemporary. I used my contacts to land such guest stars as Tom Waits and Robert Palmer and I also took charge of new technological developments such as satellite-link interviews. I produced *The Don Lane Show* for two years, my marriage broke up, then I moved to Sydney, and my new girlfriend, Daina Auzins, who'd been in *Let My People Come* with Chrissy, eventually joined me.

One morning in 1981, Chrissy came to our place. We got on well and she kept on coming, much to Daina's chagrin. There was a tension, an intensity, between Chrissy and me that was there from the word go, and it's been between us ever since.

I was writing a pop and rock column for Sydney's *The Sun* newspaper and Chrissy would pump me for information about the music industry. She asked me if I'd manage Divinyls. I was hesitant. I had never wanted to be a manager, I'd just fallen into the role. The thing for me always with bands was the magic of helping to create a sound and an image from the talent and attitudes of the musicians, stoking their ambitions and getting them started on the road to realising their dreams. That was the challenge I enjoyed, and then I'd move on. Being big time and making lots of money, while there's plenty to be said for that, wasn't really the buzz for me.

Yet I was tempted to get involved with Divinyls because of Chrissy. I was intrigued by her. She was very intense. She was very confrontational. She was challenging. She was verbose, with a clarity of speech and mind and intellect. She shared with me a feel for rock'n'roll, and a respect for its history and its ability to change lives.

One thing led to another and Daina and I split up. It was a traumatic break for us both. She blamed Chrissy, but it wasn't romance with Chrissy that came between Daina and me, just Chrissy's and my passion for music. I felt that Divinyls and I were fated to be together so, after Chrissy implored me for the thousandth time to see the band and give my verdict, I joined the seven or eight other fans grouped one night in front of the stage at the Piccadilly Hotel, where Divinyls had a weekly residency.

After their gig I sat with the band and gave them my honest opinion. I said they looked and played like they were a very young, very inexperienced band. Richard Harvey could really play the drums and you could tell he'd been around. Harve was a straight-out, bona fide rock'n'roll guy and without him they would not have had that trademark Divinyls sound. When bass player Rick Grossman eventually joined, in my opinion he and Harve were the best rhythm section in Australia. When I assessed them the bass player, Jeremy Paul, was adequate, and the rhythm guitarist and keyboard player, Bjarne Ohlin, no standout. Mark McEntee on lead guitar was brilliant.

Mark had his own style, subtle and under-played, with that rhythmic chop which is quite rare in lead guitarists, who usually like to demonstrate their proficiency at playing different notes at speed. Mark's playing reminded me of Keith Richards and Malcolm Young who are the two best rock rhythm guitarists in the world, and of the magical rhythms of Bo Diddley and Chuck Berry. However, Mark's style of guitar playing was completely unique in rock: unique sound, unique technique, totally for the sake of the song and for Chrissy's vocals.

Chrissy was a revelation. I was mesmerised by her incredible voice which was like no other voice I'd ever heard. And she had unique phrasing and a way of chewing words, changing the notes of a lyric so it took a U-turn you didn't expect. She was obviously an experienced singer, which made her shyness that night at the Piccadilly all the more puzzling. Back then, she had not developed a stage persona. She was extremely shy. She would not look at the audience. She stood back with the drummer, her head down, scowling through her fringe, pouting as if in a bad mood. She turned her back on the audience. Only rarely did she venture to the front of the stage. I couldn't believe that this was the same provocative and confrontational woman who harangued me in my kitchen. So on my first viewing I was definitely taken in, and when the band asked me for my opinion I gave it.

I told them that I loved their original songs. They reminded me of the early Easybeats—with a twist. You could tell that these songs had been cared for, nurtured and perfected, and all they needed was a bit of dirt and splatter. When they got scuffed up, as inevitably happened when played again and again in some of the roughest dives in the country, I came to see these songs as much better than very good. They were beautifully written and constructed and they were clever. To me, for as long as Chrissy and Mark collaborated, they wrote no better songs than 'Boys In Town', 'Science Fiction', 'Don't You Go Walking', 'Elsie' and 'Only Lonely'.

Chrissy invited me to see Divinyls a few more times, and after each performance we all gathered for a chat. They were getting better and better. After three weeks of this she formally asked me to manage the band. I said I'd think about it. She replied, 'But I thought you said you liked us!' Chrissy can be very persuasive. I thought hard. Rock was in my blood, but it's a hard and stressful life. Did I want that? And it was clear that with Chrissy and Mark being such strong personalities, Divinyls, for all their potential to be a great band, would not be easy to manage. Besides, I had aspirations to devote myself to writing more than newspaper articles and managing Divinyls would put an end to these. Slowly, though, I realised that I wasn't going to say no.

I met with Chrissy and said I was her man, on one condition. That we go all out from the beginning to crack the American market. If we did that, success at home would surely follow. No Australian band had ever been signed by an American label to record their debut album, but making it in the US was the challenge that would make managing Divinyls worthwhile. I wanted to go for broke in the biggest and most lucrative market on earth. It was my thinking at that stage, and still is, that the Australian music industry, as good a platform for artists as it has been over the last three or four decades, is not on the same level of musical creativity as the United Kingdom and the United States. Individuality and originality and a sense of history are not highly regarded by some of the narrow-minded types who run the Australian music industry.

Chrissy and Mark were taken aback when I unveiled my masterplan for the band, and asked what it all meant. 'It means we're leaving WEA even though we're contracted with them to do the *Monkey Grip* soundtrack and records in the future. They're not going to like that and it could get nasty. I'm going to go to America and sign you to an American record company and then we're all going to America... It means that you'll leave Australia. We may have to live in New York. We may have to live in Los Angeles. We may have to be on the road for two years. It means we're outtahere!'

A couple of the bandmembers thought I was joking, but they soon learned I was deadly serious. I certainly didn't have great contacts in

America. It was all green grass for me. Who knows the psyche that went into my scheme? What part of my ego was stoking the engine? Cracking America became an obsession—no question. And that obsession was fuelled, without a doubt, by Chrissy—and her enthusiasm and what she did and didn't want. She'd been around for quite a while, in a lot more bands than I'd realised. She'd circled the block again and again and she did not want to keep doing it in Australia. It was time to make the big leap.

First thing, we needed to get free of WEA. I didn't believe they gave two bob about Divinyls or their music. They saw us only as an item on their bottom line. Paul Turner, WEA's managing director, had just done a deal with Pat Lovell, producer of *Monkey Grip*, to put out the soundtrack EP when I told him that we wanted to quit the contract and wouldn't let them release it. WEA, of course, wouldn't let us go. So it became a confrontation between Paul Turner and me. I very quickly learned that if you had no power or money the only way to deal with most of these people was with aggression and determination. 'Unless you release us from our contract we will not record for you. We will sit out the remaining year of our contract,' I told Turner. 'We are going to be very difficult about this. We will not go the easy road.' Turner realised this was not a bullshit threat and he and I quickly reached an agreement. He would dissolve the contract if we released the EP and WEA kept the rights. Chrissy, Mark and the others agreed that this was a small price to pay for our freedom, so we said, 'Yes . . . See ya!'

Calling WEA's bluff was an audacious thing to do. They could have sued us, but they blinked. Suddenly we were an independent act with our future in our own hands. We actually amalgamated the band and made a manifesto of our mission.

With the WEA hurdle cleared, now we would find an American record company to record and release our material, and that would include new versions of those seminal songs on *Monkey Grip*. It was a whole fresh start. We taped our meetings to keep a record of business and musical decisions. Each member was expected to say their piece. We became so close, us against the world. We went away for weekends together at friends' houses in the bush or near the beach, or we'd go to each other's homes for meals and meetings which I called 'Vibe Sessions'. From the start we had vision and momentum.

I saw it as my duty to maintain harmony and keep things as democratic as possible. That was a difficult task, particularly when it got down to the division of the profits and who got what, who deserved what. We had so many meetings about whether or not the publishing money percentages should be split among the band or just Mark and Chrissy. And I did all sorts of things to inspire the team spirit.

During that early period, our roles in the band and our relationships with each other began to sort themselves out. This was tricky, because we were a diverse bunch from different backgrounds with varying ideals and talent. Divinyls was a heart 'n' soul band of talent, blind ambition and naivety. There was a lot of emotion and personality clashes were inevitable, notably between Chrissy and Mark. They were the lead performers, the songwriters, the driving force, and this power made them autocratic. They began to argue over the music and pretty much everything else and it was their clashes that would make Divinyls both great and a disaster. Their personal lives might have been a mess, but what mattered was that musically they were in sync. Bjarne, Harve and Jeremy Paul also had their idiosyncrasies. It was my job as manager to hold it all together.

I left Paddington and rented a room in Bondi Junction. There I plotted our strategy, penning our dates into my diary, keeping track of the incoming money and our expenses. I wanted us to sign with a booking agency named Dirty Pool owned by three former rock band managers whom I respected named John Woodruff, Ray Hearn and Rod Willis. Dirty Pool handled Cold Chisel, INXS, Mental as Anything, the Angels and Flowers, who would become Icehouse. The powerful agency was the instigator of a new and fairer system for paying bands in which the act would be paid the money they drew at the door of the venue and the venue would keep the proceeds from alcohol and food consumed by the fans. I was convinced Dirty Pool, so dedicated to their clients' interests, would be good for us, but I had to persuade Chrissy.

Chrissy is a naturally suspicious person, a contrary questioner who takes nothing at face value. She is obsessed with honesty and integrity. That's one of her attributes. It's also one of the most uncomfortable things about her. She was a bit suss about signing with Dirty Pool because she knew I was a mate of the partners and their acts. She said, 'You only want to be with Dirty Pool because you're friends with Jimmy Barnes!' Of course this was not so, and I was able to talk her around.

Dirty Pool would raise Divinyls' profile by booking the band to support their big-name bands. They went on a national tour with Icehouse and the British group Simple Minds.

When they started out Divinyls were not great live. They were not even good. They were merely proficient, and they were extremely conservative. They didn't hang loose. They hadn't had enough experience as a unit nor begun to explore the dynamics that existed between them. There was a lot of work to be done—from the way they played, to the clothes they wore on stage and their haircuts, to the way they related to the audience, to where they stood and their steps. Everything . . . we had to start from the very beginning. I said, 'We have to make every gig special. We have to make every gig a party.'

Chrissy, Mark and Harve were with me. They had rock'n'roll hearts. Jeremy and Bjarne were less convinced. Bjarne was a buttoned-up guy who didn't see a need for our punk-inspired edge. And Jeremy and Chrissy were at loggerheads because he considered Divinyls to be his band. In my opinion, Jeremy quite clearly was a legend in his own lunchtime because he'd been in Air Supply.

Chrissy called me Coach. I always saw myself more as a creative director than a manager. I loved to help craft an image. The managing side, the logistics and juggling money, really bored me. And I confess that that was one of my biggest faults as a manager. I hated having to negotiate with coked-up record label suits who stank of booze and fucked their secretary under the boardroom table after work. No doubt

I'm being unfair to those executives who were decent people on the up-and-up, and some were, but generally I saw them as a sleazy bunch, out to use musicians up and rip us off. And A&R and promotions people—I had no time or respect for most of them at all. I was happiest helping the band put on a superb performance, revving them up before a gig, telling them what they did right and wrong afterwards. Creating their aura.

Chrissy and I had an unspoken bond that came from both our shared desire to see Divinyls succeed and a respect for each other's talents. Regardless of what Mark may have thought, Chrissy was the power of the band. Without her, there was no Divinyls. She was irreplaceable. She was unique. So while we strove to be a democratic outfit, in the end what Chrissy wanted, Chrissy got.

Chrissy's and my relationship went up and down like a yoyo. We had some massive fights. Unbelievable confrontations. We stripped each other bare, about the band and music and personal things too. When she was drunk it was so much worse, not just for me but for everyone she came in contact with. She could be a monster, an aggressive, violent monster.

Yet at the heart of our relationship was mutual respect. I think she respected me. I certainly respected her. I liked her sassy ways. I liked her strength. I liked her balls. I liked her intellect. She was no pushover, she was a challenge, and I loved that about her. And I believed in her. I thought she was a massive talent. She wrote the best lyrics around then. Simple lyrics from the heart, which of course are the hardest lyrics to write.

With the job as manager obviously came some tough jobs. One of them was when I sacked Jeremy Paul. To me, if a bandmember is given the boot because he isn't cutting it musically, the firing should be done by the band. Any other reason and the manager should do the dirty work. Jeremy was ousted because of his lacklustre bass playing, and also because he was trying to get rid of Chrissy who, as anyone could see, was the band's strength. They were at each other's throats because of conflicting ambitions and because of Chrissy and Mark's resentment at the way he had handled the publishing deal with Castle Music. Jeremy got a cut for just three songs, but they were the best three, including 'Boys In Town'. All of this bad blood made sacking Jeremy my business and I did the deed at a band meeting at my place in Bondi Junction. He took it very badly. He really thought he was the strength of the band because until I came along he basically managed Divinyls and looked after their bookings.

THOSE DIVINYLS

8

I'd written and performed a smash-hit single, 'Boys In Town', and my career was catching fire—but deep down I doubted my worth. Any success I was enjoying had surely been everyone else's doing and little of my own. This lack of confidence was out of character, and it was evident in my performances. At our gigs I sang from the rear of the stage, lurking unobtrusively near Harve's drums, fringe covering my eyes, face turned away, not connecting with the audience.

I knew that if we were to make an impact I'd have to do more than just stand in the shadows and sing. My voice had always been different enough to get me by, and the band and our songs were good, but that wouldn't be enough to cut it in the big league where all the top bands had charismatic singers. Midnight Oil had Peter Garrett, INXS had Michael Hutchence, Cold Chisel had Jim Barnes, Rose Tattoo had Angry Anderson, the Angels had Doc Neeson, and AC/DC had Bon Scott.

I *wanted* to be wild. I wanted to be provocative. I wanted to express myself and jolt the audience out of their comfort zone. But

I wasn't game. Part of my problem was that I had written passionate, raw songs, but I was too shy to perform them with the emotional abandon they deserved.

I had been completely unselfconscious naked in *Let My People Come* and singing in *Daisy Clover*, because there was nothing of myself vested in the songs. Now it was personal. These were *my* songs, this band was so important to me, and after all I'd been through this was my chance at last to be the formidable rock singer I'd always dreamed of being. I didn't want to blow it, so I took no chances. And by taking no chances, I was blowing it. Up on stage I was no more animated than a statue.

What to do? I thought of other excellent singers and musicians I admired who took their gigs to a higher level because they were also riveting performers. There was Little Richard, James Brown, Jerry Lee Lewis, Angus Young, Stevie Wright from the Easybeats, and the deliciously dangerous Iggy Pop, who hurled himself around the stage and lacerated his body as part of the show. I realised that these stars had adopted an on-stage persona, they were in effect playing a role. Not a false role, an audience could see through fakery in an instant, but by becoming an extreme personification of their music, their attitude and beliefs, they became great. All I had to do was find the right persona for me. I needed something I could hide behind that would free me to let loose. Some kind of outfit, a mask. If only I could dress up in something that was like I'd wear in a play...then I could throw myself into character.

Making my job harder was that there were no outrageous women rock singers in Australia at that time. If I was going to shock and scandalise on stage I'd be breaking the mould. Whether they sang rock, pop, folk or jazz, female singers then were all sweet natured, accessible, non-threatening and pretty. This was a mould worth smashing into a million pieces.

The penny dropped. As the eighties got underway, Australia needed a monster, and I decided I could be it. Vince had an idea and suggested I wear something that people would identify me by, in the same way that I remembered him and Bon Scott wearing coloured jumpsuits in the Valentines. Vince and I decided on a school uniform. Vince says the first time he remembers me wearing it was at the Astra Hotel, but I did wear a version at the Piccadilly in the very early days. I also started wielding a neon tube, a prop from the *Monkey Grip* film clip, that I swung around onstage for years after. I put together an outfit that would help unleash that monster.

Vince Lovegrove

Unlike every other area of her life where, as far as I could tell, Chrissy had no inhibitions at all, in those first months of Divinyls, she had difficulty letting go. Clearly she was seeking to express herself on stage, and in a way that wasn't clichéd, but didn't have the means.

We analysed the problem. She was afraid to reveal herself by performing her songs with the honest emotion they demanded. She couldn't give that much of herself away. So we talked about it. Then we went to an AC/DC concert, and I could see it struck a chord with her. 'Chrissy,' I said, 'that's where *you've* got to be.'

Soon after, on a Friday night at the Piccadilly Hotel, I had an idea. 'Listen, why don't you wear a school tunic and white blouse,' I suggested. So she bought some uniforms and blouses and we added a suspender belt and stockings with holes ripped in them, and little flat shoes.

The first time Chrissy appeared as the schoolgirl was one of the pivotal nights in Australian rock history. She blew the roof off the old Astra pub up the hill from Bondi Beach. Never had there been such an uninhibited performance from an Australian female singer.

She was transformed. She tore around the stage like a banshee, haranguing the crowd and the band, scowling, screaming, headbanging, and all the while singing the songs perfectly, just as she and Mark had written them. The audience was astonished and terrified. She came off stage emotionally shredded, dripping with sweat, and smiling from ear to ear. Suddenly Chrissy Amphlett was one of the most electrifying performers on earth. Divinyls would never be the same again.

I didn't decide to be a provocative banshee onstage all of a sudden. That developed as a result of the heckling I would get from the audience and from other bands and their roadies. Wearing the school tunic and suspenders seemed to label me as submissive with a warped sexuality and I was often treated like dirt. I wouldn't put up with that and would lash out and say, 'Don't you *dare* fuck with me because I'm wearing this school uniform. In fact, fuck *you* all!'

I wore variations of the uniform everywhere, even on nights out in the Cross. A few years later at a US festival, I wore a little Heidi outfit that I had made in New York (way before Madonna's Heidi) and no matter what I wore people always saw it as a school uniform because I integrated it into my style.

I loved that schoolgirl. It did people's heads in and they would say, 'How could she!' I remember seeing Germaine Greer at the airport one day and she stopped and glowered at me. Being the schoolgirl gave me a freedom I'd never known. I *owned* that stage, and the audience in front of it. I could dance madly and charge furiously back and forth across the stage. I could dive into the crowd. I could scowl and yell and swear at the audience and no one dared answer back. I could smear my face and arms with lipstick and pin rubber rats onto my tunic (a tribute to my furry flatmates in Womerah Avenue) which would fling around as I danced. I could literally tear out my hair. I could wield a hatchet, a guillotine and a large glowing fluorescent rod. I could jump on Mark's back and wrestle him to the floor as he struggled to play. I could taunt the roadies to come out on the stage then throw my microphone down and as they bent to pick it up I'd kick them up the bum. I was always doing that to our roadies, and throwing water on them. I could be as frenzied and scary as I wanted to be. It was as if I was a marionette whose strings were being jerked by malevolent goblins.

RAM magazine likened me to 'a feral cat dancing a highland fling'. One observer called me 'very angry, very tense, *very* intimidating'. Another said that I had a hold over the audience, and being down there in the crowd he felt like I was 'dragging [him] along by the wrists through broken glass'.

People still swear they saw me urinate onstage. When nature called during a gig, because there were usually no facilities, I peed offstage into whatever receptacle was handy, or behind an amp, but as far as I know I never peed *on* the stage. That said, when I performed as the schoolgirl I went to another galaxy. What I did was incredibly physical with much squatting and screaming, so, you never know, I might have urinated involuntarily. Once a record producer told me that he came to see me in Divinyls in those early years and found it a jarring, unpleasant experience. He wanted to know why I couldn't just stand there and sing like everyone else.

I would rather have drunk carbolic acid. I enjoyed it when the people at *Countdown* battened down the hatches when Divinyls appeared. I relished the look of fear on the faces of those I picked on in the audience. My idols had always been the unsafe, the dangerous, the edgy, the shaker-uppers, like the punks, Iggy Pop, Keith Richards, Debbie Harry, and Jerry Lee Lewis who, when I saw him perform in the United States some years later, I was convinced was the devil. I hated self-righteousness. I hated middle-class smugness and bloated self-esteem.

I had a hate-love relationship with the audience. I never wasted time with onstage pleasantries like, 'It's so good to be with you all here in Cunnamulla!' No, I was uncompromisingly aggro.

There was something about my body and my sexuality, my physicality, that audiences found threatening. Looking as I did made my performances more confronting. Mine was not a safe body, not a doll's body. It was real. I had large breasts, I had long legs, and though small I was fit and powerful. My fringe, my pout, my outfit, my voice... the uniform, the threatening props. The whole look.

As that aggressive, seen-and-done-it-all and very well-developed schoolgirl from the bad side of town I could rebel against my straight, middle-class girlhood, against the prospect of life married to a TV newsreader. I could explore my emotions and my sexual fantasies onstage and in turn the audience explored theirs through me, although I never consciously used sex to manipulate an audience response.

My sexuality is tied up with expressing myself through music which is connected to the spirit. When I performed, sexuality naturally burst out. I don't apologise. Evoking sex and danger is better than evoking boredom.

Rick Grossman

What made Chrissy's act so effective was that she was a very attractive woman and yet so wild. You could feel the tension in the audience.

Chrissy was the master of the humiliating putdown. A bloke who didn't know better would yell something like, 'Show us your tits!' and she'd stop the show, order the lights turned on and jump down and confront him. 'Yeah, mate?' she'd yell right into his face, 'Well show us your *dick*!' The bloke would shrivel.

Sometimes I'd wonder if she was having a breakdown. I genuinely feared not just for her health, but for her sanity. Then in the middle of her manic craziness, she'd turn her back on the audience and give me a little smile, like, 'Oh boy . . . what am I doing?'

Vince Lovegrove

The audience accepted Chrissy as the schoolgirl because she was real. She's a great show woman, but not a fake. You're up there, you're totally exposed, and you can't fake it. Well, you *can* fake it but people find out in the end.

Girls considered her an ally, not a rival. That was her magic. Gay guys were crazy about her. Boofy testosterone-charged lads not so much. Her message to them was, 'Sorry fellas, your days of lording it over women are over. It's payback time.'

Tony Mott

After leaving my native England, I was a chef travelling the world on cruise ships, then I landed in Sydney and knew it was where I wanted to live for the rest of my life. I worked as a chef at the Opera House and the Gazebo Hotel and tried to get started as a professional photographer, specialising in rock and pop performers. After the restaurant closed I'd go out and follow the bands. One night I saw

Divinyls at the Piccadilly Hotel. My life changed. Chrissy was a fucking amazing performer. I started photographing her, at the Piccadilly and the Illinois pub on Parramatta Road and the Trade Union Club in Surry Hills. I chased Divinyls all over Sydney. I wasn't paid a cent, and paid my own way in, just grateful for such wonderful subject matter.

One day I summoned the courage to knock on the door of Vince Lovegrove's office and show him my pictures. He was impressed and bought one for twenty bucks which he used on a poster. I was chuffed. He told me to keep it up and show me anything new. He would put my name 'on the door' at the venue. I had no idea that that meant I could enter free, so I kept forking out my entrance money.

The first time I was introduced to Chrissy was in Vince's office, and I was shit-scared, expecting her to be the intimidator she was on stage. She surprised me by being shy and sweet, and was always generous about my work.

My career grew from that connection, and I've photographed nearly every top act in the world in the years since, from the Stones to U2 to Madonna, Nirvana, Marianne Faithfull, Janet and Michael Jackson, Bowie, the Chili Peppers, Bon Jovi and Dylan. But if someone said, 'You can have your time again. You can start your career photographing any band you like,' I'd pick Divinyls.

Patricia Amphlett

My cousin Chrissy pioneered the rock chick in Australia. Before her there was no such thing as a formidable, in-your-face female rock'n'roll performer. There's a quote I recall from a fellow singer of the sixties named Laurel Lee. Laurel, who's now passed on, said, in her lovely way, 'When we were all growing up and on *Bandstand* our desired image was that of a virtuous, virginal, clean-cut girl-next-door ... At the same time, it was desirable for the men to be perceived as wild boys of rock! So you've got the vestal virgins and the wild boys of rock. How stupid.'

And not only that, when I performed, and I'd had several hit records, I still only ever had second billing to a bloke. Promoters couldn't bear to put a woman at the top of the bill. But that's how life was, too. So you could be a big female star in the sixties but still only be second

on the bill to a bloke who might have had one hit record. You'd have
been the person who had pulled the crowd, but you could never close
the door. It was like you had to be a *man* to close the door.

Then came Chrissy. She changed all of that. She topped the bill
and she closed the door. She got out there and said, 'Righto, you blokes,
move over!' That knocks this old feminist out more than you can
imagine. It makes me feel so proud. To think that my flesh and blood
did it. My Chrissy!

I acted out a lot of my inner turmoil and anguish when I wore that
uniform. It made me invulnerable. Then I built on my persona. I took
on aspects of the personality of people I'd meet, and I'd also blend
in the feelings I'd experienced that day. Mark and I may have had an
argument, and the residual anger would be there with me onstage.
Sometimes Mark would say something caustic to me just as I was
going on, and I'd be in a rage throughout the show and nothing was
more certain than that somebody that night would cop it.

It felt good to be bad. In clubs or big venues when women left
their handbags on the stage, I'd steal the bags and sit on the drum
riser and rifle through them, holding up the contents to the audience
and then throwing them away. I'd taunt the owner to come up and
try to reclaim it. When she did I'd run off with it, and we'd get into
a tug o'war. Occasionally I'd incite people and they'd jump up on stage
to get at me, only to be thrown off by the roadies.

When I was in a particularly grumpy mood, or, as happened
more often later, was performing when exhausted or hungover, I could
get *really* nasty. A guy in the crowd was shouting abuse at me one
night when I jumped down into the throng. I found someone who
looked guilty and whacked him. Meanwhile Rick was yelling, 'Chrissy,
it's the bloke *next* to him!' And at a gig in Coffs Harbour, a creep
right in front of the stage yelled obscenities at me and tried to look
up my dress, so I ground the heel of my stiletto boot into his chest.

Stage-diving always revved things up. Sometimes I dived because
I had forgotten the words to a song and was trying to cover up; more

often I just felt like launching myself into the crowd. Rick would try to help me and accidently bang my head with his guitar as he did contortions to pull me back up onto the stage. For all the times I hurled myself into the audience I don't think I was ever groped. I just lay on top of the crowd who were all trying to hold me up, floating like a leaf on a lake.

One night a drunk in the crowd threw a full beer can onstage. It hit me on the head and knocked me out cold. When I regained consciousness a minute or so later I shouted for the house lights to be turned on. I asked the can-thrower to identify himself. He didn't, and a couple of thousand people as one pointed at the culprit and yelled, 'It was him!' and he was thrown out.

I'd always been strong-willed and uncompromising about things that mattered greatly to me, but now, as the band's success grew and I considered that we were under siege from people trying to cash in on our talent, I turned being difficult into an art form. I relished every moment of it. I believed that I made the music, and schmoozing, even if it helped sell records and attract people to our gigs, was not part of the bargain. It was Fortress Divinyls as I refused to kowtow to record companies, radio stations, promoters, disc jockeys, tour managers, financial advisers, roadies, fans and journalists. Even Vince. Given half a chance, I'd bite their head off and savour every munch.

Patricia Amphlett

My father Joe, Chrissy's dad's brother, loved her. He was one of a kind himself. After he came to Sydney he was known as Melbourne Joe. Dad was what has come to be known as a 'colourful character'. He was tremendously kind and when he won at the races he anonymously handed out ten quid notes and groceries to people down on their luck. At the same time, he had a dreadful temper.

Dad looked after the nominations and acceptances for all the horses that raced in the provincial race meetings in New South Wales— in Newcastle, Wyong, Woop Woop. It was a very responsible job and it was before computers were around and he was a walking encyclopaedia. He knew who the dam was, who the sire was, of any horse. It was all in Joe's head. This is the kind of man he was. One day a fellow came into Dad's office to register his horse. Dad always kept a photo of me on his desk. This bloke looked at the photo and sneered. Recently there'd been a newspaper article about me, saying I was the highest-paid teenager in Australia. And the horse owner made the mistake of saying to my father, 'G'day, Joe! Yeah, saw Patricia in the paper . . . says that she's the highest paid teenager in Australia! What gives her the right to earn all that money? That's a terrible lot of money. I mean, she's only a kid.' My father leant over the desk, drilled him with those brown Amphlett eyes and said, 'She's got the right because she's gotta entertain fuckin' mugs like you!'

Soon after Chrissy became well known, my father took Chrissy to the races. She was outrageously attired and was totally out of place. Stunningly out of place. The old ducks at the races were mortally offended, but Dad felt only pride.

People can't seem to cope with women who dare to be their own person.

Over the years so many people have come up to me and said, 'I met your cousin Chrissy. She's not nice like you.' I jump at them, fly right up 'em, and say, 'How can you say that? You don't know Chrissy. You don't even know me!'

I won a reputation as someone not to be messed with. My combativeness sometimes did us harm and cost us opportunities, yet it established our cred as a serious band who refused to play the industry game. It may be no consolation to those we angered or inconvenienced, but we were as brutal with each other.

I'm sure my developing alcoholism made me more difficult than I really was. Booze gave me bravado. It was a quick fix for nerves or a tense mood. Maybe I *was* sometimes an emotional tyrant. I'll own up to my bad behaviour, but at my core I believe that I wasn't a bad person. I was someone who was under a lot of pressure with a ton of responsibility as the band's frontwoman and increasingly drinking more than I could handle, which wasn't very much, contrary to popular belief.

Vince reminds me that I threw a glass of beer at him within three weeks of him becoming our manager. I can't remember if I did or not, but if I'm guilty he probably deserved it. Mark, Rick, Harve and, increasingly, Bjarne felt the lash of my tongue. Because I was obsessed with the band I didn't respect the boundaries of others. I thought nothing of calling the guys on weekends and maybe late at night because the band's business was all-important to me. They must have felt like they were a doctor on-call and I was a desperately needy patient. I didn't consider the consequences or that they may have had areas of their life that did not include me or Divinyls, I just picked up the phone and barked at them. I had drive and creativity but my people skills left a lot to be desired. I didn't care. I didn't try to be Mother Theresa. I tried to be myself. Being nice to others didn't concern me in the least. What concerned me was being true to myself.

Selfishness comes with being an artist. It's essential if you're to keep your creativity inviolate. You get so absorbed in your art that emotionally you stop growing and become self-absorbed and tedious to be near. Only like-minded people, or those who get their kicks by associating with creative people, or those out to prey on you, will hang around. Not that we were the only dysfunctional band. The guys from Cold Chisel were always feuding, Jimmy Barnes and drummer Steve Prestwich had fist fights all the time! Bon Scott was going to get the boot from AC/DC for his drinking. The Butler brothers in the Psychedelic Furs, who we would do a tour of America with, fought constantly. Then there were the dysfunctional Beatles, Rolling Stones, Beach Boys, Guns N' Roses, Red Hot Chili Peppers, Bruce Springsteen and the E Street Band, the list goes on. Sometimes dysfunction can be creativity's best friend.

Vince Lovegrove

We were an intense bunch, and a nightmare to others and ourselves. I can remember a live cable TV show we did in Pasadena, California. This was when cable television and MTV was just becoming mainstream in the US. The show was filmed in an old theatre with the seats ripped out and it went to air every Friday night. The director, sound guy and cameramen were young, but shit-hot. They had come up through the ranks, and filmed some top bands. We were one of the first Australian outfits invited on the show. Half a million people, many of whom were in our target demographic of 16–25-year-olds, would be watching, and it could mean big album sales for us.

Do you think I could convince Mark and Chrissy that the crew knew what they were doing and were up to handling Divinyls live? Of course I could not. They refused to be convinced.

Mark would say, 'Vince, how do you know they're gonna have the right sound mix on the band?'

I said, 'Mark, I'll be up in the studio—I'll be *there*. If anything's too loud, I'll tell 'em. I'll mix it with 'em. I'll *tell* 'em what to do!'

'But will they listen to you?'

'Yes, they *will* listen to me, Mark. You've got to do the show. These are the kids who are going to make or break Divinyls in the US.'

'But Vince, are they gonna know any of our songs?'

Every time we had a TV show to do, like *Countdown*, or any form of media commitment, an interview for radio, TV or the press, we went through this infuriating ritual. Every *fucking* time. I'd say, 'Chrissy, Mark, we've got a spot on *Countdown*!'

'But, Vince,' wailed Chrissy, '*Sherbet* go on *Countdown*. I don't want to go on a show that has Sherbet.'

'Chrissy, I'm the manager of Divinyls, and I say we are going on *Countdown*. You'll play your record and a million people will see it and a percentage of those will go out and buy it.'

'Well, we're *not* going to be on with Sherbet.'

We gave Vince hell, and Mark's and my stroppy perfectionism, borne of our fear of being ripped off, frustrated him endlessly. For all that, as a rocker guilty of the occasional tantrum himself, I doubt he would have wanted it any other way. Vince could be confrontational and cutting, and we would both react. Vince did coke and I drank. We *both* drank. We could be highly reactive. We were a volatile mix.

As a savvy manager, Vince knew that if our public image was bratty and punkish, it would make us seem edgier, more rock'n'roll, and he was right. He taught us all about lighting and how to look different from other bands. Sometimes we were lit so darkly that viewers could barely see us through the gloom. He encouraged our public excesses, and it came naturally to us to go along with the masterplan. He planted items in the press about our bad behaviour. A spate of stories were published that had us in some kind of strife or another: screaming matches on the street, being robbed in hotel rooms, getting pulled over three times for speeding in a single weekend, insulting other rock stars. A few of these yarns may even have been true.

Vince Lovegrove

Chrissy was an artist, and she knew I had been an artist and still thought like an artist and that's one of the reasons she got me onboard. I didn't want to let her down. From the beginning I made a pact with her and Mark that we would always take the artist's point of view. We would do what we thought was artistically right and not worry about commercially driven compromises. We'd be true to our rock'n'roll vision no matter what the cost. That, and our arrogance, hurt us. Industry people thought, 'Oh Divinyls are too much hard work,' and took their money elsewhere.

Media interviews are part of the job. You talk to the journalist about yourself and your new record. He or she writes the story. People read it. They buy the record.

In the early days, Vince kept me from doing interviews because he didn't want the public to know how shy I was, and also to build my, and the band's, mystique. When I did give an interview, I didn't know how to handle the procedure. I was terribly uncomfortable and reporters inevitably got the wrong impression.

Writer Mark Dodshon in *RAM* summed up the frustrations of dealing with Divinyls...

The temptation to write a bitchy story is always there . . . it's not that they're deliberately inconsiderate—in fact they're obliviously unaccommodating—but their irritating inability to keep appointments shows a lamentable lack of tact, at the very least. I've lost track now, but at least four times the venue and time for the interview were changed, and when we finally ended up connecting, it was in a cramped, dark, noisy make-up room at a rival magazine's office! The band's complete preoccupation with themselves and their music to the exclusion of all else puts at risk their relationship with all other parts of the industry—the media, record companies and other bands. The irony is they wouldn't be as big, or probably as good, if they didn't have this self-obsession. But it doesn't make the trip any easier for those whose job it is to put the band in touch with its potential audience . . .

Christina Amphlett's aggressive, pouting schoolgirl antics turn an enormous number of people off—but probably turn just as many on. The inherent contradiction of a strong woman wearing costumes that normally suggest innocence and vulnerability is just too confusing, too confrontational . . .

Success is obviously what they want to achieve with their music, but the personality traits that often make their songs so interesting run the risk of frustrating their ambitions.

When Vince was briefing some poor journalist assigned to interview me, he'd call the reporter beforehand and warn, 'Look, mate, there's no easy way to say this, but Chrissy is in a *really* bad mood today. For Christ's sake, be careful what you ask her or she is going to *rip your head off*.' The reporter would come into the interview loaded up with scary misconceptions about me and my mood, and the tension between us would, in Vince's eyes, make for a better article.

A lot of journalists brought trouble on themselves by arriving for our interview under-prepared, with maybe just three questions the extent of their research. I didn't suffer that. I made a point of letting the reporter know exactly what I thought of unprofessionalism.

In America I got so sick of talking to ignorant reporters that I bypassed them entirely. And I bought a little violin case that looked as if it might contain a machine gun and I'd walk into a radio station and gangster them into playing our record.

Vince Lovegrove

Chrissy would bristle, and make it very difficult for the interviewer. To an innocuous question, she'd snap, 'What do you wanna know that for? What's that got to do with anything?' Once, in America, she was being interviewed live on a local radio station and she interrupted the interviewer to demand, 'I noticed there's a nuclear silo on the way into town. Tell me why!' and gave the guy a hard time, as if the silo was his doing.

We were reaping the whirlwind, and at times I felt misunderstood. What I was trying to do and say when I was dealing with all these people in the music industry... maybe my discomfort at talking to them made my tone or my delivery awkward. Maybe I wasn't always articulate. I was, after all, new to the world of big time rock'n'roll and didn't understand the way the system worked, or the jargon. I was an artist and thought that should have been enough. I didn't know how to schmooze, and I didn't want to learn.

Phil Stafford

If a reporter had fallen foul of his editor, the most terrible punishment the editor could exact was to send the poor bastard out to interview Chrissy Amphlett. It was thought to be worse than being fed to the lions.

I was a feature writer for *RAM* magazine in Divinyls' heyday in the early and mid-eighties. I interviewed Chrissy and Mark a number of times, together and solo. Apart from having a considerable talent, Chrissy had attitude to burn and you approached an interview with her in a state of trepidation. Your best and only defence was to have an encyclopaedic knowledge of Divinyls and be wearing your cast-iron underwear. If she knew you'd done your homework and had listened to her music you were usually okay. If you hadn't, she'd find you out in a second. She'd walk out, leaving you there with your tape recorder running. Good on her. Why should she put up with unprofessionalism?

Before our first interview I had been warned about Chrissy by other music reporters, so I made sure I read everything I could about her, and she responded by being, if not exactly charming, then quirkily entertaining. At least she didn't tear my head off.

When I was working for the SBS-TV music show *The Noise* we did a piece on Chrissy and her misdemeanours, including being imprisoned in Spain. I asked if we could film our interview in a local police lock-up. She loved the idea and was cooperative and a dream to work with.

McEntee was hard going. Deeply eccentric in his own way, he was the only musician who could have kept pace with or put up with Chrissy. They struck off each other onstage—he was such a good guitar melody guy and a chordal genius—and she was an unbelievable performer and a terrific songwriter. I think her performing tended to make people underrate her writing.

I felt for Vince Lovegrove, one of the great managers of that period. He put up with a lot of shit from Chrissy and Mark. As an observer of the music scene, I thought they were virtually unmanageable.

Drugs and booze played their part in Chrissy's antics. We broke for a bite to eat midway through one interview. The waiter asked me what I wanted and I ordered a beer. Chrissy said she'd have water. 'Water?' I said, amazed. 'You're supposed to be the rock'n'roll animal!' She laughed, 'I'm what they call a two-pot screamer. I can't handle alcohol. If I have a couple of drinks now I won't be able to stop, and believe me, you won't want to be interviewing me then.'

Divinyls lived the life. They worked hard, playing maybe six times a week, sometimes two gigs a night. It was nothing for them to finish a show at the Manzil Room in Kings Cross then load the gear straight into the transport and drive to Shellharbour for a lunchtime gig.

My rudeness, which was exacerbated when I drank, manifested itself in many ways. In addition to journalists and industry honchos, woe betide the fan or even fellow musician who approached me when I was tired, drunk or generally not in the mood. At an awards show, a well-known singer came up and said, 'Oh Chrissy, I so admire your work. We really must talk.'

I replied, 'Really? About what?'

One night I was walking in Kings Cross when a fan ran up to me and said, 'I love the Divinyls, and I love *you*!' He happened to be eating an ice cream. I grabbed his hand and shoved the ice cream into his face. He stood there dumbfounded, vanilla ice cream dripping down his shirt. 'I *still* love you,' he said sadly. Why did I behave like that? Bad mood, the booze? Probably. And perhaps a little bit because I *could*. Back then I found being a monster was a lot of fun.

Rick Grossman

Chrissy and I had finished a gig in Canberra and we went out to a pub for a drink. There was a DJ perched on a stage playing records. We were sitting at a table pouring drinks from a big pitcher of bourbon and Coke. We finished the pitcher and started in on a second one when the DJ announced, 'We're honoured tonight, ladies and gentlemen, because in our midst is one of Australia's greatest singers. Let's hear it for Miss Chrissy . . . Hynde!'

Chrissy's face registered nothing. She said nothing, just stood up, grabbed the full pitcher, and calmly approached the DJ. He must have thought she was going to offer him a drink. No such luck. She tipped the bourbon and Coke all over this poor fellow and his turntables.

One night in Melbourne at a nightclub I saw Kate Ceberano and kissed her. She freaked out and ran out of the club. I was told her mother was leaving messages around that she was very annoyed with me.

Kate Ceberano

Chrissy Amphlett was bullying me. I thought, 'Why would you pick on me? I'm your greatest fan!' but didn't dare say it. I hoped she'd leave me alone. But no, she came over and gave me a long kiss on the mouth. That did it. I cried and cried and I couldn't stop. Had I been older I would have coped, but I was a young dumb-arse sook. I'd never done anything to Chrissy. I *idolised* her. She may have singled me out because she saw me as competition. It was a case of, 'Back off, kid!'.

She wanted to establish her superiority, and if bullying me didn't work, then a kiss certainly did.

What can I say? I walked the walk. Being a bad girl wasn't always an act. Twice, in 1981 and 1983, I went to jail rather than pay parking fines. There was no way I was going to pay them on principle and, besides, I didn't have the money. I preferred to wipe off the debt to the government by cooling my heels in prison. (I suspect also that Vince didn't mind me doing time because being a jailbird added to my bad-girl mystique.) Every day you spent in prison wiped twenty-five dollars off the total of the fines, which meant around two weeks behind bars each time. I'd survived prison in Spain, so how hard could being jailed in Sydney be? Quite hard, as I found out.

The first time in Mulawa prison, west of Sydney, I was put in a cell with two lesbian armed robbers. They were frightening. One night, one of them had a bad dream and woke up screaming.

The second time I went to jail, the police had waited for me offstage at the Coogee Bay Hotel to serve me with an arrest warrant. Next day I fronted up to Randwick Police Station and was put in a paddy wagon and driven to Mulawa where I shared a cell with a girl frantically scratching at her scabies.

The inmates were not all strangers. Amazingly, my old friend Candy Raymond had also been busted for non-payment of parking fines and was in prison at the same time as me. We had a lot of catching up to do. Not long before, she'd had a guest role in TV's *Prisoner*, and we both hooted when one of the guards, confusing television fiction with real life, looked her up and down and sneered, 'So *you're* back.' The other prisoners loved Candy, who was always the friendly and gracious celebrity. They had problems with me.

At that time, Divinyls had a single in the Top 10, and because I was quiet and kept to myself in the prison the girls got it into their heads that I was a stuck-up rock star. One morning Candy and I were sitting in the café when Candy started digging at me and saying, 'Say something to them! Say something!' She'd noticed the girls all stand up from their table at once, pick up their chairs and head in our direction. They were about to bash me. I leapt to my feet and held out my arms to them. 'Okay everybody,' I said, 'I'm really sorry. I've been in here before when nobody knew who I was and no one cared that I minded my own business. That's all I'm doing this time. I'm sorry you think I'm being snobby. I'm truly not. I didn't realise I was having this effect on you. Now, everybody back to my cell for coffee!'

They put their chairs down and came back and we hung out singing and talking. They sat on my bed, table and wardrobe. They explained they thought I was being like a previous celebrity inmate. 'She loved herself!' they sneered, as if this was the greatest crime a girl could commit. I thought, 'Well, maybe you all should love yourselves a little too.'

After I defused that tense moment in the café, I was accepted. I helped organise the prison entertainment, and staged a rock concert with some inmates (though that was stopped when one was sprung passing drugs to another).

My image as an ogre understandably made me an easy target and I was occasionally blamed for things I hadn't done. If the band screwed up an appointment, had an off-night, or, later, when bandmembers started leaving, I would always be held responsible. 'She's a bitch,' people would rip on me, 'it must have been her fault.' I wore it all and loved being the bad girl of the Australian music scene. Like my idols—Jerry Lee Lewis, Iggy Pop and Deborah Harry—I had created a character from within myself. I revelled in the freedom it gave me to perform.

DEMONS AND HEADACHES

The chances of a rock band succeeding are minuscule. Of all the starry-eyed kids who get together to form a band, only a tiny fraction ever make it, even in a minor way. For the rest, all those dreams and all that joyous thrashing about in garages come to zero. Why? No luck, no opportunity, bad decisions, personality clashes, insufficient dedication, or, to be brutally honest, not enough talent. A band making it to the top is a little like an embryo's journey from the moment its creators make love through the organism's journey from sperm to egg swimming in the womb and on to the big world outside. The odds are way against it, but success is as sweet as it gets.

Divinyls' dreams didn't *all* come true. We didn't quite reach the rock'n'roll stratosphere. We didn't sell millions and millions of records and become rich and famous in every country. Yet we survived for seventeen years. We gave rock our very best. We lived the life and created music that mattered.

The best of our early line-ups, Mark McEntee, Rick Grossman, Richard Harvey and, of the guys who came later, Charley Drayton,

Charlie Owen and Jerome Smith, were special people and musicians. They had to be, to put up with a full-on lead singer and all-round perfectionist diva like me. They had to be strong onstage to avoid being overpowered by my performance, and strong offstage, too, for we were a dysfunctional bunch contending with the usual suspects: drugs, booze, love, hate, death, dumb decisions, lost fortunes, law suits and raw ambition.

Rick Grossman

> The five of us back in the first half of the eighties had something special. When people started to get sacked or left, the chemistry got mucked up. Later in their career, Divinyls had terrific players, maybe even better than that first line-up, but I don't think the band was ever better than when it was Chrissy, Mark, Harve, Bjarne and me.

If you'd rocked up to the Piccadilly, the Stage Door Tavern or the Manly Vale Hotel or any of the other pubs and dives we played in the early eighties, you'd have seen me up there onstage with Mark, Rick, Harve and Bjarne Ohlin. If you'd peeped into the wings or behind our backdrop, you might have caught a glimpse of Vince Lovegrove, threatening promoters, counting the takings and generally making things happen. Meet my boys...

Mark created our arrangements and told everybody what to play. He had a peerless knowledge of chords and all the discipline from his jazz background. Shy at heart, he hid behind a prickly, awkward, downbeat façade. He communicated best with his guitar and was never happier than when he was playing. He had a unique sound and style. He wasn't flash. He didn't pose or crank out grandiose solos; he was more about melodies and rhythm. On stage he was electric. He dressed like a rock star and, as one reviewer once aptly wrote, as he played 'he bounced around the stage like he was trying to shake something off his back'. Perhaps he was.

Mark had played in other bands, but Divinyls allowed him to express himself and be a part of something wonderful. He was technically superb. He could always pull great sounds out of his amps. He had a feel for the colour of a song. He was intense and wired, existing, not always happily, in a manic world of his own. And, of course, this odd, difficult man-child who made model aeroplanes and drove stylish cars was my lover.

Mark was obsessed by his music. He could sit alone and play all day, dreaming up new melodies, new chords. Musically he was a leader, but as far as band dynamics went he was not a strong character or an organiser and wasn't a driving force, like Vince and me. Mark was always struggling for his own identity. And when you're in a band, it can be hard to be your own person. It didn't help that he was partnered with a lead singer who was the focal point of the band during the gigs and the bossiest one offstage. He responded to my overbearing ways by fighting back or sulking. We began to argue incessantly.

Mark never showed me kindness in public and started to belittle me. I wouldn't put up with that and retaliated. I was flirtatious—which didn't help matters. Mark's saving grace was his humour. He could be witty and hilarious and I could never be in a relationship with someone who couldn't make me laugh. And he did that. When Mark was funny I'd fall in love with him all over again.

He couldn't cook, so when we were sharing a house or apartment— not that we did that much because as long as we were together we kept separate residences—I had to do all the cooking and chores, and that rankled. We slept together but never spent the night in each other's arms. It wasn't a conventional relationship. We were two parts of a whole. We were attached, fused creatively, contractually and romantically. Our fighting must have made it look to an outsider as if we were deadly enemies, but while we were together we really only ever trusted each other.

Even when there was tenderness, it ended painfully. Once while we were on tour I ran Mark's bath in our hotel room and thought I'd make it special for him by pouring in some eucalyptus oil. He lowered himself into the water, and screamed. The eucalyptus was burning his balls. I picked up his dripping, writhing little body in my arms and sat him in a basin of cold water until the searing sensation passed.

'We don't get on,' Mark would tell the rock pundit and author Glenn A Baker in an interview for *The Weekend Australian Magazine* in 1991, 'but we are very fond of each other and we probably do love one another. You have to toughen yourself to Chrissy to survive. A lot of people can't take it but I had to stick up for myself at school and get used to being pushed around... I can never adequately describe what it is between us. We're close but we drive each other crazy. We don't know what we are either. It's really weird. I guess it all makes sense in the music. We reflect each other's ideas and tastes, our minds are close.'

When we started touring at the beginning of the band's career and before Mark and I got together, I would walk into a motel room somewhere on a long stretch of highway where the trucks rumbled past all night and a feeling of loneliness and emptiness would descend upon me. Typically, then, a motel room was a depressing place with dreary, generic furnishings and soggy, filthy carpet. When the band got going the quality of our accommodation improved, but not the sense of emptiness and loneliness. I never seemed to master those feelings. I would escape by playing movie soundtracks or writing songs with Mark.

Dealing with his own inhibitions, Mark rarely had it in him to comfort me when I was down. As my soulmate, I believed he should have tried. I was solicitous with him, talking him through *his* demons. I resented his lack of support most when I was criticised by fans and the press. Divinyls were very much an acquired taste, and we were just too in-your-face for many people at that time. As lead singer and frontwoman, the buck stopped with me and I was prepared to bear the brunt, yet a comforting hug from Mark wouldn't have gone astray. With hindsight he was struggling to do his best, play his guitar, write, perform. He had a full dance card. There wasn't anything left to devote to a relationship.

I was in an airport in America and saw my old hero Debbie Harry and her lover and bandmate Chris Stein hugging and kissing each other in public, so intimate, so openly loving. As I stood gazing at them I wished that Mark and I were like Debbie and Chris. And because we were shackled to each other by our music, our frankly unsatisfactory relationship went on and on and on...

Vince Lovegrove

Divinyls' best performances—by a long shot—were when Chrissy and Mark were at each other's throats. They just fired. They were fucking magnificent. Mark would play like a demon, Chrissy would perform like a demon and the rest of the band, nervous, adrenalin pumping, bounced off them. Chrissy and Mark's weird, foaming-at-the-mouth furious, loving, hopelessly dependent relationship was the magic of Divinyls.

The other guys in the band respected Mark as a musician but they were not close. Mark never had friends, so he clung to me. When Rick joined the band he thought he was in love with Mark, not in a gay way, he was just in awe of Mark's musicianship. But gradually Mark's hang-ups came between him and the others. Harve particularly gave Mark a tough time.

Rick Grossman

At a gig I tried to hug Mark because he'd played so beautifully, and he seized up and shrugged me off. Harve took me aside and said, 'Don't do that, he hates that kind of affection.'

I might not have always spent my money wisely but Mark was hopeless with it. He didn't know how to deal with money and I think he was nervous that if he involved himself in the financial side of the band he'd corrupt his creativity. He never wanted to pay bills. That irritated me because I couldn't stand to be in debt to anyone.

From the outset we owed money. It's just what happens. You need cash up-front to record and tour. The record company advances it to you and then you repay it from the proceeds of record sales and gigs. Unless you break in a big way you may never pay back the advance and remain always in the label's debt. I hated having the debt hanging over us but it never seemed to cross Mark's mind.

Rick Grossman's bass guitar gave us a growly sound. He was vastly experienced, having played in many top bands. At sound-check Rick worked at getting his sound just perfect. He combined wonderfully with drummer Richard Harvey, and together they pumped out a loud, fat, dynamic platform for Mark and me. Like Mark, Rick wasn't an arrogant player. He always strove to complement the unit. He was always supportive and good-natured. That was very important, especially when Mark and I were around causing problems. Rick also looked good on stage. He was handsome and a true performer. Yet as committed as he was to us, I didn't realise he had another friend lurking in the dark, a closer friend. Heroin. I would walk into Rick and his girlfriend's room for a chat, and they would sit there glaring at me like guilty schoolkids who'd been caught out by the teacher. Later I learned they'd been arguing about Rick's addiction, but, typically, at the time I assumed they were angry with me.

Rick Grossman

We were all at Vince's house having a band meeting. Harve got up to go to the loo and took a peek into Vince's medicine cabinet and found a container full of cocaine. Naturally, he snorted a huge whack of it. Then he returned to the meeting, and passed me a note saying, 'Go to the bathroom and check out the medicine cabinet.' I couldn't resist, so I excused myself. I found the coke and got stuck in. Harve and I each went to the loo about half a dozen times that day. When Vince returned to his stash he would have found it greatly depleted.

Richard Harvey was a good *feel* drummer. He had swing and a groove. He could flog the drums when he had to, but he wasn't just a flogger. Like his great mate and partner in crime, Rick, Harve was a good guy to have around. He was always up for a drink and a joke. A very, very funny guy. Just as Mark and I were a duo, so Harve and Rick were as thick as thieves on and off the stage and although I know a lot about what they got up to in their Divinyls years I'm sure there's plenty I don't have a clue about and that's probably just as well.

I sang and wrote and drove the band. Mark drove *me*. He never allowed me a comfort zone. He always pushed me higher, which was exhausting, but the work got done. I needed him to do that.

I yelled at and cajoled the band, and when I had to I got physical. I demanded excellence. We didn't always attain it, but we went for it. I refused to cop half-hearted commitment. I needed everyone to be on the edge if I was to perform at my best. We had to be authentic. There's no way that I, with my voice, would win a talent contest, but it's fucking *real*, and it's me. In Divinyls, it was just as much an extension of my soul as Rick and Mark's guitar was of theirs.

Divinyls was my life. I had no respite. It was a 24-hour-a-day thing. With success, there were so many different things to deal with. There was the booking agency, the record company, the recording, the contracts, the performing and touring. With Mark needing space to create, Vince and I shouldered the load. Suddenly I, who'd been a free spirit my whole life, had huge responsibility. And it was overwhelming. There were so many things to take care of, so many expectations. I got very hard, very fast.

Vince was as passionate and driven to see Divinyls succeed as I was. In many ways he was a male version of me. He was truly devoted to us. Nothing was too much trouble for Vince, and he ruthlessly ensured that our needs were met. He was more forgiving than me. He allowed us also to make mistakes and be who we were. He was an ally.

To me Bjarne Ohlin was different from the rest of us. He was a proficient guitarist and keyboard player and could write songs (much of 'Siren' is his), and he was very poised and good-looking, but there was always something mannered about him onstage, as if he was playing a part. He was very self-conscious when we were being filmed and always knew where the camera was.

I was tough on Bjarne, trying to get him to be real, and one night in April 1983, at Selinas in Sydney, it all bubbled over. Throughout that gig I taunted and poked all the guys, especially Bjarne, to get them to be spontaneous, make them mad for the sake of a bit of drama. Drama I got. With three songs to go, Bjarne decided he'd had enough of me and rammed his guitar into my stomach, really hard. It hurt, and I went to my knees. Then he threw his instrument down and left the stage.

I thought, 'At last! Some emotion from Bjarne!' but he disappointed me. After the gig there was a ceremony at Selinas where we each received a gold record. Bjarne's fury, it seemed, didn't last long and he turned up to get his award, friendly as can be, as if nothing had happened between us. The lure of showbiz was too strong. I thought he could have at least stayed away a day or two. A real rocker would have.

Phil Stafford

I had to write a feature for *RAM* magazine about Divinyls, and I went to Selinas to check them out. I had a ringside seat for one of the most shocking things I've ever seen at a gig. Chrissy had been goading Bjarne all night. She seemed to be switching songs on him to trip him up. Then suddenly she slapped him. My fellow music writers agreed it was the most outrageous thing that had ever happened in Australian rock to that stage. Bjarne retaliated by slamming Chrissy with the neck of his guitar, then he threw it down and left the stage.

Vince Lovegrove

Bjarne was the quiet one, the one who always seemed out of place to me. He was a gentle man, and a gentleman, but he just did not seem to fit into a rock'n'roll band. Not *this* rock'n'roll band.

His background was acting and at times acting seemed to be his true heart's desire. Rock'n'roll is no place for the normal and Bjarne was the most normal in the Divinyls gang, no question about that.

Perhaps he was dealt with a little harshly, but then, Bjarne was a big boy, and he knew what he was dealing with.

I *was* tough. I don't think I ever lorded it over the guys. I hope I didn't. I always tried to make my feelings known as one of the group, not someone superior.

Sometimes in the heat of the moment it was easy to forget I was a woman, and I became as chauvinistic as the blokes. Being the only female in a world of men will do that to you. Apart from the wonderful Denise Fraser from Dirty Pool, who became my on-the-road friend and minder, I was surrounded by blokes.

We lived the rock life with its many excesses. We all drank but did only a little cocaine because it was far harder to come by in those days. Alcohol was always around, there were rivers of booze, and I was beginning to find it difficult to stop at a couple of drinks.

The danger for me—and I didn't understand it then—was drinking after the show when I was pumped with adrenalin. Alcohol and adrenalin are a combustible combination, and alcohol was so accessible. For those reading this who have never performed, you're awash with adrenalin when you come offstage. It took me three hours to come down without alcohol, five hours with it. I was susceptible.

Often we wasted ourselves, but no matter how bad we felt, we still had to get up on stage every night and be great. That wasn't easy when all you wanted to do was curl up under the covers in a dark room until you felt remotely human again. It was all about discipline, and Vince and I enforced it, even when we felt worse than anyone else. Drug-fucked, hungover, hostile audience (a common occurrence when we supported big-name bands in the US), lousy reviews, poor album sales . . . didn't matter. That night's concert was the most important concert of our lives.

Rick Grossman

There was no comfort zone in that band. You couldn't hide. Chrissy kept us up to standard. She and Mark were equal musical collaborators, but Chrissy was the leader of Divinyls. Just as she could scare the shit out of an audience, she could scare it out of us. If she thought any bandmember or the crew deserved a bollocking, she'd dish it out.

Then we'd be on the road and I, or one of the guys, might say, 'Oh, I'm getting a cold,' and soon there'd be a knock on your door and Chrissy would come in. 'I've been shopping,' she'd say, 'and I've bought you all this stuff,' and dump cough drops, elixirs, tissues and medicine on the bed. All the aggression would be gone, and she'd become my Mum!

When it was time to party she could drink any of the guys under the table. This sometimes made us forget that she was a woman, and, under that hard façade, a very feminine woman. We'd get too blokey and carry on like idiots and she'd say, 'Hang on a second, there's a female present!'

I may have been female, but I was a female in a rock'n'roll band and that meant there was no room for a princess. The big theatres we played, and some of the clubs like Selinas, the Stage Door Tavern and the Civic, had passable facilities. But mostly we played in rough pubs, and wherever we were in Australia one beer barn would be pretty similar to another. There'd be an auditorium with an atmosphere more suited to boozing, gambling and meat tray and chook raffles; cheap carpet on the floor that stank of cigarettes, beer and vomit; drunk, fighting fans; steroid-addled bouncers; crap, or no, amenities; a tiny, badly designed stage; appalling sound system; unsuitable lights or lights that didn't work at all. Putting on a professional show could be trying in these conditions, but sometimes great things come from adversity.

Sound-check would be at five or six in the afternoon. The boys would get their sounds and monitors together; I would check my monitors and the sound and lighting would be checked by the roadies. I'd acclimatise myself to the stage and where the audience would be. Sound-checks can be deceiving. You do them when the venue is empty and everything sounds terrible, and later when it's jammed with people things sound and look very different, usually better. If there was a new song to learn or we had to practise something we would do it at sound-check.

Satisfied, we would go to our 'dressing room', often an office or a small shabby flat or storeroom. We'd cram in to make final plans for the show and get into our stage clothes in what passed for a private corner, maybe pee in a cup when no one was looking if there was no toilet handy, and there usually wasn't. To find some peace each of us would build an imaginary wall and hunker down behind it. People violated our impromptu privacy at their peril.

Whatever our surrounds, we'd bond before the gig by singing a song together, just something to unite us and put us in the mood. I might do some vocal exercises away on my own.

I wouldn't eat in the three hours before the show, afraid I'd feel queasy or bloated, or tired from digesting. I was always nervous and to calm myself I'd have a nip of vodka just before going on stage, and I'd keep a glass of vodka, or whatever the alcohol of the week was, near the drum riser for a swig mid-show. (Vodka was ideal because it looked like water.) I've heard Divinyls had the most exorbitant drink rider in the business.

In the earlier days alcohol worked for me. Later, when my drinking became excessive, it didn't. I never did drugs before a gig, and especially not cocaine, which split my vocal cords into three and ruined my voice.

A pre-gig intro tape would be played in the final minutes before we went on. 'Over The Rainbow', dramatic classical music or, when I was feeling perverse, a rant from the disgraced American TV evangelist Jimmy Swaggart. I found a tape of the tearful confession Swaggart made after he was busted for indulging in prostitutes and pornography and cut it up into a kind of rap: 'I have sinned against you, my Lord,' wailed Jimmy, 'and I would ask that your precious blood would wash and cleanse every stain until it is in the seas of God's forgetfulness, never to be remembered against me.'

As the intro tape trailed off we'd be in the wings. The lights would dim and there we'd be. Sometimes we'd start with 'I'll Make You Happy', sometimes with 'Boys In Town'.

I'd have worked out that night's set list. I devised a new one for almost every gig. It was terribly important for me to have the set list flow in a way I felt comfortable with and that was in sync with how I was feeling and what I wanted to say. Mark would check it to ensure I didn't have songs in the same key together too often. Our approximately one-hour set would have songs from our latest album, some older hits, and an occasional Australian cover for variety. If other bandmembers wanted to include a song, I was open to that—if I agreed with their choice. If I didn't I would say no.

I'd try to do our songs a little differently each time, depending on how I was feeling and what was happening in my life. A nuance or a twist added to our spontaneity. I wouldn't allow the band to get too laidback, and if I saw them coasting I'd surprise them with a swerve and they'd have to keep up or face the consequences.

I found our shows cooked best when there was an element of danger, a kick-arse edge to our performance. To make the air crackle and the music bleed I'd demand heaps from everyone. I'd scream at Mark, Rick and Harve for more intensity, I'd yell at Bjarne to stop posing and be real. Sometimes I'd do something really inflammatory to rev the band up, like insulting them or even, as with Bjarne at Selinas, shove or poke them. I'd dance frenziedly, waving my arms about and bashing into the amps, or stage-dive. I'd hurl water at the roadies or knock over the stage equipment so the crew would have to rush out and set it up again. I'd abuse the audience. Everyone in that house was involved. Everyone. No one was safe.

Not surprisingly, the onstage aggression infected the audience, most of whom would be drunk, and there were always fights at Divinyls shows. Men and women got stuck in. At a gig at Broken Hill, *all* the brawlers were women.

Yet the most violent people at the show were usually the blokes who'd been hired to keep the peace. I resented those bouncers, big, angry oafs frayed by dope and steroids. The venues would sell the kids enormous quantities of alcohol and then when they got drunk the bouncers attacked them and hurled them into the street. When I saw them beating up a fan I could never help myself. I'd order the lights turned on them and abuse them from the stage, and if that had no effect I plunged into the crowd and leapt onto their backs. This would bring attention to them and humiliate them. I like to think that when word got around that I wouldn't stand for their bullying the audience these thugs thought twice before throwing their weight around at a Divinyls gig.

As I've said, I didn't waste time with friendly chat or banter with the audience. To me, that diluted the performance. I'd berate them and terrorise them, sure—that was in character. I never said, 'Good night!' but just left the stage without looking back. I was always the first Divinyl to depart. Then the band would play for a little bit without me before Mark would make his exit, then Bjarne, then Harve, and the last man standing would be Rick, playing the bass line of whatever song we'd finished with—often it was 'Elsie'—over and over until he too walked off and the stage went dark.

As soon as we were back in our dressing-room the door would be locked for 15 minutes or half an hour to keep interlopers out and let the adrenalin subside. Also, if a problem, musical, technical or personal, reared during the show, Vince and I insisted that it be resolved immediately. Tempers flared at these meetings, for we'd all be as high as kites from the adrenalin of performing, our emotions far too close to the surface. Vince and I demanded total honesty. We brutally dissected each other's performances. Anyone could say anything about anyone. Criticism is painful when you invest your heart and soul, but hopefully it was constructive rather than nasty. If we gave, by our own standards, a sub-par performance, the atmosphere in that room would be that of a morgue.

Rick says he occasionally refrained from saying what he thought in our post-mortems because he feared I'd explode all over him. My defence is that it is dangerous to create a scene where the people around you only say the things you want to hear. You end up living in a fool's paradise. Later, when we got to know each other better, Rick was able to be more direct.

Rick Grossman

> Post-mortems were intense and no place for the faint-hearted. Many
> times I sat there hoping not to be singled out for criticism and praying
> for it to end. At one of these discussions I criticised a producer Chrissy
> admired. She said nothing at the time, then some nights later my phone
> rang at 2 a.m. and it was her. She went off her brain at me for what
> I'd said.

Rick and everyone else wanted me to be fiery and over-the-top
onstage, but didn't understand that I couldn't switch off as soon as
the show ended. And I wasn't doing yoga or meditation or anything
else natural to calm me down. Ours was a raucous and loud rock band.
If I had been anything other than what I was, the men in the audience
and the band would have eaten me alive.

Vince was a vital member of our post-gig discussions and always
tried to tell us the truth. He ripped and tore with abandon. Yet the
most hurtful thing Vince could ever say to me was, 'You were a
cabaret act tonight!' That was the ultimate putdown.

We all came to realise that no matter what happened on a particular
night, there'd be another gig tomorrow bringing an opportunity to
put things right.

It wasn't always fraught. Being hard on each other gave us the
freedom and the right to really get off on the many times we all played
well and Divinyls gelled as a unit. When that happened it was a
transcendent feeling.

After the gig, I'd need to party to climb down from my high. I'd
start with a few drinks, then that would tip me into wanting something
else, more booze, pot, pills, cocaine, and ecstasy in later years. I went
knocking on doors looking for excitement. 'Where's the action!' The
roadies were always able to help me out. Mark would come looking
for me and find me hanging out with the road crew and go ballistic.

Roadies live close to the edge. Things are quite different today, but
back then they were often loners without responsibilities, no families,

maybe some prison time in their past. Hard men doing a hard job—unloading the gear from our truck, setting it up, making sure the lights and sound worked perfectly and that the instruments sounded sublime, then loading it all back into the truck and driving to the next venue, sometimes in the next suburb, sometimes a thousand kilometres away. They're the unsung heroes of rock'n'roll. Sometimes late at night after a gig, I'd sit like a pirate captain and observe my cutthroats, the muscular, tattooed roadies, load our gear onto the semi-trailer, watch as those amps and lights and monitors, the drums and guitars, were packed away. I sacked my share of roadies, and drove them hard, but I always related to the crew.

So many of those concerts are a blur in my mind, but I do know that when I was performing it was the happiest I'd be all day.

I was intolerant of anyone who didn't have my passion for the band to succeed. I imagine—I know—I drove everybody nuts! Everything we did had to be executed to a high standard and in a way that was essentially and uniquely Divinyls. That included our music, our performances, sound, lighting, merchandise. I had in my sights everyone from the band, to Vince, the roadies, the promoter, record companies, our bookers and the media. Vince, too, was demanding and had standards as impossibly high as mine. I thought nothing of calling him at three in the morning, because I knew he'd be up and, besides, there were no boundaries set, to talk about an issue, and he didn't mind, not until the end, anyway, when he had other sadder and more pressing preoccupations.

Divinyls was my life and nothing else mattered. I didn't go on picnics or to the movies, or to restaurants unless it was to talk about the band. I had virtually no friends outside Divinyls and the crew. I hadn't seen Candy or Shayna or the actors from Melbourne for ages. Rick would ask me over to his place to wind down by watching a video and I'd say, 'Count me out, watching videos is not creating music or doing anything for the band. Videos are a waste of time.'

I must have been a pain. Rick reminds me of the times he'd be chatting up a girl, and just about had her on the hook, when I'd arrive and give her a terrifying look and demand, '*Who's this*?' The girl would hurriedly leave. It was so insensitive and, yes, territorial of me, but my radar wasn't attuned to others' feelings.

Divinyls had a siege mentality, us against the world. There was zero camaraderie between us and other bands. We took the view that we were all in deadly competition for audiences, record sales and airplay. I got into a lift with Todd Hunter of Dragon and Johanna Piggot of XL-Capris at Sydney's Trade Union Club and Todd said, 'Going up?'. I shot back at him, 'No, but you're going down.' Not particularly pleasant, but that's how I was. Our rivals treated us the same way. One night a very famous singer let me know what he thought of me by unzipping his fly and exposing himself to me right in the middle of a crowded bar. I laughed. There wasn't much else I could have done.

Our band fought and squabbled, but we looked out for one another. When you live in each other's pockets and tour together you become insular and protective of each other. Vince was a marvel at shielding us from outsiders. He was scathingly rude to anyone he thought was trying to take advantage of us and he tried to cocoon us from the hassles that come with touring, recording, performing and dealing with the industry.

Denise Fraser

Vince was relentless in getting the best deal for Divinyls. He was shameless and would ask for anything at all, and if he was refused, there'd be hell to pay. Vince was a rock'n'roll cowboy, and his business methods were unorthodox. He was full-on about protecting Chrissy and the band from people who wanted to rip them off and distract them from their core job—performing, writing, touring and recording. Even in the early days there was a lot of strange people hanging around that band.

Rick Grossman

Much of the tension in the band in my day was because Harve and I felt that Chrissy, Mark and Vince were the inner circle and we and Bjarne were on the outer. Vince called meetings and Harve, Bjarne and I were asked to speak our piece, but our band was not a democracy—show me a successful band that is!—and the big decisions were made by the others.

My anger was exacerbated by the paranoia that comes with drug addiction. It festered into resentment. I confronted Chrissy, Mark and Vince and they seemed genuinely shocked that I was unhappy. They assured me I was an integral part of Divinyls and offered me more money.

All in all, we were a pretty tight gang for a while, until things fell apart. It sounds corny to say, but we really felt we had a job to do. Music was changing and it was exciting. It was out of control. There was a lot of chaos in both the management and the band. Everyone was so passionate, and when people get passionate they can be irrational. Vince is an *incredibly* passionate guy. Nowadays I think he'd probably agree that he could've done a few things better. He was not a good businessman and he had a hair-trigger temper. Some of the decisions he made with his heart, not his brain, because he was one of us, not our hard-headed manager. I have no idea what happened to some of the money we made, though I know it cost a lot to do some of the things we did. I've seen Vince return from a meeting with record company executives with his shirt ripped and covered in blood, not his own.

Vince was infectious. He was so enthusiastic and he just loved music and the spirit of rock'n'roll. The edge. He wanted us to be way over the top. He would stand on the side of the stage while we were playing and be so into it. He would have killed to be out there on stage with us. Vince has been lead singer with his band the Valentines and grew up with Australian first-generation rock legends Johnny O'Keefe, Billy Thorpe, the Easybeats and Normie Rowe, and then second-generation rockers like Cold Chisel, Angels and AC/DC. He is an Australian rock'n'roll pioneer.

In the first days after I joined the band, I was convinced Chrissy and Vince were romantically involved because they were so close, and reacted in such a volatile way to each other. Mark and Chrissy? Never! You'd never have guessed it was them who were the lovers.

Vince was Chrissy's mentor. He guided her and helped her become the performer she was. He was also her psychiatrist—Mark's, too. I can't think of anyone else who would have been able to put up with the challenges they set him.

Vince Lovegrove was as much a Divinyl as any of us who sang and played. From the moment our musical souls entwined, Mark and I had a vision for the band that included being famous and respected and selling lots of records in Australia and, with luck, overseas. But it took Vince's devotion to Divinyls, hard-arsed rock savvy and audacious opportunism to turn our vision into something that approached reality.

ASSAULT ON AMERICA

Vince Lovegrove

In April 1982, after we had acrimoniously cut ties with WEA I sent tapes of Divinyls' songs, photographs and the 'Boys In Town' video clip that captured Chrissy's early, pre-feral stage act so well, to major US record companies. Then I sat back, waiting to be crushed in the ensuing frantic rush to sign us. Surely the Americans would realise what I took for granted, that Divinyls were unique and potentially the best band on the planet.

Not one responded.

Meanwhile, in the vacuum, I was assuring Australian labels there was great competition overseas to grab us and if they wanted to sign us in Australia they'd need to offer an up-front sum north of US$200 000. To a man—for this being the music business in the early eighties, all the executives were men—they laughed me out of their offices. 'If you think you can get that for an unknown quantity like Divinyls, go ahead, but you won't get it from us.'

They thought I'd drastically drop my price, but I held firm. They hadn't reckoned on my faith in the band.

Then a nibble. One morning I took a call from a guy named Roger Watson, an A&R guy at Chrysalis Records, an independent English outfit with New York and Hollywood offices that had been originally set up by the managers of Jethro Tull.

Roger Watson

At Chrysalis we had been having substantial success with Aussie-born producer Mike Chapman, who'd produced for Pat Benatar and Blondie. Mike had come across Divinyls on a recent trip to Australia to see his mum and gave me a record of theirs on his return to Los Angeles. I have a feeling it was *Monkey Grip*.

There was a name on the cover—Vince Lovegrove—and I asked Mike about him. He gave me his telephone number. After tracking Vince down we had a natter and I got the okay from my boss, Terry Ellis, to fly down to Sydney to take a look at Divinyls. We had an affiliation with Australia's Regular Records (we signed Icehouse for the world, excluding Australia) down there and the blokes who ran it, Ray Hearn and Martin Fabinyi, came to meet me—they were diamond geezers who knew Vince well. They introduced us and we became firm friends, and still are twenty-five years later.

Vince Lovegrove

Eliza Brownjohn, a Chrysalis press officer, was coincidentally holidaying in Sydney and came to check out the band. That suited us, because, good as their records were, they never captured the excitement of live Divinyls gigs. Eliza squeezed into Bondi's Astra Hotel with a few hundred sweating, boozy fans and what she saw deeply impressed her. She reported back to Roger.

On Chrysalis's books were Blondie, Billy Idol, Pat Benatar and, of course, Jethro Tull and we thought the label would be a good fit for the band. Chrysalis were rebels then. They were known for nurturing their artists, being patient, and not expecting instant million-selling albums, and they didn't try to dictate a band's musical style or image. They weren't, at that stage, corporate.

After talking to Eliza, Roger flew straight to Melbourne to see the band play at a dingy little pub in Toorak Road, South Yarra. He, too, was impressed. I took Roger to his first Australian Rules match, at the MCG, and bought him his first Aussie pie and a can of cold beer. As we walked out of the stadium the newspaper posters were screaming about British Prime Minister Maggie Thatcher's assault on the Falkland Islands. Roger tells me that ever since that day, Divinyls and the Falklands War have been inextricably linked in his mind.

It was Roger who really went into bat for us with Chrysalis, but the guy who publicly took the credit was Jeff Aldrich. When Chrysalis confirmed their interest I borrowed some money and flew to New York for a week to appoint a lawyer to handle the band's affairs, and meet with Aldrich and other Chrysalis executives. My mission was to have them sign Divinyls to a long-term record contract, book a top New York studio where the band would record their first full album, and lock up Chrissy and Mark's publishing deal for royalties on the songs they wrote.

To handle the legal formalities, my friend Jeremy Fabinyi, who managed Mental As Anything, recommended Owen Epstein, a New York lawyer who had done work for Mentals, and had represented Billy Idol and Pat Benatar in their dealings with Chrysalis. Owen was also U2's lawyer (a few years later they dedicated their first Grammy to him after he died of a brain haemorrhage).

When I arrived at Epstein's building on ritzy Park Avenue, it was 6 p.m. on a Friday. Owen had long, wavy, dark hair and wore jeans, which was at odds with his office's heavy and expensive furnishings. He invited me to sit down. I'd never met Owen, just spoken to him a couple of times on the phone, but that didn't stop him offering this very green rock band manager from Australia cocaine. He opened his desk drawer and pulled out a gram, which he split into two lines. 'Coke?' he wanted to know. I'd done a little cocaine but it wasn't rampant in Australia at that time, so I said, as nonchalantly as I could, 'Yeah, of course.' He asked me to have first snort, but I was afraid he was setting a trap, testing me to see if I'd dive in so he could then say, 'Sorry buddy, you've blown it. We don't deal with druggies.' So I said, 'No, you go first.' Owen went, 'Oh, okay,' and snorted an entire line. I hoovered up the remaining trail of white powder and for the next hour we snorted more coke together. We were humming. We must've sucked down, between us, three grams.

As we bonded, Owen played the *Monkey Grip* EP. 'Hmmm, not bad,' he said. 'The band has a lot of potential.' Then he quickly changed the subject. 'I'm going over to see Johnny Rotten and Public Image at the Roseland Ballroom later. Want to come?'

'Sure,' I said, 'but what about the record deal?'

'Oh, don't worry about that, Vinny, we're in. Chrysalis love the band.'

'How do you know?'

'As soon as Jeff Aldrich heard I was looking after the legals in America he got on my case. He wanted to sign them straight away. You'll get a good deal.'

'What do you mean, "a good deal"?'

'Vinny, don't sweat it. Come and see the show, we'll have something to eat, and meet here at ten in the morning to iron out the details.' I was well and truly shit-faced by that point, but I heard every word Owen said.

Speed, pot, LSD and booze went hand-in-hand with rock'n'roll at the time in Australia but, like cars run on petrol, the American record business was fuelled by cocaine. The PR people, the marketing people, the A&R people, most everyone we met at radio stations, the entrepreneurs, the promoters, the people in the record stores and radio stations. Everyone snorted coke, lots of it. And, as a guest in America, I didn't want to disappoint anyone! I was offered a line when I met Owen the next morning, when I had a meeting with Chrysalis's agent, and again when I faced some of the label's heavies. As far as I knew, the only person at Chrysalis Records who wasn't obviously into cocaine was the accountant.

Timing was on my side. Australians were in vogue in New York then and, after us, the Mentals, INXS, Men At Work, Midnight Oil and Rose Tattoo would ride the wave. New Yorkers were mad about Australian accents. In hotels, stores and restaurants—business meetings, too— they'd say, 'Love your accent, mate.' I don't have a broad Australian accent, but I acquired one fast.

The Frank Sinatra song 'New York, New York' tells us, 'If you can make it there, you'll make it anywhere' and that ain't no lie. New York is a tough, fast and aggressive town and no place for the weak or lazy. Fortunately, like most Australians, I had a strong work ethic. (Blind obsession will do that to you.) I went into every negotiation with the mindset, 'Everything depends on me. I'm in New York. I have to work hard. I have to work fast. I have to be aggressive . . . because these blokes I'm doing business with are Rottweilers.' One thing about New Yorkers, though, is that there is usually no malice in their aggression. It's just their way.

Helping our cause, of course, in these hard-arse negotiations with some of the slickest businessmen I'd ever encountered, was my total faith in Divinyls. My mantra continued, 'Well, fellas, this band is going to be the biggest band in the world—you can join us or not join us but you'll be making a huge mistake if you don't.' I was passionate about the people in the band, especially Chrissy, in spite of all our battles.

While I was wheeling and dealing and doing my best to talk like Paul Hogan, Chrissy, Mark and the band were waiting anxiously on the other side of the world for some news.

As soon as I returned to Sydney, exhausted and my brain turned to mush after that hectic, decadent week, I called the band together and told them of our coup. We had a deal with Chrysalis initially worth US$240,000 and a further US$100,000 to fund our tour of North America and Canada. The money would pay for us to come to New York and record our first album at the state-of-the-art Power Station recording studio on 53rd Street between 9th and 10th avenues where David Bowie, Bruce Springsteen and his E Street Band and the Rolling Stones had recorded. Our mixer would be the legendary Bob Clearmountain, who'd mixed albums for Springsteen, the Stones, the Who and the Pretenders. Chrysalis would distribute and promote the record in America and elsewhere in the world, including Australia. The advance would also bankroll a number of Divinyls gigs in the Big Apple and a full-on tour throughout the United States. If we justified their faith in us, Chrysalis would extend the deal to include more albums and tours.

The only thing not signed and sealed was the publishing deal. Chrissy and Mark demanded to know every aspect of it because, once burned, they were allergic to signing anything. Later they would form their own publishing company.

The band was over the moon. We were the first Australian act ever to sign directly to an American record label on their first deal, and a deal—the money, the Power Station, Bob Clearmountain, the gigs, the national tour, the record promotion and international distribution—that to my knowledge no other Australian band had ever been able to swing. That day, as we celebrated hard, our dreams seemed close enough to reach out and touch.

We made plans to move lock, stock and barrel to Manhattan for a minimum of three months. Chrissy was adamant that she wanted to live in Hell's Kitchen, then a notorious gangland area on the west side. Very Chrissy.

In July 1982, just before we set off for America, we had a six-week tour of Australia, including three gigs supporting the Angels. Word had spread that we had landed a major American contract, and the crowds that flocked to see us were getting bigger and bigger.

We landed amid the palm trees and freeways of Los Angeles on a balmy autumn day, and changed planes for the flight to New York. On that flight we met two very wild dancers who called themselves Suzi Sidewinder and Lori Eastside. They'd been filming a movie called *Get Crazy* starring Malcolm McDowell and Lou Reed and were going home.

Suzi, who didn't realise we'd all just arrived in LA from Down Under, poked fun at me because I kept drifting off to sleep. I wanted to have a go back at her but was just too tired to bother. She horsed around pretending to be pregnant with a pillow stuffed up her jumper, then she and Vince had a noisy disagreement over a seat. Vince always had a thing for wild girls, and they had just as much of a thing for him. Had Suzi not got in our faces on that plane, if she'd not taken issue with Vince over the seat, if she'd caught another flight altogether, the Divinyls saga would have been very different and, in hindsight, a whole lot happier.

Vince was a very attractive man and women loved him. He had an affair with a woman from Chrysalis and another from the publishing company we'd signed with. Lucky for us.

In Manhattan we rented two apartments on the corner of 57th Street and 10th Avenue, in Hell's Kitchen, a quick walk to the Power Station. Hell's Kitchen is the area immortalised in all those black and white Warner Bros crime melodramas of the 1930s starring James Cagney and Humphrey Bogart. The Irish mob had been active there since the early years of the century and was still a force.

Mark, Vince and I were in one flat; Rick, Bjarne and Harve in the other. Mark and I, still clandestine lovers, had separate bedrooms. Soon we were joined in New York by Mark Opitz, who had produced our *Monkey Grip* EP—I wanted him to produce our new record, to be called *Desperate*, which would include reworkings of some of the *Monkey Grip* songs.

At some time in those first weeks, Mark and I announced to the others that we were a couple. The news did not go down well. Some of the guys felt betrayed. Harve, especially, who'd known Mark longer than any of us, took it hard. He was furious at being left out of the loop. Harve had always carried on a little ritual. After a gig he'd come and get my sweat-drenched school uniform, fold it up carefully and take it to have it washed. After Mark and I came clean, he never did that again.

Richard Harvey

Yes, I was angry and felt let down when I learned that Chrissy and Mark were lovers. Suddenly it was the two of them and the three of us. It was the first crack in the band. A relationship within a relationship doesn't work. I don't blame Chrissy. It wasn't always fun on the road with twenty-seven guys. You take comfort where you find it.

Harve's woes continued at the Power Station. His drumming was an extension of himself. When he was happy he would pound away exuberantly. Now, feeling let down by us, missing his girlfriend back home and overwhelmed at playing in a fabled studio where so many of his drum heroes had been before him and where we bumped into Diana Ross and Bruce Springsteen at the water cooler, he cracked up and simply couldn't function.

His funk didn't last. He took a deep breath, forgave us, got his drumming groove back and again became the life of our party.

My old actress mates Tracy Mann and Lisa Peers arrived. Tracy was keen on Harve, but I don't know if they got together. It was strange having Sydney faces dropping in. I heard Rose Tattoo were staying at the Holiday Inn just along 57th Street. I saw their singer, Angry Anderson, at the Ritz rock venue and said, 'Hi, Angry!'

'Fuck off!' he replied.

Then, unannounced, Mark's wife, Linda, accompanied by his loving and protective mother, Irene, neither of whom knew about our affair, hit town. My reaction to the news? 'Ohhh shit!'

Inevitably, in that hothouse atmosphere, Linda was always going to find out about us, and there was a terrible scene. Linda was angry and hurt. Mark wept uncontrollably. He was a sorry heap of guilt. We were in the Pink Tea Cup, a soul food restaurant when Mark and Linda's favourite Human League song came on the jukebox and he sobbed at the table.

Mark was such a sensitive soul. He was in love with me, but he hated letting Linda go, and couldn't bear that he had hurt her.

That sweet sensitivity was as instrumental in winning my heart as his musical talents. Not to be unkind, but he was a 'girlie' kind of guy. He was so very small and thin, highly strung, and when he got upset his elbows would break out in eczema. He wasn't comfortable in the company of blokey blokes and wouldn't know a football from a frisbee. I liked that. And I liked that he had a savant's knowledge of aviation. He was into World War I planes and experimental aircraft and he could look up into the sky and tell you precisely what kind of plane was flying overhead. To give the impression he was less vulnerable than he was, he adopted a prickly façade, a bit like a porcupine scaring off predators.

Mark loved me, loved me enough to break up with Linda, yet our relationship was turbulent. Keeping our relationship a secret started us off on the wrong foot, made our love kind of shady, and Mark was always uncomfortable showing me affection when others were around. I grew to be the same way with him. I don't know why we kept each other at arm's length. Perhaps, as much as we felt for one another, music always came first for each of us. We were trapped from then on.

By the time we got to New York we were arguing regularly. When straight we confined ourselves to contradicting each other and bickering, and when we were under the influence of alcohol or drugs we had screaming matches that sometimes degenerated into physical fights. Usually not hard punching or kicking or anything that would do either of us any lasting damage, just slapping and pinching and rumbling. The kind of physical squabbles I used to have with Dad.

Candy Raymond

Mark was a great guitarist, but as far as I was concerned he had very little else going for him. He had an arrogance and an aggro skinhead attitude. I thought it was pure affectation, and I thought his hairdo was stupid, too. He fed the manic side of Chrissy. He kept her insecure. Mark was persuading her that anger and being nasty equalled authenticity. He convinced her that you had to be angry onstage and off. Soon she came to repress the sweetness in her nature. When she was mean, she explained, 'I'm only being authentic!' But it wasn't her anger. It was Mark's. He was the battery and she was the toy.

Mark was dreadfully insecure about us. He never said as much, of course, but he lacked self-confidence and in his heart believed he wasn't good enough for his out-there lover. He dreaded that I'd leave him for somebody new. I'd tell him over and over that he was the one and he'd calm down, yet he never stayed assured for long. Perhaps our inability to get along was the result of Mark masochistically wanting his worst nightmare—us breaking up—to come true and working to make his fear a fact. I am a flirt, and when I showed even the slightest interest in other guys he went into a steep decline, lashing out at me and accusing me of being unfaithful, which I never ever was.

Typical of Mark's behaviour was when we were out and about in St Kilda, Melbourne, with Sean Kelly from the Models. Mark got it into his head that I was keen on Sean, which, nice guy as he was, I definitely wasn't. Mark had somehow hurt his foot and I have this image of him hobbling along behind Sean and me, making caustic jokes about us while trying to keep up to hear what we were talking about in case we were conspiring against him.

The free spirit of Torquay, Spain and the Melbourne rock scene was now channelling all her energy into Divinyls and Mark. And in the end, irony of ironies, it was Mark who strayed.

I also think Mark had mixed emotions about me. The singer of any band always is the focus, and he resented the attention I got. He felt that because he was a major creative force, people should pay him a little more respect. I could understand that, but it was unfair of him to blame me for others' perceptions, and I would overcompensate.

Despite our volatile relationship, Mark and I were both aware of how far we had come—and what we had to do. New York was our kind of town. It was a buzz when Divinyls were featured on the front page of the arts section of the *New York Post* as being in the vanguard of the wave of Australian bands currently touring and releasing records in America.

In New York whispers began that I was into black magic. Another false rap, I'm afraid. What happened was I went to a fortune-teller in the East Village and she told me that somewhere a black candle was burning for me and that would bring me bad luck. I should light a white candle to ward off the evil. I believed her. That night when we recorded at the Power Station I sang encircled by flickering white candles. I'm superstitious and think now that the black candle the fortune-teller warned me about was a portent of disasters to come.

I believe in doing whatever it takes in the studio to get you in the right mood. If I was feeling great that would transmit to the finished album. It's no good a great live band known for their onstage energy coming into the studio and sitting on a chair and playing. To recapture the dynamism they're known for onstage they have to leap around in the studio, too. I would wear my school uniform while recording to re-enact my live performance. I've heard of people singing naked.

The quarter-of-a-million-American-dollars advance from Chrysalis was a fortune to us, yet it was never going to go far. As long as we were a Chrysalis act, we always seemed to be $60 000 in the red. The bills escalated from the moment we left Australia. From our advance we had to pay for airfares, accommodation, living expenses, lawyers, accountants, transport and road crew when we went on tour, setting up our shelf company, Setona Pty Ltd, through which we ran the business side of Divinyls and paid income tax. We had to pay for six weeks' use of the Power Station, the most expensive studio in New York, for Bob Clearmountain, the engineer and the second engineer, and our producer, Mark Opitz, and Vince's costs. The recording costs were ruinously pricey. Nowadays you can record digitally, but then it was tape. We had to buy boxes and boxes and boxes of expensive reel-to-reel tape.

Vince Lovegrove

The instrumental tracks were cut quickly. Not so Chrissy's vocals. She wanted the vocals to sound intimate so she refused to allow any of the band in when she was recording. She sang, with just Mark Opitz and all her candles, for hours, sometimes all night, and the guys would have to hang around in the foyer drinking coffee or playing games, bored shitless. Mark McEntee was adamant that Chrysalis people be kept away. 'Why should they come in? It's our record. They can hear it afterwards.'

As it happened, Mark Opitz had to fly home to Sydney on family business part-way through the project so Bob Clearmountain took over, recording us and then mixing. Bob had a trademark sound, which complemented perfectly some of the greatest bands in history. Yet we didn't think Bob's mix was right for us. 'Your mix is too wide. There's too much air in it. It sounds too slick and American,' Mark told Bob. 'We want it to sound Australian, smaller, like a garage band.' Said Bob, a total professional who has every right to be arrogant but isn't, 'I thank you for being so honest.' To this day, Bob tells that story and how he went back and remixed and gave us exactly what we requested.

Desperate remains my favourite Divinyls album. It's raw with a gutsy energy and comes closer than any of our other studio records to capturing the dynamism of Divinyls live. The four songs from *Monkey Grip* that we re-recorded were infinitely better the second time around. Put that down to the superior recording set-up, and also, we were a much better band than before, no small thanks to Rick who had came onboard after *Monkey Grip*. Even today 'Boys In Town', 'Elsie', 'Gonna Get You', 'Siren', 'Only Lonely', 'I'll Make You Happy', 'Casual Encounter' and 'Science Fiction' leap out of the speakers and hit you right between the eyes.

The album hit American and Australian record stores in March 1983. It reached No. 3 on the Australian album charts and spawned a series of singles.

Of *Desperate*, Jon Pareles wrote in *The New York Times* that our music fitted in somewhere between old-fashioned hard rock and stripped-down new wave 'and Christina Amphlett's lyrics are as hard-headed as anything in pop'. Pareles added that my singing was 'so peculiar it's irresistible. Her voice is hoarse and pugnacious, and every so often it erupts with quavers and hesitations and hiccups and yodels...' He said Divinyls hadn't bothered 'with the hip trappings of Men At Work or INXS... they're just making the strongest music they can. That it happens to sound thoroughly Australian—from the accents to the scrappy attitude—is less important than that it sounds something of their own.'

Wrote Christopher Connolly in US *Rolling Stone*, 'And you thought only whimsical, bland bands had joined the Australian invasion. Meet—if you dare—Christina Amphlett [whose] banzai vocals fuse the growly conviction of Joan Jett with the frenetic ululations of Lene Lovich for a vocal package that suggests a Sydney-spawned Patti Smith. The twin guitar attack of Mark McEntee and Bjarne Ohlin sizzles with an impressive urgency... The garage-band power of *Desperate* sounds to these ears like 1983's best antidote to technopop burnout.' Of course I was grateful for the glowing tributes, but I was pissed off when the American journalists kept comparing me to other performers... All fine artists but all unlike me.

RAM magazine's Phil Stafford thought that 'Make You Happy' kick-started the album 'with an amphetamine rush'. He then remarked on my 'formidable larynx. When she's not wrapping it around the lyrics, Amphlett's adding instrumental flourishes of her own, trilling, whooping and yodelling in counterpoint with the fused guitars of Mark McEntee and Bjarne Ohlin. Beneath it all, Richard Harvey and Rick Grossman graft with workmanlike precision.'

The reviews in America and back home raved about our sound. By letting us record *Desperate* at the Power Station, Chrysalis sent a message to us and the music industry at large that they were serious about Divinyls. Even so, when their heavies dropped by to watch us record we gave them the cold shoulder. Business and creativity don't mix.

The Chrysalis promotions people organised a feature on us to appear in New York pop culture icon Andy Warhol's *Interview* magazine. I turned up at the *Interview* office for the photo shoot still trashed after a heavy night. We'd partied with another heavy-drinking rocker, Robert Palmer, at the Mayflower Hotel on Central Park West. I was so exhausted and hungover I couldn't stand up so I sat on a schoolcase in my school uniform, mascara running all over my cheeks, hair in braids, as the photographer had his way. That photo was real and it was perfect. It captured our wonderful New York ride beautifully. I saw Andy with his white wig and distinctive spectacles sitting in his office behind a big glass partition, watching us. His stuffed Great Dane was standing in the corner.

We were kids in a lolly shop, chomping hard on the delights and horrors of New York City. Heroin shooting galleries were everywhere, sex and drugs were readily available and AIDS was just beginning to embark on its killing spree that took the lives of so many of New York's best musicians, actors, writers, dancers and artists.

We clubbed till the sun rose over the city's soaring towers. We saw bands... New York Dolls, the Clash and the Who, who were Rick's favourite band, at Yankee Stadium. Rick missed the show. He got so excited at the prospect of seeing Roger Daltrey, Pete Townshend and Co that he seized up and refused to go. Iggy Pop had a profound effect on me. His crazed intensity disturbed me so much that I couldn't sleep for three days. We did the drugs, made lots of love to our partners, permanent and fleeting, and were as wild as we felt we had to be.

I tried cocaine because, me being me, I was up for any thrill on offer—that was the rock'n'roll way—and everywhere I went it was thrust at me. Everyone I met seemed to have a dusting of white powder around their nose. Vince had told me how the record executives snorted it at meetings as easily as drinking a cup of coffee. I was incredulous. He was right. Alcohol, though, remained my primary social lubricant. Not so some of the others.

Harve and Rick were helping themselves to the huge quantity of drugs on offer. Rick came to breakfast one day with his eye hugely swollen, the result of snorting something that had lodged somewhere it shouldn't have and getting infected.

Vince Lovegrove

Rick and Harve were always spending our advance money. I had been watching them carefully. They'd sometimes disappear for a day or two, and I suspected they were spending the money on coke. I didn't think for a moment they were into smack.

Chris Bastic

I'd been Divinyls' road manager just before they left for the States, and they asked me to join them. My job was to help look after the instruments and source equipment for the gigs and the recording sessions. I was beside myself with excitement to be in New York. Once I knocked on Rick Grossman's door and went in. Rick and Richard Harvey were hunched over together in the semi-darkness. 'Rick, let's go!' I yelled. 'We'll explore the city!' Neither said anything. Then through the gloom I saw a little pile of ashes in front of them and I realised they were doing smack.

Rick Grossman

At the Power Station one evening I asked an engineer if he knew where we could get hold of some pot. He gave me a business card that read 'Weed Deliver', with a phone number. The engineer said, 'Ring them and ask what's on the menu tonight.'

So I rang and they reeled off all these different types of pot and I said, 'Well, I'll have that . . . I'm at the Power Station.'

Twenty minutes later a guy rode up on a pushbike with a box of pot, all colour-coded. 'There you go,' he grinned.

This was heaven for Harve and me, and we walked around in a happy haze the whole time we were in New York.

In a bar Harve and I met Rick Danko of The Band, the guitarist Paul Butterfield, and Blondie Chaplin, who played with the Beach Boys and did sessions with the Rolling Stones. We invited Danko and Butterfield to our room to lay some lines of coke. Up there, I proudly showed Danko my bass. He said, 'Fuck this shit!' and threw it across the room and into the wall. I almost cried, but the guitar was okay. It was made of graphite and so tough you could play cricket with it. Danko was off his face. Later I saw him crawling around on his hands and knees in the bar searching for a cheque he'd dropped.

There was a very hip diner we frequented near the Gramercy Park Hotel. I remember Mark coming back from breakfast and saying, 'You won't believe what's just happened. I was sitting on a stool at the counter and there was a guy either side. One got up and left. The other bloke says to me, 'Did you see who he was?' I didn't. He said, 'That was Bob Dylan.'

One night Harve was drunk and homesick and missing his girlfriend in Australia. He was getting stuck into everyone. Next morning Chrissy confronted him. She said, 'Harve, your behaviour was out of line.' He apologised. Mark was watching.

Next day, Harve was drunk again and abused us. Mark got in his face. 'Richard, I think we deserve an apology.' Harve said, 'You can get stuffed!' Mark kind of curled up and said, 'Awww . . . Don't be like that.'

Richard Harvey

Rick and I found a friendly little bar and we were sitting there when a black pimp rolled in. He was beautifully dressed and had a beautiful woman on his arm. We must have looked likely customers because he walked straight up to us, said, 'Do you do blow?' and put a bag of coke on the bar. It was like *Scarface*! These guys were gangsters. One guy tried to set me up to be a drug contact in Australia.

Chris Bastic got mugged outside Macys department store on Broadway. It was a rehearsed robbery. A guy asked Chris for money and when he pulled his wallet out to give him a buck his mate hit Chris on the back of the neck and all the money fell onto the ground. They picked it up and ran off. For three days till Vince got us some more cash we had to eat donuts. I could have hugged our roadie Errol, who turned up at our hotel and—whooshka!—he whacked a bag of cocaine on the table.

New York was sensory overload. Rick and I went to see Men At Work, who were playing at the Ritz on the Lower East Side, and we were sitting in a pizza parlour when we noticed a man and a woman sitting together on stools at a little counter eating their pizzas. The man was obviously stoned. Before our eyes, he pitched backwards off his stool and cracked his head hard on the floor. Some marines who'd come in started laughing. The proprietor walked over, took a look at the guy, who was bleeding from the head, and rang the police. 'We've got a dead one here . . .'

Vince and Suzi Sidewinder were now lovers, and she and her friend Lori Eastside had become members of our bunch. Lori was holding classes in very physical, rough-and-tumble dancing. I went along to perfect cartwheels, which had become a part of my act.

I'd never met a girl like Suzi. I was a little in awe of her, a little frightened. She told me hair-raising stories about how she had shot a man with a rifle, and was always being chased by men with guns. She said she had been a friend of the doomed, drug-addled comedian John Belushi. She was an experimenter and an adventurer. She wasn't conventionally beautiful, but had striking features and a beguiling personality. She often hung with the New York chapter of the Hell's Angels motorcycle gang. Wherever Suzi was, that's where you'd find the party.

Suzi and Vince complemented each other. Did she make him happy? I don't know that you could have described Vince as happy. He could be funny, but I don't think I ever saw him truly *happy*. Tormented, idealistic, driven, passionate, dedicated to Divinyls? Definitely. He worked very hard and was never one to sit around and relax. The American record company guys *loved* him because he was as abrasive as them, and wouldn't stand for their bullshit. They used to call him 'Vinny'.

He and Suzi moved into a little flat in Christopher Street, Greenwich Village. If he thought he would be buying a little privacy he was mistaken, but, again, our boundaries had never been defined. I called him often. I *needed* him a lot. I needed and demanded his professional and emotional support. He was our manager and I had no one else, and I believe he would not have wanted it any other way. To be honest, I resented the time he was spending with Suzi and thought he should have been devoting himself to the band. It wasn't jealousy. There was never a question of romance between us. If Vince and I had slept together it would have been like incest.

After we wrapped *Desperate* we played some prize gigs in Manhattan—at three fabled rock hangouts: the Peppermint Lounge, the Ritz and CBGBs. The crowd at these high-cred but down-at-heel joints were rough, druggy, intimidating and cruelly intolerant of acts they figured weren't cutting it. We were terrified before we went onstage, but our fears weren't warranted. They seemed to appreciate Divinyls, though they didn't know our music. And they were pussycats compared with the patrons at, say, the Comb and Cutter in Sydney's wild west on a steamy Saturday night. I like to think that in the end we intimidated *them*.

I especially remember the Ritz. In front of 2000 people, including prominent record execs and a sprinkling of rock stars, we launched ourselves onto the tiny stage and played fast and furious. I gave those jaded New Yorkers the full schoolgirl treatment. I charged around like a dervish and gripped the microphone so hard I finished the gig with blistered hands. I wasn't loose as a goose, but I sure was aggro.

After our Manhattan shows we briefly returned to Australia to hone our live performance chops on a hectic national tour before returning to America to begin the tour there in early April. While we were in Queensland the cops busted Harve for urinating in an alley, and Vince told a reporter my underwear had been nicked from my hotel room. I have no recall of the latter incident. It may have happened, but it also sounds like the kind of story Vince was busy inventing then to help create our edgy buzz.

En route to the United States, we opened for Dire Straits in Auckland. I can't recall much about that gig except for Mark Knopfler's sublime guitar playing and how the Dire Straits guys crowded around in the wings watching us, which was quite a tribute from a headline act to its support. Knopfler approached Rick afterwards and said, 'Great band, great gig.' Oh, and some Kiwi knucklehead hurling the biggest rubber thong I'd ever seen at us. It caught on the neck of Mark's guitar and hung there. That thong must have been size sixteen.

We landed in LA and checked into the Tropicana Hotel before the next day's flight to New York where the tour would begin. While we were doing lines of cocaine in Vince's room with people from Chrysalis and the publishing company, someone broke into our rooms, slashed open our bags and stole everything of value.

We were devastated but didn't have time to mope, or even help the police catch the thieves, because we were due to link up in Manhattan with another Chrysalis act, Britain's post-punk rockers the Psychedelic Furs, with whom we'd share the bill on the first leg of our tour. We gigged with the Furs at Carbondale, Illinois; then in St Louis; Oxford in Mississippi; New Orleans; Baton Rouge; Memphis; Nashville; Hartford; Philadelphia; Buffalo; back to New York; Boston; and across the Canadian border to Montreal, Toronto and Ottawa.

We worked constantly. As well as performing at night, we had endless meet-and-greets with radio stations, the press and record shops in every town. It was relentless.

Vince Lovegrove

It was a helter-skelter tour. We had no chance to see the sights. It was play, travel, play, travel, play, travel... The itinerary was meticulously planned to take in both coasts and large swathes of the Midwest. You will not crack America and make the national charts unless the radio stations in all those little towns are playing your record simultaneously with the stations on the coasts. You can be huge in New York, you can be huge in Los Angeles. That's relatively easy because if you're new and you're hip and you've got something different you'll most likely get a good reception. But most people who live in the Midwest, for example, are conservative and have never been out of their home state. They're suspicious and need to be convinced to fork out their money on a record by a band they consider 'alternative'.

On the tour I befriended Ann Sheldon, a tall and lovely young English woman who played cello with the Psychedelic Furs. We were the only girls, so it was natural that we hung out. Later, I learned that not too long after that, while in Woodstock, she was trying to steer her car while searching for the address of a party on her Filofax which was propped on her lap. Distracted, she collided with a tree with such impact that the force cut her in half.

After we parted company with the Psychedelic Furs, with whom we got on pretty well, all things considered, we played solo gigs in San Diego and at the humungous open-air three-day US Festival.

There were more than 200 000 people to see us on the day we played, 28 May 1983, at this gig which was held in the desert outside Los Angeles. Also on the bill were David Bowie, the Clash, U2, the Pretenders, Mötley Crüe, Ozzy Osbourne, Van Halen, Men At Work, INXS, the Cult, Flock of Seagulls, Stevie Nicks, Berlin and Stray Cats. Some line-up. More than 670 000 attended over the three blistering hot days of the festival, which ranks it in the five largest concerts in history.

With plenty at stake, and trying to make an impression at the biggest gig we would ever play, we decided to go all out and give the performance of a lifetime. The audience didn't know what hit them when we did 'Elsie', which I had written about an elderly down-and-out woman I'd met in my block of flats in Darlinghurst. It was probably our best ever performance of that harrowing song. Picture us, on stage in front of a giant rainbow backdrop: Mark, Rick, Bjarne and Harve playing like men possessed, me with lipstick smeared all over my face and arms, hair blown wild by a whipping wind, squatting and emitting gut-tearing primal screams as I brought that sad old woman's tale to a close. During the performance I did my old trick of leaping on Mark's back while he was playing, and for once he didn't seem to mind. We had proved we could cut it at the highest level, and there cheering us on in the front row was a group of fans I recognised from our Sydney shows—they'd taken the trouble to go all the way to America for us.

In Los Angeles we stayed at the Sunset Marquis Hotel, and Men At Work were there too. Their album *Business As Usual* was breaking big-time in the States and the spin-off singles 'Down Under' and 'Who Could It Be Now?' had raced up the American charts. The contrast between the two bands couldn't have been greater. We Divinyls, Vince and Eliza Brownjohn were being our typically raucous selves, splashing and bombing all the LA types with their tans, coiffed hair and gold jewellery who were lolling around the hotel pool. Greg Ham and Colin Hay and the blokes from Men At Work were much more reserved than us. They seemed dazed and confused by their newfound fame, unable to comprehend how or why they'd become instant superstars.

After the festival we opened for U2 in Denver, San Francisco, Los Angeles, Portland and Seattle. I wish I could tell some Bono and The Edge stories, but there was little offstage interaction between us and the far more famous Irish band.

Following a desperately needed two weeks off we did a solo show in Boston then supported the Ramones at Pier 13 on the Hudson River on Manhattan's West Side. Our monitor roadie was hopeless so I threw water all over him. He got sick of getting drenched so he wore a raincoat to our gigs. On next to Pittsburgh, Cleveland, St Louis, Detroit, Chicago, Dallas, Houston, Austin, Denver, Albuquerque, Phoenix, San Diego and San Francisco. Chrysalis made us work damned hard for our money. Our US trek, the first of many we would make, ended at The Palace in Los Angeles on 10 August 1983.

Nothing improves a band like touring and playing live. On that gruelling, criss-crossing circuit we got better and tighter. We got tougher. Attendances were far better than expected for a little-known band from Australia, and the sales of *Desperate* always leapt in the towns where we played.

Michael Jackson provided the soundtrack to our first American adventure. *Thriller* had just come out and we played it endlessly on the tour bus stereo. It was such amazing music, and I'm sad about what's happened to Michael in later years. He was a *god*.

What's that classic AC/DC song—'Highway to Hell'? Our bus driver was a Vietnam vet who talked and chuckled spookily to himself and kept canaries in a cage beside the steering wheel. The bus was divided into three sections: the front, the back and the bunks in between. We had a roadie named Kim Wilson with the worst-smelling feet. Maybe it's a roadie thing, because they always wear tennis shoes. We gave him a hard time but he didn't care. Rick told me once that he was in his room with a woman and Kim walked in, took his clothes off and said to the girl, 'Well, what's it like being with *two* Australians?' Kim was a practical joker. He's a born-again Christian now.

All of us, the band and our crew, partied after every gig. If we were staying over in town the party would take place in someone's motel room. If we had to make tracks to the next town, we turned the bus into a mobile disco as we sped through the night.

Rick Grossman

Sometime during our tour Harve and I filmed an interview with the Australian TV host Donnie Sutherland. It went well and he asked if we could do more, so our fans at home could follow our progress. 'Sure,' I told him, 'but wouldn't you rather do it with Chrissy?'

'No,' said Donnie, 'I never have a clue what she's talking about.'

We played at pubs, clubs, arenas and universities. It was endless, town after town. Like chipping away at a big wall that one day we would break down. We used a lot of cocaine. We had a Jamaican monitor roadie who was a coke-head. He was the most hopeless roadie but a really lovely chap, and he got us loads of drugs.

Robbie Robertson of The Band once famously said that the road is a fucking hard life. It is, as we found out, a bewildering and relentless grind of early-morning flights, endless bus trips along featureless highways, execrable food and dingy motel rooms. It's also what you make it, and we made memories to last our whole lives. In Nashville I heard a commotion in the motel room next to mine—Rick and Harve's. Someone was pounding on their door and yelling, in a very loud, Southern accent, 'Bobby-Sue, are you in there? Are you in bed with those musicians? Come on out before I break the door down!' Bobby-Sue, however, seemed happy in the boys' company. 'Fuck yew, Daddy!' she replied.

In another town, Rick and Harve met a girl in a bar and invited her to their room. Inside, she excused herself and disappeared into the bathroom. Moments later she emerged topless, with matches somehow affixed to each nipple. 'Now watch this!' she cried and lit the matches.

Harve could always break us up, a valuable talent when you're tired and grumpy and missing home. He'd stroll into a room wearing only a towel, then he'd somehow unclench his bum muscles and the towel would drop, leaving him stark naked. It should have been gross, but somehow Harve made it funny.

Rick tells the story of him, Bjarne and Harve walking into some godforsaken Midwest diner and the bloke behind the counter saying, 'What'll you have, gals?'

I didn't see any animosity. Our bus would pull up at a new town and all the locals would come from everywhere and want to get to know us. 'Where you from?' they'd say and when we'd tell them, they couldn't be friendlier. America loves a travelling band.

Vince Lovegrove

That first tour of America established Divinyls as an international act. We didn't sell lots of records but we definitely broke through. Radio stations knew who we were, they knew our music and played it. *MTV* put the 'Boys In Town' video on frequent rotation. We acquired a cult following. Chrysalis had no qualms about giving us the go-ahead— and the funds—to make a follow-up album to *Desperate* on our return to Australia.

When the tour circus ended it was time to go home. More recording commitments and a national tour wasn't all that awaited us when we flew back into Sydney. While we were away, Rick's apartment had been robbed and ransacked. In the real world it didn't matter who the hell we were or whether we'd been on *MTV*.

11
WHAT A LIFE!

Back home in September 1983, Mark and I moved into a room in his mother Irene's home in the Sydney beachside suburb of Manly. Actually, Mark had the room. I had the verandah.

One morning I went for a walk along Fairlight Crescent and found myself overwhelmed by happiness. At that moment I may have been happier than at any time in my life. I thought my head would explode with sheer bliss. The day was warm, the sky was a clear cerulean blue, we'd cut a hit record. I was in love with Mark. The future seemed assured.

By evening my euphoria had passed, muscled away by reality and my usual feelings of dread and impending doom wrought by the huge demands and expectations that had come to hang over our heads. Chrysalis were pressuring us to make a new album and keep touring so we could repay their huge investment. *Desperate* was a hit in Australia but hadn't done as well in America, and Chrysalis wanted hits, lots of them. While I was crazy about Mark, I knew our relationship was far from normal and I worried that we would end up unhappy together like my parents.

Sometimes my angst transformed into a terrible sadness. At such moments I found myself taking solace in that if things got *really, really* bad I could always kill myself and that would be an end to it.

I was also at odds with my hellcat persona. At my core I believed I wasn't bad. I could hear Mum saying, 'You are a good person! Don't put yourself down.' The contradictions in that, and living up to the image I had embraced, was tearing me apart.

Amid the sadness and the craziness of that time, Mark and I had a sublime aquatic interlude. Looking back, our diving adventure in Guadalcanal was one of the highlights of our life together.

It was Rick who first turned me on to diving. We went up to his family's place at Airlie Beach in Queensland and scuba'd off the side of boats. On my first dive on the Great Barrier Reef I stayed down too long and my nose bled and my mask was filled with blood, but the mishap didn't prevent me from being passionate about the pastime. I was always a strong swimmer so I took to diving easily. When I came back I said, 'Mark, we've got to learn how to dive,' so he and I did courses in Manly, including a swim with a huge grey nurse shark in the Manly Aquarium. She came gliding right at me through a shaft of light and took a terrifyingly close interest in me. She *hung* with me and while I was scared I felt safer with the shark than some record company executives I'd known. Then we progressed to diving in Sydney Harbour.

We booked a trip to the best diving location in the world, Guadalcanal, the largest of the Solomon Islands, where the water is clear and the sea bed is a graveyard for World War II wrecks and downed aircraft. We stayed in a little village near Honiara, not far from where the American and Japanese troops fought to the death on the beach, and we found dog tags and shrines to the fallen in the jungle. Oh God, it was hot! I was covered in mossie bites, which got infected when my wetsuit rubbed against them.

Accompanied by a local diver, we dived on a submarine that was just sitting there like a big grey cigar on the sand 40 metres below the surface. Even at that depth, there was crystal clarity. The sunbeams pierced the water eerily, reminding me of light shining through a stained-glass window in church. We swam inside the sub, through passageways and compartments, pushing open doors and glad not to come across skeletons. Another time we swam amid giant turtles, which resented our invasion of their caves and coral fields and shunted us with their flippers. We explored a B-52 bomber plonked on the ocean bottom. Inside lurked a nest of eels that poked their snouts out of nooks and crannies as we stroked past. The bomber was in pristine condition except for a gun turret that had broken off and lay half-submerged in the sand 20 metres away. Not far from the B-52 was a sunken troopship. It had been bombed and was badly damaged.

Mark was a very responsible diver. He had come to understand how crucial it is to ascend slowly, keeping a carefully calculated record of the time you've been under and how deep you've been. Perhaps because he was more experienced, or just stupid, our local diver was not so mindful and shot to the surface without a care. Thinking he knew what was he was doing I took off after him, but Mark grabbed me and motioned for me to go slowly. He saved me from the bends, maybe worse.

Diving took me to an ethereal, dreamlike world without gravity and teeming with strange creatures. Silent except for the sound of your own breathing and the chattering of the fish . . . truly. It was very, very relaxing, and put the life I lived on dry land into perspective.

If Mark and I had dived rather than fought we might have survived.

A large toucan hung out at our hut complex. She was obsessed with my mouth and was always trying to peck my lips and regurgitate her food all over me. She tried to come through the bathroom window when I was showering and when Mark played his guitar the rainbow-hued bird tried to pick the strings.

We scuba dived again a little later in Hawaii. An American rock manager and promoter named Barry Fey (more of him later) co-

owned a house in Maui with Willie Nelson and invited Mark and me
to chill out and write there. It was a huge tropical mansion. You could
dive from the living room into the swimming pool. We went on diving
expeditions off Maui (not as good as Guadalcanal because the sea
bed was littered with beer cans chucked off boats) and explored the
island. We set off one morning in search of the grave of Mark's hero,
the aviator Charles Lindbergh, but got lost and ended up at the top
of a volcano. Our two-hour trek took us eight.

When Mark and I got away from Divinyls we could be truly
happy together. It was good for us to share an experience that was
physical and had nothing to do with music or business. Even when
I pushed Mark off the boat into a pack of reef sharks he didn't get
mad at me. Well, he did, but not for long.

I wrote a poem about diving as a metaphor for life and love . . .

Hotel rooms and one night stands
Paint peeling off walls
Singing in bands
Late night prowling
Getting around
Standing in hallways waiting to come down
I go diving, diving
Among the wrecks looking for treasure
Beneath the sea it gives me some pleasure
Lying on the ocean floor to surface . . .
Don't want to surface any more.
I go diving, diving . . .
Promises are made to be broken . . .
Now no words are spoken
I go diving, diving, diving, diving . . .

Any break from our focus on Divinyls was going to be short. No matter
what, I was still focused on the music. Our new album would be called
What A Life! and Mark, Rick, Harve, Bjarne and I rocked up to

Sydney's Rhinoceros recording studios with producer Mark Opitz on 17 October 1983. We had some new songs, and we were fired up to cut a blistering follow-up to *Desperate*, but things didn't work out that way. There might have been albums with a more troubled history than *What A Life!*, but I doubt it.

Vince and Mark Opitz snapped at one another like junkyard dogs. They had never liked each other. (Opitz had been unhappy when I appointed Vince our manager.) Vince did not believe the material we were recording was up to scratch and, to Opitz's displeasure, on 8 January he canned the sessions. Vince knew, as did I, that a band's second album is crucial to its success and believed we needed more time to improve the songs we had and to write new ones.

I was disappointed when the sessions were called off, and felt bad for Mark Opitz, but I really did agree with Vince. We were kidding ourselves. When we went into Rhinoceros we simply didn't have the material. How could we have had? We'd come straight off the road and into the studio. We had jumped the gun and were not ready to record.

During the American tour Mark and I had written these new songs, but, speaking for myself, it's hard to write well on the road. All my energy was devoted to performing, press, travelling and partying, and I had little left in me to do anything else. Amid the pandemonium at the back of a tour bus is no place to write. So now Mark and I locked ourselves away to create some better material.

That still-born shot at recording *What A Life!* had already been interrupted in mid-December when we opened for Cold Chisel's four-night 'Last Stand' gig at the Sydney Entertainment Centre. Things must have been dire between us and Mark Opitz because his wife came up and abused Mark McEntee, Vince and me.

Last Stand was a real event, and we were happy to help out Cold Chisel. The two bands went back a long time. Divinyls had cut our teeth opening for our fellow Dirty Pool act, Chisel. We were their favourite support band, and shared a love of the rock life. The Cold

Chisel fans always liked us, or at least didn't mind us too much, and their followers and ours were equally rowdy.

Not that Chisel invited us onstage with them at Last Stand. And we didn't party together after the gigs. Jimmy Barnes and I had form. At Sydney's Manzil Room he and I had been watching a band and I said, 'Oh, I like that song,' and Jim snapped, 'It's a piece of crap,' turned on his heel and stalked away. Obviously, he and I had different musical tastes.

Rick Grossman

In Sydney then there was an incredible live scene . . . Divinyls, Mental As Anything, Midnight Oil, the Angels, Cold Chisel, the Reels, Icehouse, INXS, playing all over the country seven nights a week, and always to packed houses. When we gigged in Sydney, especially, the crowds would go off. Two-thousand-people capacity venues like the Manly Vale Hotel or the Comb and Cutter pub in Blacktown, the Sylvania Hotel, the Family Inn in Rydalmere, Selinas at the Coogee Bay Hotel, the Stage Door Tavern down near Central Station and the Sydney Cove Tavern at Circular Quay. Then there was the Governor's Pleasure pub in The Rocks, and the San Miguel Inn in Cammeray. These were the beer barns.

It was an experience playing the outer suburban pubs where your feet stuck to the carpet and there was violence every night. Here, unlike some of the more laidback inner-city venues, the audiences weren't 'cool'. If they were into you, they showed it. Same time, if they hated you, you'd soon know about it. It was trial by fire out there. I remember we arrived for a gig at the Sundowner Hotel in Punchbowl and the place was jammed. We went to our dressing-room, changed, got ready, walked out on stage and the auditorium was now only half full. Where had all the people gone? There'd been a gunfight in the car park and they'd run for their lives.

I dished it out, as any number of my victims will happily testify, and I copped it too. I learned not to let my guard down for my image and the success of the band incited people to try to make themselves look big at my expense. Sometimes my own abrasiveness was a defensive mechanism to ward off others' rudeness. Renée Geyer, a singer I have always admired, has occasionally been spectacularly unpleasant to me through the years (and once at Selinas she told Mark to 'Fuck off, sucker!' Photographer Tony Mott tells me I once gave Renée identical advice, though I have no recollection.) Renée was much more unpredictable and scary than me, or so I thought.

There was another time when a posse of rock stars ganged up on me at a benefit concert for famine relief at Melbourne's Myer Music Bowl, to which I had been asked to come along and sing solo. I was happy to join James Reyne, Neil Finn, Rob Hirst from Midnight Oil and other performers, because I believed in the cause. When I showed up I was wearing my regular performing gear, the school uniform, which seemed to enrage the others. 'How dare you disrespect this concert by dressing like that?' they said in the green room backstage. There was even a move to stop me singing. James Reyne was particularly angry. No one would speak to me. The sponsor, Coca-Cola, then said they didn't want me to go on because they were terrified I'd urinate on the stage. 'Then why,' I asked the Coke flack, 'did you invite me here in the first place?' I wore the uniform when I performed. I was really ostracised by my peers that day, and it hurt. I like to think they turned on me not because of what I was wearing but because I was successful and, maybe even more importantly, I was a successful woman.

Upsetting as it was, my peers' meanness was nothing compared to that of a stalker who threatened to kill me. He went to the Dirty Pool office and threw himself on the floor, yelling that he'd shoot himself unless I was brought to him. I never came, of course, so he started threatening to shoot *me*. He sent word that he would be coming to gigs—with his gun. For some time afterwards I went onstage with the disquieting knowledge that there may be a fruitcake assassin somewhere out there in that writhing sea of heads.

Fans could be intense. The group of girls who were in the front row of the US Festival concert and who came to all Divinyls' Sydney gigs had moved into a flat downstairs from mine in Womerah Avenue just before I moved out. They never tried to talk to me, they'd just hang out in their flat with the door open so they could see me when I came and went. Then they'd stare at me intently. It was a little weird, but not the least bit threatening.

Divinyls toured extensively. To give an idea how hard we promoted *Desperate*, in February and March 1984, after the Last Stand gigs, Divinyls played at Sydney's Balmain Leagues Club, Doyalson RSL, Newcastle Workers Club, South Grafton RSL, the Bombay Rock in Brisbane, Queensland University, Coolangatta's Jet Club, Lismore Workers Club, Byron Bay Ex-Servicemen's Club, Sawtell RSL, Kempsey RSL, Taree RSL, St Marys Leagues Club, St George Sailing Club, Macquarie University, Cronulla's Endeavour Field, Maroubra Seals Club, Auburn Baseball Club, Mittagong RSL, The Venue and the Manhattan Hotel in Melbourne, the Tasmanian Rock Festival, Adelaide's Old Lion, Findon and Bridgeway hotels and the Mooloolaba Hotel in Queensland. Beer barns, clubs and in the open air, we performed everywhere. Arrive, set up the gear, sound-check, psych-up session, do the gig, post-mortem, party while the roadies dismantle our equipment and stack it in our truck, then, tired and wired, off to the next town.

Once, pulling into Mt Isa, a mining town in the middle of the Queensland desert, we learned that the generator that powered our venue had broken down. The blokes in Mt Isa told us that our performing there meant a lot to them because visits from topline acts were rare and they rolled their sleeves up to try to fix the generator so the show could go on. They slaved away for two days, and of course we interrupted our tour to stay in town until the power finally came on and then we gave those beautiful people the show of their lives as a thank you.

At one gig I was giving a roadie we called Mark II a hard time. I poked him with my fluorescent pole, and he lost his temper and hit me on the foot with a hammer. The bloody thing broke my bones.

I kept singing, in agony. Usually my brawls with roadies were fun and games, but this was personal and management fired him.

Another time, before a Chisel show at Adelaide Town Hall, I walked into a room there and saw some roadies and hangers-on had laid long lines of white powder on a table. I usually never did coke before a performance because it shredded my vocal cords. For some reason this time I made an exception and I snorted a line. It wasn't cocaine, but speed. I had never done speed. I became ill during the gig and had to lie down flat on the stage. I simply couldn't stand. After a few minutes I pulled myself to my feet and staggered through the remainder of the show. Vince was furious with me, and he had every right to be. I couldn't sleep for two days, and Vince didn't speak to me for seven. I wished he'd been as angry at some of the others where drugs were concerned.

We didn't have wardrobe girls until the nineties, mostly because we couldn't afford them. But the beauty of wearing school uniforms or gym slips was that I could go back to the hotel, rinse them, and hang them to dry in the shower stall. Simple.

I do remember one winter, when Chris Bastic was still tour managing us, I was wearing winter tunics and they had to be drycleaned. As we pulled up outside an outer suburban gig in the band's Tarago, I asked Chris where my uniform was. He was supposed to pick it up from the drycleaners earlier that day. His face gave me my answer. He turned the vehicle, hit the accelerator and sped back into town. We pulled up outside the drycleaners at way past nine o'clock. I couldn't believe it when we pushed on the door and it opened, even though no-one was there. We ran down the aisles of hanging clothes, frantically looking for the uniform, found it, jumped back into the van and sped back to the gig. It was so surreal and I don't think we were even late hitting the stage. There was no way I could perform without my uniform.

Sometimes on the road I longed for a girlfriend, someone to chatter to about clothes and girlie things and to accompany me on shopping expeditions. Occasionally women would drift in and out of our world, but I found it hard to get close to them because they were either jealous of me and were stand-offish or befriended me so they could get close to the guys. Wardrobe girls were the worst. They seemed always to be sleeping with the band or, if they couldn't snag a musician, the roadies. I fired a lot of wardrobe girls—for causing friction in the band, or worse.

One wardrobe girl had a drinking problem and I was always going onstage in wet clothes because she'd forget to dry them. She would hit the booze backstage while we were performing, and I'd return to find her passed out and my underwear and clothes strewn all over the floor. If we remembered we'd hide the alcohol until we came off so she couldn't get stuck into it. Her saving grace was that she stuck up for me when Mark and I fought.

I took this woman and Mark home to Geelong for Christmas dinner. They spent most of the time sleeping off hangovers in the car outside the Eton Road house. When they did come inside, Dad was glad to have a drinking buddy and he plied her with beer and champagne. He adored her. Later she and Mark passed out again on my parents' bed. Mum wasn't amused.

The recording of *What A Life!* dragged on. It took another three months until things started happening again. We replaced Mark Opitz with Gary Langan, an English producer who also played keyboards with Art Of Noise, a band that specialised in experimental keyboard music featuring weird, futuristic electronic pops and bleeps, sound loops, and computer vocals. It was Jeff Aldrich of Chrysalis's idea to hire Langan to produce us. As soon as Gary arrived from London in April 1984, we moved into Paradise Studios in Sydney's Woolloomooloo and set to work.

It was immediately clear when we heard the first mixes that Gary Langan was intent on changing our sound, and wanted to create something very different from *Desperate*. Our first album had been rough-edged rock that was true to our live performances and who we were. Gary wanted *What A Life!* to be artier, more mannered and sophisticated, more Art Of Noise. He wanted to experiment with sounds and complex synthesiser programming, like his own band and all those glam bands that came out of England in the early eighties. He seemed obsessed with using the state-of-the-art and slick Fairlight Computer Musical Instrument (or CMI). To Gary, the vocal was only as, or less, important as the other instruments. Naturally, I disagreed, so Gary and I argued. I hated hearing my voice sitting way back in the mix instead of at the front where it belonged and had always been.

I honestly don't think Gary knew how to record our band. Totally lacking from those recording sessions was the energy and passion that Mark Opitz and Bob Clearmountain had achieved with *Desperate*. He stripped us of our soul and spontaneity. With Gary we recorded 'Good Die Young', 'In My Life', 'Heart Telegraph', 'Guillotine Day' and 'Dear Diary'. 'In My Life' has its moments, but 'Good Die Young' was by far the best of the batch because it was raw, undiluted Divinyls. The others are laboured, pretentious and too clever by half. To me, they sounded dated from the moment we cut them, and they haven't improved with age. I have to confess, too, that the songs on *Desperate* were stronger, by and large, than those on *What A Life!* at that stage.

We parted company with Gary Langan on 30 May 1984. After a couple of listens to everything we had in the can, we knew for sure what we'd been suspecting since we first started recording this problem child called *What A Life!* We didn't have our album. We'd had nasty firings, we'd had bitter disagreements with Mark Opitz, Gary and each other, and because we'd chewed up two recording studios, two producers, various engineers and others, we had haemorrhaged money and had a huge budget blowout ... but we didn't have an album. We went back on the road and then, at the end of 1984, the record company paid for me to go to Los Angeles to write.

I had to collaborate with songwriters Billy Steinberg and Tom Kelly, who'd co-written 'Like A Virgin' for Madonna and 'True Colors' for Cyndi Lauper, and Holly Knight, who'd penned a stack of songs for Tina Turner, Pat Benatar, Bon Jovi and KISS. Chrysalis made it very clear that they expected me to come up with the songs that would make *What A Life!* viable. Mark, my long-time collaborator, was shattered that he was surplus to requirements, and I felt for him.

Because it had been a while since we'd released any new music, we plundered the unfinished album and put out the singles 'Good Die Young' backed with '9.50' and 'In My Life' with 'Don't You Go Walking' on the flipside to keep us ticking over.

Mike Chapman, the Los Angeles-based Australian who produced Chrysalis acts Blondie and Pat Benatar, had always wanted to work with Divinyls. We met in LA and got on well, and I decided he should produce the yet-to-be-written songs for *What A Life!* and mix the entire album.

I was a long way from my comfort zone at that time. I didn't have Mark to bounce things off and I am not a fan of Los Angeles. It's sprawling, smoggy and filled with venal people. As soon as I'm there I want to get the hell out. Still, surprisingly, I did what I was told, found a flat to rent in West Hollywood and started writing with Chapman, Steinberg, Kelly and others. Holly Knight and I didn't really gel—maybe she collaborated better with guys. Wisely she went away with Mike Chapman and together they wrote what would become a Divinyls classic, 'Pleasure And Pain'. At first I had qualms about singing someone else's song, but once I'd tried it 'Pleasure And Pain' felt right for me.

'Pleasure And Pain' became the biggest single on *What A Life!*

Mike considered 'Like A Cat', a song Billy Steinberg and Tom Kelly and I had written, and thought it too 'novelty'. Cyndi Lauper heard 'Cat', loved it and asked me if she could sing it on her new album. 'Take it. It's yours,' I told her. She did a terrific job and I was glad the song didn't go to waste.

Another song on *What A Life!* that would stand the test of time was 'Sleeping Beauty', written by Mark with a very little bit of help from me.

Mike Chapman and I flew to Sydney. I introduced him to the band and Vince, and we recorded 'Pleasure And Pain' and 'Sleeping Beauty' at Paradise Studios. Then Mike, Mark and I returned to Los Angeles where Mike mixed the album at Cherokee Studios. Mike took a lot of Gary Langan's flourishes out and, not without difficulty, managed to reinvest the songs with Divinyls grunt.

The cherry on the top of the record was the title track, and we hadn't yet recorded it. 'What A Life!', which I'd written in Mulawa prison while incarcerated for not paying my parking fines, was recorded live at Trafalgar Studios in Sydney and produced by Charles Fisher, with Mark. I love that song, and 'Talk Like The Rain', too, which is my favourite on the record (but these songs weren't on the US version of the recording). I enjoyed working with Charles.

It was during these sessions that I noticed Rick falling asleep. I assumed he was bored and didn't like the material we'd written. Trust me to blame myself. I still didn't know that he had a heroin problem. If anyone ever remixes those songs, they'll find an entire track of Rick snoring.

We shot the video of 'Pleasure And Pain' in a power station in Sydney then we all dashed off to California to film the 'Sleeping Beauty' clip at a Long Beach car lot. 'Sleeping Beauty' was directed by Philippe Mora, the American-based Australian director of the bushranger movie *Mad Dog Morgan* and son of legendary Melbourne artist Mirka Mora. Philippe's wife, Pamela, who had been a Helmut Newton model, did my make-up. She was unsettled by my crooked teeth and made a little false tooth to fill in the gap.

My performance in 'Pleasure And Pain' was so over the top I've never been able to watch it. I didn't enjoy making videos. You have to do the same moves and sing the same words over and over and over, take after take. Spontaneity? Forget it. Typically you start at 5 a.m. and are still going 24 hours later. Often when I made a video I seemed to be exhausted, freezing and in a very bad mood.

What A Life! was released in July 1985, nearly two years after we first started recording. It hit No. 2 on the Australian album charts and No. 75 in America, and the single 'Pleasure And Pain' went to No. 5 in Australia and just cracked the Top 40 in the States. Follow-up singles 'Sleeping Beauty' and 'Heart Telegraph' also charted strongly here while doing little in the United States. In the end, it wasn't the breakthrough album we needed and Chrysalis demanded.

Most critics zeroed in on 'Pleasure And Pain'. *RAM*'s Mark Dodshon wrote that 'Pleasure' was 'more melodic and less abrasive in feel' than other songs on the album, and that my voice was 'mournful and fragile, yet still incredibly intimidating. It's a relaxed, masterful delivery—superbly professional and unique. Who else can howl and cry like this woman?' Indeed. In fact, when I first sang 'Pleasure And Pain' I cried. That title said lots about my life.

Vince Lovegrove

'Pleasure And Pain' was the band's biggest hit in the States up to that point. It received massive American airplay. The producer, Mike Chapman, was big-time, and he was brought onboard at great expense to sprinkle what the industry called his 'magic dust' all over the single and ensure it would be radio-friendly. Mike produced records that sounded great on radio, that came roaring out of a tinny transistor or the car radio, because that's where people hear music and decide if they're going to buy it. He knew his chops, and he didn't come cheap. We paid him $25 000 as a deposit and then he took a percentage of royalties. If you're struggling financially, like we were, that's a fucking lot of money. He was getting more than the band. Of course, if you end up with a huge hit in America, it's a bargain. Unlike Australia, if you succeed in the States, because of the economy of scale, you're a millionaire. End of story.

In his review for *Rolling Stone*, JD Considine called our sound on *What A Life!* 'loud and hard-edged, as purely physical as any metal band but tempered with the sort of swaggering rowdiness that typifies other Sydney bands like Rose Tattoo or Midnight Oil'. Considine praised Mike Chapman's production and my commitment. 'Amphlett [seems] almost possessed by the songs she sings. "In My Life" takes a bitterly ironic view of the possible means of advancement out of the lower classes. Yet even as she screams, "Modelling schools and training schools, finishing schools . . . such advantages!" with her voice dripping sarcasm, she still invests a sort of idiot glee in the chorus: "Never much happening in my life." Similarly, there's a cold fury to "Casual Encounter" that, even as she shreds the gambits of the pick-up artist she addresses, acknowledges that carnal desire is a two-way street.'

Phil Stafford of *RAM* most enjoyed the songs we cut with Gary Langan and thought our writing had a newfound maturity, 'verbalising adult fears and lingering adolescent yearnings'. He also found the band in good form. 'Apart from the trademark push and shove of the rhythm section and McEntee's consistently intelligent guitar, two aspects of Divinyls' sonic make-up step forward with renewed assurance... First, Bjarne Ohlin's keyboards, which have progressed beyond mere colouration to become an integral landmark; second, Amphlett's vocals, from the spitting venom of "Guillotine Day" to the raunch of "In My Life"... from the wrenching sadness of "Dear Diary" to the raw scrape of "Heart Telegraph" and "Old Radios". She addresses each song with the emotive quality it deserves, and injects reckless humour where it's least expected. On "Old Radios" she evokes the static between stations with a sub-guttural roar that recalls Linda Blair at her head-spinning best—growling "Oh shut-up, oh shut-up" with an almost tangible aggression.'

After *What A Life!* was released, we all sat down to take stock of our finances and were horrified. We were tens of thousands of dollars in the red. Just as well we were due to set off on a four-month Australian national tour of capital cities and rural centres, doing five shows a week, to promote our new record and try to recoup some of Chrysalis's money. That would be followed, early in 1986, with a tour of America, where 85 per cent of rock radio stations had 'Pleasure And Pain' on their playlist.

Vince Lovegrove

Chrysalis was one of the more artist-friendly record companies, but they believed Chrissy and Mark were living in a fantasy world where creative integrity was much more important than making money. There's plenty to be said for their stance, and it was one I adhered to up to a point. By failing to come up with a second album filled with new songs immediately, we had become Chrysalis's employees. We'd taken their money, and now they called the shots.

Well, we had delivered an album of new songs, but of course Chrysalis wanted an album of hits.

Just when we'd got the second album out and thought we knew the path we were on, things started to change. At the end of 1984, when the offer came for me to write in LA, the band was having a break and Mark and I advised Rick, Harve and Bjarne to go out and get session work for a while to help keep the wolves from the door. Rick played with Midnight Oil and Paul Kelly, and Harve teamed up with the Party Boys, an all-star band of guys on hiatus from their regular outfits. When Harve joined they were Kevin Borich, Marc Hunter from Dragon, Paul Christie and Joe Walsh, the Eagles guitarist.

A year later Walsh asked us if Harve could go to the States with him for a few months to play drums in another band he was fronting. Walsh had promised Harve that he would be paid much more than the $200 a week or so he was paid by us, and Harve, who I believe had grown disenchanted with Divinyls because we had yet to make it in America, was keen to go.

I couldn't handle Harve leaving us for Joe Walsh, even temporarily, because I had little respect for Walsh. For a start, I knew there would be lots of blow available and that there was a chance Harve would return to us drug-fucked, plus Joe played with the Eagles, a hugely rich, mainstream soft rock outfit from California which I didn't consider rock'n'roll. I told Harve he was selling out. Then Walsh came to my place in Manly to try to talk me into letting Harve go with him. He even sunk to sitting at the piano and singing 'Desperado' to impress me. 'But Joe,' I said, laughing in his face, 'you didn't even *write* "Desperado"!'

Harve left anyway, and, in spite of our love for a great guy and good spirit who'd been in the trenches with us, we fired him. In his place on the Australian *What A Life!* tour was a hot young drummer named JJ Harris.

Richard Harvey

I didn't want to leave Divinyls. I loved the band. I was badly hurt when I was booted out, and I bore a grudge. All I wanted to do was work with Joe Walsh for six weeks, get my US$5500 a week then return to Divinyls.

One week into the six-week tour with Joe, he and I found ourselves sitting on a beach at sun-up near Boston. He said, 'Richard, I want you to be our drummer, man. I'll look after you for the rest of your life.'

I said, 'Joe, this is just for six weeks. I have to go back to Divinyls. I've been with them for five years and they're like family.'

His mood changed abruptly. 'You're fucked,' Joe said. 'You're fucked.' That was the end of our friendly relationship.

I rang Mark and said, 'Mate, I'm definitely coming back in five weeks.'

'Err, that's no good to us, Harve,' he said. 'We're going on the road in three.'

'But Mark, I've signed on with Joe for six weeks. I have to play with him when we support Foreigner at Madison Square Garden. Look, put your tour back two weeks and I'll pay everyone's wages for that period until I can come home.' Divinyls were getting $200 a week, so that was $800 a week from me. That's how bad I wanted to be back in Divinyls. Mark said, 'Uh . . . Okay, I'll talk to Vince and Chrissy,' and hung up. He didn't call back. Soon after I phoned Vince and said I could be back in Australia in four weeks. Vince said he couldn't postpone the tour because the band desperately needed the money.

Then I got a letter signed by Vince, Chrissy and Mark saying that Divinyls no longer required my services. I went back to Joe and said I was available to sign up with him full-time. 'Man,' he said, 'fuck off.'

Joe did me a favour. If I'd stayed with him in America I wouldn't have survived. They would have found me dead of an overdose. The life, the drugs. Those boys were heavy-hitters. Joe still owes me four-and-a-half grand.

I came home and over the next years I sat in with the Party Boys, Dragon, Hippos, even did a short stint with Joe Walsh and Waddy

Wachtel in Joe's band Creatures From America when they toured Australia. I bought a new car with the money I got playing with Joe in America for those six weeks, and I still have it today.

In 1989 I had a bad car accident. My face went through the front windscreen of my Volkswagen. It felt like someone had hit me full in the head with a shovel. I had glass in my eyes and my face was cut to pieces. I busted my nose and teeth and damaged my ribs. It took 200 stitches to put my face back together.

I work on the council these days. There *is* life after rock'n'roll and it's called local government. I play in a good band that does mainly covers at leagues clubs and RSL clubs. Rick Grossman is a good mate, but I haven't seen Vince at all and Mark just once since they sacked me, and I only recently caught up with Chrissy.

Vince Lovegrove

Harve's departure cost the band a luminous raconteur. He was a bloke always up for a laugh, a drink and anything else that was happening. He was the ultimate rock drummer, and knew how to roll with the backbeat. Most drummers think straight out hard rock beats are what it's all about, but what you don't play is as important as what you do. It's the space in between that made Harve the drummer he was. That and his ability to feel that roll and swing, something most drummers only dream about.

But Harve was always a little unhappy, slightly bitter about money, conditions, or the set-up of the band, the length of the tour, the places we stayed. Even so, he wouldn't directly voice his opinion, not even when I tried to push him. He preferred to whinge on the quiet or sulk in a dark corner.

Our *What A Life!* shows were sell-outs. After all that time in the studio and writing, it was a wonderful release to perform live again. So many years later, it's all a blur, but I remember a one-day rock festival at Flemington Markets in Sydney where we blew Mental as Anything, Machinations, Dynamic Hepnotics, Electric Pandas and GANGgajang off the stage. And as far as I could see, our co-act Jimmy Barnes suffered the same fate at a Myer Music Bowl gig in December.

Reporter Beldon Cable in *RAM* captured the electricity of our *What A Life!* performances in his review of an October show at Cronulla Workers Club: 'Divinyls are back with their edges sharpened to the point of frustration—frustration with the time it's taken to get back to this, their undeniable element: an unseasonably hot and steamy night in the suburbs, an environment in which they've always excelled... tonight they left scorchmarks on unwary ears. Blowtorch guitars, Grossman's thundering bass, a new drummer who substitutes finesse and momentum for colourless thud, fresh keyboard injections and that familiar, full-throated wail: Amphlett never sounded so wounded, so animated, so emotionally convincing. She's now a full-blown actress, the inflated parody set off with moments of chilling realism. Some of this pain *is* real, most of this humour is black, the stage antics curiously compelling. Like a road accident, you can't look away... Like a witch in a party dress, the costume's mere deception: world weariness clothed in youthful innocence. The sex is threatening, a million miles from cheap titillation. The noise is overwhelming, yet imbued with a curious symmetry: the songs sound so *new*—of course some of them are—yet the standards are anything but... "Siren" sounds slower, yet it still tears like a blade through butter. "Boys In Town" addresses everyone of them [in the audience] tonight, whilst "Elsie" drags out the drama like slowly tensioned wire.'

If only Beldon Cable knew what was going on behind the scenes.

I was drinking more heavily by then, and there were drugs. Never heroin, though. I know it sounds unbelievable but even at this point I *still* had no idea Rick was addicted to smack. He must have had his own places to score that none of us knew about.

Rick Grossman

To me, the period making *What A Life!* was when cracks first appeared in our united front. There was a fair amount of angst, and it reminded me of the low times I'd had when I was playing in Matt Finish. I was in a hotel room in Ballina and I'd read a book called *Dispatches* by

Michael Herr and in it there was a story about American soldiers shooting themselves in the foot to be sent home from Vietnam. I thought, 'I could get a hammer and smash my hand and I could be out of here.' At this period with Divinyls there was exhaustion and there was mad behaviour. A lot of drugs. All around me people were behaving in a very irrational way, as passionate people sometimes do.

Part of my unhappiness was because I felt hardly done by. I felt left out of things, and not helping matters was my low self-esteem, a condition I've had all my life.

I remember looking at a Divinyls cover and Chrissy standing there saying, 'Well, Rick, what do you think of this?' I thought it was horrible but instead of saying so, I looked at her and said, 'This is *so* good!' because I knew that's what *she* thought. In Divinyls, I wanted to be included in the decision-making and the songwriting and I had ideas about our performing, record covers and so on, but I was too fearful to speak up. I was in awe of Chrissy and Mark. I saw them, especially Chrissy, as incredibly talented people and I wanted to be like that.

I also think, with hindsight, that a lot of my resentment could have been drug-induced paranoia. I was in the throes of heroin addiction and it's a common attitude for people in that condition to blame others for their state and to consider life unfair. Chrissy and Mark copped the brunt.

While things were not always great offstage, there was never a time when I thought Divinyls weren't a truly great performing band. When we were all up there playing together it was a magic feeling. We all loved each other then, with the possible exception of Chrissy and Bjarne.

Divinyls were on the verge of disintegration. We were assailed on all fronts by drugs and alcohol, debt, frustration and our failure to break in America, and our own inherent dysfunction.

Things had changed with Vince, too. When he told us Suzi was pregnant, I was so happy for them. Troy Lovegrove was born on 25 June 1985, and Suzi and Vince were married on 19 July of that same year at the old stone registry office in Sydney's Macquarie Street, just off the Botanic Gardens. It was a small affair and a happy one. Suzi wore black lace. But Vince's focus moved from Divinyls to his family and nothing would ever be the same. Through it all, Mark and I survived as creators, performers and lovers. We didn't exactly have a choice. We couldn't walk away. We were caught in the same trap. We were contracted to the hilt to continue making music together, and even if we hadn't been, at that stage of our lives we wouldn't have considered doing anything else. For us, living the dream, or nightmare, as it was becoming, was all we knew.

ROAD RAGE

If we thought we had our work cut out for us on our first assault on the US in 1983, on the two *What A Life!* tours we made in 1986 we paid our dues and a whole lot more. After those drama-filled treks, rock'n'roll held no more surprises for us.

It hadn't taken us long to get used to our new drummer. JJ Harris was an energetic, hilarious kid and a gifted drummer, though, as we would discover, he was more at home playing live than in a recording studio.

Soon after JJ joined we learned that things hadn't worked out between Harve and Joe Walsh and our old mate had returned to Australia. It was tempting to invite him back, but as far as we were concerned the door had closed.

We flew out of Sydney on 14 January for the first leg of our US tour. We'd be supporting Aerosmith, a once mega-band who were making a comeback, in Portland, Seattle, San Francisco, Oregon, Reno, Las Vegas, Bakersfield and Fresno.

Divinyls had cut our teeth opening for more established acts in

Australia, and we'd never had a problem. Okay, you know that the majority of the crowd hasn't paid to see you and are hoping that you'll finish soon so they can see their heroes, but fans of Cold Chisel and INXS grew to like us and gave us a good hearing. As we gathered momentum, at some Australian gigs we got a better reception than the headline band. This, sadly—and painfully, was not the case when we went on before Aerosmith, whose mostly redneck male fans were among the most hard-core in rock.

Vince Lovegrove

It was a rite of passage for any band supporting Aerosmith that if you survived their rough fans you were made of the right stuff. AC/DC opened for them and rode out the storm, got noticed and became bigger than Aerosmith ever were. I thought Divinyls would kick arse with Aerosmith and our long-term future in America would be assured. I knew exactly what we'd be letting ourselves in for when I signed on with the American rockers, but I didn't tell the band. As hard as it was going to be, most acts would kill to open for Aerosmith, and it was a coup when we got the job.

These morons hated us for showing up, they hated us because they'd never heard our songs before, they hated me for being a woman. So they pelted us with full beer cans, coins and wet paper towels compressed into rock-like hardness and rained M-80s—big firecrackers—onto the stage. My response to them was 'Fuck you!' I was determined not to let them see how much they were frightening me. Every night, we came offstage covered in cuts and bruises and with our ears ringing from the exploding bungers. Rick's eye was closed and blackened by a flying coin.

The first night we came under attack I burst into tears in the dressing-room. I felt like a shell-shocked survivor of the Blitz.

After the second gig, Aerosmith's leader, Steven Tyler, apologised to us and said, 'Just hang in there. Please don't leave! I'll introduce you.' From then on he'd walk out before we started playing and ask his fans to give us a fair go. It made little difference.

We had a meeting and decided that in future if any of us was hit by a flying projectile I would calmly and with dignity halt the show, explain to the crowd why they were making it impossible for us to continue, and then we'd start playing again. If they continued to toss things we'd go straight off.

The only fans I ever encountered who rivalled Aerosmith's for craziness were the Ramones'. When we opened for the Ramones at Pier 13 in New York in 1983 they came armed with aluminium cans which they'd squashed flat so the edges were razor-sharp and serrated and they skimmed them at us like Ninjas throwing star knives. We did our best to dodge the missiles but didn't always succeed.

Aerosmith were nothing like their fans. They were nice guys. Rick hung out with them, and Steve Tyler told me how he had nearly been killed when he crashed his motorbike. He took off his shoe and proudly showed me where the exhaust pipe had burned a hole in his foot. He was lovely. When he performed, I'd sit on the side of the stage, up close, and he liked that. He'd turn around and see me and grin. As a performer and as a man, Steven Tyler excited me.

Rick Grossman

We didn't know it when we signed on, but Aerosmith fans always put the support act on the rack. It was a blood sport to them. That made working with Aerosmith bloody stressful and, with our tiredness and cocaine and Scotch whisky consumption, it brought a lot of the tensions within the band to the surface.

One night we were midway through a gig in Seattle, and the pelting started. I looked around and there was no Mark. He'd left without a word. I thought he was changing guitars, but he didn't return. It was impossible for us to keep performing without our lead guitarist so Chrissy, very angry, stopped the show and led us off as the crowd booed. We found Mark in the dressing-room. Vince and Steven Tyler were there. I was in a rage at Mark's unprofessionalism. 'What about our plan that Chrissy addresses the crowd? You were meant to tell her if you got hit!'

Mark came back at me with a smart-arse remark and then turned it all around and blamed Chrissy for the fiasco. I lost my temper. Me, who has had only two fights in my life. I picked up a garbage bin and threw it at Mark, then I grabbed him by the throat and shoved him hard up against a wall and began punching him. Everyone was shocked because I'm usually so mild-mannered. Vince was yelling, 'Stop it! I can't believe you're doing this!' Much of my anger was because Mark had abandoned us, but I realise now that at least a few of my punches were repayment for Mark's difficult and divisive ways.

'Are you happy now, Rick?' Mark gasped. 'How do you feel now, Rick?'

I shouted, 'Fantastic! Great!' as my stored-up resentment came out in one big, ugly, but thoroughly justified, torrent.

Things calmed down, but as we were getting ready to return to our hotel, Mark muttered darkly, 'I'm not fuckin' getting into any car with Rick.'

I lost my temper all over again. I slammed him into a shower stall and banged him against the wall.

Later, back at the hotel, I felt awful about what I'd done. I wasn't up to fronting Mark just yet, so I went to Chrissy and said, 'I'm so sorry.' I remember exactly what she said. 'Rick, I despised you for 30 seconds when you were beating up Mark. But then I thought, "You know, Rick's right!"'

Just then, we looked down the hotel corridor and spotted Mark trying to slink into his room. Chrissy took off and started hitting him.

Vince Lovegrove

Chrissy was so disgusted with Mark [after he walked off stage] that she called a car and went straight back to the hotel. She knew we'd blown it.

Eventually he knocked on my hotel-room door. I thought he'd be filled with remorse, but no. 'Right,' he said, 'have you cancelled the rest of the tour?'

'I'm not cancelling the rest of the tour, Mark. We'll be back onstage tomorrow night.'

'Well, I'm not going on unless you sign a contract with me and the promoters that nobody in the audience is ever going to throw anything at me ever again. Right?'

I looked at him and said, 'Are you serious?'

'Yeah, I'm serious.'

'Mate, you've just lost me. If that's going to be your attitude, you'll never make it in America.'

That night Chrissy and Mark had a huge fight and she punished him verbally and physically.

The tour went on—*with* Mark—but he and Chrissy travelled separately for the next couple of months. She refused to be in the same room with him. She refused to travel in the same car. They didn't speak for some time. Then, of course, relations thawed and they got back together.

Mark did himself, and Divinyls, some damage that night. Word got around that he'd stormed off the stage, and in future negotiations promoters would say, 'But what about that temperamental guitarist? He's not going to freak out again, is he? He's not going to screw things up?'

He had also made a mockery of the tough image Chrissy and I had created for Divinyls. And we *were* tough. We played tough music. Chrissy was extremely tough, as a person and a singer. Rick was tough, but didn't show it. I had always thought Mark was tough, but after Aerosmith I had my doubts.

Things were changing fast. In Suzi I had a friend and a lover at last to confide in, and I held nothing back. I told her how the challenge of making Divinyls the best band in the world had faded. I had no ambition left to be a big-time band manager in America. 'What would we do if I just bailed out?' I would ask her. 'How would we survive? Who would manage the band in my absence?'

The band started squabbling over money. We had meetings where we'd examine our finances and justify expenses. Often they were heated affairs.

The bottom line was we had spent all the Chrysalis money and gone further into debt with the label. The money we owed could only be reimbursed by more relentless touring and new recordings. We were in a vicious cycle.

Touring in America and Australia are different beasts. Australian music fans go to gigs in droves, but are also content to hear bands on the radio and see them on TV videos, and if they like them they'll buy the records. In the States, they prefer to see acts live. They want to make sure they're real. So to pull it off there, you have to hit the road, and America is a bloody big country. It is like touring 52 countries.

At first, we found touring the US fun and an adventure, going from gig to gig, town to town, state to state. Lots to see, lots to do. But we weren't a major band and it wasn't as if we were playing a big stadium, having three days off and flying to the next city. We mostly played one-night stands in small halls and clubs, night after night, travelling from one to another crammed into a tour bus. You arrive at a town at midday. You check into the hotel. You go down to the venue and do a sound-check. You do a radio interview. You go back and do the show because you're on first. You finish the show. You're all hyperactive after the show so you party. Every town has a party. There's booze, there's drugs, there's women, there's a record company whose people want to introduce you to the guys at the radio station and the record stores. Suddenly it's long past midnight. You crawl back to the hotel to get an hour or two's sleep and at 6 a.m. you're on that bus bound for the next gig. This goes on for months. You live in each other's pockets. You eat fast food. You don't exercise. It is deeply boring. Only the strong survive. If there is any animosity between bandmembers, rest assured it will blow up into a massive issue on tour. Being on the road is demoralising, it's exhausting. It's rock'n'roll.

You seek relief in sex, alcohol and drugs, though we were not a band that played stoned or drunk. Chrissy would have a gin and tonic or a vodka before she went onstage. That was all. Mark, too, never needed to rely on drugs or booze to perform at his best. Adrenalin did the trick. I didn't think Rick was drug-affected either, but in hindsight, knowing the extent of his problem, he could have been. If so, he kept it well concealed. Later, when I did know of his addiction, I didn't try to help him. I didn't want to interfere. I didn't really know how I could help. I had my own problems and Rick was far from my mind.

My role as manager of the band had its own separate evolution. When I began, I was on hand 24 hours a day, on the road, at rehearsals, in the office. At the outset I was managing and directing their career, being tour manager, business manager and publicity manager. Chrissy had become quite dependent on my feedback on her live performances. But as Divinyls' status in America grew I was needed more in offices, overseeing finances, keeping the books and having meetings with record companies, lawyers, accountants, agents, promotions and publicity people. But I just didn't want to know about setting up taxation schemes, insurance policies, investment banking. This was not my scene. This was not why I took up with Chrissy's gang. As the band became more successful I was forced to wean myself off the road, away from the action that I loved, away from the music.

By the beginning of 1986, as it all unravelled, my love for Suzi and Troy was deep and growing deeper. I wanted to be with them more than the band. Suzi gave me the strength to see my role with Divinyls in a different light.

The constant struggles with Mark and Chrissy and the ongoing battle to pay back Chrysalis's advance was taking a toll on me. The band was well on the way. Success was not inevitable, but likely, if things went to plan and luck was on our side. We'd not cracked America by any stretch of the imagination, but we certainly had a seat on the merry-go-round. Either Denise Fraser from Dirty Pool, who was now with us full-time acting as our on-tour organiser and Chrissy's confidante, or Tom O'Sullivan, who by this stage had effectively become Divinyls' manager, were my proxy. Without Tom and Denise the tent would have been pulled on the entire circus. They were extremely capable people and could do what I was doing. Perhaps they didn't have my passion, but they were far better at handling the finances. My thoughts, more and more, were straying to life after Divinyls, and I was thinking, among other things, of managing other up-and-coming bands, such as the very talented Australian outfit Electric Pandas. The buzz for me, of helping a band get up and running and into the race, was all but gone with Divinyls.

While Denise and Tom travelled with the band, Suzi and Troy and I took every opportunity to dash up to Niagara Falls or have a weekend in New York together. We'd travel down to Wilmington to meet Suzi's Italian–American family.

When Divinyls returned to Australia for a February tour after the Aerosmith gigs and before the upcoming March and April American shows with the Cult, we stayed in the States and Suzi, Troy and I moved into the Warwick Hotel on West 54th Street in mid-town Manhattan. Suzi showed me another side of New York. She introduced me to her friends, musicians, dancers, actors, artists.

Suzi and Chrissy's friendship had blossomed. They were both wild, and Chrissy could see how much Suzi meant to me. Being with strong and funny women, such as Suzi and Denise Fraser, was good for Chrissy. She was obsessed with the band, and when with them had no choice but to be one of the boys, and it wasn't easy for her.

Drugs and alcohol were affecting everybody—myself included. I look back on some of my behaviour then—it was rash and it was aggressive and sometimes extremely foolhardy. Once I got into a fight in a club. I was off my face when a fellow bumped into me and I turned around and said, 'What do you think you're doing!' and we brawled and ended up with torn shirts and bloodied faces. My lip was badly split.

I bashed a Chrysalis executive. He deserved it, but cocaine and alcohol—and a touch of paranoia—had undoubtedly poisoned my disposition and made me over-react. This ugly little episode took place at a meeting at Chrysalis's office in Manhattan and present were some marketing people, the guys who dole out the payola to record stations and record stores to ensure the label's records got played and displayed. (Anyone who doesn't believe that level of corruption exists knows nothing about the American record industry because that is exactly what it was like. And *is* like.)

I was criticising Chrysalis for not supporting the band, and my blood was boiling. I accused the men in the room of not stocking our records in the right markets nor of keeping promotional promises they'd made. I had prepared a report backing up my accusations and I presented my findings vehemently but without menace. Then one executive adopted an aggressive tone and said, 'What you're saying is bullshit. Don't come in here and tell me how to do my job because I know what I'm doing and you've got to remember that we have heavy contacts in this business and you don't want to upset the apple cart because if you do you could personally be in danger and your band can be dropped like that.' He punctuated his tirade by snapping his fingers in my face.

I went berserk. He was a bulky guy, but I grabbed him by the lapels of his coat, lifted him off the ground and pushed his face against the window. We were twenty floors up. I said, 'Don't you fucking *ever* threaten me again. And don't threaten to drop the band. If you do I'll come back here and I'll throw you out of this fucking window. *And I will have no remorse.*' He was white-faced and trembling when I set him down again. I left the office and went to the president's office and gave him my report. 'This proves your marketing man is a liar and I want something done about it.' I walked out. We never dealt with that marketing honcho again.

In America, record companies employ so-called experts to advise them on music trends, what records are likely to be hits, and record covers that are likely to sell. Chrysalis showed their guru a proposed image for a Divinyls release. The shot showed Chrissy, her dress hitched up and her hand on her suspender belt. The guy shook his head. 'Too risqué,' he declared. 'Americans won't like it. You'll have to airbrush out the suspender belt.' Chrissy took offence, and I didn't blame her. He hadn't the remotest idea what Divinyls were about. There was no way we were ever going to delete that suspender belt.

As the Divinyls–Cult tour proceeded I found myself thinking that I truly was fed up with being manager of Divinyls. I'd had enough. I decided I would stay onboard for the gigs back home and then return for the final shows we were booked to do with the Cult through the United States, but after that, I just didn't know. At the end of the

Aerosmith gigs the band and I had gone on a cocaine binge to celebrate the end of that sector of the tour. I thought to myself as the party raged around me, 'I won't be on the road again with this band. I'm too old for all the angst, and the drugs and the booze. If you don't escape you could end up dead.' I was going to get a life, and it was going to be with Suzi.

I started to plan my exit. With the band's agreement I contacted Barry Fey and Chuck Morris in Denver. They were two of the biggest promoters in America, who had pioneered U2 in the States and were Divinyls fans. They would manage the group in America and I'd retain control in Australia and other countries. Chrissy had only recently said, 'Maybe we need some big names in America to look after us . . . to perhaps take us that further step.' No question she had a point, too. I made some bad financial decisions; I can't even remember what they were now. I wasn't a moneyman, or a businessman. I could be both tough as nails and pathetically weak and indulgent. Who knows how these things are judged? How can you ever look back on anything and say, 'Would it have been different had it been done another way?' I don't live my life like that.

Barry and Chuck thought it was a terrific idea, and the wheels started turning to swing the deal. I would not have considered handing Divinyls over to these Americans had not the very competent Denise Fraser and Tom O'Sullivan been there to hold the band's hand in my place.

Like Vince, I took a set against some of the Chrysalis guys. I became convinced our record label didn't understand us. They told me, 'You aren't having any hit singles because your teeth are buck and crooked. Your appearance is holding the band back.' They told me to have my teeth straightened. They wanted me to look conventionally beautiful like their other artists Debbie Harry and Pat Benatar. That was not me. It wasn't real. I was enraged, then I thought that if they were prepared to foot the bill for braces I'd wear them. And I did, but in the end they stopped paying for the ongoing dental treatment so I took the braces off.

Americans are obsessed with white, perfectly symmetrical teeth. They didn't understand that my buck teeth were as much a part of me as my voice or my spirit. Americans take out loans to have their teeth fixed like Australians pay off their houses. They whiten their teeth so much their gums recede and then their teeth fall out, and it serves them right.

Years later, when I was up for the role of Judy Garland in *The Boy From Oz*, the producer took one look at me with my snaggly teeth and thought I was perfect for the part. 'Judy had buck teeth too!' he declared. I guess that gives me the last laugh.

The pressure was on with the record company. We knew we had a huge debt and I wanted to pay it back—but we needed their support to do it. Mark and I argued with Chrysalis over what we considered their half-hearted promotion. During our US tour we spent a few days going around to the radio stations to meet the DJs and programmers so they'd be able to put faces to our music and play our records. We'd do three, even four cities in a day. Get on a plane, fly to a city, be met by the Chrysalis promotions man in the area who'd drive us to the radio station, meet the staff, get driven back to the airport, hop on a plane and fly to the next town. It was demanding, especially for people like Mark and me who only wanted to play our music and were Z-grade schmoozers. At one radio station in the Midwest I saw our Chrysalis publicity guy pushing other Chrysalis records. He had a stack under his arm. He was supposed to be working for us. We expected loyalty and focus from our record company. So I said, 'Mark, let's go!' and without explanation we walked out onto the street and—shades of my Torquay days—stuck out our thumbs to hitch a lift back to the airport. The rep ran after us, yelling, 'Come back!' but we refused to return to the station. We had cut off our nose to spite our face, but a principle was involved. When word got back to the Chrysalis head office, they were not impressed.

All my focus, all of us—Vince, Mark, Rick, Bjarne—had put everyting on the line for Divinyls. On that American tour things started to get dark and crazy. At the end of the Aerosmith tour, we returned to Australia to do a show at Thirroul Leagues Club on the south coast of New South Wales and two sold-out headline gigs at Sydney's Enmore Theatre. Backstage at the Enmore I was with Suzi and noticed she had some angry-looking sores on her back. 'What are those?' I asked her. She thought they may have been shingles.

A fortnight after that, Mark and I had an argument, and I moved into a small private hotel in Kings Cross—alone. I called Vince to let him know where I could be reached, and he broke the news that Suzi had, that day, been diagnosed with AIDS.

I was in deep shock. In tears, I caught a cab to their place in Point Piper. An ashen-faced Vince let me in and I found Suzi bathing Troy in the kitchen sink. She was trying to smile but was obviously distraught. I threw my arms around her and kissed Troy and, feeling desperately inadequate, I told her how sorry I was, and that I loved her. Vince meantime was manic, pacing about the house. I looked into his eyes and saw only fear and rage.

Vince, unhinged by grief, did not accompany us back to America for our gigs with the Cult. I hadn't realised this was something he'd been thinking of even before Suzi was diagnosed. I guess this shows how disjointed the band had become.

Vince Lovegrove

Since we'd met, Suzi had had frequent bouts of feeling ill, and would break out in rashes and sores. Neither of us knew why. I certainly didn't suspect AIDS. Of course I'd heard of the disease, but it was not yet the epidemic it would become. As far as I knew it was purely a gay person's disease. I can remember one morning in Greenwich Village, Suzi and I were out shopping and there was a demonstration. A group of gay men had set up trestles and were handing out pamphlets about AIDS. 'What's this?' I asked Suzi, 'a gay rights demo?'

'No,' she said, 'they're educating people about this new disease, AIDS.'

We looked at each other and I said, 'Well, we don't have to worry about AIDS because we're definitely not gay . . . but just to be sure we don't catch it from them, let's cross to the other side of the road.' That little incident will be burnished in my mind for as long as I live.

Soon after Troy's birth and our wedding, Suzi was feeling ill and had another attack of what she thought were shingles on her back, so we went to the doctor. He examined her and said, 'Mmm, that is a bit like shingles but shingles are rare in someone your age, and you say they've come and gone for years. Are you sure you're not HIV-positive?'

'What's HIV-positive?' we said.

'It's the precursor to AIDS. Nine times out of ten it develops into full-blown AIDS.'

'But I thought only gay people got AIDS,' I stammered.

'Well, no . . .'

Suzi was tested and found to be HIV-positive. We had a second test at St Vincent's Hospital. I was at the office and the phone rang. It was Professor David Cooper from the hospital. 'Vince, the tests are back. They're positive again. I've told Suzi. She's at home—I think she needs you.' Tests also confirmed that Troy, who was a sickly baby with rashes around his mouth, was HIV-positive as well.

Suddenly our lives had been turned upside down. There were so many questions.

'What's going to happen?

What's the prognosis?

Will they die?

How long do they have?

What am I going to do?

Will I be able to work?

If not, how will we live, how will I be able to pay the medical bills?'

Because of my situation with the band, I had to know the prognosis to see how much time Suzi had. I went to see Professor Cooper alone. He told me Suzi had around eighteen months to live.

Sadness hung over Divinyls like a shroud. The American tour had to proceed. We were contracted, in debt and would never have been released from our obligations. With Vince staying back in Sydney caring for his stricken family, tour manager Tom O'Sullivan took his place and Barry Fey and Chuck Morris, who Vince had engaged in return for a percentage of our take, became our American managers. Vince and I had one of the early email machines, one of those where you cup rubber attachments onto the earpiece of a phone and the message is sent. As we travelled from town to town, Vince's grief and anger poured out of the email contraption. I tried to respond, but there was no email etiquette then, and I sent messages that Vince misinterpreted and he sent emails that I misconstrued. Everything fell apart by email. Vince and I were suddenly enemies and there was no sane dialogue between us. He had been my confidant and support, and now he turned me away. I felt weak and powerless. Grief makes us behave irrationally, and who am I to judge a man as grief-stricken as Vince was then? Because of the circumstances, and the atmosphere created by drugs and alcohol, none of us had the tools to deal with this escalating tragedy.

At the start of the tour, there was no love lost between the Cult and Divinyls. The plan was whichever band was selling the most records in a particular region would headline the gig there. As a topline British rock outfit, that compromise rankled with them, as it did with us. Both of us thought we deserved to be headliners all the time. Before long neither band was speaking to the other, a potential disaster since we'd be travelling together for the next two months to Boston, Detroit, Philadelphia, New York, Pittsburgh, Cleveland, Washington, Milwaukee, Minneapolis, Dallas, Kansas City, all through Texas, Salt Lake City, Denver, Los Angeles and San Diego.

One godawful night in Detroit, Divinyls and the Cult were in the same snowbound hotel bar and the air was rancid with animosity. It was like a Mexican stand-off between us. I was in a bad mood, distressed about Vince, warring with Mark, tired and drinking too much, and pissed off in a major way by the Cult's arrogance. I broke the ice by mixing up a concoction of garbage, slops and water from the hotel kitchen that looked and smelled exactly like vomit and putting it in buckets which I placed at the hotel door of each member of the Cult. What I was saying was I thought their snotty attitude sucked. Of course, the Cult thought it was hilarious; they were not used to feisty Aussie women, and we all hit it off from then on.

Well, that's not entirely true. The Cult's lead singer, Ian Astbury, who today is a friend, got so angry in Denver when his band had to go on first, that he kicked an amp in his fury and broke his foot. For the rest of the tour he sang from a wheelchair.

That night in Detroit I bought a rabbit-skin coat from a groupie in the hotel bar for $100. I was freezing and she was broke. I still have the coat, and each time I see it hanging in my wardrobe a faint smell of vomit assails me. I hope it's my imagination.

Rick Grossman

In Denver, I went with Richard and Tim Butler of Psychedelic Furs to see a U2 gig. Richard or Tim kept telling us he was great friends with The Edge. We went backstage and when The Edge saw the Butlers he said, 'Well, well, it's the Brothers Grimm.' The night went downhill from there. Later we were all at a bar and there was a houseband playing. Bono, very, very drunk, walked onstage, took the microphone from the singer and started singing. The band's drummer grabbed Bono and threw him off the stage. Bono said, 'Do you know who I am?' and the drummer said, to the cheers of the house, 'I couldn't give a rat's arse who you are. No one sings with us without an invitation.'

I might have been more concerned about the tour if we hadn't had the help of a genuine rock'n'roll legend, the amazing Phil Kaufman. Let me tell you about the man known as the Road Mangler...

Phil is like Groucho Marx with a short, barrel-like body and 10 000 tattoos. He was what our sad little outfit badly needed. A walking streak of one-liners and rock sensibility, Phil made his name when he went way beyond the call of duty as tour manager for the great seventies country rocker, the extremely wild Gram Parsons.

Gram and Phil had made a pact that if one of them died, for whatever reason, the other must take his body out into the Southern

California desert to Joshua Tree National Park, where they had spent many stoned and drunken nights, and burn it, so the ashes would rise into the desert night and not be interred in some sad little suburban cemetery.

Parsons was in a drug-fuelled downward spiral, and just a few months later he overdosed and died. Phil stole Parsons' body from the morgue and with a friend named Michael he drove it to Joshua Tree, stopping on the way for some beer and five gallons of petrol. Right near the Joshua Tree National Monument, a large rock formation, Phil and his friend unloaded the coffin from their van. As Phil explains it, 'Michael said, "Let's get out of here," but I said, "No, we gotta pay tribute to our buddy." So I started to open up the casket and Michael got really spooked. "Oh man, don't open the casket, don't open the casket." I said, "We have to see Gram." So we squeaked the lid open and there was Gram, just laying there dead as he could be. We said a couple of things. I took the gas, poured it all over him. Took a cigar, took a big hit, got the big red thing on there, and just tossed it in, and boy, it went "Ka-boom". The body started burning; we could see it bubbling in there. Then a strange thing happened. The ashes from his body went up in little dust devils into the desert night, straight up. There was a billion stars and Gram joined them.'

In his time, Phil was also road manager for the Rolling Stones, Led Zeppelin, Marianne Faithfull, who was a hero of mine, and Emmy-Lou Harris, who sang with Gram and was his lover. Phil got Emmy-Lou to gigs on time for years. Not long ago, I ran into Phil and Emmy-Lou and he introduced me to her. I said, 'Hi, I love your boots.' Her response was a withering look and I can only imagine the terrible stories Phil had told her about me. I loved him, even though he wrote in his autobiography *Road Mangler Deluxe* that I cut the crotch out of my underwear before each gig—which I never did! I cut holes in my stockings, but never in my crotch.

Phil took no shit from anyone, and was incredibly organised. These were valuable traits on that Divinyls–Cult tour. With him pulling the strings the logistics of touring—booking and catching the flights and the buses, checking in and out of hotels, eating—ran like clockwork. Whenever something had to be done, Phil did it to perfection. I've never seen anyone carry so many bags at once, each one with his little colour-code sticker on it so it couldn't get lost. He was always happy and never complained or shirked a job. Every band should have a Phil Kaufman.

He cared for all the guys in Divinyls, but was especially good at looking after me. When I was angry or sad, which was always, he'd make me laugh. One morning I was sitting in a hotel lobby feeling blue when he bounced up to me and said, 'Christina, I'm your greatest fan. I'm such a big fan that I've got your name tattooed on my arse.'

'Noooo! You do not!'

'Yes, I do, Christina.'

'Show me!'

With that he pulled his pants down right there in front of everyone and sure enough, there were the words 'Your Name' tattooed on his bum.

Another time he said, right out of the blue, 'Christina, did you know that my cock hangs below my knee?'

'No way, Phil!'

'Yes, it does, Christina. Look, I'll show you.' Then he rolled up his trouser leg and there was a tattoo of a rooster on his leg. He had these tatts done just so he could make jokes.

No one defused a tense situation like Phil. One of the Cult guys would be being snooty or impossible and Phil, who stands about 5 feet 2 inches, would go straight up to him and flip him on the nose.

The morning after the fake-vomit episode in Detroit, we were due to leave for the airport. Phil switched on the ignition of our Lincoln limo to warm up the motor then got out to load up, but he inadvertently locked the keys in the car. I was standing outside freezing in the snow. Phil calmly and purposefully walked past me back inside the hotel and emerged with a hammer. Then he proceeded to smash the window of this very expensive vehicle, reached in through the gaping hole, opened the door and packed us in as if nothing had happened. The hotel doorman looked on aghast, but there was no time to open the car door with a coathanger. The plane was waiting and we had to catch it. We drove all the way to the airport with a blizzard blasting through the shattered window.

Phil recently made a movie about himself and Gram Parsons, called *Grand Theft Parsons*, with Johnny Knoxville of *Jackass* fame playing the Mangler.

Phil Kaufman

The Divinyls . . . a wild crew. Great times . . . if only I could remember them. These days I can't remember what I had for breakfast. I'm glad to be out of that scene. I play golf now, with a lot of other old rockers, like Alice Cooper. We used to talk about pussy, now it's prostates.

How did I get involved with Divinyls? I got the short straw. Barry Fey called me and said we've got an off-the-wall band on tour. They're trouble. I can't think of anyone who can keep them on the straight and narrow but you. I thought, 'What the hell . . .' I met 'em in New York. I had the flu. I was coughing and gagging and puking.

We went out on the road with very little money or, as we used to say, a few dollars and no sense. Divinyls were always squabbling with the Cult over who'd play last. I'd get in Chrissy and Mark's ear, tell them we weren't the support act, we were just going on first. I also gave them the idea of always insisting on having the same size lettering as the Cult on the handbills and posters, so they seemed equal, no matter who was playing first or last.

One morning Chrissy had had enough of the Cult. She came down to breakfast late. Both bands and I were already there after a hard night's partying. We were shaking like a marimba band. She just fuckin' lit into them. She got right in the face of Ian Astbury. 'Don't you fucking treat us like shit! You shit!' She just bit the head off that boy. From that moment on, the Cult were always, 'Good morning Chrissy! Good morning Miss Amphlett!'

She was an unforgettable performer. Before a show she'd be pissed off, after a show she'd be pissed off, but during a show, *Rrrrrrr . . . the school uniform, the hatchets, and those Mick Jagger lips!*

What was she like as a person? What, as opposed to what she was like as a cocker spaniel? Or a carrot? I remember her more as a rutabaga than a person. She was a sweetie on the inside, with a terrifying exterior. Chrissy and Mark had a strange relationship. I don't know what the hell was going on there. One minute they were screaming at each other, next they were gettin' on.

So Chrissy denies cutting the crotch out of her tights? I stand by my story. I'm sure she did, but then again I was afraid to look closely.

On the final day of our tour, in Seattle, we partied in my hotel room. On my bedside table was my loaded .38 sitting right beside the night's takings. I always travelled with a gun, but was sure to keep it in my suitcase when I was flying because carrying a gun in hand-luggage is a serious crime. Next day at the airport I farewelled both bands and their entourages and they hugged and kissed me and thanked me for everything. It was a touching scene. They flew off. My plane was to leave later so I whiled away the hours over a few Bloody Marys in the airport bar. When it was time to board my flight I walked through the metal detector and alarms went off and lights flashed. 'What the fuck's happening?' I wondered. What was happening was that I was in deep shit. Rocket, the Divinyls' roadie, had taken my pistol out of my suitcase and slipped it into my carry-on bag when I wasn't looking. I was arrested and only released after some very fast talking. The police kept my .38 and some months later I copped a hefty fine.

Divinyls had the talent and the songs, and a good following. They should have been the biggest band in the world. Why weren't they? Ah, I don't know. Lack of label support, bad management and booking, their own mistakes. They opened in the States a lot for other bands and opening acts have it tough because often when they play the gig is only a third full, and those who are there are only interested in the headliner. Maybe it was a combination of all these factors. You know, it can be hard for a band from Australia, England, Canada or wherever to break in the United States. Some acts just don't translate, and Americans tend to prefer the homegrown act. The Beatles and the Stones are notable exceptions. Kasey Chambers opened for Emmy-

Lou. She was terrific, but she didn't break. The act is good. The music is good. The writing is good. You know what? I don't know what happened.

Just like on any rock tour I've ever been on, there were drugs. If you didn't have a little vial of coke you could forget about getting into parties. It was 'Hello, my name is Phil and I've got cocaine.' 'Oh! Come on in, Phil!'

Drugs did Divinyls no favours. I remember JJ hangin' out with the drummer from the Cult, a crazy guy. There'd be a lot of biker guys and they'd go off with them and I'd still be trying to find JJ the next day.

Rick Grossman was a force for good, and Bjarne and JJ were nice guys. Vince wasn't around and every day there'd be miles of email messages from him all over the floor. There was something very bad going down in his life. And with all the arguing between Chrissy and Mark, it wasn't really a *joyful* tour.

Vince, Suzi and Troy's tragedy, fighting, drugs and mishaps, Vince's crazed emails. That's what I remember most about being on the road with the Cult.

Vince was beside himself and often made no sense, but he succeeded in making one thing clear. He was thinking of quitting as our manager to be with Suzi and Troy. He said that caring for them through their terrible disease would be a full-time job. As much as it hurt me to read Vince's messages, I couldn't pull myself away as they spewed from the machine onto the floor. Mark said, 'Get away from them! You're going nuts!'

There were many things said in that insane, two-month-long flurry of emails, but all that really counted was when Vince told Mark and me that he was leaving the band, effective immediately. He had advised a dismayed Chrysalis and Mike Chapman, who had agreed to produce our next album for Chrysalis after the label had classified *What A Life!*, for all its Australian success, a failure.

Vince was recommending that Mark Pope and Richard McDonald, two former Dirty Pool managers who had broken away and had been managing Jimmy Barnes, take over the management reins. They would succeed Barry Fey and Chuck Morris.

He was also asking to be paid $120 000 that he insisted he was owed in unpaid commission. Mark, Rick and I freaked. We were not equipped to handle this. Vince was our brother, and we'd all been through so much together. We had fought with him and made his life miserable, but we loved him for himself and what he had done for us. Now his life had been torn apart, Suzi and Troy were dying, he was leaving us and, because he now needed to pay for their escalating medical bills, he was demanding money that we simply didn't have, money that, as far as I was concerned, we'd never had because it was to be repaid to Chrysalis. It was tour support money. We were broke, we owned no homes, no cars. Everything we made above our living expenses was owed to Chrysalis. We wept for Vince, but we were also terrified about what was going to happen to us. He was angry and we were angry.

Soon after, I sent Vince a cheque for $5000—all I could lay my hands on—but the damage to our relationship, personal and professional, was done.

Vince maintains he came to our rented house in Los Angeles (in, ironically, Highport Street) to tell us he was leaving the band, but I have no recollection of this. One of us has got it wrong. I know that Chuck Morris from our American management, concerned by my drinking, sent a lady round to see me and I started going to a twelve-step program. I was in and out of it, I wasn't committed. There was that, and a lot of fear and confusion and maybe I shut down. I did not know how to cope at that point. I felt very alone.

Throughout that crazy tour and the drama with Vince, Mark and I fought bitterly. It had started with the Aerosmith tour incident—after that he was particularly fragile and needy—but he confined his vulnerability to when he and I were behind closed doors. In public Mark kept up his bad-boy façade. In a Texas airport waiting for a light plane to take us to our next gig we were both exhausted and pissed off with each other and the world. Mark said to me, in a loud, cross voice, 'I'm going to the shop. Whadya want to eat?'

I said, 'Doesn't matter. Something nice.'

He went off and returned with a beautiful sandwich with chips and a carton of flavoured milk for himself and a small, bruised, sad-looking apple for me. 'Here y'are,' he snapped and shoved the apple at me. Everyone was watching his little power play. I took the apple and threw it at him, hitting him in the groin. He yelped and picked the apple up and hurled it right back at me. It missed and hit a bystander. Then Mark tossed his carton of milk all over me. I was drenched in it. Denise hustled me off to the bathroom to wash it off, but it was a hot day and I reeked of rancid milk the whole flight.

During a hiatus in the Cult tour, with all the anxiety that was happening back home with Vince, Phil Kaufman decided we needed cheering up and drove the guys in our band; Rocket, our sound guy; Denise and myself to the Rosarito Beach Hotel just over the Mexican border. It was a faded relic of glamorous days gone, where Marilyn Monroe and the other starlets of the era played in the 1950s.

Weeds grew around the once beautiful mosaic swimming pool and bad renovations had marred its gorgeous interiors. Denise freaked out as soon as she got there and was convinced the place was haunted. We all sat at the bar, knocking back tequila shots and trying to drown our sorrows. While we were getting fired up, some guy with a gun came up and threatened to shoot me. I told him to go right ahead. At that point I didn't care. I wanted to die.

On the same trip, we bought a whole bunch of firecrackers and sat on the beach and let them off as we all got more and more smashed. Denise wouldn't sleep in her room because she was terrified of the ghosts and bunked in with me. Rocket disappeared with a couple of older women with brassy hair piled high. As we waited for him outside the hotel the next morning, we watched him walk like a cowboy in a spaghetti western, staggering up the middle of the dirt street toward us. His once white clothes were coated in mud and vomit. What became of the women he wouldn't or couldn't say.

It was far harder being on the road in a foreign country than at home, where everyone knew us and our songs. Apart from our single 'Pleasure And Pain', American fans were unfamiliar with our music. Often their lack of response made me think they hated me, so I bit back by being even more obnoxious than usual.

We did a gig in Houston, Texas, and the audience was totally into itself. They didn't dance, cheer or yell. They just stood silent and still with preoccupied expressions. It was as if they didn't even notice that we and the Cult were playing for them up on the stage. It was kind of other-worldly and I'd never seen anything like it. That's because I'd never played for an audience stewed to the gills on ecstasy. We had never heard of this new drug. Then, all of a sudden, it was everywhere. Of course, soon enough, the road crew got a stash of pills for us. I didn't indulge because I had a radio interview to do early the next morning, and Mark didn't either. Everybody else did. Both bands, the road crews and all the hangers-on.

At 7 a.m. I was sitting in the foyer waiting for Denise Fraser to drive me to the radio station. All around me were people in an ecstasy trance. Denise finally arrived in the lobby and she was *wasted*. She sat beside me and slumped against my shoulder. 'Denise,' I said, 'you're supposed to be looking after me and I'm the one looking after you.' Denise wasn't driving *anywhere*, so I made my own way to the radio station.

Denise was a champion. A dear friend and, except for that one time, a terrific support for me. It helped that she was a woman, and we went out shopping and doing girlie things, away from all the men. She was tough, smart and very practical. And, the great thing, she loved Divinyls.

Denise Fraser

The Cult tour sticks in everyone's mind. Insane, hysterical. It was so *Spinal Tap*. Everyone was fighting. Divinyls with the Cult, especially over who was going to go on last at their Los Angeles gig when all the Chrysalis heavies were there. The arguments . . . Chrissy with Bjarne. Mark with Rick. Chrissy with Mark, always Chrissy with Mark. I was a bit surprised by the intensity because I'd seen them together at their home and it was ordered and there was a lot of love. I still have no idea what their relationship was about.

Back in my Dirty Pool days, before Vince took me into the organisation as his personal assistant, Chrissy had sniffed around me, checking me out. She must have decided I could be trusted because she gave me the job of looking after her axolotls and canary when she went on tour. I'd been away a couple of times to America with the band, but I really had my work cut out for me on the Cult tour, because I was doing a lot of Vince's work.

They had a punishing schedule. Vince sensed that with all those men around, Chrissy needed a female friend to go shopping for clothes, cosmetics and props, or for a drink, or just a coffee. I think she valued my input. We shared ideas about women in music. Still, Chrissy worked hard at maintaining her privacy and her take-no-crap-from-anyone image, and ours was not the kind of relationship where I could sit her down and say, 'Why are you upset? Having a lovers' tiff? Are your emotional needs being met?'

Just because we'd bonded didn't mean she was easy on me. I was terrified of going backstage after a gig if things hadn't gone well. I'd shudder, thinking, 'What am I going to be facing tonight?' Chrissy would come up to me and pump me with questions: 'What was the show like? What got screwed up in "Siren"? Was the sound right? The lights?' If I didn't have the right answer—or, at least, the answer she wanted— she could be so . . . She'd suss me out and if she thought I was lying she would be so angry. When I told the truth, and she disagreed, she would sulk for days. I tried not to be there sometimes.

The guys learned from the word go not to mess with Denise. They treated her with respect. She and I were the exceptions. Females generally were considered fair game, especially by our lot. Promotions girls, record company girls, caterers, back-up singers and wardrobe girls, all they had to do was enter our little den and the blokes would draw straws to see who made the first move. In the vast majority of cases, they scored.

In Boston we were playing in a theatre and after dropping our gear off in the dressing-room we went to have a snack. While we were gone someone stole our carry bags, despite security guys being posted everywhere. This was not good, but what made it worse was they contained our supply of coke.

With some qualms, we told security we'd been ripped off. They searched the premises and found nothing, then, when we were performing, one of the guards noticed a man in the audience with a cache of bags stashed under his seat. We were in luck, for our thief happened to be one of the three or four dumbest people alive. He'd stolen our things, then hung around to watch the show. Duh! The security staff pounced. Our bags, and dope, were returned to us. Then before they called the police they searched the crook and found a packet of pot in his pocket. 'Oh,' one of us said, 'and that's ours too.' So this idiot was busted *and* lost his dope in one fell swoop.

For all our problems, our gigs were a hot ticket. Celebrities found it cool to come and see us play. Olivia Newton-John was in the crowd at one of our Los Angeles gigs. I saw her leave halfway through the show. I met her some time later and all she could think of to ask me was whether I had any children. David Byrne and Talking Heads had a real thing about us. Grace Slick from Jefferson Airplane rolled up one night; I met her afterwards and she was very quiet. Bruce Springsteen went on the record saying we were one of his favourite bands, and years after at the Sunset Marquis his sweet wife and E Street Band member Patty Scialfa told me she and Bruce had played our music on their honeymoon. Ted Nugent turned up wearing two guns on his hips and a sheriff's badge. Stevie Nicks was tiny in high heels. Rick, a Rolling Stones fan like me, came upon Bill Wyman in a bar and summoned up the courage to approach him. 'Bill,' he stammered, 'you're an absolute hero to me. But what do I say to someone like you?' Bill smiled and replied, 'Hello would be a good start.'

Elton John was a VIP guest at our gigs at the Roxy nightclub in New York. He eyed me and asked me to go for a ride with him in his Rolls-Royce. I wasn't very happy with how I'd performed that night and was feeling a bit antsy so I turned him down—not that anything untoward would have happened!

In early May 1986, we returned to Australia to meet our new managers, Mark Pope and Richard McDonald, and to endure a disastrous experience that my life, as mad as it had been, could never have prepared me for.

GUILLOTINE DAYS

Back in Australia, Vince made my life, and Mark's, a misery. Few of us, thankfully, get the chance to learn how we would behave in the face of overwhelming tragedy such as that which Vince was suffering, but I could understand his plight had driven him over the edge. Not that this knowledge made his behaviour easier to bear.

Vince waged war in the media. He wrote a vicious article about me in the June 1987 issue of *Australian Penthouse* magazine, under the heading 'Wild Child'. It branded me as a fake who lied about my background and fabricated my rock'n'roll cred. He claimed, quite erroneously, that a past lover had 'blown his brains out'. He also brutally revealed that I had an abortion the day after we filmed the 'Pleasure And Pain' video. That alone was a devastating act that betrayed our friendship and the intimate details of our lives that we had both shared. I know he blamed me for things he himself had been a party to. In another article he wrote, 'Together, Amphlett and McEntee are a whole person, apart they're not. I see them both as completely ruthless and very selfish, with no regard for anyone but themselves. When I left, I compared myself to running a boarding school for brats, and it was those two I was talking about. I still feel that Mark McEntee is a really nasty piece of goods, a man with no friends... Their day hasn't come yet but it had better come soon because I think they're running out of time, running out of friends, and running out of steam. There are bodies strewn everywhere.'

For once, in the face of these scathing attacks, I didn't fight back. I kept my silence. Engaging Vince in a slanging match would have played into his hands. He was spoiling for a high-profile battle.

Nor had Vince forgotten about the $120 000 he said we owed him. The $5000 dollars I had sent was not going to placate him. He hired the most aggressive lawyer he could find and came after us hard.

Vince Lovegrove

I did things I'm not proud of. I was grieving but I give no excuses, only apologies for hurting others as a result of my grief. It all felt the right and fair thing to do at the time as I lashed out. Why should I be the only person going through agony? I was desperate. I feared for my loved ones.

My lawyer, Warren 'Mad Dog' Morgan, wrote to Chrissy and Mark stating my claim to the money. They maintained they didn't owe me a cent and in fact I owed *them* money. So Mad Dog said, 'See you in court.'

Next job was to serve Mark and Chrissy with a subpoena. I couldn't afford to pay a summons-server so, in between setting up a support network for Suzi and Troy and attending to their daily blood tests and other medical necessities, I had to serve the summons on Chrissy and Mark myself.

One night Suzi, sick as she was, and I went out to serve the summons together. Driving down the street in Balgowlah, north of the Harbour, where they were living in Mark's mother's house, we saw Chrissy and Mark climb over a fence and get into Mark's car, an old funeral flower vehicle. We roared up beside them. Mark floored the accelerator and tore off with Suzi and me in hot pursuit. There followed a Keystone Kops chase through the streets of Balgowlah, down the

Bradfield Highway and across the Harbour Bridge. It was deadly serious, but we were laughing so hard at our mad adventure that tears were coursing down our cheeks. We had both begun to accept our fate. Suzi's and Troy's impending deaths, my survival. Our perspective on life began to run a little loopy, a little perverse, a little black. At one point, Suzi remarked, 'How ironic! Two people in a funeral car being pursued by someone who'll soon be in a hearse!' Both cars ran red lights. Mark would wait until the last possible second to make a turn, hoping we'd shoot ahead the wrong way, but somehow I stayed with him. Eventually he had to stop at a red light. I screamed to a halt behind him, then Suzi leapt out of the passenger seat and slapped the subpoena under Mark's windscreen-wiper.

Chrissy and Mark declared that they would fight the case. By then I had too much to worry about and no money at all to pursue the court case, nor the time to prepare evidence. I gave up. Divinyls' managers Richard McDonald and Mark Pope were refusing to send me the accounts or even to communicate with me. Suzi and Troy needed all my love and care, and Suzi had decided she wanted to make a documentary film about our battle with her disease which had progressed to full-blown AIDS. We hoped *Suzi's Story*, which was screened in Australia and all over the world, would raise awareness of AIDS.

I remember the day Vince and Suzi chased us. Mark and I were living in Mark's mother's boarding house. It was large and it must have appeared to people that we were living in a mansion, but she was renting the rooms and we were living in one of them. Vince may have thought we had plenty of money, which wasn't true. Mark was driving a 1959 funeral flower car. As we were preparing to go to a gig we heard a commotion. We looked down the street and saw Vince and Suzi yelling up at our window. It was the saddest thing, and I thought it was especially sad that Vince would have Suzi there in her condition. Mark and I left the house the back way and climbed over the fence to avoid them. I didn't know they were serving a summons. I thought that in typical Vince-style he wanted a confrontation. We jumped into Mark's car. We had to get to the gig and we were late. They saw us pull out and drive down the street and gave chase. Vince rammed our car from behind. I looked at them and they were laughing. It was mad and it was so, so sad.

When we came to a stop, Suzi ran up to my window and was crazed and threatening to bite me. By then I wouldn't have cared if she had.

Eventually we got to the gig. Everyone was waiting for us. The place was packed. Management was freaking out, wanting to know where we'd been. From that point, because of all the shows that had been booked, we had to have protection. Mark Pope's brother was in the police Tactical Response Group and organised some guys in the squad to look out for us when they were off-duty. It is not my nature to hide behind anyone, but the show had to go on.

I was terrified of Vince. Like me, I suppose, there was a dark side to all that drive and passion which manifested itself in a capacity for violence. He'd had a physical fight with the Chrysalis marketing man in New York and a pub brawl, and when he lost his temper he was not a pretty sight. When he was trying to serve that subpoena on us, he was like an avenging angel. There was nothing funny about that car chase, and there was nothing funny about Suzi, my old friend, threatening to bite me. It was a tragic and undignified incident for all concerned.

I know Vince thinks Mark and I were uncaring towards him. In fact, my heart was broken, but I wasn't equipped to deal with the tragedy of Suzi and Troy. I felt helpless. Mark was sad for Vince too, but, again, didn't have a clue how to express his feelings. When Suzi died on 14 June 1987, we sent Vince a card:

'Dear Vince, We thank you for showing us *Suzi's Story* and presenting Suzi with the dignity she possessed and deserved. She was the bravest girl that we have had the privilege to know. We send our deepest sympathies to you, Troy and Holly [Vince's daughter] and share your hopes for the future. Sincerely, Mark and Christine.'

We meant what we said, but I know it was too little, too late. Six years later Troy died. He was nearly eight.

Throughout all this horror, I was an emotional wreck, and drinking more heavily than ever. I was unable to deal with the situation. I was up against a person I thought was crazy. I felt guilty that I'd hurt Vince, but I didn't know what I was responsible for and what I wasn't. In all of that madness my boundaries were blurred and I thought I was responsible for everything and nothing. And Suzi, whom I wasn't allowed to see, was dying, and Troy was dying too. And Vince, who had been my friend, mentor and muse, now hated me. I had nobody to confide in. Mark was no use in situations like this. He wasn't a bad person, but he was not a strong person, and he too was bearing the brunt of Vince's fury.

Vince Lovegrove

After Suzi's and Troy's deaths, life took on a new perspective. Nothing in this life is as bad as losing a wife and a child, but, in a way, surviving it made me a better person. After living and working in England for twelve years, I'm now packing my bags to return to Australia with my beautiful partner Julie to start a new phase of my life. For a year or two after the bust-up I wrote off the whole Divinyls episode as an exercise in the worst kind of bad karma, but then I realised it meant little in the larger scheme of things.

It is surprising how when things are really bad, you can keep going. I learnt during this time that if you can get through the hard times— eventually you start to be able to move ahead again. I kept my focus on the band, on music, and hoped for better things. In 1988 I came into a little money by way of a publishing advance from Chrysalis. They wanted new songs and they wanted them fast, so they forwarded me $60 000. I had never owned property and now, finding myself in the rare position of having some cash, I took the plunge. I put the $60 000 down as a deposit and took out a mortgage on a two-storey, four-bedroom house in Pine Street, Manly. Then, right on cue, interest rates soared to 19.5 per cent and I couldn't afford the repayments. Mark and I weren't living together, he would just visit and spend the night, so I moved all my belongings into one room, put a lock on the door, and rented out the rest of the bedrooms and the living room to boarders. I could now add the occupation 'landlady' to my curriculum vitae. Mark's mother, Irene, who was a landlady herself, taught me the ropes, and even collected the rent for me when I was away on tour.

There I was, a famous rock star, renting out rooms. There were up to eight tenants in my house at any time. One was named James Bond. True. He was always falling asleep on the couch with a lit cigarette and more than once he nearly burned the whole place down. A pair of Scandinavian bicycle racers enjoyed waxing their legs in my kitchen. And I was always springing tenants cooking in their rooms. When I'd catch them I'd bang on their door and tell them off like a landlady in a Tennessee Williams play. I was reading a lot of Tennessee Williams then. It was no fun coming home wasted after a gig and finding a sink full of filthy dishes. No one ever washed up but me. Once when I was away on tour, junkies broke into my room and stole my collection of Johnny Cash records, as well as anything else they could carry away.

It was a relief when we went to Los Angeles in October 1986 to rehearse the album that would become *Temperamental*. We went without Bjarne Ohlin. Five years down the line, we'd finally come to a parting of the ways. And then we lost JJ Harris. Early on in rehearsals, it was evident that producer Mike Chapman was unhappy with our young drummer.

Richard Harvey

I was at home in Sydney and the phone rang. It was JJ. He said things weren't working out in the studio. I realised he was crying. He said, 'Harve, how do I play *feel*? They've told me I have to groove and swing a bit more, what do I do?' Well, it's instinctive. If you ain't got it, you ain't got it. You can't tell someone how to swing. All I could suggest was that he go out and buy some Frank Sinatra records and listen to how Frank's band played. What happened to JJ was similar to what happened in the Beatles. Their first drummer, Pete Best, just couldn't cut it in the studio so their producer George Martin replaced him with Ringo.

JJ was a tremendous live drummer, but Mike Chapman thought he wasn't good enough in the studio and we had to let him go. He was young and didn't have much studio experience. It was a tough thing to do to the kid. Of course, I got the blame.

We auditioned a number of replacement drummers. We set up a kit in the studio and drumming hopefuls arrived at designated times. There were some likely candidates, including Dallas Taylor and Clem Burke, the drummer from Blondie. There were also some unlikely candidates, including a cocksure young dude who airily refused to use our drum kit, saying that he not only had his own kit outside in his van, but his own personal roadie to lug it around for him. While the roadie was setting up his drums, this wannabe excused himself, explaining that he had to change. He returned wearing a parody of a drummer's outfit, and he was deadly serious about it. Tight T-shirt and pants, high boots, head- and wristbands. Doing our best not to laugh in his face, we asked him what he would like to play. 'Only Lonely', he declared, then as Rick played the guitar parts this poor guy laid into his drum kit. He was abysmal. No, he was worse than abysmal. He was hopeless.

In the end, the job went to American Tommy Cain. Tommy was very good-looking but really stiff, and I couldn't stand him, but I was so beaten down I shrugged and said, 'Whatever.' Our new manager, Richard McDonald, wanted him because he looked good.

In late December, the first Australian Made gig was held in Hobart, and the shows continued through January 1987, in Adelaide, Melbourne, Perth, Brisbane and Sydney. Taking part in the huge and now legendary celebration of Australian rock were the top bands in the land. Our line-up for the series of monster open-air gigs was me, Mark, Rick, Tommy Cain, a truly gorgeous American keyboardist named Kenny Lyon and another American, a guitarist named Frank Infante.

Frank, who was with us briefly after he'd been fired by Blondie, was another good-looking guy, but he struck me as narcissistic and paranoid, deeply suspicious about the most innocuous things. He was a good guitarist... until he drank. When he did he lost all sense of being a member of a group and tried to hog the limelight, which would throw our act off-kilter and I would have to dress him down. Frank wore black and would stand and stare at himself in the mirror when he thought no one was looking. To bring him down to earth I made a point of jumping on his back in the middle of a song. Mark revered Frank, and I noticed that he took on his character and mannerisms. My diary entry for 28 January that year reads: 'Mark is intimidated by Frank. Frank is not playing. Destructive. Kenny is a good musician but is too scatty to lead. Rick doesn't know where to begin. I'm just getting frustrated.'

All the Australian Made bands flew around the country together in the same plane. We all got on surprisingly well. It was good to catch up with an old mate in Michael Hutchence, who was a sweet man who said in one interview that he wanted me to have his baby. We had many deep and meaningfuls. INXS's drummer Jon Farriss was a show-off and was always twirling his drumsticks on the plane trips and I felt embarrassed that our drummer, Tommy Cain, couldn't. He would try—but then drop them in the aisle.

Tommy may not have been able to twirl his sticks, but he could pull girls. One tactic was to write his phone number on his tom-tom head in big numerals so when the overhead cameras at the gigs focused on him anyone of a mind in the audience could jot it down and call him.

Of the topline acts, Mental As Anything went on first, followed by I'm Talking, the Triffids, the Saints, Divinyls, the Models, Jimmy Barnes and INXS. We tried our hearts out, and the crowd response gave me goosebumps. *RAM* magazine reported of the Perth show: 'Divinyls crack "Science Fiction" for starters. A saucy flash of knickers from Miss Amphlett, a few impressive high kicks and the minx with the boofy red hair has the audience in suspenders. A performer to her toecaps, she swings a giant prop tomahawk at amps and fellow musicians, and has the roadies scuttling to right the mic stand that she is forever knocking down, as if to taunt them.'

While there was unusual camaraderie among the musicians, it was fun to see all the different bands' managers, not least Mark Pope, Richard McDonald and INXS's Chris Murphy, who were the brains behind Australian Made, squabbling about who was going on first and last, the sound and light gear and the filming of a documentary.

Around this time Rick's heroin addiction was worsening. He had always been so handsome, but now the smack had made him look pale and wasted. He was suffering frequent asthma attacks. He could not string two words together and his teeth were furry and green. He had always been so professional, but now he had no energy, and, as I've mentioned, fell asleep in meetings and rehearsals. God knows how much money he was spending on heroin. Sometimes he looked as though he'd been beaten up, and he told me later that he had been bashed when he went out scrounging for his smack. At Australian Made, I saw Rick walk out of a Portaloo where he'd been shooting up and fall flat on his face, unconscious, as everyone looked on.

Rick's last gig for us was in Mooloolaba, Queensland, on 8 February 1987. When Rick told us he had to leave the band Mark and I were angry, then we understood. Mark sobbed bitterly in front of him, sobbed and sobbed.

After his last gig Rick checked himself into a rehab clinic in Bangalow, northern New South Wales.

Losing Rick broke my heart.

Rick Grossman

I was in a ward at the clinic, feeling like death, and the TV was on. Suddenly there on the screen was an old Divinyls video, and I was in it. Another patient looked at the TV, looked at me, saw my eyes glistening with tears and said, 'Nooo . . .' My self-pity was compounded

by the fact that while I was in rehab, the band returned to America to
record *Temperamental* in Los Angeles . . . I felt so alone.

When we returned to LA to record *Temperamental,* Divinyls bore little
resemblance to the starry-eyed bunch who'd recorded *Desperate* in
New York in 1983. Only Mark and I remained. Machinations'
drummer Warren McLean had replaced Tommy Cain, Kenny Lyon
was on keyboards, and Tim Millikan from Australian rock band
Tootieville was Rick's replacement on bass. Mark and I moved into
an apartment in West Hollywood. Sadly, adversity hadn't drawn us
closer together. Arguing was our natural condition. We went to see
Concrete Blonde, a band I loved, and later went out with my girlfriends
in the Go-Go's. All I remember is drinking too much, swallowing a
handful of pills and Mark punching me in the face and chasing me
around the block.

Our first attempt at recording *Temperamental,* at Rumbo studios,
was short-lived. Neil Diamond was cutting an album in the next room
and complained about our noise. We got the boot and relocated to
Sunset Sound, not far away. Sunset was a legendary recording studio
where Los Lobos, Tom Waits and Bonnie Raitt had cut albums. On
my way to the loo I found my path blocked by the hulking figure of
Brian Wilson. I said, 'Excuse me.' And one of rock's true geniuses just
stood there with a vacant expression, like he'd been lobotomised. I
said again, 'Excuse me.' Still no reaction. I had to climb under his legs
to go to the toilet.

Released in mid-1988, *Temperamental* was Divinyls' first album
without the old tried and true line-up, and Chrysalis had made it
clear that it was our make-or-break record. Top 10 in Australia would
be welcomed, but if *Temperamental* did only moderately well in
America, as *Desperate* and *What A Life!* had fared, we'd be skating
on very thin ice with the label, which in the years since 1983 had
become a lot more hard-headed, corporate and less artist-friendly.
They were still coming to terms with Vince's departure.

Temperamental contains some of Divinyls' best songs, written by Mark and me throughout the emotional maelstrom of the exits of Vince, Bjarne, Rick and JJ. Who says good can't come from bad? The title song, 'Back To The Wall', 'Hey Little Boy' and 'Punxsie' (a song about a coat I owned) became staples of our gigs and, with 'Pleasure And Pain', 'Boys In Town', 'Only Lonely', 'Science Fiction' and 'Casual Encounter', still turn up on lists of Australia's top songs. 'Better Days' remains a favourite of mine, a strong and optimistic song. But, to me, 'Back To The Wall' nailed those dangerous days best. It sketched our feverish angst and whispered of things to come:

> We are living in desperate times
> These are desperate times my dear
> There's no way out of here
> There's no way out my dear
> I've been holding back all my tears
> Just so the pressure don't show
> Like a time bomb ticking away
> I might blow up some day

Chrysalis in Australia spared no expense hyping *Temperamental*. The country's top music writers were invited to a sumptuous launch—a meal in a restaurant, then a gig at the Roundhouse in Sydney's east and a party later. There were newspaper and magazine reports of me drinking too much cheap white wine and 'unleashing a torrent of abuse' at some hapless woman who'd once forgotten to organise for my name to be on the door at some concert. Mark was seen by one reporter playing air guitar 'like a ghost convulsed in electric shock'.

That night there was much made of my decision to finally discard my trademark school uniform in favour of a leather dress, shirt and a black feather boa. Getting rid of the tunic after all those years was a no-brainer. I was older, we were a new band, with a new record and under new management. The first incarnation of Divinyls was over, and we were moving on, for better or worse.

RAM's Phil Stafford was at the launch gig: 'As always, McEntee surveys stage right from behind his fringe, slashing and caressing his lump of wood with equally self-absorbed intensity. But it's *her* they're all looking at: the band watch her for secret cues, the front rows simply gawp or mouth the words ... the males pump the air, eyes locked on the object of their fear/fantasies/infatuation. The females simply wonder just how this screaming/whooping/crooning harridan could ever share their sex, much less why their boyfriends are so fascinated by her every move ... a lascivious smile [curves] around that characteristic pout. She rubs her crotch offhandedly, crouches cat-like on the drum riser, splaying her legs for theatrical effect. Not so much a come-on as coy confrontation, it's the actress in her, played more for graphic realism than cheap titillation.'

Later, Stafford cornered me at the after-party. He asked me about my new look and songs. My reply gives a glimpse of me in post-gig manic euphoria mode. 'It's much more direct, truer, I've been in jail a long time, often felt like I couldn't walk out that door, so now I feel I'm out of jail. I really feel it's better days—I feel ... fuck it, I'm just me and I don't fucking care what anyone else fucking thinks. And it feels really scary; sometimes it feels like I've lost my guidelines, but still I feel a lot happier. It's harder, it's so much harder now, 'cos we have so much more to do, so many more decisions ... I feel responsible. Finally I can say, "Right, the buck stops with me." But the strange thing is I'm no more together than I used to be. I'm probably less together. I'm more crazy, more bad-tempered, more grumpy ... I was grumpy before but I'm more so now. It's like ... I try to be good, I try to be nice to people, but some days, when you're dealing with as many people as I am, I'm not. Everybody's a shit some days. I have my shit days. Don't you?'

Reviews of *Temperamental* were positive. Singled out were the strength of our material, Mark's playing and my 'lecherous' singing. With its more ragged, rougher sound, many saw the record as an improvement on *What A Life!* American *Rolling Stone*, however, begged to differ. Their reviewer called Mike Chapman's production 'a wall of smudge, compromising the ultimate punch of Mark McEntee's guitar work and Chrissy Amphlett's wild child chants... like all four Shangri-Las rolled into one—with a snatch of pre-exorcised Linda Blair.'

On the back of months of full-on national touring, *Temperamental* scorched up the Australian charts, and in July we were back in the United States showcasing the album. Under new management of Nick Wexler and Danny Heaps, who handled Public Image Limited and Robbie Robertson, we returned to our old stamping ground, the Ritz in New York City, where *Billboard* magazine's Jim Bessman caught our show. 'Amphlett proved once again that she may be the hardest, harshest female singer in rock, even resorting to tearing her hair out or painting her face red with lipstick while singing... she has exchanged her school uniform for a clinging black dress.'

Back in Australia for more *Temperamental* gigs, we changed managers once more. While we were playing at Selinas at the Coogee Bay Hotel I was contacted by the venue's booker, Andrew McManus, who hinted he'd be interested in managing us, despite his lack of experience. Mark and I had not been happy with Mark Pope and Richard McDonald—we were at loggerheads. I can't remember what about, nor the rights and wrongs, except that it was a dispute about money. So we gave Andrew a hearing.

Andrew McManus

I came to Sydney from the Gold Coast on a rugby scholarship, played on the northern beaches, and then at twenty-one I took a job managing the Rose Bay Hotel in the eastern suburbs. When I started, that pub was making $23 000 a week and after a year it was raking in 57 grand. What helped our bottom line was the off-course betting and after-hours card games I organised and the then-illegal poker machines I'd set up out the back. When we got wind of a police raid, my mate, a butcher, would hide the pokies in his freezer. From there I managed a pub in Mudgee then got the call to work at the Coogee Bay Hotel.

I first hooked up with Divinyls when I was booking at Selinas. I was an employee of the Coogee Bay but also had a share in the financial success of the nightclub. I hired Divinyls through their manager Richard McDonald. We had them for two nights and sold out both times. I became very interested.

After the first of the two gigs, Richard approached me and asked if he could get some cash for the band.' I didn't have a problem with that. It was all cool. I was organising the cash when the phone rang.

'You don't know me, I'm Chrissy Amphlett.'

'I saw you on stage last night,' I said, 'I know you very well.' In fact I was flabbergasted by her. I haven't seen Chrissy perform since 1994 but then, and prior, she was far and away one of the world's best. She owned the stage. Whether there were 50 people in the audience or 50 000 she could captivate them and have them eating out of the palm of her hand, watching her every movement. She was like a cat onstage. You didn't know what she was going to do. Crowds love that, and that night at Selinas the people had gone crazy for her.

Chrissy continued, 'We've got a problem with our manager at the moment. I don't want to go to the length of saying that I won't go on stage tonight if you give him that money, but I don't want you to do it.'

Richard turned up wanting the money. I told him, 'No.' He carried on a little bit and I stood my ground.

At the end of the second show, I met Chrissy and Mark McEntee for a drink and said, 'What's the deal with your management?'

'We're just cheesed off,' Chrissy explained. 'All the dramas. We've had management issues for years now. The band's been out on the road for so long and we've never really made any money.'

We agreed to meet again a week later at the Bellevue Hotel in Paddington, which was then owned by Ray Stehr, a racing friend of mine. There was a small private room out the back where we could talk. Chrissy and Mark listed all their problems, including how they thought they'd never be able to pay off their Chrysalis advance and it had become a millstone around their necks, and told me again how they were broke. I said, 'Make me your manager and I'll show you how to bank $20–30 000 a week.'

Chrissy said, 'If you could do that we'd be over the moon. We'll cut ties with Richard and Mark.' ,

I set to work planning their next gig, in Jindabyne in the snow country. I cut and shredded the road crew. I organised budget accommodation. Chrissy and Mark could have their own room and everyone else would share. We worked out promotional tactics to pack the venue. All of a sudden Divinyls were a professional outfit. After four nights at Jindabyne we were rolling in cash. We'd made the money I said we would.

I can remember one morning being down in the kitchen of our hotel with Roger Mason, who was the keyboard player of the band then, making breakfast for all the guests after we'd all been up all night celebrating.

Next, I booked more tours and started thinking of ways to get Divinyls away from Chrysalis. I enlisted the support of John Anderson at EMI Publishing and a lawyer named Peter Thompson, who had advised Chrissy and Mark when Vince was trying to get them to pay him the $120 000.

I had never managed a band before. It was a great learning curve. Today I'm one of Australia's leading promoters with multi-million dollar homes in Toorak and on the Gold Coast, a number of luxury cars and such clients as KISS, Andrea Bocelli, Jethro Tull, Motorhead, Mötley Crüe, Fleetwood Mac and Deep Purple. And everything I've learned I put down to my apprenticeship with Divinyls. In spite of what happened down the track I'll always have a place in my heart for Chrissy and Mark.

Even at the age of twenty-six, Andrew was larger than life. A big, bluff man, he affected waistcoats and gloves, lots of flashy rings, and he carried Benetton luggage. He had thick skin when he was being taken to task by someone he liked and respected, such as me, but if an outsider tried to take advantage of him, or us, he loved a fight. He was a lot of fun. He had a wicked sense of humour and tried hard to please. Mostly he succeeded. Taking him on as manager wasn't a tough decision. He was a lovable rogue. He could have been the beefier Antipodean cousin of Arthur Daley, the shady wheeler and dealer played by George Cole in the old English TV series *Minder*. He was always cutting corners and doing deals. Even today, established promoters will tell me how he tricked them. Andrew loved drama, he was physically very brave, as the numerous altercations he got into while rescuing me attest, and he was never, ever boring. He was a generous soul, too. I can still hear his wheezy laugh. His friends were 'colourful identities'. When he'd take us to their homes in Sydney's eastern suburbs they'd have huge televisions and the races would always be on and bets being laid.

No matter what dramas were playing out, about money, managers, bandmembers or with Mark's and my tumultuous love affair, I was still the girl from Geelong living my dream, and another unexpected chapter in my stage life was about to unfold.

Right then I received a phone call that broadened my performing horizons and led to an opportunity a decade later that may have saved my life.

14 TASTING BLOOD

Starring in a stage musical was the last thing on my mind when I took a call from Australia-based producer Wilton Morley, son of the late English actor Robert Morley. He said he was a Divinyls fan and asked if I was interested in starring in the Australian production of *Blood Brothers*, a powerful attack on the British class system.

I was surprised and flattered and asked Wilton to tell me more. He wanted me to play Mrs Johnstone, an impoverished and abandoned single mother of eight kids, 'so cruel with a stone in place of her heart'. She gives birth to twins, Mickey and Eddie, but is forced to adopt Eddie out because she cannot afford to keep him. Eddie grows up in a privileged family while Mickey is raised in poverty by his mother. The boys meet again as men, neither realising he is related to the other. They have become products of their environment. Eddie is a successful businessman, Mickey a criminal. Trouble flares and they shoot each other, leaving Mrs Johnstone to mourn the tragedy of the two brothers.

Written by Willy Russell, who had penned the play and film

Educating Rita, Blood Brothers was a hit in London's West End. My sons would be played by the fine young singer and actor Peter Cousens and a raw and little-known actor named Russell Crowe.

My first instinct was to say no and stick with what I knew. With all the personnel changes, the band was in a state of flux and at that time we were still getting to know our new manager, Andrew McManus. Besides, was I up to it? I hadn't done a musical since *Oklahoma!* at the Geelong Musical Comedy Company (I refuse to count *Let My People Come!*). I also had qualms about performing someone else's music after singing my own for so long.

Wilton took my reservations onboard but insisted he really wanted me. He told me that such stars as Carole King, Petula Clark and Kiki Dee had all played Mrs Johnstone and if they could do it, so could I. And he would fly me first class to England to meet Willy Russell and the man who would be directing *Blood Brothers*, Danny Hiller, an experienced stage and television director. They would tell me more about the role and the play and see if they agreed with Wilton that I was right for this demanding part. I would be onstage virtually the entire performance, singing all the big songs and portraying the despair and pain of the beleaguered Mrs Johnstone. I made no promise to Wilton but the least I could do was go to meet Willy and Danny.

When I arrived in London I stayed at, of all places, the Piccadilly Hotel. Needless to say, it was far, far more salubrious than the bloodhouse of the same name in Sydney's Kings Cross where Divinyls had our start. Then I took a train to Leeds, in England's north, where Willy Russell and Danny Hiller were conducting playwright workshops. I knocked on the door of the address I'd been given. It was a big old house, with the headstones of dead children and the poet Sylvia Plath, who gassed herself in 1963, in and around the grounds. As I came down the driveway in my short dress and fishnet stockings the wannabe playwrights peered at me from the windows.

I was ushered into Willy Russell's bedroom, and there was the playwright drinking wine. A broken glass was on the floor. The room was in chaos. He and Danny Hiller interviewed me at length. During the grilling, they impressed upon me that Mrs Johnstone was the show's pivotal character; the success of the show depended on her. They thought I'd be ideal, but told me to think hard about whether I wanted the role. They'd be in touch. I really liked both guys, but wasn't sure I needed all this extra pressure in my life. The money would be very good, and very welcome, yet a disastrous performance could destroy my reputation. After joining Willy and Danny and the playwrights at dinner, sitting at one long table, I caught the train back to London.

Danny Hiller

> Chrissy struck me as bright and fast-thinking and when we met in Leeds it was obvious she'd studied up on *Blood Brothers* and Mrs Johnstone. She had hooked right into her character's character. She also understood the class system and the damage that Margaret Thatcher had done to the United Kingdom. After Willy and I met her we both said, 'Yeah!'

Back at the Piccadilly Hotel, the London one, I was lying on my bed all but convinced that I would turn down their offer—just too much to lose, too much responsibility—when Danny rang. 'Well, what do you think?'

'Danny, I don't want to do it.'

'I think you will,' he said with a chuckle.

'No, I definitely don't want to do *Blood Brothers*. I'm a rock singer, not an actress.'

'I think you should.'

'Danny, nothing against Willy. I just don't want to sing someone else's songs. I have my own material to sing.'

'Christina,' continued Danny, undeterred, 'do it.'

'Why *should* I?'

'I just think you should.'

How could I argue with such logic?

•

While in London I accepted a lunch invitation from Chrysalis Records. They sent a stretch Jaguar limo to pick me up and take me to the restaurant. Things went downhill from there. In our party was a female executive who was so horrible to me. She looked at me with total disdain and snapped, 'Well, who are you? Do you sing? What's the name of your band?' She was a shocker. It seemed fitting that at such a venomous lunch I came down with food poisoning. On the way back to the Piccadilly, angry and ill, I vomited in the back of the limousine, then I perversely asked the driver to stop while I got out and did some shopping on the Kings Road. I was only in London for a short time and I'd so looked forward to doing some shopping and by God I was going to do it, sick or not. I got back into the car with my packages, vomited again, then did more shopping. Making a mess of Chrysalis's Jag was the least I could do to repay them for such a miserable lunch.

The next day, still feeling bad, I went to Heathrow for a flight to New York for talks with American music honchos. My plane was delayed and because Wilton had bought me a first-class ticket I was upgraded to Concorde, which was a thrill. If I was going to feel dodgy, I can't think of a better place to suffer than on Concorde. Plane-mad Mark turned green with envy when I told him of my ride into space.

At some time on that journey I decided I had to do *Blood Brothers*. Danny Hiller's persistence had paid off. Bowing to pressure wasn't my style, but I respected Danny, a tiny man with an iron will, and, as my co-star Russell Crowe would find out, balls of steel. A true professional from whom I learned so much.

Rehearsals for the August 1988 opening of *Blood Brothers*, at Sydney's Seymour Centre, began almost immediately upon my arrival home. Danny was there to hold my hand in our rehearsal room at the Sydney Showgrounds. He introduced me to the cast, including my 'sons' Russell and Peter, and Bob Bain, who played the sinister narrator and a host of other roles.

The first thing Danny told us was, 'Don't try for a Liverpudlian accent just yet. Speak in your normal voice for now, and we'll get a voice coach closer to opening night. Concentrate on your lines, movement and understand your character.' I did as Danny said, but of course Russell couldn't resist reading his lines in a thick accent. That made me feel out of my depth. (Russell would later tell a journalist I was nervous, which I thought was unkind.) My first day of rehearsal was not a happy one as I told myself I'd made a huge mistake. I felt so inadequate. The next day was better and the one after better still.

Danny Hiller

She was an honest-to-God talent and it was a thrill working with her. It couldn't have been a breeze taking on that demanding part with no formal training, leading a cast of experienced actors. I know she was under pressure from the band not to do it. They were afraid they'd lose her to the theatre. Mark McEntee demanded to be allowed to oversee her singing. I checked with Chrissy and she told me if I didn't want him involved then I had her blessing to tell him. So I did.

Chrissy had no safety net. The musicians were strangers, the songs were unlike anything she'd sung before, she had to speak convincing Liverpudlian. This was a huge ask. Leaving rock to tread the boards was a career risk. She was a brave girl, and a professional, always at me to help her: 'Tell me how you want me to do it!' Like a sponge. Each night she was at the theatre half an hour earlier than necessary.

The first day of rehearsal it was obvious she was nervous. She sat alone up the back with a big hat obscuring her face, and said little. So I asked her to come and sit next to me as I worked with the other actors. Gradually she came to feel comfortable and began to participate. After a few days she sang her first song and the entire cast sat there with their mouths open. The power of that voice...

Early on at rehearsal I tried not to draw attention to myself. I stood at the back of the stage as I had with Divinyls before I became the schoolgirl, but as my confidence grew I moved to the front. It helped that I had *found* Mrs Johnstone. I based some of her on my Aunty

Rose, Dad's sister. Then, with some help from an accent coach who taught me to speak from the back of my throat, I managed a convincing Liverpool accent. Add dowdy clothes and hairstyle, and slumped posture to suggest the hardness and sorrow of her life, and suddenly, again having cloaked myself in costume and mask, I *was* Mrs Johnstone.

Danny had warned me there was no easy way to learn lines. It was a matter of endless repetition until you were confident enough to go off-script, then you had to react naturally to the situation and the other actors. Most of the other castmembers went out of their way to help. Peter Cousens would always tell me when I began talking too fast.

The songs, such as 'Tell Me It's Not True' and 'Marilyn Monroe' were beautiful: sweetly melodic, yet dripping with menace and a sense of doom.

Danny Hiller nurtured me. 'You'll be great, love!' he endlessly insisted until I began to believe him. He shielded me from the snobbery of some of the established actors in the cast who resented that a rock star with no formal theatrical training had landed such a major role and, what's more, was being paid more than them to play it. Too, it infuriated some that I had my own dressing-room with fridge and phone while they had shared dressing facilities. Nick Wexler, my American manager, assured me that stars always had a phone and a fridge in their dressing-room. What was a girl to do? I didn't feel bad. I knew that Wilton Morley was counting on my Divinyls fans to swell the audience each night, and if I was to pull off this performance I needed to feel comfortable.

I learned to channel my defiance at my co-stars' resentment into Mrs Johnstone who was beset by similarly mean-spirited people and an unfair social system in her sorry life. On opening night, I was quivering with nervousness. The last thing I needed was when one actor looked down his nose at me and in an upper-crust accent sneered, 'Well, this is not rock'n'roll now. How does it feel to be in the *theatre*?' but I used the outrage I felt at his snide remark in my performance.

Mrs Johnstone's jaw set more firmly and her anger at her plight bubbled. 'Thank you very much, mate,' I thought. 'I'll have that!'

It was strange performing to a quiet and still and seated audience. If I forgot my lines, missed my cue or strayed from my accent, I could hardly stage-dive to distract the crowd's attention! I was terribly nervous, and calmed my nerves before each show with a glass of white wine. (To some of my co-stars, this was another strike against me—not good. Simply not done in the theatre.)

Peter Cousens

When I heard Chrissy was to play Mrs Johnstone I was dubious. Of course I knew her as a rock star. I had no idea whether she could pull off a lead role in musical theatre. I guess I was a little suspicious of actors who were not formally trained. I had come from NIDA and was a technically correct formal actor and singer. Possibly, too, I was a bit full of myself. Chrissy, and Russell Crowe, for that matter, were instinctive actors. She was coddled by the producers, and paid ten times more than we were. She had her own dressing-room while all us other actors had to share and she made a huge fuss because she didn't have a personal phone. The producer had Telecom install one and run a line out of her room and down the passageway.

Chrissy did just fine. Her acting was assured and she sang with extraordinary soul. She channelled her life as a rock star—all the drugs and alcohol and existing on the edge—into the character of Mrs Johnstone who, with all those kids, no husband and no money, was also an outsider.

Russell and I played Chrissy's sons from children to adulthood. I found being Chrissy's 10-year-old very bizarre. I remember skipping around the stage like a little boy and Chrissy was so real as my mother that tears came to my eyes. There was a wonderful emotional connection. She was incredibly open and brave and compensated for her lack of technical acting skills with a huge heart and a quite wonderful voice. My sister was so affected, she could only come to see *Blood Brothers* once.

My total immersion in my role and singing those gorgeous Willy Russell songs got me through. The audience gave me a standing ovation on opening night. I lapped up the applause, all the while knowing that *everybody* gets a standing ovation on opening night. The real test would be in the following performances when the less-easily impressed ticket-buying crowds showed up. Happily, they enjoyed my Mrs Johnstone too, as did the reviewers, whose notices were rapturous.

Danny Hiller

Chrissy had bad butterflies on opening night. I spent some time with her in her dressing-room before the curtain went up. She said, 'How can I possibly expect the audience to like me when I don't even like myself?' She had nothing to worry about. Her portrayal of this tragic yet brave and dignified woman was heartbreakingly good.

Mary Amphlett

I think Christina's forte is acting. What she put into *Blood Brothers*! I didn't even recognise my own daughter when she walked out onto the stage. When I heard her sing I said, 'Good God! It is Chrissy!' To see all those people in tears . . .

Sitting next to me in the theatre were two young gentlemen and as they returned from interval one asked me if I was enjoying the show. 'Oh, yes,' I replied. 'Very much so.' And he asked me what I thought of Chrissy Amphlett. I said, 'That's a very hard question to ask me because I'm her mother!' He exclaimed, 'Chrissy's fantastic!'

Danny Hiller, he was very taken, too. After the premiere he said to me, 'What do you think of your daughter now?' And it was just the way he said it. We were all so proud.

Mark couldn't find it in him to share in my happiness. Whether he didn't enjoy my being in the spotlight without him, or feared that I might quit the band to act full-time I'm not sure. Maybe a little of each. From the moment I told him I was going to be in *Blood Brothers* he moped. Even on opening night when everyone was saying, 'Well done!' he lurked sourly in the shadows backstage.

I think Mark also resented the friendships I made doing the show, people very different from those in rock. Danny, Willy, Wilton, Russell, Peter, and the wonderful company manager, Kevin Hanily, whom I adored. I bonded with Kevin from the start. A sweet and gentle, though outrageously foul-mouthed, gay man in late middle age who was nicknamed 'Handbag', he'd always check that I was okay and take me aside for a gossip. I had my own hairdresser, who styled my hair in an old-fashioned way each night. He was about to have a sex change. He was replaced by a woman with arched eyebrows and piled-up hair named Pamela Blake, who was known among the dancers as Hungry Pam for a reason that remained a mystery to me.

Blood Brothers was produced on the cheap without understudies. We had to go onstage no matter how bad we may have been feeling. Usually that's not a problem for me, but one night after a show I stayed up until 6 a.m. doing ecstasy, took a pill to knock myself out, and turned up at the Seymour Centre that night with a hangover that made me throw up. It was so unlike me to hammer myself before a gig of any description, but this time I got carried away. This night, too, I knew Jim Barnes and Michael Hutchence were in the audience and I so wanted to show them I could cut it. I delivered my lines then went to the wings and vomited into a strategically placed bucket. I told everyone backstage that I had stomach flu. Kevin Hanily called a doctor to give his fallen star an injection to settle her stomach. Somehow I got through the show and vowed I'd never do anything so stupid again. Years later, Kevin told me he knew *exactly* what was wrong with me, but never gave me up because it would have meant dismissal. Why did I do it? Why did I jeopardise all my hard work with such stupidity? I don't know.

I got to know Russell Crowe during the run. Russell is a larrikin, and that appealed to me. His art comes from the heart more than the head, same place as mine. Also like me, he was a problem child. Today, as an Oscar-winning star, Russell has a reputation for being difficult and pedantic. Remember the big strife he got in for throwing a telephone at the head of a New York hotel employee? One in a series of confrontations. His victims should know that he's been pulling stunts like this for years, and was exactly the same when he was an unknown.

Danny Hiller was not intimidated. He relished the chance to butt heads with Russell, and would pound him on the chest when he felt he needed to project his voice more. It was fine with me, too, because I was just as driven as Russell in my own field and got on well with him. Russell was always a frustrated rock'n'roller. He sang under the name of Russ La Roq as a kid in his native New Zealand and still tries to mix singing with acting. He kept giving me demo tapes he'd made. He asked me what I thought of his singing and I told him I didn't think he'd found his voice yet and to keep trying. He accepted my advice.

However, to many in the *Blood Brothers* cast Russell was a pain in the arse. Even though an acting novice, he was fond of telling the other actors—such as Peter Cousens, an acclaimed young performer with an impeccable theatrical background—how they should be playing their parts. When Russell tried this with me at rehearsal, Danny Hiller punished him by making him kiss me 100 times on the cheek! Danny had to harness him. Russell had some good ideas but for the sake of harmony in the company he needed disciplining and Danny was tough enough, and respected enough by Russell, to do that. But Russell blew it when he broke Peter's nose.

Peter Cousens

Chrissy found herself in the middle of the unpleasantness between Russell and me. He and I were getting on well until a particular week when things got out of hand. Right at the end of the show, just before we shoot each other, my character, Eddie, is at a meeting and Russell as Mickey bursts in with a gun and confronts me. He has to kick a chair, and he started kicking it into the audience. There followed a kerfuffle while the audience had to deal with the flying chair. It broke the tense atmosphere on stage and that irritated me. Then when we shot each other Russell insisted on throwing his heavy gun into the air as he fell, and it would invariably land on me, which bloody hurt. I put up with this for a while, then after one performance I went up and mouthed off at him in the dressing-room. I called him an 'amateur prick'. He swung a punch that missed. Other actors separated us, then suddenly Russell lunged forward and headbutted me in the face, breaking my nose and blackening my eyes.

We were ordered by Wilton Morley to write a note of apology to each other. I did so. Russell refused, and was sacked. When word of his attack on me got out to our peers they said, 'Who is this bloody New Zealand actor? He'll never work again.' Yeah, right.

Danny played Russell's part for the next week until a replacement actor could be found.

For all Russell's faults, I was sad when he was sacked. After he was fired, he defiantly came up to the theatre bar. He sat down beside me and said, 'Hello Mum!'

The show didn't long survive Russell's demise. After three months, Wilton Morley ran out of money funding his production of *The Rocky Horror Show* in New Zealand and *Blood Brothers* was never staged outside Sydney.

The same people who resented my being in the show blamed me in part for its early closure. They said if I'd taken a pay cut, the production could have continued a little longer. I was never going to do that. I still had to keep the band going while I was absent and that cost me money, and, after all, Wilton had approached me, not me him.

In the days after *Blood Brothers'* premature closing I felt empty. It was a good production and even though it was set in the north of England its themes were universal. The cast was excellent, especially Peter and, while he was there, Russell, plus Zoe Carides, who played the girl Russell and Peter fought over, and Danny Hiller, a gem. Wilton, a happy-go-lucky guy in the great tradition of seat-of-their-pants theatrical entrepreneurs, was always up for a friendly drink with Danny and me at the Bourbon and Beefsteak bar in Kings Cross after the show, even when he knew he was in dire financial straits. Wilton left Australia and is now running a restaurant called, appropriately, Mad Dogs and Englishmen in Florida.

Blood Brothers was a special time for me. It gave me confidence that I could do more than sing in a band. That I would survive if Divinyls broke up.

While I would have enjoyed taking on other theatre roles, not necessarily musical theatre, but straight acting, the band came first, and Nick Wexler and Danny Heaps had planned a new American tour and Andrew an Australian tour, promoting *Temperamental*. So it was goodbye to Mrs Johnstone and back to my first and greatest love, rock'n'roll.

TOUCHING MYSELF

As empowered as I was by my theatre role I still had the drama of the band's money woes dragging me down. Divinyls parted company with Chrysalis. The butterfly had flown. We still owed them more than a million dollars—unpaid reimbursement of their advances for recording, distributing and promoting three albums, and supporting all those tours, yet they let us off the hook. Chrysalis knew, as did we, that we'd never be able to repay such a sum. They figured that because *Temperamental* hadn't broken us in the States, we were never going to make it there and they'd be smarter to write off our debt as a tax deduction. 'It's time to split,' they said. 'We can't do anything more with Divinyls.'

The revenue from our Chrysalis albums would continue to go straight to Chrysalis, though the publishing royalties would continue being paid to Mark and me. It was gracious of Chrysalis to cut ties without a nasty legal battle, which they could have brought on if they'd been inclined, and it meant we could start again. I thank our lawyer, Peter Thompson, for extricating us, with help from Andrew McManus.

Andrew decided to shop us around. With financial help from John Anderson at EMI Publishing he organised a producer with access to a studio in Mullumbimby, on the far north coast of New South Wales, to make a demo tape of some of our new songs. (Andrew promised the fellow he could produce our new album—which was never a chance—if he'd work cheaply.) He then made appointments to play it for A&R guys at likely record labels in the US and UK. 'Love Is A Gun' and 'Need A Lover' were two of the songs on the tape which, it has to be said, was rough. One track had a strange buzz, as if crickets had flown through the studio window in the middle of the recording session.

Capitol Records, when they heard it, wanted to sign me as a solo singer and songwriter, but I refused to leave Mark in the lurch. It would have broken his heart, and mine.

Andrew McManus

I truly felt I'd be able to waltz right into these big overseas record labels with my five-song demo tape and they'd fight among themselves to sign us. I received a rude awakening. They didn't want to know. Divinyls' reputation had preceded me. Everyone knew they'd left Chrysalis owing heaps of money, and Chrissy and Mark, who really *were* the band at that stage, were notoriously difficult.

Just when I thought my mission was hopeless, Virgin Records called me. They were interested in signing Divinyls because they thought Chrissy had it in her to be another Madonna. A songwriter who worked with Virgin named Billy Steinberg was the deal breaker. Billy had written 'Like A Virgin'. Then Freddy DeMann, Madonna's manager and Michael Jackson's former manager, got involved. Freddy could take Divinyls to the heights, he boasted to Chrissy and Mark, but that he, not me, would be their manager. Chrissy, to her credit, said no deal unless I was still in charge of Divinyls in Australia. Freddy agreed.

I was in London at the time, and Chrissy and Mark flew in to break the news. I was devastated, but had no choice but to agree. If DeMann could pull it off in the States, the band's profile in Australia could only soar exponentially.

Maybe to raise my spirits, I shouted Chrissy and Mark tea at the Ritz Hotel on Piccadilly. It was so beautifully genteel, and far removed from people's image of the pair. They were on their very best behaviour. Mark, in fact, loved scones and his tea in nice cups. And the three of us took a trip up to Nottingham, where we hired a little gate-house near Sherwood Forest so Chrissy and Mark could do some writing. I would run through the forest where Robin Hood once robbed from the rich to give to the poor listening to Elvis Presley's *Aloha From Hawaii*, then after dinner I'd go down to a little pub and have a pint with the locals while Chrissy and Mark created.

I'd received a call from Billy Steinberg. He said, 'Now, this guy Andrew that you've sent ... he's not ... he's not going to be ... suitable for America. I've asked Freddy DeMann to consider managing you guys. I think you should get on a plane now and come to Los Angeles and meet Freddy.' So we did. His office was right next to Lucille Ball's old headquarters, and as a Lucy fan that was okay by me. Said Freddy, in his squillion-dollar suit, 'Chrissy, Mark, you're going cheap so you're a good buy for me. I think I can do something with you. I'll take 15 per cent of everything you make.' That's how it was, strictly business. I made it clear to DeMann that if I was to agree to him handling our affairs in the United States, Andrew had to stay on as our Australian manager.

Andrew cried when we told him, but then, trouper that he is, accepted that it was a good idea. He realised he still had a part of us, and if Freddy DeMann couldn't break us big in America, no one could.

I never told Mark, but Freddy was another who wanted to work only with me. He felt Mark wasn't necessary. I told Freddy in no uncertain terms that we were a package deal.

Once the deal was done Mark and I moved to Paris to write. We holed up with our eight-track in a 400-year-old apartment writing 'Love School', 'Make Out Alright' and 'Lay Your Body Down', going outside to eat and visit the Paris Air Show. Then Virgin set us up in Los Angeles. The idea was we would write for six months, at first the two of us and then with Billy Steinberg and his collaborator Tom Kelly.

With a swag of new songs we would then make a new record, to be produced by David Tickle (who'd cut records for Prince, Sting, U2 and George Michael). Fingers crossed it would be a US hit.

Andrew told us later that Freddy hired the experienced road manager Bert Stein to keep an eye on us and to keep him in the loop.

'I Touch Myself' is the biggest hit Divinyls ever had. It made No. 3 in America and No. 1 in Australia. It may not be our best song, but it's the one most people think of when they hear our name. That song was born in a café in Los Angeles where I met Billy Steinberg to write lyrics. He came with a notebook of ideas, including the words 'I Touch Myself'. He wanted to see which ones I responded to. The idea of doing a sexually explicit song that would still get played on the radio appealed to me.

The next day, Mark, Tom Kelly, Billy and I rendezvoused again and through trial and error wrote 'I Touch Myself'. Billy, years later, told the Song Facts website, 'What I like about the song is that in spite of the chorus boldly [being about masturbation], the verse was sort of more poetic and kind of meaningful. It says, "I love myself, I want you to love me, when I feel down I want you above me, I search myself, I want you to find me, I forget myself, I want you to remind me." Those words, I think, are very strong.' Agreed.

The new album would be called simply *Divinyls* and the other songs we took into those recording sessions at Jackson Browne's Groove Masters Studio in Santa Monica included 'Make Out Alright', 'Lay Your Body Down', 'I'm On Your Side', 'Need A Lover', 'Love School' and 'Bless My Soul (It's Rock'n'Roll)'. Joining Mark and me for the sessions were Randy Jackson (yes, *the* Randy Jackson who is now judging TV's *American Idol*) on bass, Benmont Tench of Tom Petty's Heartbreakers on Hammond organ, and a beautiful and extremely wild young African-American guy named Charley Drayton who played drums.

The first time I laid eyes on Charley he was wearing a baby-pink leather jacket with a broken record coming out of the shoulder. He had beads and chains, hair like a poodle and the most adorable face.

Charley was richly credentialled, having played in Keith Richards' band X-Pensive Winos, and he'd worked with Neil Young, Herbie Hancock, Courtney Love, Seal, Iggy Pop, Janet Jackson, Mariah Carey and our old touring mates the Cult. We specifically asked for him after we learned he had played drums on one of our favourite tracks, the B-52s' 'Love Shack'. Even though he was only in his early twenties, Charley was an old soul. After working with the cream of rock, jazz and the blues, nothing threw him.

Occasionally Mark would complain to me, 'Charley is so arrogant,' but he wasn't. He was simply very sure of himself and opinionated about music.

He had every right to be. He grew up in Brooklyn, New York. His grandfather, Charlie Drayton, was a bass player with Billie Holliday and Lena Horne. Charlie passed away when Charley's father, Bernard, was five. Bernard became a recording engineer and recorded what turned out to be the great saxophonist John Coltrane's last album. Bernard took Charley to sessions, concerts and clubs and by the age of three, Charley knew he would be a musician. At thirteen he was headhunted to attend the prestigious Music and Art High School on 135th Street. He began playing in clubs at the same time, and was a professional musician at twelve. At fifteen he was on the road with Chaka Khan and was soon playing bass and drums in X-Pensive Winos and the house band on the *David Letterman Show*. On 30 September 1989, on the US TV show *Saturday Night Live*, Charley helped Neil Young perform what Young's biographer Jimmy McDonough in his book *Shakey* called 'easily Neil's greatest electric live broadcast performance . . .' The song was 'Rockin' In The Free World'. Drayton, 'in flashy leathers and ripped jeans, tumbleweed hair obscuring his sullen face, lumbered around like a prehistoric mutant marking territory'. Young was inspired, blew the set and the song apart, and later rated Charley 'so great'. The performance ends with Neil enveloping Charley in a big hug.

Recording with Charley and Randy was a revelation. Unlike any other drummer I'd worked with, Charley plays to the singer. He *considered* me, instead of connecting only with the bass player. He had a special groove and feel, which I hadn't experienced because coming from Australia I'd never worked with black musicians. And Randy was an amazing bass player. With those two cooking behind me, I was in rhythm heaven.

The norm would be for me to record guide vocals, then Mark would come in and lay down all the parts, and by the time I came in to record the actual vocals the record would be a *fait accompli*. Now, for the first time, I really enjoyed the recording process. I'd never worked with musicians as generous and as talented as Randy and Charley. I loved it too that when there was a break in recording they'd go out to buy shoes, or food. Both guys loved to eat.

Mark was in heaven, too. Charley and Randy were knocked out by his playing, and he blossomed in the glow of their approval.

The only sour note came when we were recording 'I Touch Myself' and suddenly the studio was invaded by Virgin suits and management. I realised that 'I Touch Myself', being the obvious single from the album, was the only track they were excited about. We all thought, 'What about the other songs?' Charley, by then so passionate about the project, threw his drumsticks down in protest and walked out. Eventually the studio was cleared, I herded the band back inside, and we recorded the track. In less expert hands, 'I Touch Myself' could have been a quickly forgotten novelty song, but it has become something of a classic. Only recently I was driving near my home in New York and it came onto the radio. It picked me up and carried me with it. 'I Touch Myself' has stood the test of time and I'm proud of that. I can't tell you why it works, it just does.

Whether playing our music or just hanging out, I felt instantly at home with Randy and Charley. We made a French-Moroccan club called Ponana Souk in Los Angeles our meeting place. There'd be me, Mark, Charley, Randy (who, unlike the rest of us, didn't touch drugs or alcohol), and sometimes Freddy DeMann and his wife Candy. The owners were friends of one of the guys who created Cirque du Soleil so the entertainment was acrobats, stilt-walkers, fire-eaters, a unicyclist and topless dancers. This went on until 2 a.m. when the doors were closed to the public and for the enjoyment of invited guests, Ponana Souk transformed into an ecstasy den complete with topless dancers. I was always impressed that Charley, who was very rock'n'roll, could party hard until the early hours and always turn up at the studio looking great, feeling great and ready to go.

Charley Drayton

There was definitely anticipation [when asked to play with Divinyls]. I'd receive offers to record with various musicians and singers. I'd weigh them up, then go into the studio. In 1990 I got a call from the co-producer of Divinyls, a band I didn't know, who wanted me to play drums on their new album. I was talking to my friend Babi Floyd and said, 'Who are these Divinyls?' He said, 'You gotta do this ... The band rocks. Chrissy Amphlett is fabulous, but a little crazy. You gotta hear their first album *Desperate*.' I said, 'You've convinced me. But maybe I'll wait till I do the new record with them and *then* I'll hear *Desperate* so I don't go to Los Angeles with any preconceptions.'

I hadn't met anyone from Divinyls, but I was told with this band *any* door could open. The first thing I noticed was Chrissy's energy. She walked into the room, not over-confident, but she knew what she had to accomplish there. She was dynamic and had a vision for the way each song should be done. Mark did too but he wasn't as articulate. Mark was in her wake, light on words at first. Working with Divinyls was a pure rockin' experience for me and the talent of Mark and Chrissy made the session memorable. The group assembled there for those few weeks grew into a real band. Making that music taught me so much.

'Make Out Alright' was the first song we recorded. We took up our places ... and Chrissy was over at the far end of the room with a handheld microphone. When she sang, I had never seen or felt anything like it. Most singers in a studio put down a vocal track and then say, 'Okay guys, you know what the song is, I'll see ya later.' Chrissy was with us all the way, ten hours a day. She kept inventing ways to make a song better. She was an instrument, not just a singer. Being with her was like being in school.

Until we cut 'I Touch Myself' the recording had been pretty quiet, no one had been bothering us. Then I turned up at the studio and all of a sudden all the execs from Virgin had come down and were in the studio and that pissed me off, so Randy and I walked out. I said, 'We gotta go!' and went shopping in Fred Segal's department store in Santa Monica as a protest. Then we went to eat.

'I Touch Myself' was Divinyls' big success, but I felt, after the fact, a poisonous kiss. It's too commercial sounding in comparison to the album's other material. Its success gave the record company ammunition to demand similar sounding songs.

Randy Jackson had just met Sly Stone's manager, and when we were re-recording 'Lay Your Body Down', Randy happened to mention that Sly might drop by the studio. Sly was responsible for some of the greatest funk and R&B ever recorded. He had battled addiction, but I'd heard he was now sober. Freddy DeMann had been in the studio. He was annoyed with me because I wasn't afraid to show my personality and independence in sticking up for Chrissy and Mark. We were at the point where we were close to getting the right take on 'Lay Your Body Down', but we weren't there yet. Freddy said, 'That's great! That'll do. Just put Chrissy's vocal on it and it's finished.' I turned around and gave Freddy a long, long look. Freddy soon disappeared.

Soon after, Sly Stone came in, wearing a cool brown suit and looking better than he had for ages. He filled the studio with positive energy. If only we'd asked him to play. I stuck as close to him as I could during his time in the studio, hoping some of his genius would rub off. Sly listened to 'Lay Your Body Down' for a while then said, 'Yeah . . . catchy . . . catchy tune.' Now 'catchy' is a very blasé and vague word when most people say it. But coming from Sly somehow it was a great compliment. He left the studio. We all said, 'Don't worry, we're gonna play with Sly one day.' But we never did because soon after he disappeared again. That experience taught me that if you want something real bad, you *make* it happen. You find a way to pop the question.

Imagine the experience I had when I returned home to New York and heard *Desperate*. I was jumpin' up and down. It gave me such joy hearing it after I'd worked with Chrissy and Mark. We had something fresh and different from other Divinyls' recordings. I was impressed by Richard Harvey's drumming. Harve has a special gift. I appreciate what he brought to Divinyls. He was so inspiring. He had a confidence that he knew he *owned* that music. He had a special rapport with Rick Grossman. They were connected, on and offstage.

When we parted after that last night at Groove Masters we promised to stay in touch. We knew there was a future for us together somewhere, sometime, somehow.

Once we released the album US *Rolling Stone*'s Jim Farber wrote that '"I Touch Myself" is one of the catchiest songs ever written about masturbation. It is perhaps the truest tribute to Amphlett's urgent talent that she can make even self-stimulation seem inclusive... *Divinyls* is the most cutting record the group has had since its debut album in 1983 ... the guitars are harsher, the hooks grab harder, and Amphlett's vocals slice through the mix ... Few singers can locate the rage that lies behind the lust like [Amphlett]. She sings with an eroticism that is almost vengeful, hurling out phrases brimming with violent need.'

A No. 1 single was every band's dream—but for us things were careening out of control and the hysteria around the song wasn't a blessing.

Andrew McManus

On 31 December 1990, Divinyls were playing a big New Year's Eve gig at Cronulla Leagues Club. 'I Touch Myself', the first single from the new album, had just been released. As we prepared to go onstage Virgin Australia called me. 'Andrew, you're managing the band that has the No. 1 single on the Australian charts.' I told Chrissy, Mark and the guys and we cracked a bottle of champagne, then another. Suddenly we remembered we were on in 30 minutes.

That was one of the great Divinyls gigs. The band rocked. Fifteen hundred people were packed into the 1200-capacity venue. Bloody hot, 34 degrees outside and even hotter inside. Early into the gig I noticed a big ugly dude with glazed eyes and sweating like a pig in the front row. He looked like bad news, and he was. Just as I reminded myself to keep an eye on him, I saw him spit right at Chrissy. Again and again, great gobs of spit. She was carrying on but giving him the evil eye. I thought, 'Fuck this!' and just as the big bastard leaned back, about to spit at Chrissy again, I jumped down off the stage and punched him right under the chin. A perfect uppercut. He went down like a sack of spuds.

Chrissy always knew I'd stick up for her when things got nasty. I enjoyed getting in the trenches and throwing my weight around with unruly fans, even punching out stroppy crew members if I had to. When Chrissy was feeling perverse, which was almost always, she would take advantage of me by stage-diving into the middle of the toughest looking blokes in the house. She knew I'd wade in to rescue her, even if I copped a beating. Once I leapt into the fray with a broken leg. I thought Chrissy was in trouble so I didn't think, just bounded in, plaster cast and all. I looked at Chrissy to see if she was still in one piece and she was laughing at me.

We filmed the 'I Touch Myself' video in a nunnery in Pasadena. The director, Michael Mann, was not well known then, but his films *Heat*, *The Insider* and *The Last of the Mohicans* have since made him one of Hollywood's most acclaimed directors. He may indeed be a wonderful director but he was rude to me, threw things around the set and wasn't at all open to suggestions. The video was nominated for an *MTV* award and Mann sniffed, 'Oh, it's the worst thing I've done.' That didn't stop it from being constantly screened all over the world. Oddly enough, Australia was the only place where it was banned in general exhibition hours.

We worked hard to get to this point—we had a song that could springboard us into major recognition and success in the US and we couldn't back off. However, the years of constant touring and partying after gigs had taken their toll and I wasn't sure how long I could keep going. There is only so much rock'n'roll life one body can take.

EXCESS

10

I thought I was going to die.

After an Australian tour in 1991, I was staying in Sydney, where I found myself in the loft of an old friend, a stylist, in William Street. I had spent the night bingeing on alcohol and drugs and I'd collapsed in a sumptuous pile of velvet theatre curtains that my friend had somehow acquired. My stomach was convulsing uncontrollably, just like John Hurt's in *Alien* before the monster bursts out.

I was dry-retching internally. Torn between horror and helpless despair, I watched as my stomach jerked and juddered. The pain was enormous. I tried to vomit to rid my body of the poison but nothing came up. I was too out of it to even call for help. I thought, 'I'm going to die right here and these velvet curtains will be my shroud.' After 30 minutes of agony I passed out and when I awoke many hours later my stomach was still. The seizure had passed. I'd survived. Before long I was looking forward to my next drink.

By 1991 and '92, after 'I Touch Myself' and the *Divinyls* album came out and we were touring Australia and fifty cities and towns in the United States, my alcoholism, for that is what it was even though I didn't admit it, was veering out of control. I regularly drank before gigs and always got hammered at the parties afterwards. I would only screw up *really* badly around once a month, but I was often drunk during those endless, grinding tours, or at least tipsy.

It didn't take a lot to get me plastered. I had never been able to tolerate too much alcohol, and a bottle of wine would do the trick. I drank even though drinking made me ill. With my low tolerance I would get drunk very quickly, then I'd be sick.

Alcohol was having a negative effect on my relationships, my disposition and my health. I knew in my heart that I sang better sober, and at one point I made an effort to cut down, and tried to go onstage without drinking first. Then people, including executives from Virgin, told me that they thought my more sober performances were not as powerful as when I'd had a drink, and I came to believe that I couldn't perform without alcohol. So, ever the professional, I gave myself permission to get pissed at every opportunity and because Divinyls had the biggest drinks rider in the business, with vodka, gin, bourbon and beer on constant call, there were many opportunities.

The result was increasingly nasty flare-ups in public and private with Mark and Andrew and anyone else who crossed me—and pathetic scenes like my curtain call in the William Street loft.

When Molly Meldrum heard that we were booked to play *Countdown* again, he said, 'Uh-oh, the bitch is back! I thought we'd got rid of her.' No such luck.

Joe Turtur

I joined Divinyls as a drum tech for Australian Made in 1987, and stayed with the band until 1996. At first I was shit-scared of Chrissy. After three years we developed a mutual respect and got on better, and even partied together. I helped her acquire her props, the fluorescent tube, some mirrors and other things.

I lasted longer than any other Divinyls roadie. Many got sacked or weren't prepared to put up with Chrissy's shit. She was ferociously devoted to the band, but when she was drinking or stoned she got crazy and would just go off. Maybe she was putting on a front. It must have been difficult being the only woman among guys. I think sometimes she was looking to enjoy some of the camaraderie all the blokes had, but because she was a woman she couldn't let go. Sometimes I suspected she was softer underneath than she let on.

There was always ecstasy, cocaine and booze around Divinyls. My job was to go into the next town and suss out who the local drug dealers were and buy the stash.

During the 'I Touch Myself' tour there was a problem one night with the sound system. The band was playing too loud and the promoter wanted us to stop. Chrissy refused and incited the crowd to riot. 'They're trying to shut us down!' she yelled. Brawls broke out all over the place. We hit the cocaine very hard that night, just went for it! Next morning at the airport, Chrissy and Mark were shouting at each other. It was scary to see. She was wired after the gig, got wasted, and then she had to front at a radio station to do interviews.

After a gig at the Brisbane Expo, Chrissy went ballistic because other bands on the bill had used our sound system and had not set it up right for us when we closed the show. We were terrible. She called a meeting and tore strips off everyone. 'We're the fucking headline act, and the other bands can have six channels, but they don't touch our twelve.' I'd taken some pills and was sitting off to the side a little out of it, chuckling to myself. Chrissy kept eyeballing me throughout her harangue. I reckoned I was history but was too stoned to really care. When she finished she came to see me, smiled and said, 'Whatever you're on, I want some!'

In Sydney we often stayed at Peppers Hotel in Double Bay. It was a palatial hotel with a pool where I was raucous and did my trademark belly flops to annoy the guests. On one visit I was in my suite, with prints of Norman Lindsay's naked women on the baby blue walls and a white four-poster bed, when a pipe burst in my bathroom. I called the concierge then sat on the bed with my door open waiting for the plumber. Billy Thorpe and the Aztecs were staying at the hotel too.

Billy's room was at the end of my corridor. Then one of Billy's band, Warren 'Pig' Morgan, appeared at my open door. He had assumed that I was sitting with my door open like some goddamned groupie waiting for Billy to pass by so I could pounce and drag him into my bed! He said, 'Oh, you don't want to get involved with Billy, Chrissy...' As if I was *remotely* interested. 'Piss off!' I yelled. 'I wouldn't touch Billy Thorpe with a bloody bargepole!'

I never stopped to think why I drank alcoholically. I learned much later that some people are born predisposed to alcoholism, and I'm one. Dad drank heavily, and so did some of my uncles. Add to this the pressure of performing night after night, the gruelling life on the road, the long, boring stretches, the tension with Mark and Vince, money woes, drug-induced mania and delusions of invulnerability, the need to maintain the post-gig adrenalin high by heavy partying and the ready availability of alcohol and I came to see that it would have been odd had I *not* drunk.

Alcohol was my prop. I leaned on it. It relaxed me, and gave me the strength to cope with sad, rundown hotel rooms and unpleasant jobs like being witty and on my best behaviour for music industry executives at dinners and parties. I came to rely on a glass of vodka before I went on stage, and when I was tired a swig of something would rev me up.

Alcohol got all of my cravings going. After drinking I'd progress to pot or coke.

Somewhere back in the early eighties my behaviour when drunk had begun to get more and more extreme. A few drinks would lead to arguments and punch-ups, the kicking of doors, the smearing of ice cream on the face of a startled fan. By the early nineties my heavy drinking and the fiascos that ensued were a part of my life. I think an alcoholic is someone who cannot guarantee their behaviour when they drink or who continues to drink after negative consequences. That was me.

I was also a blackout drinker. I would drink and pass out. Or I would drink and stay conscious but have no recall when I sobered up.

Alcohol made me angry. It broke down what few inhibitions I had. It exacerbated my frustrations. I would become not very nice to be around, lashing out at friend and foe. I was a woman who could be unkind when drunk, and who spoke her mind, telling people what I thought of them without thinking how hurtful I was being. People don't always need to hear the truth, or my version of it.

To help me perform while hungover I would have the doctor give me Stemetil to ease my stomach and throbbing head, then to bring me up again I had a capful or two of Catovit, a pink, sticky potion I bought at the chemist that contained about five times as much caffeine as a cup of coffee. I'd wash it down with a swig of vodka. Sometimes the Catovit bottle leaked and my bag would be awash with pink goo.

It was no big deal to empty the hotel room minibar. The trick was always to have the party in someone else's room so they'd have to foot the bill. Some of the boys would drink the little bottles then refill them with water so they'd be long gone before their con game would be discovered.

I remember during this time being a target, drunk or sober. We had a night off in Brisbane and a few of us went to a club run by a transvestite in the red-light district. The moment I walked in she was all over me physically and wouldn't leave me alone. I started barking at her like a dog. She was hugely offended and had me and everybody I was with thrown out onto the footpath—and we were stone-cold sober!

Andrew thought he was doing the right thing by appointing my physical trainer, a martial arts expert named Mick, to be his trouble-prone star's minder. Oddly enough, Mick seemed to *attract* trouble.

Andrew McManus

Chrissy, Mick the kung-fu guy and I were staying at the Banks Hotel in Melbourne when for no reason a tall Yugoslavian guy wearing a leather jacket in the hotel bar knocked Mick unconscious. Then he pulled a gun. I dived through the air and tackled the bloke. Chrissy kicked his gun across the floor. Bouncers came at us from everywhere and threw the gunman, Chrissy and me down the stairs. As we tumbled, I kept punching the Yugoslavian fellow, and my nose was broken in the melee. Later, the hotel manager told me he'd be adding the damages bill to our account. 'Fuck you!' I said. 'We're not paying a cent.'

Chrissy and I got into another big punch-up in Melbourne, at the Car Club. We were on the drink and being loud and rowdy as usual. Chrissy got into a screaming match with a barman. All the time we must have been under observation, because later that night someone hit me over the back of my head and stole $5000. I came to after 20 or 30 seconds, returned to the bar and made a huge fuss, shouting and throwing my arms around. Security grabbed me. Chrissy, this time, came to *my* aid. The bouncers got stuck into both of us. First they tossed her into the gutter. Then they grabbed me and threw me out. Through the pain we looked at each other and grinned.

There were no teetotallers or health-conscious people in our band or crew. They wouldn't have been welcome. We were all big beer-drinkers, wine-drinkers, whatever-takers. Even though I wasn't on stage, I felt like I was, because I was so much a part of Divinyls. At the end of a show you couldn't help but be on a high, and that's when the drinking would start. The big wind-down. It could last 8 or 10 hours. You'd fall asleep and then have to get up the next day and drive or be bussed or fly to the next venue to get ready for the show.

Brawling, stage-diving, I put Andrew through hell . . . Yet I think he *enjoyed* rescuing me. Andrew was always very protective, and I wasn't used to that. He made mistakes, some bad mistakes, but he'd always try to make things right.

Even though the time between drinks got shorter I still had to work and I'd push myself through the hangovers to keep going. The show had to go on! Freddy DeMann was cajoling me to dance onstage like Madonna and Michael Jackson and hired a choreographer to help me work on steps and routines. I refused to do it. He couldn't get it into his head that Divinyls were a rock'n'roll band and I was a rock'n'roll singer. Choreography, to me, was not real.

Virgin organised for Mark and me to interrupt our American tour for a day and fly to London to mime 'I Touch Myself' on *Top of the Pops*, a cheesy television pop show. Virgin pulled rank and we couldn't say no. They were probably right to do so. An appearance on *Top of the Pops* meant big record sales and 'I Touch Myself' became our only hit in England. I hated my faked performance and I hated the pink outfit they made me wear.

Lightning struck twice. In London, unbelievably, I came down with food poisoning again after a restaurant meal with record company executives. Shades of 1988, the unpleasant woman from Chrysalis and my vomitous visit to the Kings Road. Then the limo driver had to contend with my illness; this time it was my fellow Concorde passengers en route back to the United States the next morning. I was violently ill and must have ruined everyone's dream flight. I certainly screwed up Mark's. For years he had wanted to fly on Concorde and now his great adventure had become an exasperating and messy ordeal. I had considered staying in London till I recovered but we were booked to play that night and 'cancel' is not in my vocabulary.

Mark and I had stayed in touch with Charley Drayton and when it was time for our next American tour we contacted him. Unfortunately, Charley and Randy were not available for this tour so we employed an American named Gerry Angel to play drums, and brought from Australia the Models' keyboardist Roger Mason, Jim Hilbun from the Angels to play bass, and the brilliant guitarist Charlie Owen, who'd made his name with a number of top indie outfits. Charlie, about whom Paul Kelly wrote the ballad 'Charlie Owen's Slide Guitar', went on to play with more indie bands, most notably Tex Perkins' Beasts of Bourbon, remains a friend and an inspiration to this day. He has a wonderful nature and fitted in so well. A master guitarist, he played sublimely with Mark, each one complementing the other. We were mischievous together. Jim Hilbun, unfortunately, didn't gel with us as well as Charlie. It bothered Mark that Jim played a fretless bass—only jazz players are supposed to play these—and it bothered us both that Jim had a disconcerting habit of taking off all his clothes in front of everyone in the dressing-room.

Charlie Owen

Divinyls were one of the rare bands to straddle indie and mainstream. They were indie in spirit, but had a large following. Best of both worlds. Before I joined Divinyls, and long after I left the band for that matter, I played in indie bands. The people I played with were disdainful of mainstream acts, but they made an exception for Divinyls. Chrissy's singing, Mark's brilliant playing, and their killer attitude made them more independent than any of us.

When I was asked to audition for the band I thought, 'Oh wow!' I wasn't Chrissy and Mark's first choice. They wanted another guy, but he was in America. I was in Australia and available. Andrew McManus invited me to meet Chrissy and Mark at their house in Manly. 'Understand this,' snapped Chrissy, who impressed me as being very matter-of-fact and formidable, 'you'll be playing rhythm guitar. You *won't* be playing any lead.'

'No, no, no,' I assured them. 'That's cool.' And then they asked me to go outside and sit in Andrew's car while they compared impressions. I put on a Divinyls tape and dozed off. Then Andrew came down, got into the car and told me I'd passed muster.

I got off on the wrong foot. Before signing on with Divinyls I'd given my word that I'd play with another band at a gig in Brisbane on the same night that Divinyls were playing at Selinas. I couldn't get out of it. I explained my predicament to Chrissy and Mark and they said it would be fine so long as I flew to Sydney after the Brisbane gig in time to play with them later that night. I organised a flight, and sure enough I arrived at the Coogee Bay Hotel shortly before Divinyls went on. The band was on fire and I was on such a high that I forgot myself and in my exuberance launched into a solo. It sounded terrific, but this was not *done* in Divinyls. My job was to know my place, do my bit and sound exactly like the record. Chrissy rushed over and slapped me out. 'Don't you ever do that again!' she barked.

For a short time after that Chrissy was a little stand-offish. Then one night I cut my leg somehow backstage. She came over to me just as we were going on and said, 'Oh, Charlie, you're bleeding. Let me get you a bandage.' Then she took me by the hand and we went onstage together. That's how I knew I'd been accepted into the fold.

I've been privileged to play with the greatest rock singers in Australia and Chrissy is right up there with them. May even be the best.

Once Mark and I put the band together we were ready to head back to America. The craziness followed us. There was a Cuban wardrobe girl who stole some of my clothes when we were filming the 'Love School' video in New York, then blamed another wardrobe girl. We sacked the woman she accused, and invited the Cuban on the road with us. We sure could pick 'em. She seemed insanely jealous of me, and tried to compete, whining, 'Oh, Chrissy, *how* can I compete with you?' Once, just before I was about to go onstage she accidentally on purpose ripped my dress.

This girl, who was quite beautiful, slept with some members of the band. Meanwhile my clothes kept disappearing. I told our American road manager, Bert Stein, a gentle soul, that I was sure she was the thief but he wouldn't believe me. Then Mark finally caught her in the act and Bert fired her.

Charley Drayton joined us at Ocean Way studio on Sunset Boulevard in Hollywood to cut a cover version of the Rascals' hit 'I Aint Gonna Eat Out My Heart Anymore' for the soundtrack of *Buffy the Vampire Slayer*. Also on the session was Charley's good friend Darryl Jones, who'd played bass with Miles Davis, Sting, Madonna, Peter Gabriel and currently with the Rolling Stones. We were trying to do a rockier, different version of the old R&B classic. At first, Mark had a block, and then he and Charley dreamed up a new riff, everything changed and the instrumentation came together. I was having problems with my vocal because I found parts of the melody tedious. I asked Charley to help. He rewrote the melody and the song took flight.

Mark and I thought, 'This guy is really happening. He is *so* supportive.'

While in the studio we also recorded our take of the Troggs' 'Wild Thing' for the soundtrack of the Yahoo Serious movie *Reckless Kelly*, and Roxy Music's 'Love Is The Drug' for the *Super Mario Bros* film. The film director Ridley Scott rang up and asked us to do a version of 'I Wanna Be A Cowboy' which didn't work out.

Charley Drayton

The project producer for the *Buffy* soundtrack was a scrumpy little guy named Ralph. He was a nervous man and I knew he was gonna lose Chrissy and Mark. While Chrissy, Mark, Darryl Jones and I were in the studio trying to find a formula for the song Ralph, in the control room, just kept talking and offered nothing but counter-productive nervous energy. What we were hearing of 'I Ain't Gonna Eat Out My Heart Anymore' we didn't like and we knew we had to dig a little deeper. Ralph kept babbling. I told him, 'Ralph, stay in the control room. Be *quiet*. Do not say *anything* until I get back to you.'

We four reinvented 'I Ain't Gonna Eat Out My Heart Anymore'. I played around with the drum beat and came up with a feeling we knew would be good. Then we jammed on that for a little while. Mark and I tried to chase down what the signature hook was going to be. As we were playing, Mark got so immersed in the music that, like a mad scientist, his head went down, and down, lower and lower as he concentrated. He played two bars and I yelled, 'Hey, stop! Play that again!' He'd got it. The song unfolded. Then Mark was on his feet, playing his part like a man possessed. With Mark, you had to stay cool and encourage him and push him and you could count on him to come up with something wonderful. While all this was going on, Chrissy stayed cool. Just one out-of-place word from her could have brought Mark crashing down. She was so relaxed. We knew we were on our way.

Chrissy was due to put down her vocals the next day, and Felix Cavaliere from the Rascals, who'd written and sung the song years before, would be coming by to play organ, along with two sisters Ralph had signed to sing back-up.

That night, Darryl and I went out and had a couple of drinks. When I got back to my room at the Hollywood Roosevelt hotel, Chrissy called. She said, 'I need your help on this song, I still need to find my way into the melody.' I promised to try to come up with something. I switched the lights off and turned on my cassette recorder by the bed, and the melody began to unfold. One thing led to another as I vocally scribbled all over Felix's song. Next morning I called Chrissy and told her I thought I had something. She said she'd need me beside her in the studio to sing it.

I said, 'Ralph, you're gonna have to take a back seat again today.' We got it down in three or four takes, then Felix came in, and the energy was elevated by the creator's performance.

We were pleased with the recording of the song but unfortunately the mix was Ralph's responsibility and we didn't like the way the song sounded in the film. When Sony in Australia decided to release it as a single, we suggested mixing it again. It was a Top 10 hit, the most-played single in Australia that year, and really showed Divinyls in a new light.

Darryl Jones says that during those sessions in Los Angeles Chrissy looked at me differently. He said, 'Do you see the way she looks at you?' I had the reputation of being blindsided by beauty. I certainly had no inkling that Chrissy was remotely interested. I had no clue. I didn't even know that she and Mark were together. Then again, few people did.

The next single we did together was 'Wild Thing'. Chrissy and Mark asked me to produce it and I went to Australia. I'd just left the X-Pensive Winos. My number had come up. Keith Richards and I had not confronted a situation that had arisen between us. I had to stick to a decision I had made and I left the band.

In January 1993, I flew to Sydney to cut 'Wild Thing'.

These were more good times with Charley Drayton and we told him we'd love him to come to Australia to tour with us. He said he was currently tied up touring and recording, but he'd give our suggestion some hard thought.

Then Freddy DeMann dropped us. Suddenly and brutally. It was Madonna's fault. She said she wanted to start her own record label, Maverick, and needed Freddy to run it. He said yes, then cut ties with all his acts, including Divinyls. He didn't tell us face to face, but in an ad he took out in the *Los Angeles Times*. That's how Bert Stein found out, too, that he was history. Within days, our business managers had packed all our paperwork in boxes and had them delivered to Bert's door.

It got worse. We'd signed a merchandising deal with the US company, Winterland, and to complete the deal, we were to do a series of gigs in Europe with Simple Minds. Then, in one of the last things Freddy ever did for us, he changed his mind and suggested we not do the gig. 'It'll all be on the cheap,' he explained. 'A waste of your time.' So we pulled out. Our lawyer didn't read the fine print on the Winterland contract, and nor did Mark and I, so we had no way of knowing we'd breached a T-shirt merchandising contract. When we first agreed to tour with Simple Minds, Winterland had paid us $US250 000, which was soon depleted when we paid tax on the sum, our lawyers, Wexler and Heaps, and Freddy DeMann, who was due his commission. Mark and I were left with $AUD50 000 each. But, when the tour was called off, he and I, as Divinyls, were responsible for repaying Winterland the entire $US250 000 sum, which, with interest, was getting larger every day. We didn't have anything like that kind of money. In the end the debt would blow out to $AUD650 000, but more of that later.

Mark and I took our frustrations out on each other. We fought incessantly and intensely. While we were recording 'I Ain't Gonna Eat Out My Heart Anymore' the riots that followed the police bashing of Rodney King were being waged in the streets of Los Angeles. Mark and I were in the middle of a riot of our own when we started to smell acrid smoke and heard the sound of windows shattering.

Nothing seemed strange to me at this point and the negative energy around Mark and me seemed like it was seeping into our souls.

Back in Australia, Andrew drove us hard. He had to, so we wouldn't go under. It seemed there wasn't a city, town or outback pub that we didn't play. Our hard work paid off because *Divinyls* sold well, but touring took a heavy toll.

One night at a Gold Coast gig, I fainted towards the end of the performance. I pitched forward and lay there, unable to move. Although the show was all but over, Andrew ran onstage and offered everyone their money back. He didn't have to because by playing as long as we did we'd honoured our contract. He thought he'd make himself look a big man, and claim the lost money on our insurance policy. Most of the audience, meanly I thought because we'd given them a great time, took him up on his offer and collected their entry cash at the door. I was taken to hospital and had blood tests. Unfortunately they showed that I had marijuana in my blood which invalidated the insurance. We were in the red $20 000 on the gig. I considered breaking into the hospital's administration office and stealing the test results. Then I thought better of it, took the twenty grand out of my own bank account, not that I could afford it, and paid it into the band's kitty. That was one expensive joint.

Andrew McManus

Today I can hold my own with anyone, but I was a green businessman in those days, and way out of my depth with the sharks in the record industry, especially the Americans who chewed you up and spat you out before you even knew you were on the menu. To save money, as well as being Divinyls' manager, I was booker, tour manager, marketer, bodyguard, did the accounts, and put the band in front of crowds.

I came up with an idea to increase our exposure and sell more albums, as well as do some good for the community. I wanted to close off Victoria Street, Kings Cross, and have Divinyls put on a free street concert. Volunteers moving through the crowd would collect money for the homeless kids of the Cross. I met the police, the fire brigade and the council and finally got it all approved. The big day, a Sunday afternoon, was hot and sunny. In a nod to Divinyls' past, we set up the stage outside the Piccadilly Hotel. More than 15 000 people showed up and gave generously. Not even a generator breakdown three-quarters of the way through the set could spoil that wonderful gig. Chrissy, in her garter belt and fishnets, went off! In gratitude the punters rushed the stage and thrust money at her. She stuffed it down her bra. I said to myself, 'I know where some of that money's going!'

During this time we did quite a few charity concerts. The Kings Cross gig was close to my heart, because it was in aid of Father Tim in Roslyn Gardens, who did a fantastic job caring for the underprivileged and dispossessed in the Cross. Andrew is wrong about me ripping off money but right about one thing: it *was* a wonderful gig.

We were due to go onstage at 5.30 p.m., but at 4.30 p.m. Victoria Street was empty. 'Oh God, no one's coming!' I thought. Then suddenly, at five, the street filled with people. It was a human tide, on the street and footpaths, sitting on cars, on balconies, in trees.

At another charity concert we did in Melbourne I met a street kid named Storm. She was desperately troubled, and no wonder because she'd been raped by her father and uncles. No wonder, either, that she would murder two women in prison. She wrote me some poetry.

Andrew McManus

There was recklessness in the air at that time. At 4 a.m. after a gig in Tasmania we were all crammed into a van on our way to the next show. We were behind schedule and doing 140 kilometres per hour. It was pouring with rain and pitch dark with no street lights. We were all drinking bourbon. Someone said to the driver, 'Hey, slow down!' We all went, 'No, speed up!'

Against my better judgment, Andrew booked us to play at bikie picnics and hangouts. 'They have a code,' he'd say, defending his decision. 'They *always* pay their bills, and they pay them in great stacks of cash that they keep in the back of a truck. No bouncing cheques with bikies.'

I always felt uncomfortable performing in front of bikie gangs. These weren't urban kids with attitude, they were genuine bad guys with prison records for assault and rape. At an open-air gig on a bikie property at Bindoon in Western Australia, they stretched out in front of us as far as we could see. We hired eight security guards in case of trouble, not that they'd have been of any use to us if things got out of hand. The bikies were speeding off their faces and their girlfriends wallowed topless in the mud. Lucky we were a loud band because we were competing against the revving of Harley-Davidsons.

Andrew McManus

I was wrong about bikies. They didn't *always* pay their way. We did a gig for the Rebels in Tasmania. The gang's leaders had guaranteed us $20 000 but not as many of their brothers turned up as they hoped so at the end they could only pay us ten grand. 'That's all we've got, mate. Take it or leave it.' Valuing my life, I took it, but I didn't dare tell Chrissy and Mark I'd been short-changed.

Back in Sydney I called some of my rather more colourful mates in the racing game, including the notorious George Freeman, who was later gunned down. George and co gave me some sure things for Randwick. I risked $5000 of the $10 000 the Rebels had handed over on the horses which, of course, all won. I collected $12 000 in winnings. I put ten grand into the band's coffers, which squared off the Rebels gig, and kept two for myself.

Divinyls, with me on the cover naked under a fishnet dress, hand covering my breast, was a huge hit in Australia. We had believed the album and the spin-off singles would send us into the rock'n'roll stratosphere in America, too, but apart from the smash hit 'I Touch Myself', our Australian success proved to be a false dawn. While the series of follow-up singles to 'Touch' did okay in Australia, they didn't do well in the United States. And because of that, and because Mark and I couldn't decide on a producer for our proposed new album or what songs we wanted to do, Virgin, just like Freddy DeMann, abandoned us.

Once more we were without a label, and Andrew McManus was again our sole manager.

This was a heartbreaking setback. For a while there, we were one of the most famous bands on Earth. We had lived it up in five-star hotels, flown Concorde, been wined and dined in the world's best restaurants. We had cash flow. We had hope. Now we were nowhere. Of course, I told myself, booze would help me cope. Cheers!

For the next two years or so, we lived off touring in Australia, publishing royalties from a couple of greatest hit compilations that Chrysalis put out and our soundtrack cover versions of 'Wild Thing', 'I Ain't Gonna Eat Out My Heart', 'Love Is The Drug' and 'To Sir With Love'. The money we made from these covers was much needed and gratefully received.

Andrew continued to flog us. We were basically on a non-stop tour. He seemed devoted to us. He put up with our shit, got us out of trouble and made us feel special. He pulled strings so we could fly business class and stay in the best hotels in the towns we played. His ploy was to tell the proprietors that other bands on his books (of course he had none) were scheduled to pass through town after us and if the hotel-keeper could see his way clear to giving Divinyls a reduced rate, why, he'd make sure the other bands all stopped at the hotel too. Think of the business! Those proprietors are still waiting.

We hired a new bass player from America, Jerome Smith. He was recommended to us by Charley Drayton. Jerome was a demon guitarist, but like a big child and extraordinarily reckless and a little irresponsible. On the flight to Australia he realised he hadn't bothered to get a work visa. Unfazed, he breezed up to the customs officer at Sydney Airport and announced he was here to play with Divinyls. Amazingly, they gave him a visa on the spot when people in his situation with less chutzpah would have been on the next plane home.

Jerome was a rarity: a black guy crazy about AC/DC. He was a big man and thumped around on stage, especially when he'd been drinking. During gigs I felt he was crowding me out of the spotlight, trying to overshadow me, and one night after a show I came down on him like a two-ton amp. I tore strips off Jerome in front of everyone. I didn't believe there was any other way of dealing with him. I didn't feel good about it later because normally if I had to lay down the law in a major way I'd do it one-on-one behind closed doors. I think this was another sign that I was spiralling out of control and not thinking straight.

But it wasn't always drama, drugs and alcohol. We did have what Biccy Henderson, our tour manager on and off through the nineties, called 'peaceful moments'. We weren't always temperamental rock stars.

Mark had bought a 200-hectare farm at Delaney's Creek in D'Aguilar in the south-east of Queensland, and we left Manly and moved up there. On hiatus from touring we'd return to the farm to lick our wounds. The place had once been a grand estate belonging to a tin magnate—Mahatma Gandhi, former British prime minister Harold Wilson and, the story went, Queen Elizabeth, had all stayed there—but now it was falling apart. There were snakes in the roof. The house was filled with clunky old antiques left behind by past occupants. Mark's mother, Irene, decided to turn the farm into a dairy. By day I made sandwiches as they worked, and at night I slept out on the balcony of the dark old house.

Mark and Irene were always busy working on things together. I felt an outsider and resented the way they set me adrift on that isolated property. There were bottles of malt whisky in the kitchen cupboard and after they had gone to bed I would creep down from the balcony and drink shots alone. I was so unhappy, so lonely.

When some land came on the market a few kilometres down the road I bought it. While a small and basic farmhouse was being built, I lived there alone with only some foxie dogs for company in a corrugated-iron shed with a makeshift shower and toilet. In these hard-scrabble days I thought of the irony: I had just had a No.1 single and yet was living like a yokel.

When bandmembers and roadies visited, they shacked up in a house on Mark's property we called the 'music cottage'. Once Mick, the martial arts expert who got punched out by the Yugoslavian, dropped in. Mick developed an immediate animosity towards Baron, Irene's Anatolian Shepherd dog. Baron lunged at Mick, and he punched the dog between the eyes, which soured its view of the world even more.

Still nursing a grudge against humankind, Baron leapt at me as I got out of my 1950s jeep and savaged my arm. Mark pulled the dog off me. While I was recovering from the shock and the stitches, neither Mark nor Irene seemed overly concerned. I lay alone for three days on a li-lo on my concrete floor, covered in the mini foxie dogs I was breeding and reading Patrick Süskind's *Perfume*. My sense of smell, either because of the dogs or the book, became very pronounced.

In the early nineties, Divinyls hit a purple patch. Mark, Charlie Owen, Jerome and I were really cooking and our set list, after all those years, was formidable. Having been treated to 'Boys In Town', 'Science Fiction', 'Pleasure And Pain', 'Back To The Wall', 'Temperamental', 'Punxsie', 'Casual Encounter', 'Hey Little Boy', 'Make Out Alright', 'Lay Your Body Down' and 'I Touch Myself' any audience was going to go home happy.

Then, in 1993, Charley Drayton, our saviour during the 1990 *Divinyls* recording sessions, took up our offer to play with us Down Under, and Divinyls took a quantum leap.

Charley was a consummate drummer and bass player, yet almost as important was the effect he had on the rest of us. Just as he had done in the studio in Los Angeles, he was endlessly supportive of Mark and me, helping us to focus on our music and offering his broad shoulders to weep on. He was a good man, stable, calm and positive. He took the pressure off, set a professional tone. It was just what the doctor ordered.

Charley indulged me. He was like a cheerleader, telling me I'd performed well. 'I love the way you never give up!' he'd say, hugging me. And he adored Mark, respecting our talent and rising above our craziness. He was inspiring to work with and I think Mark needed to be inspired at that time, in his playing and writing. Like me, he was troubled, jaded and exhausted after so long doing what we did and having little to show for it.

Charley was no goody-two-shoes. He hit alcohol and drugs hard then, and was right at home in our madhouse. Yet, as I had noticed in Los Angeles, no matter how much he knocked himself about the night before he was always fit, focused and together when it was time to work. He could be moody and was capable of not speaking for days when in one of his periodic dark patches.

He was also exotic and when he went to a nightclub, with his good looks and bright clothes, jewellery and out-there accessories he brought the place to a standstill.

Clothes and food mattered to Charley. He dressed in frock coats, with chains hanging off him. Anyone else may have looked ridiculous, but on Charley Drayton it looked right. He was a wonderful cook. When I first met him he opened his coat and the inside pockets were filled with little bottles of sauces and spices.

Charley did a big favour for Divinyls. The gigs that followed his arrival were among the very best we ever did.

His first live performance with us was at the concert at Boggo Road jail in Brisbane on 31 July 1993, which has gone down in Australian rock history as one of *the* great gigs. He was literally hours off the plane from New York. If you watch the video of the concert you'll see me beaming at Charley, who is pounding away on his drums with a beatific expression. He made a big difference to us, just like that.

Charley Drayton

Chrissy told me later that she really wanted me to play with Divinyls but never asked me because she was afraid that I would, and things would work out, and then I'd leave to go on to something else. It would be too much of a tease. When she invited me to play with Divinyls at the Boggo Road concert it was on the understanding that it was only a temporary hiring.

After the performance, I had back spasms, a result of my weight fluctuations, the long flight and the show. Chrissy came to my rescue and massaged my back. This was the first time in four years she had showed me more of her caring side.

We went on last at Boggo Road, after the other two acts on the gig, Billy Thorpe and the Aztecs and Rose Tattoo. Both of these bands tried to top us by playing louder than we could. They failed. When I watch the video of that gig I realise, without false modesty, that when we were good we were very, very good. The band had kind of come down . . . the groove had slowed a little. It was a bit more behind the beat, whereas early Divinyls was right on the beat or ahead of it. Which was great, but this was good too.

Andrew McManus

Boggo Road was the creepiest venue we ever played. It was no longer a prison, but there were still cells, which of course I sold off as corporate boxes. We went down to a dungeon beneath the cement quadrangle which looked just like a mediaeval torture chamber and it chilled us to the bone.

I had an altercation with Rose Tattoo. They were playing too loud, trying to make us sound wimpish in comparison when we came onstage after them. I told their manager Michael Browning to lower the volume. He told me to 'Fuck off!' so I pushed Browning off the stage. He fell 5 metres into a pit.

Adjoining the section of the prison where we played was a still-functioning women's prison. I knew one of the inmates. It was Storm, the street kid and incest victim I'd met at the charity gig in Melbourne. By now she was covered in tatts and had a big scar around her neck where she'd literally tried to cut her head off. Storm was notorious in prison for her homicidal tendencies. I can't imagine what went through her head when she heard me singing not 200 metres away.

One fabulous gig was not going to turn things around. Divinyls may have been getting the sound right professionally but personally Mark and I were striking a very discordant tune.

17
SPLIT

Mark and I were falling apart and the words of Divinyls' Steinberg/Kelly song 'I'm On Your Side' were taking on a sad and prophetic resonance.

If Mark and I had never met, a lot of good music would never have been made, but quite possibly we would have been happier people. We very near destroyed each other. The comical bickering that characterised our first months and years together became something much darker as time went by. By 1992 and 1993, Mark and I were nearing the end. Our physical attraction for each other and our creative partnership had kept us together through some horrendous scenes. But suddenly sex and creativity were no compensation for a deeply flawed relationship that was making us desperately unhappy and fuelling our addictions.

Mark, like me, had very low impulse control. He was argumentative and manic when he was drinking. Apart from rare times with Charley, he couldn't relate to anybody else apart from me. And while he was clinging to me, we were beating each other up. It's the old cliché, we couldn't live with each other and we couldn't live without each other. I went along with it. He was such a major part of Divinyls I felt I had to cosset and protect him so he could create.

There was something about each of us that ignited the other, that exacerbated our nastiness and potential to be cruel. That would have happened without the alcohol and drugs, but those substances made us worse. Much worse.

We abused and sometimes even physically attacked each other, though not in a way that would cause each other real harm. We slapped, bit, pinched and kicked, screeched and chased each other like naughty kids in the playground. For all that, it was deeply destructive behaviour.

Apart from music, our basic values were different. Mark was very much into appearances, and even when we had no money he usually found a way to wear expensive clothes, buy a rare guitar or the latest model plane to make, and drive a swish car. I loved clothes, too, but cut my cloth to fit my budget. And I couldn't have cared less about cars. I never lost my solid, middle-class way of viewing life.

Incidents lurch to mind like skulls looming through the gloom on a ghost train. Once in Melbourne we were staying at the Carlisle Hotel where all the bands stayed. The place oozed rock'n'roll history, and Mark and I left it with a legend of our own. The night started out badly when tomcats urinated on the bonnet of our hire car while it was in the parking lot of the gig venue, and as we were being driven back to the Carlisle afterwards the nauseating stench of tomcat piss permeated the car. Mark and I had argued earlier in the evening, and once in our adjoining rooms at the hotel we continued the argument. After a bit Mark cried off and went to his room. I wasn't finished with him and ordered him to open the door. He refused, and as he cringed inside I dug at his door with the heel of my cowboy boot. I dug for about an hour, until I had made a large hole. When I reached through the hole to unlock the door Mark grabbed a fire extinguisher and sprayed foam all over me. Meanwhile, a large crowd, including the rest of the band, had gathered in the hallway, observing our antics. We didn't care who was watching. When I checked out I was presented with a hefty bill for the damage.

This was minor theatrics compared to the time I almost killed Mark. We were in Los Angeles. He and I were sitting in the front of a convertible we had leased, with Mark in the passenger seat. The car was stationary at the top of a steep driveway but the motor was on. I wanted to go to one destination, Mark, of course, to another. We were shouting at each other. I released the handbrake and got out of the car which, with Mark inside, rolled down the drive, picking up speed, and plunged into undergrowth which stopped it from tumbling over a cliff. Luckily, Mark was able to leap free before it stopped and wasn't hurt. I don't know what I would have done if he'd been injured.

It seemed that even when Mark and I were having fun together things ended in tears. Again in Melbourne in some hotel, for a laugh I took my clothes off and covered myself in newspaper. Mark began chasing me around the room. I ran into the bathroom and tried to skid on a towel that was lying on the floor, tripped and sprained my foot. For the following week, each night before a gig, my family doctor, Peter Lewis, had to give me an injection to deaden the pain enough so I could pull my boot on and go on stage. I was in agony the whole time.

I can remember Charlie Owen and me at a café in Sydney's Darlinghurst. It was 10 a.m. and we'd been up all night and were still plastered. Don Walker from Cold Chisel was having breakfast and Charlie and I wobbled in and sat down beside him. The whole place was staring. We didn't care. Then we walked back to Don's house and tried to write a song. Other times I'd find myself sitting in a dark room in Kings Cross doing coke with strangers and not having a clue how I'd got there. These are not highlights of my life but if I want to tell my story they have to be included.

When I was drunk I'd call friends all over the world from my hotel room, then in the morning have no recollection of having done so.

When I went to the reception desk to pay the bill it would be humungous. 'Did I do *this*?' I'd ask, hoping there was some mistake.

Shayna Stewart

> When Chrissy was in a really bad phase she would phone me at three
> or four in the morning and she'd be completely mad. Raving. But, you
> know, obviously needy in some way . . .

To me, drinking ramped up the fun. It made the moment last, and last. As long as I kept drinking the party couldn't end. I'd walk into some place and think, 'Oh, this is boring!' but once I had a drink it wasn't so boring. I drank to make everything bigger, better . . . more of a trip. And Charley Drayton was like that. Charlie Owen was like that. Vince and Andrew were like that. Harve and Rick. Mark was like that. Mark was probably just trying to keep up with me. That's how we all were.

Mark and I had so many fights, they lost meaning. We were never contrite afterwards. We never even discussed them. By then we had found something else to be at each other's throats about.

Andrew McManus

> Chrissy and Mark in their final months together were completely
> unmanageable. Chrissy was usually juiced up, and Mark threw terrible
> tantrums.

By this stage there were more low times than good times. I coped with the disaster my life had become by drinking and taking more drugs than I ever had. I surrounded myself with people who drank and did drugs, perhaps to make myself feel better about what I was doing. It had reached the stage when the only time Mark and I could really sit down and talk civilly was after we'd had a drink or done cocaine. Then the come-down was horrible.

In spite of my image as a man-eater, I was always faithful to Mark. I *was*, as God is my judge! I don't believe he can say the same thing.

One night I arrived at Benny's bar in Potts Point and surprised

Mark with a woman. I knew at once by their stricken looks that they had been together. It was getting ugly.

Mark would jealously berate me if I so much as looked at another man. In New York I got smashed and went home with a guy who was an art director. Absolutely nothing happened. Nothing would have happened even if I hadn't passed out. When I returned to our hotel the next morning Mark assumed I'd slept with the fellow and he was devastated. He never forgave me for something I hadn't done. Maybe he justified his flings this way.

There was a woman who worked for a record company who had a crush on Mark. I didn't take her seriously as a rival and went out of my way to be kind to her. I even bought her lingerie. She responded by trying to humiliate me. In an Indian restaurant in London the waiter tipped his tray of drinks and ice all over me. Sitting there drenched and freezing, my dress ruined, I glanced at the woman and she looked like the cat who'd swallowed the cream. Maybe I'm being paranoid, but I believe she paid that waiter to up-end his tray, and maybe to do something else as well. The next day I came down with food poisoning.

In 1993, we hired a new wardrobe girl. I could see Mark was attracted to her and she to him. One drunken night Mark, this woman and I ended up in bed together. I soon came to my senses and kicked her out.

Then a friend whispered to me, 'Do you know Mark's having an affair with the wardrobe chick?' I didn't. Everyone else did. Mark returned to me, as he did after each of his flings. I believe he truly loved me. But I was a really hard person to love. Sometimes when I would start to drink, Mark would look at my glass and he'd be so afraid. I drank alcoholically, and Mark wasn't equipped to help me cope with my disease. Yes, he slapped me, but I didn't blame him. How could I have? He had landed himself the lover from hell.

In time I, perhaps subconsciously, began pushing Mark onto other women, hoping he'd fall in love with one of them and we could break up and put an end to our agony. I just wanted it over, yet I didn't have it in me to call our relationship off. I couldn't bear to hurt this sad, sensitive soul, nor did I want to disrupt the band.

Then, towards the end of 1993, along came Gabby, a beautiful model and a very sweet girl. This time Mark didn't come home.

It was over at last. I was broken-hearted and cried for three days, then I said, 'Okay. That's that. Time to move on.'

Mark and I continued as songwriting collaborators and as Divinyls, but that was all. No more emotional torture, no more insane jealousy. I felt an enormous release. After twelve years being yoked to him, I was free.

I met a guy named Simon. He was an artist. Simon was good-looking and fun, and an on-the-rebound antidote to Mark. But after all those years with Mark, it was weird being with someone new. Simon was most impressed that I was a rock star and I liked that. There was no way I would take him on the road with the band, though. It was a novelty having two separate lives, with band and romance not intertwined.

Then I fell in love with Charley Drayton and a whole new life opened up.

TAKING THE PLUNGE

18

Charley and I became lovers in 1994. We were staying at Peppers Hotel in Double Bay. Up until that magical night, Charley had seemed to keep his distance from me, in spite of the time, after a stoush with Mark, when I drunkenly blurted out that I fancied him. There had been a couple of uncomfortably charged moments following that. Was Charley trying to head off Mark's jealous accusations, or did he fancy me more than he let on and didn't want to precipitate something that would unbalance the band's dynamic? Maybe he genuinely felt nothing romantic for me then. I still don't know, but I do know that for both of us, from the time I split with Mark, something was stirring.

In Darwin on New Year's Eve 1993, Mark and I had had another of our drunken arguments and I ran out into the night, determined to find some crocodiles and throw myself to them. Charley chased after me. He took me by the shoulders and calmed me down. We sat and talked till the early hours. In my inebriation I blurted out that I was attracted to him, then instantly regretted it. The next day we flew out of Darwin, and Charley was given the seat next to me. I was so embarrassed that I'd opened up to him. But he made it okay.

He then flew back to New York for some gigs. I don't think I even said goodbye. We didn't speak for a couple of weeks, and then he called me. He told me he was seeing a girl, and I by then was dating Simon. Phew. So there was nothing to us, after all.

Charley returned for more touring with us, and then came the night at Peppers when we slept together. We told no one that we were lovers. We didn't want to announce anything until we were sure it was for real.

For the next couple of months we sneaked around. We went to each other's rooms, via the fire stairs, in the dead of night. No one guessed a thing, including the roadies, which was incredible because those guys are bloodhounds when it comes to sniffing out affairs.

Charley and I decided to test our love. We would catch the Indian Pacific train from Perth across the Nullarbor Plain to Sydney. If we could survive living in each other's pockets for four days non-stop, and still loved each other by journey's end, we would come clean.

We boarded the train and to our dismay we had been given two sleeping compartments. That wouldn't do. I bribed a porter and we were immediately relocated to a suite. It was a huge compartment with two double beds and gold wallpaper, a stereo and a private bathroom. Outside our window there were kangaroos and emus racing the train, flocks of pink flamingos, and the vast, vast desert. Until then the only wild Australian animals Charley had seen were roadkill on tour. Aborigines waved as we sped by their camps and Charley, an African-American from Brooklyn, waved right back. Each morning at six the porter brought us tea and in the evening we'd dress for dinner and dine *a deux*. I felt loved and human for the first time in a long while. Charley and I talked and loved and laughed. I quizzed him about every woman he'd ever slept with and instead of feeling threatened I embraced his past. A good sign, I thought. By the time we arrived at Sydney's Central Station we knew this was for real.

Charley Drayton

I realised that I wanted to be Chrissy's lover as well as her friend. Yes, I had been unsettled by the rubdown she gave me after the Boggo Road concert. And while we were recording the album in Los Angeles we all stayed at a hotel near Sunset Boulevard and on a few occasions after a recording session I'd go to my room and unwind with a Bloody Mary and then walk the corridors, stopping at Chrissy's door and coming *so close* to knocking and seeing what would happen when she opened it. Each time I held back, afraid that she'd say, 'Sorry, Charley, you've blown it. Goodbye.' I wasn't prepared to risk our professional relationship. It was way too tall to mess with. And there was intimate tension when we were in Los Angeles recording 'Love Is A Drug'. Chrissy needed a stereo to listen to mixes and she asked me to drive her to an electronics store on Wilshire Boulevard. We were in the car together hanging out, and there was undeniably something in the air between us. The silence was *loaded*. Afterwards, we went to an Italian restaurant on La Brea and couldn't look each other in the face.

I went home to New York after Boggo Road. Then Chrissy and Mark called me and asked me to tour with them in Australia in mid-1993. I returned, rehearsed and went on tour. The last gig of the tour was a New Year's Eve show in Darwin. There were conventions going on, so Chrissy and Mark had a suite in a hotel while the rest of us stayed in a motel further out of town. After the show we were all in Chrissy and Mark's suite and they were fighting, arguing once again. I'd had enough and left. Jerome, Charlie Owens and I sneaked downstairs into the lobby and climbed into a cab. Just before we set off, Mark and Chrissy appeared in the lobby, still arguing. Chrissy saw us and ran away. She was distraught. 'I'm running, I'm running, I'm running away,' she sobbed. 'I'm going to throw myself to the crocodiles. I'm tired and I can't take this any more.'

She took off down the street that suffocatingly steamy tropical night in her Michel Perry high heels. I'd never seen her run like that. Afraid that she meant what she said about the crocodiles, I leapt out of the taxi and chased her, running over stuff I couldn't see, crashing through undergrowth and down rough dirt tracks. She ran so fast. And when I finally caught her I was astonished by her strength. I grasped her wrist to try to tell her to calm down and she wrenched away from me and hared off again. 'Hang on, Chrissy! Calm down!' Had she been alone who knows how it would have ended.

Very early in the morning we ended up in a park. It was a wild scene. There were Aborigines and homeless people. I grabbed her wrist again and I could barely hang on as she struggled to get away, she was beside herself in tears. I tried to reason with her and we talked for what seemed like hours. At one point Chrissy wanted to make a confession, that she had strong feelings for me. She wanted to come back to my room. I said as much as I wanted her to, she couldn't.

Next morning the band left Darwin to fly to Sydney, where I was to connect with a flight home to New York. Mark and Chrissy were allocated seats together but refused to sit next to each other, so I was given the seat next to her. Everyone was hungover. Feeling embarrassed because of what she'd said a few hours earlier, Chrissy wouldn't talk. Then, just as we were landing in Sydney, she said very softly, 'Charley, I can't believe you'd ever speak to me again after I put it all out there last night.' I told her, 'I love you. We'll speak. This isn't the last time we'll ever see each other.'

We did speak a few weeks later when I was back in New York. We had a five-hour telephone conversation. We went to sleep while talking to each other on the phone.

I later came back to Australia to do more gigs with Divinyls. The first night back I was in my room with Jerome in Peppers in Double Bay, and the door opened. It was Chrissy with a bottle of wine and a glass in her hand. She opened up her bathrobe to reveal the bathing suit she wore underneath. That was the first time I had seen her like that. I pulled Jerome to the side and said, 'Jerome, whatever you do tonight, you are not to let me out of your sight.' Chrissy was lying on the couch, flirting with me like crazy. A party sprang up around us. The room became like a mosh pit. Later there was just Jerome, Chrissy

and me. Then Jerome disappeared. Chrissy had bribed him to leave.
We cuddled on the terrace. That was the start of us . . .

On the road we had an affair . . . We didn't want anyone else to know
at this stage in case it didn't work out. And we knew Mark would be
furious. Even though he had Gabby, he still needed some kind of
ongoing control over Chrissy. I didn't want to hurt Mark. My respect
for him was boundless. And I respected his and Chrissy's extraordinary
musical relationship and didn't want to destroy it. At each new town I
cased our hotel, checking where the staircases and fire escapes were
so I could secretly go to her room at night. It was dangerous, and
romantic.

By the end of the run, in Perth, we had decided we wanted to be
together. We were in a hotel and had separate rooms. I was never in
mine. I lived in Chrissy's suite and I don't think we ever had clothes
on the whole time we were there. We were just loving each other. It
was a beautiful time.

We thought we had better put ourselves through a final test, just
to see if this was love or just passion that would dissipate when the
novelty wore off. We would take the train back across Australia to Sydney.
But we couldn't just go alone together because everyone would suspect
we were lovers, so we had to go through the charade of inviting
everyone and hoping like hell no one would take us up on our invitation.
Incredibly, Mark of the whole bunch was tempted, so Chrissy picked
an argument with him to put him off.

The train trip was wonderful, and I took the chance to be honest
with Chrissy. I told her I loved her. I told her I wanted to be with her. I
told her she was drinking heavily and that if we were to have a long
and happy future together she should think hard about giving up the
third person in the relationship—alcohol. 'Chrissy,' I said, 'I don't want
to lose you.'

As soon as we got off that train, our mood was broken when Simon
was there to meet me. Charley had organised with Jerome to pick
us up, but somehow Simon found out and turned up as well. He

raced up to me and I gave him both barrels. 'How fucking dare you just turn up unannounced! I didn't ask you to meet me. Leave me alone!' Understandably, Simon was terribly upset. But at least the deed was done.

Not so easy was breaking the news about Charley and me to Mark, even though he had a gorgeous lover of his own in Gabby. Andrew agreed with Charley's idea to tell Mark in a public place because he'd have to control himself there. We asked Mark to meet us in a café on the footpath outside Peppers Hotel. I told him Charley and I were together. He told us to fuck off—emphatically.

It was a revelation to be in a relationship whose foundation wasn't animosity. Charley *never* argued. He couldn't be bothered. Even I was much calmer, though I suppose it takes two to fight. Occasionally when I was drunk, I would lash out. Charley would hug me, soothe me, talk to me and tell me it was all okay. I would dissolve in his arms.

Charley Drayton

I loved Chrissy and looked out for her, but she could squash my buzz. I'd find what I thought was a good hiding spot for the evening, a place to drink, mingle and get high. Then, soon enough, I'd get a warning that Chrissy was on her way there. I knew if she'd left the hotel she'd be ready to party. I'd tell the crew, 'I'm bailing, I'll see ya at the next spot.' Eventually Chrissy would catch up, soon you'd run out of hideaways. This was all in good fun, but my buzz would go flat, while Chrissy's would be in first gear.

Sometimes although exhausting, she could be very entertaining. I've seen her walk up on big nasty people, read them their rights, tongue-lash them, chew 'em up. Other times, I'd have to intercede and kindly extricate her from the situation. Next day or day after she'd ask, 'What happened the other night?'

Don't know how we got through a few of those.

Eventually, Mark accepted that Charley and I were lovers and in love. Our fights continued, but now it was only the music we argued about. With Charley around, Mark was careful never to overstep the mark. Charley continued to treat Mark with respect. He loved Mark, and never threatened his position in the band. Charley was also a marvellous help to Andrew in matters concerning the band.

I broke Simon's heart. For a few weeks after I called our relationship off I'd arrive at my hotel room and he'd be there in bed. I'd make him leave. He rang me every day for the next year. I felt terrible about hurting him but needed to follow my heart.

In 1994 Charley took me back to New York for a couple of weeks. I knew Charley was a highly respected musician. From Keith Richards and Neil Young down, he was held in high regard by rock royalty. When we went to see Marianne Faithfull, I went backstage and she was so affectionate to him. I watched him accept her adulation in his stride, as if it was his right.

We lived in his apartment on the corner of 43rd Street and 11th Avenue in Hell's Kitchen. His mother, Isadora, came to visit. She looked me up and down and wobbled her head. She didn't like me at all. She'd heard of my reputation and feared I was going to take her precious son to live in faraway Australia. It didn't help my cause when I went with her and Charley's father, Bernard, to see Charley play a gig and I got drunk. I don't know what I was thinking but, as I've said before, it doesn't take much to get me there.

The following Christmas we were back in Australia staying at my farm and Mum came up to meet the man I loved. Charley cooked her a soul food lunch of corn bread, barbecued pork and chicken, rice, macaroni and cheese, and did his impersonations of a Frenchman, Mike Tyson and President Clinton. She almost wet herself. She was also extremely impressed at the way he stood up to me. She'd never seen a boyfriend do that before. Mum will be a fan of Charley's for life.

Charley was a romantic, always buying me presents and surprising me with treats, and he made a huge fuss of me on Valentine's Day. I'd melt.

Another gift was the space he gave me. He was neither controlling nor jealous. He had his own life and work away from me and Divinyls. He continued to live, tour and record in the States with topline acts between Divinyls commitments.

Charley was Divinyls' biggest fan. He collected all our past albums, singles and bootlegs, and still buys Divinyls memorabilia on eBay. In turn, the boys in the band and the road crew were in awe of him. When he toured with us, he always had his own room that he decorated with scarves and bright materials. There'd be tea made—Charley adores exotic teas—and incense burning. Music was always playing. Everyone gravitated to Charley's room. Most hotel and motel rooms are sterile, not Charley's. Entering it, you'd feel you had stumbled into Aladdin's Cave.

Charley even brightened up those eternal bus trips as we travelled the bush and the outback. A 2000-kilometre bus trip is deadly boring no matter how many videos you watch or tapes and CDs you play. Then there are the ubiquitous ramshackle motels with the ubiquitous green, slime-covered swimming pools that await at the end of each day's journey. But because Australia was a novelty to Charley, he was astounded by the scenery and animal life that I'd come to take for granted and his wide-eyed enthusiasm was catching. For this somewhat jaded rock'n'roll singer it meant I saw my country anew.

Charley Drayton

We performed every show as if it were our last. We played to encourage each other and make the best out of what was happening. No matter what state of mind we were in we always gave it our all and if the crowd served us extra attitude, it would be an added challenge. Whether the gig was for a small crowd or a drunk crowd or a tired crowd at 2 a.m., or a bunch of miners in Mt Isa, our challenge was to make it the best for them that we could. Chrissy would always go out of her way to make a show special, even when she was at a physical or mental low.

Depending on how we felt, we'd dissect all the segments of a song and take a ride on that. Early on, Divinyls' arrangements were always the same. In later years, the band had the chops to explore and experiment with songs.

A wiser, saner woman would have been looking to change things. But even with Charley in my life, my drinking and drug-taking was preventing me from focusing, sorting out my priorities. I was in a pattern, a routine from which I couldn't see my way clear to escape. And my excesses were fuelling my predicament. It was time to get off the Divinyls train and sort myself out, to change my life and my whole way of doing things, but to do this I had to stop drinking and at that stage I wasn't equipped to do it.

UNDERWORLD

As far as the band went, all I could do was start thinking about a new record label—and a new album. We'd been living on the proceeds of our endless touring and what royalties came in. Now, in 1994, it was time to have another crack at a big hit album. Andrew set about trying to get us a label, and I went to the United States to write songs with Billy Steinberg and Tom Kelly. One was a ballad called 'I'm Jealous'. Nothing I've written has been 100 per cent autobiographical, but I'm sure the seeds of the song were sown in those days before Charley rescued me, and I was eating my heart out over Mark. The bitter lyrics, which included the lines 'I'm liable to do anything/I might kick her face in', were a fair reflection of my feelings towards some of the women involved with Mark.

The new song was to be on our next album, if we could get someone to sign us up, but to make some money in the meantime we decided to record 'I'm Jealous' at Woodland Studios in Nashville while we were on tour in America and then try to place it on a soundtrack.

'I'm Jealous' was produced by Peter Collins, who'd worked with Bon Jovi and it was engineered by Kevin 'Caveman' Shirley, a South African who'd produced for Baby Animals in Australia before linking with Collins in America. Since 'I'm Jealous' he has gone on to become one of the world's finest producers, working on albums by Aerosmith, Black Crowes, Little Steven, Iron Maiden, Led Zeppelin, Journey and on *Frogstomp*, the multi-platinum debut album by silverchair. Recently Kevin sent me a piece he'd written (for his book—which has not yet been published) about the nasty vibe at Woodland as we cut 'I'm Jealous':

Kevin Shirley

I've always thought Divinyls were amazing. Chrissy Amphlett's voice is so sexy and sluttish, and her accent adds a raspy illusion which makes her sound like a smoky-voiced prostitute in a Kings Cross junkie choir, all attitude and enigma! Mark McEntee is her perfect foil, with his razor-edged guitar tones and riffs, and the passion and magic between her voice and his guitar was so sublime, it seems that they were always destined to be lovers, which they were for a long time.

When I first heard Divinyls, I was blown out of the water; like an inedible rainbow reef fish dynamited off Hin Muang in Thailand's Andaman Sea. I must have listened to the *Temperamental* album, which Mike Chapman produced, a thousand times, and can hear it in my head now without playing it, with its armadillo mix all spiky and tight . . . the title song, the gorgeous 'Punxsie', 'Hey Little Boy' with its sixties 'hoo-hoo' backing vocals . . . what an album! So, when Peter Collins asked me to stay in Nashville and record a new song for the band, I was delighted. We moved into Woodland Studios to set up the session on 20 July 1994, just a few days after I'd wrapped up the Bon Jovi 'Always' sessions, and were ready and waiting for the band—who sauntered in the following day at about four in the afternoon, obviously they'd just woken up and been driven to the studio. The air was so tangibly thick with tension right from the beginning, you could have cut it with a knife—thicker even than Los Angeles summer smog, but a lot cooler in the artificial airconditioned studio environment. Drummer

Charley Drayton and bassist Jerome Smith came into the studio, and I got them to play a little, and set up the sounds for them for the session. Jerome was very animated, and Charley was more reserved, but very professional. I, as usual, tried to be very upbeat to give the session a sense of urgency and fun, but it was a mime song and dance act for the blind!

Chrissy came into the vocal booth to get a sound, and muddled along—trying to find the key and learn the lyrics of the song from a cassette of the demo in a very non-committed way, and then she disappeared. Mark came in about half an hour later, and noodled around on the guitar—seemingly in the dark as to the song's structure, composition or arrangement. It was patently obvious that the two of them were not talking . . . no one was happy. Mark had his new blonde Australian girlfriend with him at the studio, and Chrissy was with Charley—and the song we were recording, 'I'm Jealous,' was written by Chrissy (with Billy Steinberg and Tom Kelly) about the break-up of her and Mark's relationship . . .

You got a new girlfriend
But I still love you
I can't stand the thought of her
Having a piece of you

What she got that I don't?
What she do that I won't?

You must be blind
Take a good look at her
She's not your kind
I don't know what I'd do
If I saw her with you

I'm jealous
I'm jealous
I'm jealous
Out of my mind

I come around and see you
'cos I want to remind you
But what if she's there?
How would I find you?

You've got a new baby
But I want you back again
I'm liable to do anything
I might kick her face in

What she got that I don't?
What she do that I won't?
You must be blind
After all we've been through

I'm devoted to you
I'm jealous
I'm jealous
I'm jealous
Out of my mind

And it hurts
And it hurts right here
In my heart is a bloody tear
I thought that you were so sincere

You got what you wanted
And you got out of here . . .

I'm jealous
I'm jealous
I'm jealous
Out of my mind.

It's all there in the lyrics! Anyway, we finally got the band together and
started running through the song. I was blown away by Charley's feel
on the drums, and was later quoted in *Modern Drummer* magazine as

saying he was the best drummer I'd ever worked with; but I was about to make a blistering faux pas. In a light-hearted attempt to keep the session alive, I had remarked that Charley and Jerome were sounding amazing, and added that 'it must be that natural rhythm', which unbeknown to me, didn't go down at all well with Chrissy, who thought that I was making an ugly racial stereotype—which with my South African heritage was tantamount to discrimination. If anyone had bothered to find out anything about me, they would know this to be without any validity, but in the self-centred, insular and very frosty environs of the studio, no-one even cared.

Cutting the basic tracks was straightforward enough. I think two or three takes would have nailed it, as Charley's pocket and groove were flawless, and Jerome just stuck to him like chewing gum to a boot on a hot day! Recording Mark's guitar was quite a bit more difficult, but his ideas were great, and we finished the guitar without Chrissy hearing a note of it.

When it came time to do the vocals, Chrissy didn't even bother listening to the track in the control room first, she just went into the booth and we ran over the vocals quite a few times, and she went home. Peter and I stayed on to compile the vocal, and then I Fedexed a copy to the song's co-writer, Billy Steinberg, as Peter wanted his opinion on the vocal. I was surprised, because I'd never seen anyone give the songwriter that respect in the studio—and Billy replied first thing the next morning with some very salient points about adjusting the melody in the chorus, which Peter took note of, and then he had Chrissy re-sing the parts. The difference was very positive and the song came out great. We had an ocarina session player come in and lace some ethereal parts all over the song, but I'm not sure they were ever used, as the band hated the sound of it. The ocarina is an ancient shell-shaped, flute-like instrument, and is probably most famous now as the instrument played on the *Legend Of Zelda* video game.

Once the track was recorded, we moved back to Emerald Studios, site of the Bon Jovi sessions, where I mixed the song, and its many versions (with ocarina, without ocarina, etc.). It's a very dry mix, with

Chrissy's vocals standing very proud of the instruments—and it only took me about one hour to mix. When I had finished, I went out into the lounge area where the band were sitting uncomfortably quiet, and I said, 'I've finished the mix.' All four of them just looked up at me, said nothing, didn't smile or make any gesture and didn't move—so I went back inside and got my already-packed bags and walked out. As I walked by them sitting in the lounge on my way out, Charley tentatively asked 'Where're you going?' and as I got into the taxi I replied, 'I've got to go to the airport. I've a plane to catch!' closed the car door, and headed for the airport to go to New York, where I'd been booked to mix an album for Doro Pesch, starting the next day. A singularly strange experience, but to this day 'I'm Jealous' is one of my favourite mixes. And I still think Divinyls are amazing.

The tension Kevin felt heightened everything. It wasn't a good time and it seemed we were all looking for an escape—and alcohol and drugs were the easy release we chose.

Andrew McManus

Trouble and chaos dogged us in Nashville. Charley and Jerome hired a convertible and prowled around town. Then, because two black guys had robbed our hotel recently, they were stopped and searched by the cops three or four times in a morning's drive. Those redneck bastards couldn't believe Charley and Jerome could legitimately be riding in such a swish motor. Then Mark's girlfriend Gabby had a few drinks and antagonised some good old boys at the waffle house next to our hotel and the police were called and a guy thrown out. He threatened to return with his gun and finish us off. I moved us all to another hotel.

What caused me most grief was when Mark stuffed up a dream of mine, to visit Elvis's mansion, Graceland, in Memphis. It's a six-hour drive, but we set off together in plenty of time to have a good stickybeak at the estate. This would be a highlight of my life. Then, on the way, Mark decided he was ravenous and insisted on stopping for a lengthy meal. I tried to get him to hurry but there was no rushing Mark. We arrived at Graceland five minutes before those big gates clanged shut for the day. I had just enough time to buy a fridge magnet and a couple of books. Then we set off on the long drive back to Nashville in thick silence.

The day after we recorded 'I'm Jealous' I flew to Los Angeles. In my luggage was the tape of the track, which I was to play for Jeff Aldrich, who chose the songs that were used on *Melrose Place* and on the label's big-selling soundtrack album. It was a crucial meeting because if he liked the record, and me, it would mean a good payday for us. I checked into the Sunset Marquis the day before our 10 a.m. meeting. I was determined to have a quiet night and then, straight and sober, catch a cab to Giant. Of course, this didn't happen. A friend had got wind that I was in town and it was my birthday. At 9 p.m. there was a knock on my apartment door. I opened it and there was my mate, with John Lennon's son, Julian, in tow and a big bag. Within half an hour there were twenty people in my room, partying. So much for my quiet night.

At nine the next morning, an hour before my appointment with Jeff Aldrich, I hustled the last of the revellers out of the door. I showered quickly, thinking, 'How the fuck can I pull off this meeting? I'm too wasted to talk. I'm too wasted to *think*!' I finally got my arse to Giant. I sat in the reception foyer drinking glass after glass of water thinking, 'Keep it together, Andrew ... keep it together.' Right on ten, a secretary approached. 'Oh, shit!' I panicked. 'I'm on.' But to my immense relief, she said, 'Mr Aldrich is running half an hour late. He's terribly sorry.' I tried to tell her, 'That's perfectly fine,' but was incapable of speech. Anxious and paranoid, I gripped the arms of my chair hard and took another long gulp of water and sweated on Jeff Aldrich, much as a condemned man sweats on the electric chair. Eventually Aldrich arrived and I was shown into his room. I sat opposite him in front of his huge desk with its photos of him and various mega rock stars. He talked about 'I'm Jealous' and Divinyls. I attempted to respond but my lockjaw prevented conversation. Finally he said, 'You know, Andrew, I like you. You know why? You don't butt in!'

Mission accomplished, I returned to the Sunset Marquis and slept for three days.

We were all on the toboggan. There must have been something about 'I'm Jealous' and cocaine. The night before I had to film the video for the song in Sydney I drank too much at the hotel where I was staying, the Ritz-Carlton. Charley was in the States. Andrew put me to bed, where I remained for all of half an hour before going back downstairs and disappearing into the night. At a bar I bumped into a very well-known singer I knew who, naturally, had some cocaine. We went to his room and did lines all night. I can't remember going to bed. I *can* remember my alarm going off at an ungodly hour. I was due on the set. I felt so awful. I felt as though I was insane. I wanted to die. I arrived only a little late, and soldiered on at the shoot for six hours until midday, when I began to feel *really* ill. Like when I got wasted during *Blood Brothers* and my stomach convulsed in the loft in William Street, I knew with stark clarity that I was destroying myself. Yet as soon as I felt better, my fears dissolved and I recklessly turned again to consuming as much alcohol and drugs as I could lay my hands on.

I went to a Robert Plant and Jimmy Page gig at the Sydney Entertainment Centre. I was wearing a thousand-dollar Helmut Lang PVC suit and I'd had a few drinks. I was backstage and the band was just about to walk on and I yelled out to the drummer that I thought Charley Drayton was a better drummer than him. The poor guy's face dropped. A man carrying a hurdy-gurdy told me to 'Fuck off!' Then somebody grabbed me and stuck a backstage pass on my suit that completely ruined it. Mark was there and tried to look after me. I could see the look in his eyes that said no matter what I did, he still loved me. The next morning, I went to breakfast in Double Bay, and Page and Plant and their tour manager Nick Pitt walked in. I just sat there, embarrassed to the roots of my hair.

Charley Drayton

Chrissy's idea of winding down after a gig was to find someone to give her a joint so she could go to sleep. We knew if she smoked that joint she'd still be up the next day. If it was Charlie Owen, he would take his guitar to Chrissy's room, and they'd work on beautiful songs, explore new ideas, then share a bottle of wine and the wine sometimes kept flowing and flowing. Partying and craziness would follow.

Nothing would ever stop Chrissy getting to the stage but towards the end she needed certain things to get there. She'd be so sick the doc would come in and give her an injection of Stemetil which would make her so sleepy she would have to take a capful of Catovit accompanied by a glass of vodka to get her back up there. This didn't happen every night, but once a week or fortnight. Chrissy was a binger.

Even though we were all getting wasted we were still focused on the band, the music. Andrew knew Chris Gilbey, who was head of the international record label BMG's Australian office. After talking to Andrew, Gilbey convinced his masters in Los Angeles to take a chance on us. BMG would bankroll the recording of our next album, and distribute and promote it worldwide. We celebrated; we were back in business.

We wouldn't have partied quite so hard had we realised that a terrible blunder had been made, one that would all but destroy the band and sentence Mark and me to years of heavy debt. As I understand it, Andrew and Gilbey were asked to advise BMG head office how much it would cost to get the band to Los Angeles and record there. They told them $280 000. Delighted at the low quote, BMG took us on with enthusiasm. Which turned to fury when, halfway through recording *Underworld*, the money ran out and BMG realised they'd been quoted *American*, not Australian dollars. We didn't have $US280 000 to make our album, we had only around $US160 000.

I don't completely absolve myself or Mark from not picking up the error. Strictly speaking it wasn't our job and the responsibility for the negotiations with Chris Gilbey and BMG producer Keith Forsey in Los Angeles, who would produce the album, was Andrew's, but in earlier days when we were control freaks and pored over every minute detail of Divinyls business, desperately trying not to let anyone burn us, such a disaster would not have occurred. For all that, at the time of the fiasco and for years after, I was beside myself with rage at Andrew. As our manager, I held him responsible for the debacle. He tried to explain how it had all been a terrible misunderstanding, but I didn't want to know.

Andrew McManus

The mistake wasn't my fault. There was confusion between BMG executives in Sydney and Los Angeles. I always understood we'd need $US280 000. The other guys got it wrong. Why would I go to America to record and think I'd be paying for it in Australian dollars?

We were in the deepest shit. I asked BMG for more money, but they laughed and told me, 'You're kidding! You are not getting another cent, but we want our album for the agreed-upon sum and if we don't get it we're going to sue you.' It got really unpleasant. I paid nearly $50 000 of our debts with my Diner's Club card. We all returned to Australia. Chrissy and I were at each other's throats. We were having terrible arguments. She thought I'd *planned* this disaster. It was a simple misunderstanding, complicated by dealing with executives in another country and a number of those executives being coked out of their brains most of the time. An arbitration meeting was called between Divinyls and BMG, in Sydney, and after long and expensive deliberation involving many lawyers and a judge it was decided that BMG would forward a little more money to allow us to record the rest of the songs for *Underworld* at Festival Records in Sydney on the cheap. Charley Drayton would produce.

We were sinking in a quicksand of debt. Mark and I owed more than half a million dollars to Winterland over the aborted Simple Minds tour merchandising deal. We owed BMG for all our expenses to date, for our advance on recording *Underworld* and for the new recording sessions in Sydney to salvage the album. We owed money to the lawyers who represented us at the arbitration, and it cost us $5000 a day for more than a week to pay Sir Laurence Street, the former Supreme Court Chief Justice who'd been brought in to preside at the mediation between us and BMG. Andrew was present but I refused to talk to him. If things had been bad before, they had just got a whole lot worse.

THE BITTER END

20

In late 1995, before we went into the studio to cut *Underworld*, we tried to raise some money by doing a national tour with American rockers Joan Jett and the Blackhearts as our support band. The shows did well, but to help shoulder the costs, including a light plane flight to Kalgoorlie, where only a handful of locals and some mangy dogs turned up because there was no publicity organised, Andrew got backing from some businessmen in Perth. Apart from a recollection of sitting in a hot tub one night with Charlie Owen and Joan Jett, who happened to be wearing a blonde wig, my memory of what happened at that time is vague. I was too distraught and frantic and wasted to remember. There are many different versions of the deal with the businessmen, a contract may or may not have changed hands, but the bottom line was Divinyls, that is, Mark and I, didn't get paid. In fact the businessmen said we owed *them* money. We were also up for our touring costs and those of Joan Jett and the Blackhearts. More lawyers were necessary, and with them came more crippling bills. Another financial fiasco.

Divinyls owed nearly a million dollars and Mark and I found ourselves pursued by a horde of angry creditors.

Andrew McManus

That last tour, I've always said, was three or four weeks too long. I was trying to milk every cent, so we put on many extra gigs. This cost money, and some shows were not a success and the promoters lost money. The group fell apart. Prior to that tour, 99 per cent of our tours *had* made money. I had always put the band out at just the right time on the back of whatever record was in the charts. The Joan Jett tour was a disaster.

At the end of the tour, Mark and Chrissy got into a fight at Peppers in Double Bay. Onlookers said they saw one dangling the other off a second-floor balcony by the legs. The police were called. Then at 1 a.m. one morning I got a call from Peppers' manager. 'Can you get down here quickly? Chrissy Amphlett has gone berserk. I want her out of here. Now!' I drove to the hotel, and there was Chrissy in the foyer, drunk, and making a huge scene, dressed only in a white towelling robe.

That was it for me. I'd had enough. I went to my room, packed my bags and drove to the Gold Coast. I'd worry about recouping my $50 000 later. I had to get out of that scene.

At the time oblivious to the BMG money shortfall, we went to America in early 1996 to cut *Underworld*. We had some excellent songs, including a bunch of rootsy rockers and the raw ballads 'I'm Jealous' and 'Come Down To Earth'.

A producer for *Underworld* had been appointed. Keith Forsey was an Englishman who'd produced Billy Idol's 'Rebel Yell', the soundtracks of the movies *The Breakfast Club*, *Beverly Hills Cop* and *Ghostbusters*, and he'd won an Oscar for co-writing 'Flashdance—What A Feelin''.

It was ill-fated all the way. We were to record in San Francisco and Andrew had booked us to stay on houseboats, which was a disaster because when the tide went out, they just sat on the mud. It reeked.

Charley and I went straight to a hotel, the rest of the band moved out next morning. The San Francisco studio was a shambles, too, because Metallica were rebuilding the studio next to ours, filling our space with thick, noxious dust. My throat was clogged.

We moved to Track Record studios in Los Angeles. I wasn't keen on being produced by Keith Forsey. I feared he was too 'pop' for us, and wouldn't be comfortable with our gritty garage rock. Charley, too, was dead against using Forsey. But BMG told me I was being difficult and in the end I reluctantly acquiesced. Also, Forsey had a reputation as a serious party boy, and I was trying, at that point, to change my life. I hadn't been drinking. Then to familiarise himself with our songs, Forsey insisted on over-rehearsing us, which made us jaded and cost us the spontaneity that made our records raw. I could have choked Forsey when I caught him laughing and pulling faces while I was recording my vocal for the intense and demanding 'Come Down To Earth'. Charley was horrified. Forsey was on another planet. Of course, in such an environment, I started drinking again.

Then, after two weeks the money ran out and the sessions were over. What did our 160 000 bucks buy? Two finished tracks, 'Sex Will Keep Us Together' and 'Heart Of Steel', and some guide vocals and guide guitar tracks for the other songs.

Kevin Shirley

I was in Sydney when [Chris Gilbey] called me and asked if I could meet him in his office in North Sydney. He explained that Divinyls had been recording an album in Los Angeles with producer Keith Forsey, but that they had blown [their budget] and the record company had nothing to show for it. He asked if I would take the multi tracks [from the aborted session], which were in his possession, and [mix them], and I agreed. I took the multi track tapes to the now defunct Rich Studios and set to work on them. Some songs were major productions, and others were nothing more than guide tracks, with a scratch vocal and a scratch guitar track—and I genuinely put every effort into making them reflect the band, which I had enormous respect for, and represent its music. My thought was that it was better that someone who cared for the band was doing this underhand job, rather than someone who didn't really have a rock feel for them; and I managed to mix a whole album out of the tapes, and mastered them with Don Bartley at EMI in Sydney.

I thought I'd done a great job, considering the material I'd been given to work with; but sometimes the naivety of being creative hides the ulterior motives of the shaman businessman. So, I think Chris Gilbey may just have been trying to shock the band, because he sent them a copy of 'your new album', and they were not happy—not unhappy with my mixes as such, but because it was their unfinished work. I bore the full brunt of their distaste and animosity, but Chris's tactics worked, because the band reconvened in Sydney, with Charley Drayton producing, to finish the recordings properly . . .

Charley Drayton, my Black Knight, agreed to turn all this unfinished material into an album, all on the skinniest shoestring. This was so unfair. Charley was brave to take on the job of trying to save *Underworld*. If the album had any shortcomings they were not Charley's fault.

Kevin Shirley

In an ironic twist of fate, I was working in Studio B at EMI's Studio 301 in Sydney, mixing the *Blue Cave* album for Hoodoo Gurus, while on the same floor Divinyls were tracking in Studio A. We shared lounge and kitchen facilities, but in a silly, petulant and pre-pubescent display, someone in the Divinyls camp (Charley!) had insisted we split the facilities into two halves and had a floor to ceiling partition built with gobos (the 2-metre-high moveable modular sound insulation walls used in the recording studio for instrument separation) and covered with black curtains. Gaining entrance to the studio through the dark, velvet maze was not unlike entering a photographic darkroom.

On the rare occasions we bumped into each other, either getting a coffee or just passing, it would be a totally silent meeting, unless one of us was caught off-guard, in which case you may have heard a faint primeval grunt from me . . . At one point, Mark and I had gotten over the grunting, and I offered him a drink as I was getting ice from the kitchen for my Jack Daniels. He accepted, and about two hours later, Charley came to find Mark, and we drunk the entire bottle and were gossiping away as only two obliterated drunkards can—off our heads. I can still smell the Jack . . . As it transpires, I have become very friendly with Charley and Chrissy in recent years, and respect them as people and as musicians, very much. I've bumped into Jerome once or twice but haven't seen Mark since.

Charley Drayton

When they asked me to finish the record in Sydney I was asked to repair Keith Forsey's work, and recut some tracks. One was 'Come Down To Earth'. I said I thought the song was special and to choose any day during the sessions when they felt in the mood to do it. When we did it, we recorded 'Come Down To Earth' live, and Chrissy's performance was raw. It is definitely one of my favourite tracks.

The critics were not so kind to *Underworld* when it was released mid-1996. Jeff Apter in *Rolling Stone* thought its sound was 'typically Divinyls' fodder: raw, rootsy and a tad too familiar. Mind you, there are some musical highpoints: "Come Down To Earth", a song of genuine emotion, and "Open Windows", which surprises with pseudo classical guitar and deftly-styled harmonies . . .' Andrew Masterson in Melbourne's *The Age* newspaper noted, 'Over their careers, Christina Amphlett and Mark McEntee have progressed from being exciting newcomers, to welcome staples, to veterans. They have contributed much—and much that is memorable—to Australian music. This album, sadly, is unlikely to be remembered as one of the highlights. As always, the pair deliver songs anchored to themes of love, passion, sex, jealousy and broken hearts. In the past, the mixture relied in equal parts on the chunky rollicking rock of the arrangements and the pleasingly schizophrenic mixture of sex kitten, bitch and femme fatale incorporated in Amphlett's dinstinctive voice. Amphlett's voice is still there, although, it seems, leached of much of the urgency and anxiety that coloured it before.' If my voice reflected my state of mind while recording that jinxed album, I'm not surprised that I sounded a shadow of the Chrissy of headier, more promising times.

Underworld flopped in America and was only a steady seller in Australia, not coming close to matching the chart performance of our previous albums. Still, 'I'm Jealous' and 'Come Down To Earth' compare with our best work. Soon after the album's August 1996 release, Mark and I sang 'Come Down To Earth' as a duo at a benefit gig at the Metro in Sydney. Charlie Owen, who was working with Beasts of Bourbon then, was there:

Charlie Owen

'Come Down To Earth' was a song I heard a lot when *Underworld* came out, but I wasn't prepared for the way Chrissy and Mark did it that night. Chrissy sang so intimately, so emotionally, it was difficult to watch her, and Mark accompanied her with sublime classical guitar. The audience, expecting the usual full-on rock, was shocked, and delighted. It was one of the best gigs of the decade.

After the BMG debacle and the resulting bad feeling, we parted company with Andrew McManus and appointed Grant Thomas, who loved *Underworld*, as our new manager. Under Grant, we continued to tour the album throughout 1996. I was physically and emotionally fried. A burnt-out case. I was disillusioned, deeply disappointed. I was beginning to suffer anxiety attacks onstage because of my alcoholism. I wouldn't know what I was going to sing. I couldn't remember the words to songs. I'd be standing up there going, 'What are the words to "Boys In Town"?' That was terrifying.

Charley Drayton

Things were not going well. No one was happy. Many things began to wear on us. The music was suffering. Our support was diminishing. Charlie Owen had split. There was the debt. The Chris Gilbey–Andrew McManus US dollar error, and how we scrambled and cut corners to finish *Underworld*. Mark and Chrissy's spark was waning. They were not going the extra lengths to make a song great. Things were getting darker.

We channelled the darkness we felt offstage into our performances.
We played up-tempo songs such as 'Pleasure And Pain' and 'Guillotine
Day' mean and slow. The break was due and necessary.

Our last gig on that tour was at a venue in the outer suburbs of
Melbourne. I can't remember the date or the name of the venue. All
I recall is that the stage was very low and we were tired, angry,
disillusioned and wasted. None of us knew it that night, but it was
the last time Divinyls ever played. I had devoted sixteen years of my
life and all my emotional energy into Mark and the band. It was time
to leave it all behind—but like any parting it would not be easy.

THE ANGEL AND THE DEMON

Very bad things can happen on Christmas Day, as we all know. Tensions simmer and boil over in the high summer heat as unrealistic expectations, family dynamics and too much alcohol poison what begins as a happy occasion. Well, very bad things happened to me when I spent Christmas Day 1996 with my sister Leigh and her husband at their home with Mum, my nephew and my sister's husband's aunt. Then, at the end of the disaster, a very *good* thing happened. I survived.

Having just gone through the roughest patch of my life, I was so looking forward to the big celebration as a desperately needed chance to embrace my family and remember happier times. Charley was back in the States and I needed to be around people I loved.

Of course, Christmas Day in Australia, unlike in many other lands, is about drinking alcohol and of course, being alcoholic, I got caught up in the spirit. I had never drunk to anaesthetise myself against my problems. I got plastered to have good times and keep the party high going. As I joined in the family fun, the euphoria that coursed through me as those first few drinks kicked in made my problems seem less severe. So I drank more.

I drank all morning and by the time we sat down to eat Christmas lunch I was irrational. I had decided to kill myself so I began giving all my jewellery away. Leigh, Mum and everyone else were looking at me aghast. Mum kept trying to take my champagne glass away. Despair and alcohol had sent me into meltdown.

I sat at the table scowling and distracted as Leigh brought in the Christmas chook. My sister is a wonderful cook, but either the bird was bad or having me around in my state had got to everyone. The lunch was a disaster.

After lunch we visited Leigh and her husband's friends. I think I broke their record player. By then my euphoria was long gone, replaced by a sullen anger at the unfairness of the terrible things that had happened to me. I argued with Leigh's husband in the car on the way back to their place. He said, 'How dare you embarrass us in front of our friends!' The day had taken on a nasty edge.

When we arrived home, Leigh's husband bundled me up the stairs to a bedroom. He put me onto the bed and left the room. Lying there, so very sick and sad and all alone, my woes snapped at me like hyenas savaging a wounded gazelle. I was assailed by a stark realisation of my sorry situation. The enormous sums of money I owed, my disease, Mark's abandonment, Andrew's role in my insolvency, Divinyls' thwarted dreams, Charley being so far away. I thrashed and flailed hysterically, crying out and throwing things.

Then I realised I wasn't alone in the room. I could see black wings and I could see white wings all swirling around me. I still wonder today if they were the wings of angels and demons. I swear they were, and I believe that they were having an almighty fight for my soul. Leigh was in the room trying to hold me down on the bed as I kicked and screamed, and Dr Peter Lewis, our family doctor, was injecting me. I bit him on the arm. Then the Valium did its work and I passed out.

Leigh called Charley in New York, who talked her through the experience for nearly two hours, and made it very clear, if she and

Mum didn't know already, that this was serious, that their sister and daughter was in desperate trouble.

When I regained consciousness a day later, it was as though I had been cleansed. I had had an epiphany. I was beaten. I had stopped struggling. I had given up trying to keep the life I had been living together. From now on, whatever happened, happened. All I could do was try to stop drinking, pay off my debts and reclaim my life, happiness and reputation. Of all those resolutions, the most unattainable seemed to be the recovery of happiness. I had been sad at heart for such a long time.

Leigh and Dr Lewis took me along to a twelve-step program in Melbourne. Then a woman called Joan Trotter took me into the city to a meeting where there were a lot of rock-bottom, recovering alcoholics who had brain damage, and that really frightened me. 'That's how you'll end up if you keep drinking the way you are,' she told me. Miraculously, the obsession to drink left me that day. Sadly, a couple of days ago I received a message via my sister from Dr Lewis telling me that Joan was in a hospice battling breast cancer, which had gone through her body. They kept asking the family to come in and she kept rallying. I rang and spoke to her while she was in physio. She was proud that she had walked twelve steps that day. She also told me that I had been a hard case. Since our phone call, Joan has died but I am glad I was able to speak to her and thank her.

Everyone's different. Some people have to white-knuckle it, for me the obsession just vanished. Elvis had left the building. Nor was I tempted to take drugs. I had only ever wanted them when alcohol had lowered my defences and I was on a party high. In the surreal environment after a gig it was the thing to do.

I called Charley often. He was in America touring and recording. I told him of my hopes to stay sober and become solvent. He was happy for me.

Dr Lewis recommended that I see an elderly psychologist named Eric Gaudry, now retired in Queensland. Dr Gaudry was an expert on alcoholism. I went to stay on my farm, alone again, and made an appointment to see him. He didn't mince his words. 'You have a very serious disease, alcoholism,' he told me, 'and you're in the second of three stages. You are hanging by your fingernails. The third can prove fatal.' He counselled me to understand my disease and what sacrifices I would have to make to stay sober. His words and the time-tested twelve-step suggestions set me on the way to sobriety.

At my farm at Delaney's Creek in the clean, warm Queensland air with my five dogs and two cats spoiling me I began to rally. I spoke to Charley on the phone every day. He was a rock. I didn't deviate from the program. Every day I felt better than the day before.

Getting sober didn't guarantee that I would never fall off the wagon in the future, or make my debt disappear, but somehow with a clear head and gathering strength I could at least address ways of staying away from booze and figure out sanely and sensibly how I might pay off the money I owed instead of, like in the bad days just past, collapsing in despair and drinking more. I was determined to survive. Not even when writ-servers came down the dirt driveway to my farmhouse door did I go into a tailspin. I took their pieces of paper and put them into my 'to do' basket.

When I felt strong enough I went to America to be with Charley in his apartment in New York. He hugged me and made me feel like a queen. After spending some time with him, his love gave me the strength to fly back to Australia to face my creditors in court.

Andrew McManus had chosen to take his demands further, and his case against Mark and me—to reimburse him for the band's expenses he said he put on his Diner's Club card while we were recording *Underworld*—was heard at Coolangatta. The area outside the court was thick with reporters and cameramen. I had anticipated an ugly confrontation with Andrew, but, weirdly, considering how hard he came after us, Andrew was his usual Arthur Daley-ish charming self when we collided in the corridor. He gave me a smile and an 'I wish this didn't have to happen' shrug. His lawyer put Mark in the dock and accused him of being a drug addict, which was not true. When I stood up I ignored the vitriol and stuck to my story:

that we owed Andrew nothing. Then it was Andrew's turn to be grilled by our lawyer. In the end, the judgment favoured Mark and me.

We didn't fare quite so well in some of the other cases in which we were being chased by creditors for a combined sum that was now huge and continually growing as interest accrued. We also had to find the money to pay the lawyers and accountants acting on our behalf. We had the option of declaring ourselves bankrupt, which would mean that apart from basic living expenses any money we earned in the future had to be paid to our creditors, or we could try to clear the debt and start all over again.

Two particular creditors sent Mark bankrupt. He simply had no choice. I had been brought up to pay my bills, and somehow managed to keep my creditors at bay. I would regain my good name and trust in my talent.

Mark's bankruptcy made matters twice as bad for me. Creditors, knowing they'd be getting nothing from Mark, now beat a path to my door. Instead of sharing the load, the burden of debt was now mine alone.

To raise money, I sold my house in Manly. I sold my car, after painting over the scratches my dog Dobro had etched in the duco. I put my farm up for sale, but no one came to the auction. The royalties I received from songwriting went straight into the grasping hands of creditors. With the help of Grant Thomas and my accountant, Carmen Curtin, I contacted all the people and organisations to whom I owed money and we worked out a repayment schedule. Some, relieved and surprised that I had no intention of cutting and running, agreed to reduce the amount. Others wouldn't budge and continued to hound me for immediate payment.

Even after I had sold my assets, I was still a few hundred thousand dollars in the red. I was far from physically and emotionally healthy, and all I wanted to do was sleep, but there is no rest for the wicked. I had to find work. But what? I could plug on with Divinyls, maybe do some solo or guest gigs, but for now I had to get away from rock'n'roll. I had to do something entirely different for a bit.

I was living in New York, but back in Australia the debts kept mounting, interest on interest, the summonses kept being served. I came to dread the phone ringing because it would usually be Grant Thomas with more bad news from home. I felt like a punching bag. And I was alone—except for Charley.

Then came a godsend. In August 1997, the producer Ben Gannon who was planning to stage a national tour of a new musical, *The Boy From Oz*, the story of the late Australian singer Peter Allen, called me. He said he'd seen me in *Blood Brothers* and asked me if I would be interested in auditioning for the role of Peter Allen's mother-in-law, the tragic diva Judy Garland.

I hesitated for a moment as doubts about whether I could pull off such a momentous role crowded in, then I remembered Danny Hiller's words of ten years before, 'Chrissy, I think you should do it,' and I told Ben I was very interested.

And Judy Garland was a hero of mine. She was a strong and talented woman who overcame tremendous obstacles, many of her own making such as self-destructiveness, addiction and debt, to be an enduring star. I could relate to her struggle. And there was the all-important added incentive that if the show ran and ran, I would be able to make a dent in my debts.

'Auditions are starting now,' said Ben. 'Be on the first plane to Australia. We'll put you up at the Sebel Town House.' I protested that I wouldn't have enough time to research my character. Ben replied that if I wanted the part I should board that plane, pronto.

As I threw some clothes into a suitcase and Charley drove me to JFK airport, I thought that if I could only land that role and get my creditors off my back, there'd be nothing stopping me from, like Judy's immortal character Dorothy in *The Wizard Of Oz*, living happily ever after, not with Toto but with Charley Drayton. All those years ago when I had played Judy singing 'Over The Rainbow' before I went onstage I'd thought it was just a nice song. Now I knew it was an omen.

Lesley Shaw, *The Boy From Oz*'s company manager, met me at Sydney airport and drove me straight to auditions in a room at the Sebel, presided over by the fierce and demanding director Gale Edwards, who had worked in London's West End and on Broadway. Before my ordeal, for auditions always freaked me out, Lesley and I sat on the footpath outside and had a calming coffee. The irony struck me. In other years I would have chilled out with a vodka. My dear friend from *Blood Brothers*, Kevin Hanily, 'Handbag', with his limp and his gorgeous, jolly face that made him resemble a Franciscan friar, was at the door. 'Hi!' he beamed. He didn't leave my side.

Gale Edwards was waiting for me in the rehearsal room. The musical director, Max Lambert, was there and, unlike Gale, he was warm and welcoming. Gale's cold and snappish manner made it clear that she did not want me. I auditioned and under the circumstances I thought I did fine. Not so Gale. I went to my hotel room totally deflated and wondering why the hell I had let myself in for this crap.

The next day, to my surprise, I was called back for another audition. Over the following week I was called back five times. After each audition, Gale dismissed me without giving a hint of how I was faring. Finally I summoned up my courage and asked her, 'Have I got the role?'

She erupted, 'How *dare* you ask the director a question like that?' Before I'd felt deflated, now I felt brutalised. I wanted to slink home, but I didn't. Life for me was all about not giving up.

Ben Gannon took me to lunch to comfort me. He reiterated that I was perfect for the part, but agreed things were not working out with Gale. I was resigned to missing out.

Later that night the phone rang in my room. I can't remember who it was from the company who called. All that mattered is that he or she told me I had the part.

The role of Judy Garland was a gift. I met many lifelong friends while working on *The Boy From Oz*. Handbag, Ben Gannon, Fran Moore, and Stephen Maclean, who was one of the show's creators, were all supportive and encouraging and probably have no idea how much I needed them at that time. Sadly, Stephen, who now lives in Thailand, is battling cancer.

Stephen Maclean

Chrissy and I bonded immediately. We first met at the Sebel when she was auditioning. Chrissy was a star in her own right and had been through the whole celebrity thing. And there was that voice and her presence, as I recall it very still and regal, as if she'd suffered and prevailed, which of course she had. Plus, she had one snaggletooth, just like Judy Garland. She also had the long legs and the short torso. I had always admired what Chrissy did musically, and the image she created for herself and used onstage. The bad schoolgirl. Chrissy, of course, didn't sing like Judy and only resembled her in a superficial way when she was made up, but because of what she had gone through in her life, she was able to give a wonderful *impression* of Garland, rather than a superficial impersonation. We could have hired any number of Garland impersonators to do that . . . Chrissy got the part because she had Judy's soul.

The day after I was told I had the part there was a scheduled press call at the State Theatre when the announcement would be made that I would play Judy. I was told that Gale Edwards said, 'Chrissy's not very glamorous. I hope she dresses for the press call.' She needn't have worried. I wore a gorgeous jacket with black velvet tails, leggings and little high-heeled black suede boots. Very Judy. Gale approved.

Before the media were invited into the State Theatre's foyer for the press conference, I sat by myself in an office feeling totally inadequate, and like a complete outsider. Then Handbag grabbed me by the arm and ushered me into that wonderful old theatre with its ornate mishmash of art deco, Gothic and Italian decor. There, before the huge plush velvet curtains as carved plaster cherubs looked down upon us, he made me kneel beside him. On your knees before a higher power is a good place to be sometimes. I was filled with hope and strength. When I fronted those reporters, I felt confident. The announcement made all the papers and TV news reports.

Then I was on the plane back to Charley. I had five months to prepare for the role. But I still had to stay sober and pay my debts. As reality set in, my heart sank at the struggle I would now have to undertake. 'Fuck,' I shuddered. 'What have I just done?'

I enrolled in acting and singing classes. I tried to get deep inside Judy's head and each time Grant Thomas rang with more bad news I channelled my fear and anger into the alter ego I was creating.

Stephen Maclean

I took my Judy Garland videotapes to Chrissy in New York. She was remarkable the way she absorbed the key and vital aspects of Judy's character. She took me to a function at the Chelsea Hotel and there was a fellow there who was the president of the Judy Garland Society. He was the keeper of the flame of the Great Goddess Judy. When he learned Chrissy was portraying Garland on stage in Australia he contemptuously looked her up and down. His eyes bored into her as he asked exactly how she proposed to play Judy. Chrissy replied, very coolly, 'Sympathetically.'

She and I went down to Greenwich Village to eat and by chance this fellow was sitting at another table in the restaurant. Chrissy said to me, 'Quick, give me a really obscure fact about Judy.' I did, and Chrissy yelled across the room to the Judy-phile, 'Hey, did you know . . .' and reeled off the fact. He was dumbfounded and shrieked, 'Hi Judy!'

That time in New York, Chrissy, Charley and I went to visit Louis Armstrong's house in Queens. Chrissy had a reverence for great artists that extended far beyond the narrow world of rock.

Nine months had passed since that fateful Christmas Day. It's true that whatever doesn't kill you makes you stronger. I was still being bombarded by writs and still following my twelve-step program. I felt in much better shape, and very proud that I hadn't weakened.

I still felt great sadness, resentment and anger and sometimes, to my disappointment, self-pity. My ego was in Monte Carlo and my self-esteem in Bangladesh. I was all over the place and I could be self-righteous in my new-found sobriety.

I was speaking to my sister on the phone one day, and she told me how worried she was that I would drink again. Well! How dare she tell a recovering alcoholic that she was worried I might drink again... I just might because of that! I feel awful to admit I wrote her a letter and pointed out all *her* faults. I know I really hurt her.

My New York sponsor, Denise, an Irish-Catholic from Hell's Kitchen, greatly cared for me. She knew my spiritual muscle was weak and it needed building up to cope with what lay ahead. She suggested that we go and stay at a monastery in upstate New York, where the homeless people from the Bowery and the addicted go to confront their demons, helped by the tough but loving care of New York's Irish and Italian priests and nuns. I'm not Catholic but that didn't matter. Because I was someone who'd been to hell and back I was given food, shelter and life-affirming advice.

The monastery was old and beautiful. In my week there it snowed and the grounds were covered in swathes of white like prayer rugs. The place rang with laughter. Those priests and nuns were good-hearted people and like most Irish and Italians were brilliant at telling jokes. Yet on some floors there was not a sound. We were not allowed to speak, because, as the priests explained, they were 'professional pray-ers' and needed silence. I found that a particularly hard edict to carry out.

I sat in a little friary and thought about where I'd been and where I wanted to go, and of my love for Charley and for life, and how I had nearly lost it. The rest of my time was comprised of anointing healing, prayers, lectures and heart to hearts with the priests and something we called Saturday Night Live. Anointing healing was when we women all lined up and picked a priest into whose ear we whispered our biggest fears. They would listen intently, anoint us and in so doing take our fears away. Saturday Night Live was a ritual in which we walked in, wrote down our woe, or burden, on a piece of paper and placed it in the burden box. And then we would sit in the dark with Father Joe and yell out the things that were frightening us. There were Harlem accents and Bronx accents, and one Australian accent.

My diary entries in the second half of 1997 give an insight into my desperate state of mind as I struggled with sobriety, debt and the challenge of playing Judy Garland. While I was at the monastery, I emerged from the darkest period of my life with renewed strength. Reading those feverish entries, it is clear that I was beside myself. My ravings and reflections, in turn vengeful, rambling, hopeful, raw, brutally honest, incoherent, are testimony to the torment I was enduring. Here are some of my musings...

Welcome into my life today... the prayers the women sang were very moving. So much pain I felt... I feel a lightening of all my burdens putting them in the burden box. I think we need a burden box at home. I will not take anybody's judgment of me anymore. People putting themselves above me or judging me. I'm not a bad person. I might've done things that were beneath me or bad and I will have to do better but I'm not a bad person. I didn't know what the right thing was to do. I had no guidance. I had no idea what was right... I was suspicious. I thought everyone had turned against me. But they hadn't. I was being helped. I surrendered straight away. It was like I had a breakdown and it was all over. Everything then changed. I started on a new path. One not so filled with bills. Although I think about myself a lot, I'm aware of others as well. I hope I'm getting out of the rut I was in. I couldn't get out of it. I was stuck. This last year I've had support, love and caring and I feel better. I've had a lot of financial worries and I feel betrayed and realised how I surrounded myself with no love and no depth. Half the situations [I am in are the result of] impetuous decisions. I wonder if [I'll be able to] do the play.

I'm scared to go and look at the fax... sometimes I just wish it would go away. It's been nearly a year and nothing has gone away. You know, I could just roll over and go to sleep. Black out all the financial worries that I have. I don't know how I'm ever going to rid myself of all of this.

I have to stay healthy so that I can work and get clear of all these debts. It makes me feel suicidal. I feel so alone ... This has been a humiliating experience for me ...

Welcome into my life. Grant upset me last night, he was so het up that I could feel the panic and fear welling up inside me ... like when my father used to yell impatiently when I was a child and I would get frightened and blank and cry.

Reading over these words is hard—the rawness of my soul and my honesty to myself are confronting and bring it all rushing back. My manager at the time, Grant Thomas, helped me—he did what he could for me in his way. He would buy my farm and looked after the details of my *Boy From Oz* contract but there were times when I hated everyone—and no one more than myself.

Good morning, welcome into my life ... I'm just trying to keep things fair. I was unable to see the stranglehold the whole thing had on me and what were the truths and what were the lies. I'm still angry as I'm writing this, it brings up feelings of remorse, regret, stupidity. Does this anger shape me to be a more aware, compassionate person? What does it do to benefit me in the long run? I have grown in the last year. I value sanity. I value sane thinking. I value honest people and don't look upon them as square and boring.

My confidence went so low ... Diamonds were never real diamonds and gold was never real gold.

I was getting all the poison out of my system in my diary. Working through the process. I was coming to realise that I was as much to blame as pretty much anyone, and through that realisation arriving at a kind of peace. I also realised that in alcoholism I had a disease, not a socially acceptable disease like cancer or multiple sclerosis, but a disease all the same and one that I shouldn't feel ashamed of.

I can't have any of that low-level stuff with no boundaries or values. It is a part of my life that's very painful and I really am not proud of having ... how far I went down. I just wanted to escape reality. I thought

I was above all the things touching me. I thought I was invincible! I thought these people would not rub off on me, that I could survive, but I know I lost everything because I didn't value or appreciate what I had. Fear of being alone, not being able to cope on my own. I feel so much stronger, braver, centred. I have made giant steps. Always was so dependent. And my alcoholism made me more and more. And the people I associated with enabled me. I think it will be another year before I'm clear of all this. I would like to write a book on the truth . . . if I could remember it. Who I really am. And how can I do that with my parents still alive? I don't want to inflict any more pain on my parents than they feel now. As a teenager, I had no idea I could really protect myself. I wasn't valuable. I just didn't have a sense that I was precious. I was always someone else's to own . . . and do what they wanted with me and push me around. It's only now that I feel I'm really worth something. I'm now appreciated. That I have talent. I thought it was drugs and booze that added . . . it gave me that edge. I never thought I was pretty. Now I'm getting glimpses [after being] ten months sober that I am . . . and I am realising what my strengths and weaknesses are. I am talented. I am good. I was hurt by being in such a competing and cutthroat world. I lost belief in myself as I've never had a strong support system and everybody questioned my abilities. Mark didn't, he encouraged me. But we were both insecure and delicate. We were in the deep-end and I was ill prepared . . . no one is ever prepared. I had style. I was too good. But I became a liar. Disconnected. I pray for you and I invite you into my life, to show me the way. I want to do this properly now. I am grateful. I am sober. And to stay sober and creative I want to make, not break, things. I don't want to end up like Stevie Wright . . . in a caravan.

I was trying to find my soul. I was trying to plug into a higher power. Michael Hutchence, my old friend, died on 22 November 1997, while I was in the monastery. It was an electric shock to my heart and made me recognise the survivor I was.

Trying to come to terms with Michael's death and why I wake with a pain in my tummy. It's all very sad ... Michael Hutchence died yesterday. Welcome into my life. I need you to help me with this. I am angry because he did this. I have felt all the things he felt. Insanity, self-pity, self-absorption. He has a child of fifteen months. How could he leave her? I can't stop thinking about it. I'm in pain. It brought back all my pain, the misery. Everything. My behaviour. And so all of this happened, too, Michael died among all of this ...

During one of my trips to Australia to confront summonses and have more meetings with my lawyers and accountants, I stayed at the farm, which I still had not been able to sell ... and found the place infested with rats.

I listen to the rats up in the roof making all that noise. I wish they would go away so I would be rat-free. My roof would be empty. Not the sound of scurrying feet pushing around what I left for them to eat. I could be rat-free and my roof would be empty. Do you know how I'm feeling? Rat, ratty. Quite ratty. I don't like to hear them in pain ... because I'm poisoning them ... because there's a rat plague. I don't like to hear them in pain. I only feel the same. I don't want them to suffer. I just wish it could be over, poor little things. I have to sell everything ... the less I have on my plate, the more freedom I have. Just a whole lot of lawsuits. Sometimes I feel deflated. I like having responsibilities. I'm working well. I'm not ... so I suppose this is best. Just five dogs and two cats and furniture and clothes and me. How does that feel? I'm resigned to the fact. Thinking of Mark makes me angry. Andrew makes me angry. My career is embarrassing. The positive? I'm getting through all of this. Feel exhausted ... get very depressed with the predicament I'm in ... Sometimes I think I should go on Prozac. I feel depressed. Powerless. It all got too hard for me today. I must write some songs. I feel suicidal ... I'm losing everything and I feel such a victim. Positives? Charley! New York! All my animals. The weather. My lovely clothes and shoes. Grant has been helping me. I have to look forward to the positives. Feeling extremely tense ... listening to tapes, imagining

worse, bad tapes, fear of rejection—rejection is part of life. Ego going
through the roof. Need massage—*badly*. Terrible tension and feelings
of uncomfortableness. Feelings that I can't handle things. Overwhelmed.
Can't cope. Sat up until 4.30 worrying about Charley's family.

It may not have sounded like it, but I was trying to live, think and
feel like a normal person for the first time in what seemed like
forever. I didn't know how to relate to normal people. In my diary I
addressed the higher being I had come to know at the friary.

Hold my hand today as I need you now. I seem to get carried away
with other people's stuff instead of staying with my own. I need to feel
comfortable with myself. I'm very open but I really can't forget you today.
Don't forget me. Don't forget me. Someone rang very early this morning,
I wonder who it was. I don't like myself when I get . . . I would like to go
to an art gallery this week and see some paintings. That would be my
artist date with myself. I need to find some books on Judy Garland. I'm
going to put on some beautiful music in a moment. I hope I can help
people instead of being helped. And without being jealous. My voice
is jumping out of my throat. I really want to sing—to see how it is going.
Just to see how my voice is going. I love my animals and I'm happy I
come from a family that does. I do, but I'm not really prepared and this
is what I really need at the moment. I'm getting stronger and I've grown.

I'm trying to survive but I'm not bitter. And I'm in a good relationship.
I have a good paying job next year which will give me back [my life] . . .
I must sell the farm. It'll take a while but I must put it on the market.
Drought is here [on the farm]. Terrible drought. Thank God for another
morning without shame and a hangover! I feel good. I don't want to
get drunk because I just can't handle it. Your weaknesses get used
against you and you don't know what's happening around you. I just
dreamed . . . I was in a rock'n'roll band again and I watched an Indian
being killed by an insect. My eyes are stinging.

A year after the angels and demons battled over me I returned to
Sydney at Christmas to rehearse for *The Boy From Oz*, which would

premiere in Sydney at Her Majesty's Theatre in March 1998. I wrote in my diary: *I'm nervous about singing these songs... singing... I'm really full of fear. I've been waking in the night full of fear. My fears are rising to the surface. I am lost, and very afraid.*

At least I was being honest with myself. After all I'd been through to stay standing, to stay alive, I was going to go through with it and give it my best shot. I would achieve all the goals I had set for myself. One day at a time.

Nearly dying is a wonderful motivator.

OVER THE GODDAMN RAINBOW

I flew from a bitter New York winter into the bright blaze of Sydney summer. As I landed at Kingsford Smith airport I felt excited and terrified at what lay ahead of me. I rented a little terrace at the bottom of Elizabeth Street in Paddington. The lurid bougainvillea and elegant wrought-iron balconies of the old suburb lifted my spirits.

Saying goodbye to Charley in New York broke my heart. With him so far away and also working hard, we were going to be apart for longer than either of us could handle. We had no choice, and resigned ourselves to astronomical phone bills.

With no Charley to pamper me I settled on the next best thing. I moved my animal family from the farm into Paddington with me. It was just me; Minky, my big chocolate-brown Himalayan cat; Dobro, a Dalmatian; and Saki, a mini foxie. And Judy Garland moved in too.

I immersed myself in Judy. I listened to no music but hers. I replayed tapes of her speaking voice over and over so I could grasp her slightly nasal Mid-west accent. I watched videos of her movies and absorbed her gestures and the way she moved when she sang. I had trouble nailing Judy's regal though uncertain gait until at rehearsal one day Stephen Maclean suggested I walk like a fashion model. That worked. Stephen's advice was a wonderful gift.

The key to this part, I decided, was not to try to be a mirror-image impersonation of Judy, but to deliver a finely nuanced performance.

I turned up for my first rehearsal at the Betty Pounder studios at the back of Her Majesty's Theatre. There was no one there to hold my hand. Running the show was my nemesis, director Gale Edwards. Gale made us all sit in a circle to read the script. She seemed pleased with my attempt at Judy's voice. She could see that I'd worked hard to master the part, and that broke the ice between us.

Gale is a perfectionist and a hard task-master and she drove all her actors relentlessly. Her demands were exhausting. I kept my head down and worked my butt off.

Not helping Gale's disposition was that the script was being written by Nick Enright as we went along. Nick would write some lines and show it to Gale who would change them if she felt it necessary. Gale is very creative in the moment and knew exactly what she wanted— and Nick would rework it.

We all learned to leave our ego at the rehearsal-room door. We were involved in an intensive creative process and under Gale, this production was no place for the faint of heart. Gale was a terrific actor's director. When I needed her, she was there. She could free me and move me. When I got stuck, she could always get me to the next place in my performance. I've been fortunate that in my two musicals to date I've had directors as good as Gale Edwards and Danny Hiller.

Stephen Maclean

Chrissy was always afraid Gale was going to fire her, and I would take her for a drink—always non-alcoholic!—in the Sebel Town House bar to reassure her that that wasn't going to happen. Knowing her reputation, it was interesting and a little surprising to me that Chrissy had insecurities. Now, she is the only performer I know who I think of first as a person and a performer second. She's very real.

Gale announced she expected us to be off-script within two weeks, so she could see whether she had a first act. I shuddered at the thought, then I said to myself, 'What the hell. I'm confident of being able to portray Judy now, and after all I've been through, learning some lines will be a breeze.' It wasn't, but somehow through those long days of rehearsal and at night at home poring over the script with Minky, Dobro and Saki curled at my feet, and again in the early morning, the words and lyrics ingrained themselves in my psyche. It got to the point that I didn't have to remember them. So long as I was in character as Judy, the words and songs burst forth.

Kevin Hanily and I became very close. I confided in him and he in me. Handbag, who was around 65 then, was HIV positive and was feeling very out of sorts but couldn't tell anyone for fear of being sacked. His secret was safe with me. It was the least I could do after he'd kept quiet about my hangover during *Blood Brothers*. Handbag would come up into my dressing-room and we'd chat and, as a recovering alcoholic who'd been sober for twenty years, he devoured my recovery books.

One night, Handbag busted. After all those years on the wagon he hit the bottle. When he called to tell me, he was at his sister's. I drove out and picked him up and took him to a twelve-step meeting. He had begun drinking again because he was angry at being HIV positive.

The 4.5-million-dollar production's opening night at Her Majesty's Theatre was a gala event. My moment in the spotlight was spoiled somewhat when some seedy little man thrust a summons at me at the stage door. These people really know how to pick their moment.

I was a nervous wreck when, as a tipsy Judy Garland, I staggered on in front of a packed house in the first act. I comforted myself with the knowledge that Judy would have been feeling just the same way.

At show's end, I received an ovation like rolling thunder. I shook and my eyes glistened as the yelling and clapping resounded around the vast theatre. Gale Edwards said, 'You'll never know how good you were tonight,' and from her that was high praise indeed.

And then I received a gift that meant far more to me than praise. Waiting for me in my dressing-room was Charley, who'd flown in from New York to surprise me. As I entered he stood and applauded. I took one look at my cool dude and wept. As Charley always did when I was being emotional, he yelled, 'Cut!'

We all stayed up late waiting for the reviews in the morning papers, and they were all we could have hoped for, and much more.

Ben Gannon

Chrissy's performance in *Blood Brothers* was amazing. It would have been extraordinary at any time, but the fact that it came from a performer with no theatrical background made it more so. I called *Blood Brothers'* producer Wilton Morley the day after I saw the show at the Seymour Centre in Sydney to tell him so. I never forgot Chrissy's Mrs Johnstone, and when we were tossing names into the ring to play Judy Garland, I said, 'Why not Chrissy Amphlett?' Blank looks. 'Are you mad?' To humour me, it was agreed to fly Chrissy to Sydney for an audition.

When she showed up that first day in August 1997, we'd been auditioning for ages, and were finding out how hard it is to find someone who can play such a well-known and beloved performer as Judy. Yes, we'd seen Garland impersonators who got the look and superficial mannerisms right. There was a girl we auditioned who did a Judy Garland act in the clubs who was technically amazing. She thought she had it in the bag, but was completely soulless. We'd tested excellent actresses who could sing and do the Garland tricks and in the right clothes and make-up could look the part. Yet what they all lacked was Judy's essence. How to explain it? Someone who was trampled by life, knew heartbreak and addiction, but like a wind-up toy, put her in front of an audience and she'd perform her battered little heart out. Chrissy stopped us all short. She so obviously had that same never-say-die, get-knocked-down-and-pick-yourself-up-again spirit. It was only much later that I learned, because she never let on, that she was going through a terrible period in her life. Yet she walked into the Sebel looking like a star, and she rose to the occasion. Because of everything that had befallen her, because of all those Divinyls shows, the good ones and the bad ones, that she performed for all those years, because of her emotional baggage, she had Judy's spirit, and that's something no one can act. Chrissy's amazing voice was a bonus.

I knew as soon as we saw her audition that day that Chrissy was the best choice, the only choice. And Max Lambert, in his heart, knew too. He remarked, 'The audience will buy Chrissy as Judy in two minutes flat.'

At the start, when it was becoming obvious we were going to offer her the role, people had reservations. 'Are you sure this is a good idea? She's rock'n'roll. She's got a reputation for being difficult and temperamental. What if she goes off the rails? *Blood Brothers* was on and off in a flash. We're hoping to run for two years. What if she decides after a few months she doesn't want to be tied up for the long term?' I said, 'Trust me,' and I was right. We did around 750 shows and she was the only cast-member who didn't miss a performance. Chrissy never acted like a rock star. Apart from a phone in her dressing-room, she never wanted anything special. She was low-key, quiet and dedicated. She never partied after the show. She went home, took care of her voice, hung around the house all day, then came to the theatre early to prepare.

Chrissy took an enormous risk playing Judy. Showbiz is littered with the carcasses of actresses who've dared to portray her, and failed. Garland fans are extremely protective and are usually affronted when someone tries to play her on stage or in a film. If the actress doesn't measure up, and often even if she does, the critics will shoot her down in flames. With *Blood Brothers*, which was dark and edgy theatre, Chrissy's rock star cred pulled her fans through the door. And Divinyls were huge at the time, 1988, with a tremendous following. *The Boy From Oz* was different. It was a traditional musical. Most of those who came to see it were female and over 45 and while some may have heard of Chrissy they most probably weren't fans. They didn't pay to see *her*. Chrissy got the part on her merits alone. It was a complex role. We took licence with Judy's character. In our show we needed her to be Peter Allen's muse, a wise and worldly woman who had hit the heights and now was passing the torch to Peter, telling him how to be a star and to stop doing all those tinselly versions of cabaret songs. She had to come across as someone strong enough to influence someone as tempestuous and charismatic as Peter Allen.

Chrissy was amazed by the adulation she received. She *triumphed*. Often the best people don't realise just how excellent they are because there's something in their head, the thing that made them great in the first place, telling them they have to strive for more.

What really won the audience over was her first song, 'All I Wanted Was The Dream'. That proved she had the chops for this kind of musical theatre and always got her a big cheer. She thrived on the applause. People ask me how a performer can get themselves up every single night, night after night, and deliver their best performance. My theory is that an enthusiastic audience fuels entertainers. Their cheers are payback for all the work and anxiety and the performer responds with a memorable show.

People were surprised by Chrissy's comedy skills. Her delivery was perfect and she got every laugh. Judy was very dry and witty and had terrific comic timing and, happily, so did Chrissy.

When we took *The Boy From Oz* to Broadway, casting Hugh Jackman as Peter Allen, we gave serious consideration to having Chrissy reprise Judy. Then we realised that you simply can't have someone who is not an American portraying this great American icon in America. US audiences would have taken it as an insult and not turned up. We would have been tempting a kicking. It wasn't that I didn't think Chrissy was good enough. She was. And I'd have no trouble casting her as Judy in London's West End, anywhere but in America. I know she was disappointed because she knew she could do it perfectly.

The show played all the capital cities. Night after night, month after month, year after year, I was onstage. The flu, headaches and summons-servers did their worst, but I kept turning up. Never once did I let on, except when having a heart-to-heart with Handbag, that things in my life were anything but wonderful. It became a point of honour to me not to miss a performance. The toughest night was when Pam, our gorgeous ticket-expert and recovering alcoholic who was my twelve-step program sponsor, died from cancer. I was distraught, but on I went and I used my sorrow to make Judy's plight more poignant.

Todd McKenney, who played Peter Allen, worked hard. His was a back-breaking role, singing and dancing and onstage virtually for the whole performance. He needed support from his co-stars and we tried not to let him down. Todd and I didn't exactly get on. At my entrance, he would stand with his back to the audience and pull faces to try to make me crack up. It was so one-sided because if I ever tried doing it back to him he would be outraged. Once or twice it would also amuse Todd to kick me in the shins when we were dancing, and as a fine dancer he knew exactly what he was doing. If one of the guys in Divinyls had tried such antics I would have punched him out, but this was not Selinas, it was Her Majesty's Theatre. I toughed it out and didn't crack. Todd flung himself around on stage, like Peter Allen did, and injuries were inevitable. He missed a few performances, so I had to work with understudies, which I found difficult because I'd rehearsed so closely with Todd.

Mum and Dad came to the opening night in Melbourne in May 1999. To Dad, that was the night I finally passed muster. All those years when I was a rock star paled in importance to what he'd just seen, his daughter receive a standing ovation for playing Judy Garland in a big glossy musical. 'You've really made it now,' he gushed as he hugged me. 'You've *really* made it now.'

At the party afterwards, Dad naughtily plucked *two* beers instead of just one from the drinks tray every time the waiter hustled by. He danced with me, danced with me beautifully. As he took me in his arms, I noticed that he seemed a little frail, but then I was swept away in his sure grasp. It was as if my feet weren't touching the floor as we glided across the room. He was proud.

Mary Amphlett

> I went to Sydney for the opening of *The Boy From Oz*, but Jim didn't go. I think that was the start of him not being well. So when the show came to Melbourne he was so thrilled, and he said to me, 'Mary, I loved it. I'm so excited for Chrissy.' Someone asked Jim to rate the show, and he replied, 'Nine and a half out of ten!'

Ben Gannon got it wrong. I didn't have a perfect performance record. I missed two shows, one on the evening of 27 July 1999, and the matinee the following day. I had a good reason. Charley Drayton and I were married at the farm at Delaney's Creek on a cool, clear Queensland Tuesday. Mum was there, and Lesley Shaw, and Grant Thomas, who gave me away in my ailing father's absence, and his girlfriend. There was a celebrant, and my naturopath and her son filmed the ceremony. I wore a Comme des Garçon dress and had had my hair done at the local beauty parlour. Charley, who whipped up a soul food wedding feast, wore a turn-of-the-century priest's coat, which by the end of the day was smeared in cake we'd rubbed over each other in an old American custom, and his tears. All my dogs wore bows, and howled in unison when the celebrant asked if anyone present could show cause why we shouldn't get hitched.

We flew back to Melbourne on the Wednesday and I was back on stage that evening. Charley returned to New York. There was no honeymoon. For us both, the show had to go on.

My goals to stay sober and pay my debts and find happiness were being achieved. Apart from my basic living expenses, all my wages each week went to creditors. I paid Winterland. I paid lawyers and accountants and tour operators. By the end of 1999, my mountain of debt was a hill. I was so proud that I was clearing my bills on my own, and knew that if the show lasted just a few more months there would be no one left to put their hands out. No one in that production knew I was in such financial strife. They thought I was a rich and glamorous rock star without a worry in the world. I didn't confine my acting to the stage.

The final venue of *The Boy From Oz*'s more than two-year run was in Perth. After the curtain came down for the last time there was high emotion, tears and hugs, among the cast and crew as we basked in the glow of a job well done. In Dad's eyes I had made it.

I'd kept the promise I'd made to myself when I regained consciousness after my Christmas Day breakdown three years before. I was solvent at last. I had stayed sober. In my twenty years as a performer I had co-written songs with Mark McEntee that are on the personal soundtrack of thousands of people's lives. I had truly given my heart and soul, sometimes my blood, to my audience. I was a happy woman. And I was in love, more in love than ever, with Charley Drayton. And what was really great was that, after everything, my husband was in love with me.

NO REST FOR THE WICKED 23

Today, my sobriety is the foundation for my peace of mind. Now I have some inner strength to deal with life on its terms. Don't think I'm not tempted from time to time. I'll be sitting in a restaurant or club and a waiter will pass with a tray of drinks. The smell will remind me of glamorous and exciting times. And then I will think where alcohol led me and try to put such thoughts out of my mind. There was nothing glamorous about the way I was, unable to guarantee my behaviour when I drank and continuing to drink after negative consequences. At first I only drank when I worked. Later, of course, I drank whenever I could. The dreadful scenes, the despair and remorse, the damage I did to my mind and body, and to others' minds and bodies. Not that I'm apologising for a thing. I never, ever apologise. I was what I was, and now I am what I am. I needed to go through the dark to find myself and my own uniqueness.

Everything that happened was a small price to pay for following my dream.

People ask me what I'm up to these days. They want to know why

I don't return to Australia. 'What?' I reply, 'and get a job as the nasty judge on *Australian Idol*?' Seriously, the short answer is I'm leading a full and happy life in America with Charley and our dog Holiday, in an apartment in Riverdale, New York.

I'm a long way from home, a stranger in a strange land, but being with Charley is more important to me than anything, and if that means that I spend time away from home, Australia, that's the way it has to be. Geography doesn't matter. What does is that I love and am loved.

Charley and I don't argue. There's no need. He's a man who is comfortable with his talent, his strength and ability to love. He apologises when he's wrong, which is not very often, and never holds a grudge. His love is unconditional, yet his integrity makes him steely. Mum always says one of the reasons she loves Charley is because he doesn't put up with any of my nonsense. She's on the money there. Charley and I have a thing where when he's listening to the traffic report while we're in the car I always talk. He says, 'Shhhh!' I keep talking. He says, 'Chrissy!' I say, 'Okay, I'll shut up.' We enjoy being together, while treasuring our independence. He's away a lot playing and recording all over the world and I have projects of my own. Charley has his world, so do I. If for a moment either of us felt our marriage wasn't right, it would end. For now, every morning when Charley wakes up he smiles across the pillow at me. The big grin is because he is happy to see me.

My husband is a hopeless romantic. I'll walk into the bathroom and there'll be little love lollies all around the bath, and when we visited Japan, where he was playing, I opened the door of our hotel room and he had sprinkled flower petals, love letters and antique Japanese gifts through the room.

Like Mum, I'm not domestic. Charley is head chef. His domain is the kitchen. And his tea cupboard is always full of the best green teas from Japan, Indian teas, the most fragrant teas. He drinks tea all day. Unlike me, he doesn't touch coffee. He cooks as he plays music, testing different ingredients and styles, blending, fine-tuning.

Charley and I performed together at New York benefits for the firemen killed in the 11 September 2001 terrorist attacks, for AIDS research and the victims of the Bali bombings (we did 'I'm On Your Side') and the South-East Asian tsunami.

In 2002, we cut a bluesy electronic version of 'Before Too Long' for the Paul Kelly tribute album *The Women At The Well*.

I sang 'St James Infirmary', the old funeral dirge I performed with my autoharp on the streets of Europe three decades before, at a fashion show at New York's hip Maritime Hotel for my dear friend Nick Morley's then label, Buddhist Punk. Charley played marching funeral drums for me and organised all the music for the night... The theme was pirates and I felt at home among the skulls and crossbones. The gig took me back... on the bill at the after-party were some guys from Guns N' Roses and, of all people, the Cult, our old American tour mates from the eighties. Ian Astbury and I swapped war stories from the road. Steven Tyler, whose fans threw missiles at us, was there, and Boy George. The models included Charley, to my mind looking more gorgeous than any of the girls, and the daughters of Mick Jagger and Keith Richards. I managed to get tangled up in my pirate outfit and fall down the stairs before I went on. I lay sprawled on the floor as young, tall, thin, blonde women stepped over me without a care, their eyes only for the rock stars. I really hurt myself. I had my leg and ankle iced and when the time came to sing I stuffed my swollen, throbbing foot into my big pirate boot and toughed it out. Like when the angry roadie clobbered my foot with his hammer, no one knew I was in agony. It was a moment of dejá vu.

I continue to write songs which may or may not ever be heard by the public. My music has been slower. There's a couple of faster songs but it's more groove-orientated.

I'm often asked to reform Divinyls, but I've jumped off that particular train and, while never saying never, it's hard to think of getting back on.

Living here with Charley I hear music all the time. The music he plays and listens to, music in the street and blaring from passing cars. There is so much to take in in New York. My love of music has never diminished. As ever, I like straight-ahead basic rock, but my musical knowledge and taste has broadened. I can appreciate different styles and rhythms. As a performer, I was always driven by rhythm, and I've grown to be even more into rhythmic music, from funk to salsa, and that's helped my phrasing. As I've travelled in such places as Puerto Rico and the West Indies I've heard music I didn't know existed. I absorb a lot of different kinds of sounds and it comes out in my own singing and writing.

Like everyone else, I was shattered by the events of 11 September 2001. From my toes up through my body, I've never experienced such fear. I called Mum in Melbourne to tell her I was okay. Charley's close family gathered together, quietly deriving strength from each other. Charley's father, Bernard, cried. He had seen the planes hit the World Trade Center from his rooftop in lower Brooklyn. For days after, we heard sirens and could smell the acrid smoke that drifted up the island from Ground Zero. While sorrowing, the family didn't discuss the atrocity. At a family barbecue, I asked Bernard why. 'Because terrorism is nothing new to black people,' he said. 'We've been victims of terror for 300 years.'

Happily, Charley and Keith Richards are mates again. The rapprochement came in 1995 when the Rolling Stones were touring Australia. A friend called us at the farm where we were staying to say he had just seen Mick, Keith and the guys on a televised press conference in Brisbane and Keith had said, 'I have a good friend in Australia and I need to connect with my mate.' He meant Charley. Charley went to the Stones' hotel and I didn't see him for two days. Keith arranged for a limo to pick me up at the farm and take me to Brisbane for the gig. I got so excited that I partied hard the night before and slept all the next day. The limo came and left without me.

One night I heard squeaking footsteps in the hallway of our apartment in New York. Suddenly Keith was in the room. Contrary to his rapscallion image, Keith is a very real and somewhat self-effacing man. And he is elegance personified. That night he wore a

long cashmere coat that reached the ground, tight blue jeans and
sneakers. I have a memory of him sitting at our kitchen table drinking
vodka and smoking joints. After a dinner in Connecticut at the end
of 2004, Keith kissed me goodbye, right on the moosh. He had been
smoking, drinking and eating all night and I have never tasted sweeter
breath in my life. It was so clean and fresh and *healthy*. I was
astounded.

Mum and I are as tight as ever. Through my tempestuous life she has
lavished on me the same unconditional love and support she did when
I was a little girl, and she still spoils me rotten. It was important to
me that I clear my debts and even at the worst of the worst times in
my life I still managed to love myself a little. I thank my mother for
instilling in me the values of responsibility and self-confidence.

Mum has been ill these past years. She had a heart attack in the
early nineties and a pacemaker was inserted in her chest, and a couple
of years ago she had a thyroid malfunction then skin grafts on her
leg. She was in hospital when it became clear to her that the old family
home in Eton Road, Belmont, was now too big for her. I flew to
Australia and, bossing around a horde of estate agents and solicitors,
sold the house for an excellent price. I then bought a sunny and more
easy-to-manage townhouse in Belmont where she lives today. I moved
all her belongings and furniture from the old house while she was
laid up so she could move straight in. It's not unusual for me to call
Mum twice a day from New York.

Dad died two minutes into New Year's Day 2003. Our relationship
had been loving but distant—he had never acknowledged any of my
relationships. When Mum told me Dad was dying of cancer I came
to Australia and visited him in the palliative care ward. He looked
frail and obviously didn't have much longer to live. I would massage
his feet. He was crotchety with Mum and me because he didn't want
us to see him in such bad shape. He was incorrigible to the end,
gambling the snack money that Mum had brought him with the others
in the hospice. One day, we both broke down and I said, 'I'll come

and see you again, Dad.' And he said, 'I wouldn't worry about that, Chrissy.' And I didn't know whether he meant 'Don't bother coming to see me because we don't get on' or 'Don't bother coming to see me because my time is up and you've got a life to live.' Mum assured me that the latter was true.

After he died I went through his belongings and found he had kept all my elocution reports.

Kevin Hanily, Handbag, had long been on borrowed time, yet in the end it wasn't his AIDS that killed him. He had a fatal heart attack at his home in Melbourne while ironing a shirt. In his last years, my old backstage friend from *Blood Brothers* and *The Boy From Oz* helped in the mission on Roslyn Street in Kings Cross, handing out blankets and warm drinks to the homeless people and junkies. 'The remedy for feeling as awful as I do is to go out and find someone worse off,' he said. When I was in town I'd whisk him off for a coffee. He asked if I would sing 'Amazing Grace' at his funeral. 'You have to sing it, Chrissy. If you don't, the job will go to Tina Arena, I fear!' I said I'd be honoured to, but when Kevin passed away I was in the United States and I didn't find out he'd died until after the funeral. And, yes, it was Tina who sang the lovely old hymn.

Handbag was always close to his sister, who lived in Melbourne. With terrible irony, a couple of months after he died, she was in the street leaning on her car and talking to a friend when an out-of-control car smashed into her vehicle and she was killed instantly.

Andrew McManus and I are friends again. For a while we didn't speak, then things thawed. He wanted to make things right between us. He's a big teddy bear, a good man and a good-natured man. I was always his girl, and he was so protective of me and he's still that way. Today he is one of the wealthiest and most successful promoters in Australia.

I rang Rick Grossman recently and said, 'Rick, you've got children. What will they think when my book comes out and people read about all the things we did?' He said, 'Chrissy, they already know. I told them long ago.'

I was angry with Rick for getting addicted to heroin and having to leave the band. He moved on and cut us off, but I know now that's what he had to do. We have always been friends and have talked right from the late eighties to now. These days Rick has beaten his addiction, although it wasn't easy for him, and he is one of Australia's best and most respected musicians. He's in the Hoodoo Gurus, he teaches guitar to young rockers, and counsels drug addicts. He has a lovely family. A normal, happy man, responsible and dependable, Rick is a dear, dear friend.

This book has brought me in touch with Richard Harvey and Vince Lovegrove after nearly two decades of not speaking. I invited Harve to dinner while I was in Sydney to talk about his Divinyls days. Dapperly dressed and periodically going out onto my balcony to puff on little cigars, he was still very funny, and before launching into an anecdote he would stand up and hold court, just as he used to. Yet I got the impression Harve was still bruised by the circumstances of his departure when he left us to play with Joe Walsh and we didn't let him back into the band. He was one helluva drummer, and maybe life hasn't panned out for Harve as it should have. When somewhere around midnight he said goodbye to me and disappeared into Kings Cross, our old stamping ground, I felt a little sad.

I'm glad Vince and I are talking again. In 2004 I called him and asked if he would share his memories for this book. He enthusiastically agreed, and I deeply appreciate that. He has endured a lot in his life, much more than I could ever have done. Those terrible days when Suzi and Troy were diagnosed with the AIDS that would kill them, and he left the band, not surprisingly changed our relationship forever. We caused each other pain, and time will tell if we can ever be good friends again, but I will say this: Vince is a good and loving father and a talented rock historian, writer and documentary maker.

Last night I dreamed of Bjarne Ohlin. We haven't spoken since he parted company with Divinyls nearly twenty years ago. In my dream Bjarne was angry with me and made bitter accusations, then he calmed down and we were friendly. I woke up feeling good, as if another piece of baggage from my past had been collected and carried away. I wish only good things for Bjarne.

Mark McEntee and I have also buried the hatchet, and we've usually shared positive moments when we've caught up in the eight years since Divinyls last played. In the end he gave me some money to contribute to the Divinyls debts that I had already paid. All that said, at this moment, Mark and I are not speaking. Surprise, surprise! I'm not totally sure why.

Mark has much to be proud of; we both do. I believe Divinyls are— for we have never officially broken up—a very good band that on occasions approached greatness. We made music that defined the era in which it was created and has stood the test of time, though we were even better live than on record. As they say, you had to be there. I worry that Mark has been overlooked as a guitar player because of my presence and antics. That may have contributed to the air of disappointment I sense in him. He should never doubt that he was— is—one of the great guitarists, and a hell of a songwriter when he applied himself.

I'm sad that we're not better friends. We have a lot to offer each other. I respect Mark and I hope he appreciates what we achieved together. In the end the excesses of the rock'n'roll life tore us apart.

Working on this book has picked me up by the scruff of the neck and made me look at my life, with all its pleasure and pain. I'm quite clear now about my legacy and what I was, and wasn't, responsible for. I'm happy with that. The fact that I survived to write it is a miracle in itself. It's clear that someone, something, has looked after me. I hope, on that terrible Christmas Day in 1996, that the angel with the white wings won.

It was never my way at the end of a gig to exchange pleasantries with the audience. To thank them for coming to the show and wish them a safe journey home. I preferred to leave them in the moment of our songs, with nothing more than memories of a great gig. To me that was enough. But, as I reach the end of my story (so far), I'm

going to make an exception. For all of you who've accompanied me
on my journey from Belmont to the Big Apple via heaven and hell,
I say thanks for staying with me for the ride.

Just don't ask me to apologise.

THE UNEXPECTED

Life rarely turns out how we expect. Reading again the final words of the first edition of *Pleasure and Pain*, I am reminded that my life was rich and busting with endless possibilities. I was healthy and fit; I had paid my dues; I was married to a beautiful man.

If someone said to me I was about to be stricken with multiple sclerosis, a cruel and debilitating illness that would change every aspect of my life, even threaten my very existence, I would have laughed, then said, 'I don't know much about multiple sclerosis. Isn't having MS the reason why the former Olympic runner Betty Cuthbert and my old friend the great harmonica player Jim Conway are in wheelchairs?'

But today, sitting on the porch of a magnificent 210-year-old farmhouse in Connecticut, loaned to me for the summer by dear friends Will and Sandrine Lee so I can work on this final chapter for the new edition of *Pleasure and Pain*, my body stiff and aching and deeply fatigued, I know exactly what MS is.

There can be no more perfect place to gather my thoughts and commit them to paper. It is high summer, yet under the huge and spreading trees in the yard, the air is cool. I smell blossoms and grass being cut. The sounds I hear are of leaves rustling in the warm dusk breeze, of a creek nearby that meanders over old stones, of deer and voles rambling in the undergrowth, and my Pekingese, Holiday, yapping for her dinner. Inside the three-storey house are open fireplaces, paintings and photos and mementoes of my friends and their loved ones, a TV tuned to the station that plays old black and white movies 24 hours day, and musical instruments which I am not compelled to pick up and play.

The first time I acknowledged that something was terribly wrong with my body was in early 2005 when I was staying in an apartment in Challis Avenue in Potts Point, Sydney, working on the first edition of this book. I had the sensation of pins of needles in my feet. Thinking they were simply cold I pulled on a pair of socks. But the tingling didn't go away for quite some time. This is weird, I thought.

When I finished writing the book, my publishers hosted a party at the Eastern Hotel in Bondi Junction to celebrate the end of the project. I didn't feel well all that day and by 7 p.m., when the party got underway, I was feeling dreadful. Instead of mingling with the guests, I plonked myself in a chair and held court there all evening.

In the following weeks, the pins and needles came and went, in my hands as well as my feet.

I met a friend named Tess Strelein for lunch and when I told her about my pins and needles she said I should see a doctor sooner rather than later because she had an inkling something serious was the matter. Tess's inkling became a certainty moments later.

When it was time to leave the cafe I got up from my seat. My legs buckled. I crashed to the floor. Plates and cutlery went flying. The other diners looked at me disdainfully as though I'd been drinking. I'm sure I heard someone say, 'Oh, yes, Chrissy Amphlett, off her face again.' I looked up from where I'd fallen and protested, 'I'm not drunk, I'm just not well. Really!' But I don't think anyone believed me. Tess helped me up and said, 'I know a really good doctor. Will you see him?'

I didn't see Tess's doctor, but I did have a CAT scan of my spine and hips, which was clear, and I made an appointment with an osteopath who told me, 'Chrissy, you're just running really hot.' I thought he meant hormonally.

Things got worse. In addition to the pins and needles I started to experience grinding fatigue. It overwhelmed me. I had trouble walking up the stairs to my apartment. One night I put my head down on my pillow and it felt like it was breaking in two.

My flight back home to New York was horrific. When I disembarked from the plane in Los Angeles to go through Customs before boarding again for New York, my messed-up digestion was playing havoc with my stomach. It felt like it was full of chewing gum. The pilot of the plane recognised me and came over to tell me how much he had enjoyed my music. As he was rabbiting on, I couldn't help it, I farted, or, as my mother would have preferred me to say, broke wind. Appalled, the pilot's face contorted into a look of incredulity and disgust. He actually turned and ran from me. I could only stand there, stricken and shattered. Back on the plane for the final, five-hour leg from LA to JFK airport in New York, I was so sore and uncomfortable I had to sit with my feet in the air. I could not relax my legs, which were tingling and buzzing.

Over the following weeks I continued to suffer pins and needles, lassitude and depression. I was dizzy and nauseous. It was as if electric currents were coursing through my body. I felt cold at my core. Not just on my skin, but in my bones. It was as though a boa constrictor was squeezing the life from me. I dragged my right foot. My digestion wasn't working and I was full of gas. And there was pain in my ribs and my hands and my feet at different times. My right foot began twitching and my right hand would flex involuntarily into a claw.

I went to a doctor, who prescribed sleeping pills. Sleep was bliss, but I'd wake up and find my pain and discomfort was real and not a nightmare. What on earth was wrong with me?

After some blood tests I was told by one specialist I had rheumatoid arthritis.

There had been signs in past years that all may not be well with me. I'd been diagnosed with poor circulation, and from time to time I'd had panic attacks, depression and fatigue. A hot day would lay me low. I'd fall inexplicably. Once when I was doing a show at the Queensland Performing Arts Centre my body had been mysteriously paralysed for half an hour. But I ascribed all of these symptoms to the rock'n'roll life I'd lived.

I booked in to see a rolfer, a masseur who specialises in deep and painful massage of the soft, connective tissue of the body. Every second day he dug his fingers between my ribs to separate them; he prodded and jabbed my thighs and groin, even probing inside my mouth to massage my cheeks to unlock my jaw. That's what I required for relief, because by then I had knots in my forearms and shoulders and my hands were curled and cramped. Then my foot would go all twisted and I couldn't stop it. I couldn't get comfortable in bed.

I knew in my heart I was in strife, but I was in denial and spoke to no one about the awful changes that were attacking my body, not even Charley. He was playing on the soundtrack of the movie *Across the Universe* then and I didn't want to bother him. I tried to hide my symptoms. Perhaps, I *almost* convinced myself, I was undergoing hormonal changes.

I was also consumed by anger because my body, which had served me so well through so many experiences, was letting me down.

My condition grew worse. I fell down often because I couldn't feel my foot on the pavement. One night, I didn't have the strength to get out of my hot bath. My body had gone limp. Charley heard my feeble cries for help, wrapped his arms around me and lifted me out. I later found out that in the old days losing your strength while in hot water was a way of diagnosing MS.

One day I visited Charley on the *Universe* set on top of the ABC building on Broadway. It was the middle of summer and on my way there I could barely drag myself along 19th Street. It took me an hour to walk one block. When I finally arrived I hauled myself up the steps and into the building, and all around me were bright young actors and dancers with verve and energy. I felt one million years old.

Later, in around July 2005, as I went to meet my old manager Andrew McManus at the Algonquin Hotel in the heart of Manhattan, bustling, busy New Yorkers jostled me out of their way and cursed and glowered, making exasperated sounds as they pushed past. One man shoved into me and I fell down. It seemed to me, as I was sprawled on the footpath with this angry-eyed bastard berating me, that he was every man who had ever been brutal to me. At last, some passers-by helped me up. I called Charley and he told me to put one foot in front of the other and make it along the quarter block to the Algonquin. It took me 30 minutes. Inside the hotel I staggered into the lounge, sank into a deep armchair and had a glass of cold water. There, where Dorothy Parker, Robert Benchley and the other members of the Algonquin Round Table once met and swapped witticisms, I cried.

For the first time in my life I began noticing disabled people. They'd always been there, in the streets, all around me, but until I became one myself I guess they never really registered. Suddenly I could empathise with them about their daily struggle, the cruelty and prejudice they had to deal with. I saw one middle-aged woman, beautifully dressed and groomed, making her way in a motorised wheelchair along Madison Avenue and I was filled with awe and admiration for her.

Each night I hit the internet and Googled my symptoms. I know it's dangerous to self-diagnose, but I couldn't help myself. Again and again, the various medical sites threw up different diagnoses, including MS. Finally, in late August 2005, I summoned the courage to see a neurologist.

That done, my dear chiropractor of many years recommended to me a Park Avenue neurologist who had the reputation of being a great diagnostician. Because I still didn't know what was wrong with me, this was in his favour. I told him my symptoms and he conducted various tests on me: a lumbar puncture to withdraw cerebrospinal fluid from my spine for diagnosis, and also an MRI, during which his nurse stuck needles all over my body and ran an electric current through me to see if my nerve pathways worked. That was excruciatingly painful.

While my neurologist was analysing my results I had to fly to Sydney for the launch of *Pleasure and Pain* and do a national publicity tour. My symptoms came and went, and sometimes I felt so bad. However, I steeled myself to put whatever was happening to me to the back of my mind until I returned to New York. By doing this and devoting all my energy to the book release and tour I got through everything. Despite my stiff leg, no one was any the wiser that I was ailing.

Tour over, I flew home and on Tuesday 3 January 2006, I called on the neurologist. He didn't mess about. 'Oh,' he said, 'you've got MS . . . Didn't I tell you before you left?'

I broke the news to Charley, who was on tenterhooks out in the waiting room. He just looked at me, waiting to take his cue from my reaction. Then when he saw that I seemed to be stoically accepting my diagnosis, he hugged me. In reality I was in shock.

That night at home he lay alongside me and asked me how I was. I said, 'Charley, let's get a divorce. Not only did you marry an older woman, you married a dud.' He held me tightly and said, 'Chrissy, we're in this together. This is life. These things happen.' I thought, 'Yes, they do. But not to *me*. Not now. After I've beaten my demons, given up drinking, paid off my debts, and finally found happiness and contentment with Charley. I've made amends and now look what's happened. This *is* life. But life isn't fair.'

Multiple sclerosis is a disease of the nervous system in which the protective sheath, whose medical name is myelin, around the nerve fibres in the brain and spinal cord are damaged and plaques or lesions form in the scarred sections. The scars, or 'scleroses', scramble and impede the messages that are sent along the nerves. According to the experts, common symptoms include pins and needles, weakness in the limbs, extreme tiredness, dizziness and loss of balance and coordination, blurred vision, foot-dragging, hand and foot tremors, incontinence, digestive issues, memory lapses, speech difficulties. I certainly ticked a number of those boxes. The cause of MS is unknown—though genetic or environmental factors may be involved—and there is no cure. However there are medications, such as Copaxone, to ease the symptoms. MS can be progressive and it is unpredictable. Every sufferer has his or her own set of symptoms, with some people becoming severely disabled and others going on to lead a perfectly normal life after the initial symptoms. About 2.5 million people in the world have MS, and 70 per cent of sufferers are female.

Officially, my diagnosis was 'relapsing-remitting MS' in which acute symptoms occur, last a while, maybe a week or a month, then go away, then return.

A nurse came to our house and instructed me on how to self-inject the drug Copaxone (glatiramer acetate) with an auto-injector into different parts of my body. (I now inject daily, and alternate between seven injection sites over a week.) Copaxone's function is to reduce the incidence of relapses in my form of MS, relapsing-remitting multiple sclerosis. Turning myself into a pin cushion became my daily routine.

After you inject yourself there is an after-sting, as painful as a wasp bite, that lasts five minutes or so. Lumps and red welts spring up around the puncture. I have never grown used to self-injection. Every time I do it is an ordeal. Charley hates needles, so early on I tried to do it privately. Before too long he was helping me set the contraption up and leaving it for me on my night table, just in case I conveniently forgot!

I was also prescribed an anti-depressant/pain medication in one, plus a sleeping pill. My neurologist wasn't one to over-medicate and because I found all the muscle relaxants too strong I had to find other ways, like physiotherapy and swimming, to keep the stiffness at bay.

The drug Copaxone is supposed to reduce further exacerbations by up to 30 per cent, but while I could function, still the symptoms recurred. When I learned that stress can exacerbate the condition I made sure I avoided conflict and drama and unpredictable situations. It wore me out to focus on too many things in my life at once, so I did one job at a time. Multi-tasking for me was a thing of the past.

I read everything about multiple sclerosis that I could lay my hands on. The MS Society sent me a book about ways to manage the disease, and I read Teri Garr's inspiring book, *Speedbumps: Flooring It Through Hollywood*, about her own MS (like me, Teri had suffered symptoms on and off for many years before she was diagnosed in 1999). I read and read and read, and there was so much conflicting information. Some people's symptoms were mild; others went blind, lost their speech, died. Some people's MS progressed slowly, others' quickly; I read that because I was older my MS would not be so bad; and I also read that because I was older my MS would be worse than had I contracted it earlier in my life, and there was a chance I would be in a wheelchair within a year. I was like a headless chicken, running this way and that, listening to every piece of advice and trying every treatment.

Each morning I would wake gasping and anxious and for a second or two I'd wonder why I felt so distressed, then the grim truth would settle upon me: I had MS, and I could have no idea what the illness had in store for me.

Soon after my diagnosis, at one of the lowest points of my life, I wrote of my frustration and despair in my diary: 'I drag my foot across the kitchen floor and it makes a sweeping sound. Maybe I can be useful after all and should attach a swiffer pad to it and swiffer the floor. My right side still aches from falling on it with the full weight on my breast. My once pretty ankle is stiff and swollen and my toes curl under. My leg muscles are taut and stiff and burn with pain. I look at myself in the mirror and my face is puffy from too much sleep but sleep is my solace and I want escape. I dream dreams in which I am walking but can never get to my destination. I see women walking in the street without limps or stiffness and I envy them. I used to be able to do that, but took my health and fitness for granted. The woman I saw on Madison Avenue in the motorised wheelchair... will that be me? Not everybody with MS ends up in a wheelchair. Some people have exacerbations then incur no further damage. Others progress very rapidly. I don't know which category I fit into except that I know my particular MS is not the worst kind. I think it's somewhere in the middle. It's an unpredictable disease that affects each person differently.

'I don't know much about this disease even though I have read countless books and articles. It makes me feel like a failure as others have gone into remission and cured themselves. I can't. Why can't I just cure MS like I have been able to fix other things in my life? Multiple sclerosis robs me of my self-esteem and the place I occupied in this world. I feel powerless and beat and worthless and insignificant and dirty.

'I feel *wrong*. I burn myself again on the oven as I am clumsy, my right arm is weak and I drop and smash things to pieces on the clean kitchen floor that has given me a sense of order and control in the chaos. I imagine what it is like for Charley to live with my MS 24 hours a day. He must be longing to get away on tour. Away from depression and his sick, dependent, depressed wife. He doesn't complain when I have run the bath too hot and I go to jelly while soaking and he has to lift me out as I can't get out on my own. The endless trips he makes driving me to doctors. He was brought up not to be a slave, but he has become one, a slave to MS, and that's no life for a young man in his prime. I feel sorry for him, not for myself.

'When I am out I stagger and fall on people like a drunk and they glare and sometimes abuse me. I apologise but they look at me with anger, believing I fell on them purposely. Yet I realise that if someone does offer me help, it is a gift to be grateful for although I find it difficult to take their arm.

'I try, as much as possible, not to rely on others. I am isolating myself, withdrawing. I find it hard to reach out and ask for help, even making a phone call to a friend for a chat. I have no small talk, only seriousness. I try to read to take my mind away to far-off, wonderful, healthy places but I can't concentrate. I feel acutely the sadness in the world, the suffering, the unfairness. I am brought to my knees. What is the reason for all this? Is life all about suffering? Is there meaning in what's happened to me. Is having MS a calling? I think of suicide and how to do it and I buy Derek Humphry's book *The Final Exit: The Practicalities of Self-Deliverance and Assisted Suicide for the Dying*, but I never read it because somehow I lost it in the apartment somewhere . . . Or maybe Charley saw it and confiscated it?'

Charley went on tour as the drummer with the singer/songwriter Fiona Apple and when he returned after a few months away I could sense something was different. I asked him, 'What's wrong?' Glancing at my messy, pill-bottle-strewn night table and other reminders of my illness, the look on his face implied, 'I've come home and it's just MS again.' I felt so sorry for him. It made me try to make life as good as it could be for Charley, and lift my spirits and be conscious of not having my illness the centre of attention all the time. I would not mope at home. Even though the last thing I felt like doing was socialising, I made the effort to dress up and go out with Charley to parties, concerts and dinners.

I also tried to strengthen my legs and fire up my nerve force. I worked out with an Australian trainer and sports scientist named Todd Philpott who trained at a gym at the Thomas Jefferson sports complex in Spanish Harlem. It was way over the other side of town but it got me out and about. All the security guards were big black women with guns on their hips. Todd is a sweet, special guy. He has only one leg, but that doesn't stop him being super-fit and a terrific trainer. He was a champion hand cyclist and helped rehabilitate war amputees. Todd and I were the only white folks who regularly attended the gym— everybody else lifting weights and exercising was Spanish or black.

Backtrack now to September 2005.

Ben Gannon, who had produced *The Boy from Oz*, invited me to his apartment on Central Park West. Uncharacteristically, because my taxi had waited at the service entrance rather than the front door, I was late, and, equally uncharacteristically, he was annoyed. I realised later this was probably because the cancer that had dogged him for years had returned and his health was flagging. His irritation with me, however, did not prevent him offering me the role of Judy Garland again in a new production of *Boy*. This time it would play in arenas throughout Australia and Peter Allen would be played not by Todd McKenney but by the brilliant Hugh Jackman. The director would be Kenny Ortega who had choreographed Madonna, the Academy Awards and directed the *High School Musical* movies (and before Michael Jackson's tragic death in July 2009 was going to oversee his 50 farewell concerts at London's Millennium Dome). What could I say? Of course I said, 'Yes!'

Then I had an MS reality check. I had committed to an enormous and gruelling undertaking: 42 shows, one after the other, constant travel, and my role was especially demanding. I asked my neurologist, 'Realistically, can I do this?' He said he thought that I could if I kept my medication up, steered clear of stressful situations and didn't get over-tired. And, he added, 'No one need know.'

Obviously, I could not tell a soul in the production that their Judy, who was going to dance and sing in big production numbers and show-stopping ballads and get lifted high into the air above the stage, had MS. If they'd known they would not have let me take part in the show.

At the press conference officially announcing the show, in Sydney on Monday 13 February 2006, I was stricken with terror. How on earth was I going to get through this, and then the entire run of such an exacting production, without letting on about my illness? My symptoms had subsided but every day was uncertain. I had not had another incident like the one in 2005, perhaps because of the Copaxone and my other treatments, including handfuls of vitamins. But because I prided myself on my professional standards I was afraid of being sacked, of messing up on stage or simply being too ill to maintain the hectic schedule.

At the press conference, when it was my turn to be introduced I walked as briskly and normally as I could to the podium to be interviewed and photographed, I felt my leg stiffen at the knee. Perhaps Hugh Jackman noticed, or maybe he was just being the perfect gentlemanly 'son-in-law,' because he ran to my side, took my arm and helped me up the stairs onto the stage. He was so gentle and kind, and his support and compassion for me did not flag for the entire run of *The Boy from Oz*.

During that frantic fortnight I recorded my day's doings in my diary, and reading it again brings back that nightmare...

'Monday 6 February: So anxious... Doctor writes out a prescription for a stronger antidepressant... Gives me three different drugs to read about. I have to learn more about what's happened to me...

'Thursday 9 February: Still anxious and tired but body OK... Go to sleep then wake up early still feeling tired after a long night's sleep. Go to gym and work on legs, ride bike for 12 minutes, massage, aromatherapy 50 minutes. Very relaxing. Put shoes on and can't walk in them very far. Have to take them off because ankle collapses. Start to feel very anxious. Denise comes over. I put wedges on and can't walk in those either. Right arm and hand feel weak, legs in pain, pain in hand. Feeling uncomfortable. Pins and needles in hands. Ring Mum.

'Sunday 12 February: Wake up with headache. Go for swim. Water feels good. Headache. Legs feel weak. Arms feel weak.

'Monday 13 February: Press conference day. Wake up early. Stretch. Buttocks tight... right hand weak, right leg weak. Make-up and hair, run through the press conference. Have trouble getting on the stage.

'Tuesday 14 February: Qantas interview. Take a drug to ease the stiffness in leg. I run around seeing doctors just like... I don't know what I'm doing.

'Thursday 16 February: Make-up. Interview, *Sydney* magazine. Go to meeting at St John's, light the candles. Interview, *Sunday Life*. Seven o'clock massage. Fly to New York. Arrive Friday the 17th.'

•

Back in the Big Apple I began preparing for *The Boy From Oz,* which would start its run in Melbourne in August. As I had before, I immersed myself in Judy Garland. I obsessed over the songs, and the script. This time, however, in keeping with the arena version of the show, I wanted to play Judy with more of a sense of fun than previously.

On 2 March 2006, Charley and I were guests at Keith Richards' wife Patti Hansen's and their daughter Theodora's 50th and 21st birthdays respectively at the Pink Elephant club on West 27th Street. Keith was happy that his friend Charley was there. My wonky body ensured that I remained seated most of the time, but it was such a happy party with such great music that I threw caution—and my pain and stiffness—to the wind and got up and danced, even though I remained in the one spot doing the bump with jewellery designer Carolina Barbieri. I felt so happy and glamorous. Keith sat high up on a deck in the venue presiding over all his guests and Patti looked gorgeous dancing with everyone in a short black dress. Lisa Fischer, the Rolling Stones' beautiful and talented back-up singer, came over and told me I looked great and wanted to know my secret. 'Great sex!' I said. Little did she know that I had another secret: MS.

By the early hours when the party ended, I could barely walk and I staggered and shuffled out holding tightly to Darryl Jones, the bassist with the Stones who played on Divinyls' 'Ain't Gonna Eat Out My Heart,' and Charley. I was flushed with fun and excitement—and for one evening I was able to forget that I was stricken with multiple sclerosis.

There was a memorable interlude in June when Shayna Stewart, my dear friend from early singing days, came to visit me. We flew to New Orleans together, almost one year after Hurricane Katrina had battered and drowned the legendary music city. In our hire car, Shayna confided to me, 'Chrissy, you know I'm going blind in my right eye?' and I said, 'Well, don't worry; I'm going to be crippled by MS.' Feeling a bit like we were disabled versions of Thelma and

Louise, we both cracked up. I hadn't laughed out loud for a long, long time and we laughed all the way back to Manhattan.

Walking around New Orleans I ran into a Divinyls fan, Charles Alexander, who had lost all his memorabilia—T-shirts, posters, photos—in the hurricane and had had to try to replace it all. He came to our hotel with his treasures and I signed the lot. It was the least I could do. Charles took Shayna and me around the city and I couldn't believe there were still destroyed houses and debris piled everywhere—even abandoned boats sitting at traffic intersections. It was heartbreaking.

My sadness at the destruction of this musical Mecca aside, Shayna and I had a good time together, taking lots of photos, eating delicious food, browsing in vintage clothing stores and listening to music. Baton Rouge, the town that gave us the name of the group we sang in all those years ago, was only a few kilometres away.

I summoned the courage to buy a cane. I chose one with a beautiful black wooden handle and a silver top. Todd Philpott later broke it accidentally at the gym . . . but I wasn't too upset because I didn't really need it.

By and large, my illness was under control on that trip, except one very hot day when I became disoriented. I had no idea where I was or what I was doing. My confusion passed when I found a cool, quiet place to sit and regather my strength.

In late June that year I was back in Australia, knuckling down to rehearsals for *The Boy from Oz* at the old Capitol Theatre in Sydney's Haymarket. As rehearsals got underway I began to panic. They wanted me to wear high heels in my Hong Kong opening scene, and I knew performing, let alone dancing, in heels was out of the question. I was beside myself with worry until Kenny Ortega conveniently told wardrobe Judy should wear pants and ballet flats, on the grounds that she would have done in Hong Kong.

And they kept changing Judy's dying scene, where she ascends to heaven, something like 15 times and I always wore heels. For a while

I had to climb a large flight of stairs on the stage, then the director decided I should stand on a platform, without a railing, that was raised by a hidden hydraulic lift high up, at least a couple of storeys, into the ceiling of the arena. With MS, my balance was awry and every night I felt I might fall into the chorus line of dancers far below. God bless my dresser, Ron, who was waiting for me on high to help me off my platform to safety.

On the first day of rehearsals, Kenny Ortega threw me a huge challenge. He told me he wanted Hugh Jackman and me to do the intricate and high-energy Tramp Dance, which Judy had danced with Fred Astaire. I could have refused to do it, but turning down an artistic challenge has never been my way. I started out gingerly doing the steps and suddenly my leg collapsed under me, I fell down and for a while sat on the floor, embarrassed and shocked. No one said a word. After what seemed like an age I smiled and regained my feet with the gallant Hugh's help, and got stuck into the Tramp Dance again. The choreographer Kelley Abbey and her assistants Troy and Lisa were so patient with me, as was Hugh, who is a very quick learner. For the first few shows I was a bit shabby, but gradually I got the hang of it and pulled it off.

To survive in the show I realised I had to follow my doctor's orders to 'manage your disease'. So I kept up my injections and underwent physical therapy sessions in Sydney through rehearsals.

Around this time, I went to a doctor who tested my hormone levels. He declared me low on testosterone and gave me the hormone over a three-week period to build up my strength and stamina, and increase my physicality which was so important when playing to a large arena.

After I had the injections, I knew what it was like to be a man driven by sex. I didn't enjoy feeling like a man and wouldn't recommend it. My skin was breaking out and I became obsessed by penises, scouring the internet for pictures of them. I wanted to dominate men—not have sex with them, just dominate them. Poor Hugh, I was getting so strong. 'Judy' was pulling him around by the arm like a toy boy. One night, prowling the back streets near my hotel I felt like a she-wolf.

When I told my neurologist back in New York I had taken the hormone he was furious. I didn't care. I was prepared to try anything for the weak muscles in my right leg and hand. Looking back today, I know I never want to feel like a she-wolf again!

In early August 2006, after five weeks of rehearsals at the Capitol Theatre, *The Boy from Oz* began its 42-show nationwide arena run at Melbourne's Rod Laver Arena. The crowds flocked in and they loved the show. We received a standing ovation every night. Hugh was magnificent. I have never seen such energy or professionalism. He was on stage the entire show and sang and danced himself to a standstill every night. He must have known I was performing under duress, but never once did he complain to me or the producers. He had endless patience. He is a superb dancer and a quick learner, much quicker than me.

At the end of our dance together I had to emphasise a downbeat with a wave of my hat to conduct the orchestra and my timing was sometimes off, but whenever I missed the beat he'd laugh, and I'd laugh too.

In between my scenes when Judy wore heels, my dresser Ron, who had no idea what was wrong with me, sat beside me in the wings, uncomplainingly massaging my legs and feet which would cramp and knot and clench and hurt like hell. I was terrified every time that lift whisked me to heaven and, between my final scene and the curtain call at the end of the show, my legs would stiffen and it would be all I could do to return to the stage to take my bow.

In spite of that, at times I could be really silly and have fun with the cast and crew. It was the way I coped. Once a trouper, always a trouper.

Late at night I'd go to my room and fall into bed. I would be exhausted but all the rehearsing and dancing seemed to fire up my nerves to function better, although my neurologist would almost certainly disagree. But it did take my mind off my diagnosis.

Ron was my co-star Colleen Hewitt's dresser too and when she saw him massaging my legs she must have wondered what was wrong with me.

Despite the cancer which by now had spread to his liver, Ben Gannon, was his usual self, a hands-on whirlwind of perfectionism. What is it about theatre people? Not even liver cancer can stop them. Ben was doing what he loved and *The Boy From Oz* was his baby. He was inspirational and had the whole company's respect. Though clearly dying of his cancer he was ever-present, cajoling us, demanding that we give our very best.

His illness had made him even more brusque than before. Once he saw me strapping my ankle and snapped, 'Well, I hope I'm going to get my money's worth out of you.' I didn't take offence because I knew he was sick, but he would never have said such a thing before.

Ben knew I kept liquorice in my dressing room and often sneaked in to help himself. At the last Sydney show, just before we went to Perth, he was in my room. I knew he was not well enough to accompany the show to Western Australia. We hugged and both wept. We knew this was the end. I never saw Ben again. Sadly, he died a few months later.

It seemed to be a time of death. Just after Ben died I went to a funeral in Harlem of a young black woman, a Drayton family friend. She had left two young children behind. I hadn't known her but I went to the funeral in support. I held it together until her children arrived at the funeral home. Seeing them, my heart broke for them, and I grieved for Ben and also Stephen Maclean, who had died of cancer the year before in Thailand. There I was, the only white woman in the congregation, and the only person sobbing. Everybody else was able to contain their emotions. I was a mess.

In early 2007, I went to Manhattan's Waldorf Astoria Hotel for a meeting. Sitting there, in a suite as big as a ballroom, were my old partner and bandmate Mark McEntee and his girlfriend Melanie,

Charley and Andrew McManus, the Divinyls' former manager. The suite was Mark and Melanie's. Andrew had flown in from Los Angeles that day to propose a Divinyls reunion tour to follow our 7 December gig headlining the huge Homebake open-air music festival in Sydney to which we were already committed.

We all agreed that there was a demand for a tour. Our fans in Australia had never forgotten us, in fact they were as hard-core as ever, and our songs had come to be considered classics of Australian rock. The band would be me and Mark, my Charley would play drums, lovely Jerome Smith on bass and the mighty Charlie Owen would play guitar.

At that point I told everyone about my MS and that I felt I could do the concerts so long as I had plenty of rest.

In the following months everything fell into place. We would play Homebake then set out on a month-long national tour. Then, we would gather again in March for the second leg of the series of gigs. These shows would be the profit-making ones. Andrew, always our biggest fan, agreed to be financial backer, hire the venues, and to pay for the recording and distribution of an EP of new songs I had written, including 'Asphyxiated', 'Don't Wanna Do This' and 'All Pretty Things', that we would showcase at Homebake and on tour.

In a portent of things to come, because of commitments Mark couldn't leave his home in Perth to come to America to record the new music. Andrew and Charley bent over backwards to accommodate him. With Andrew footing the bill, Charley and our friend, engineer Pat Thrall, set us up in the Las Vegas Palms Casino Resort's state-of-the-art recording studio, Studio at the Palms. Pat and his wife Zoe, who was the studio manager, put Charley, Holiday and me up at their home. Zoe had been an engineer way back in 1983 at the Power Station when we cut *Desperate*.

In the studio Charley, Pat and I built the basic treatments for the songs. They hired a satellite link and recorded Mark in Perth, which was difficult and expensive, and mixed his guitar tracks to what we were playing in Vegas. Thanks to Pat and Charley the recordings sounded great. I sang all the vocals in the Thralls' dining room, where Pat had built a vocal booth for me. Zoe would arrive home from the Palms tired, but she would always be my supportive audience when I was cutting the vocals.

Las Vegas, in the middle of the desert, was inferno-hot, so I could only leave the house at midnight when a breeze sprang up. I would take Holiday walking in the gated community. Charley and I met a fellow dog walker in Colonel Tom Parker's widow, and we would often walk past king of the blues BB King's two touring buses on our route.

Recording in Las Vegas was fun. When we were all at the studio, recording rhythm tracks with Richard Fortus, including the rhythm track for my song 'Kill Her With Love', the producer Timbaland was producing the now-notorious MTV awards show in which Britney Spears had her famous meltdown. Timbaland and his entourage were in the studio next to us in the Palms. We were separated by a green room where you eat. I learned that he didn't like dogs, probably in the wake of a scandal then going on in which a high-profile NFL player was caught staging to-the-death dog fights, so I tried to keep Holiday out of his way. We kept to our studio and Timbaland kept to his.

One day, however, Holiday followed me to the loo and on the way she ducked into the green room where Timbaland and his team were sitting. I scuttled in after her, apologising profusely to everyone in the room because, I confess, I didn't know which one was Timbaland. One guy there took one look at tiny Holiday and declared, 'That dog ain't no killer!' At about 10 centimetres high, she certainly wasn't. I said to Holiday's defender, '*Exactly*, now would you mind her for me while I go to the bathroom?' That broke the ice. Everyone laughed, including, I think, Timbaland. Zoe was listening in her office freaking out.

During that *Boy From Oz* tour, I took a call from Mark Pope, who was working for Australia's Rock'n'Roll Hall of Fame. He said the Divinyls were going to be inducted in a big ceremony at Melbourne's

Regent Theatre on 16 August 2007. He wanted to know if the band would come together to play a song or two at the ceremony.

The night before the ceremony, Andrew McManus hosted a dinner at his home in Toorak. He invited Charley and me; Rick Grossman and Vince Lovegrove from the old days; Charlie Owen and his partner Kylie; and Mark and his girlfriend Melanie. Andrew thought it would be a good idea to make sure we could all be in the one room and not murder each other. He needn't have worried. It was a lovely evening. His then girlfriend, whose name was Nicki, cooked a roast.

Finding time between my appearances as Judy Garland, we had had some rehearsals and it all felt good. Obviously I was in no condition to rampage like a banshee across the stage or dive into the crowd. Apart from my MS I was 15 years older, but I tried to compensate by putting all my energy into my singing.

Mark Pope asked Hugh Jackman if he would induct us into the Hall of Fame on the big night, and Hugh said he would. Then something came up and he pulled out. I was furious with him, but I directed my anger into my rehearsals of the song 'Taught By Experts' in *The Boy From Oz*. Then Hugh decided he *could* induct us and all was forgiven—I was glad, because it's very hard to be cross with Hugh.

During our acceptance speech, I singled out in the audience my old adversaries Angry Anderson and Billy Thorpe (sadly, Billy would die of a heart attack not long after). Tongue in cheek, I accused them of giving me a hard time back in the day. With a grin, Mark chipped in, 'Good on you, Angry!' Angry yelled out that he was mean 'because I was in love with you, Chrissy!' Funny way to show it, don't you think! We then played a blistering set, and ripped the Regent apart.

Mark and I got on well, considering what happened between us before and that we'd scarcely spoken in years because his only email contact is via his girlfriend. He is not into computers. He can be so sweet. Deep down he has a poet's heart. At the Hall of Fame, Mark asked me, 'What's up with your leg? You're limping.' I replied, 'Nothing. I'm fine.' I was taking my medication religiously, and my determination was not to succumb to my illness, and to keep moving.

Then there was our controversial appearance on the final of the TV talent show *Australian Idol*, early in December that year. One of the contestants had sung 'Boys in Town' and it had gone down well with a whole new generation of music fans so we were invited to perform on the show's finale. It wasn't our scene at all, but we agreed to hype our tour which was about to commence, and our new CD.

Rumours were spreading by then that I was drinking or on drugs because I had fallen and stumbled a few times in public. Then, on *Australian Idol*, after we performed we were interviewed by the host Andrew G. All was well until it turned out that the show's satellite had crashed midway through our song, so we had to do it all again. They quickly pulled the set together as it had been half broken down, and we ran to our places from everywhere. Charley walked to the drum kit and away we went, again.

By the time Andrew G approached me with his microphone to re-do our interview, I was pumped with adrenalin and feeling pleased we had pulled off the performance on live TV without a hitch or glitch. As a joke (and referring to the fact that we'd completed our interview only a short time before) I looked at him with a confused expression and said, 'Oh, who are you?' Everyone thought I was being rude to him. I wasn't, I was just trying to be cute. The rumours that I was off my face intensified.

So to put an end to the whispers, which could have hurt the tour, and hopefully to inspire some other MS sufferers, I went on 'A Current Affair' with a sensitive Richard Wilkins and came out about my illness. I reiterated that not all people with MS had led the rock'n'roll life, and that I had stopped drinking eleven years previously. I wanted to alert fans that if they bought a ticket to a Divinyls gig, I might well fall over. My statement made front page news all over the country. I made it clear how hard it was for me to go public about my condition, and bridled when it was suggested that I was only doing it to sell tickets.

The tour went well. I didn't fall over on stage. The crowds loved seeing us again and our reviews were good. It took us no time to get into the zone. There were fewer histrionics but more music, and that reflected where we were at the time. Older and wiser but still rock'n'roll. I felt the band was better than ever, and that I was singing as well as I ever had. In a strange way, my MS improved my singing. I was moving around less!

It's not a chore for me to sing the old Divinyls songs. I never forget the words, they're in my body. To me they never get stale. I imbue them with what I'm feeling at exactly the time I sing them and that keeps them as fresh as the day we wrote them. And while the new material was well received by audiences, I was disappointed that we couldn't get any of it played on radio.

When we finished the first leg of the tour I was elated and deeply satisfied with how it had progressed. I couldn't wait to go on the road again in March. Andrew was especially looking forward to the second leg of the tour, because excitement about us was in the air and he would get a financial return on the pretty large sums he had outlaid so far.

Then, without warning, Mark McEntee pulled the plug. He was oddly incommunicado for a while and then, on the phone, he told Andrew that he didn't want to play some of the shows on the tour, and that he had commitments back in Perth. He would not be talked out of his decision to stay in Perth and help Melanie with her fashion business. He left Andrew, and the rest of us, high and dry. I feel so sad for Andrew, who backed us and lost a lot of money. I feel sorry for the band members who turned down other lucrative gigs and reorganised their lives to tour with Divinyls. I've not spoken to Mark since, so I have no idea why he made the decision, but without him there is no Divinyls.

I'd always denied that the band ever broke up—saying that we were still together, but 'just weren't playing at the moment'. Today, in the light of Mark's not wanting to tour, I am finally prepared to say that Divinyls *are* dead. Let him help Melanie sell her clothes, let him make his model aeroplanes. I don't care. I wish him well.

Very early the following year, 2008, I was back home in New York when a girlfriend sent me an email from a young Australian woman with MS who had gone blind and couldn't walk. She had been cured after six ayahuasca ceremonies with an Austrian neurologist and now head of shamanism for the Ecuadorian government, named Dr Valentin Hampejs, who lived on a small farm with his family in the Venezualan Andes. The ceremony involves the ingestion, accompanied by praying, rituals and the use of religious iconography, of a beverage extracted from the rare female ayahuasca vine, a plant with chemical properties that can induce altered states in human beings and so heal or change attitudes.

I checked out Dr Hampejs' credentials, contacted him and for around $US2000 booked three weeks at his retreat in the mountains. I then fasted for a month, and stopped taking any medication—no Copaxone, no sleeping pills, no anti-depressants—because it could react with the ayahuasca.

Charley knew how desperate I was to go to see Dr Valentin, which is what I came to call him, so he didn't try to talk me out of what was, at best, an uncertain trip and at worst, a dangerous trip. Many friends did—to no avail. They told me I was crazy, but I was doing this to get well and also to prove that I could still function by going alone on a great adventure.

On 27 February 2008, my alarm woke me at 3 a.m. I climbed out of bed, showered and collected my bags, then Charley drove me to the airport. On the day I had gone to book my ticket, a 49-seater plane, just like the one I would later be flying in, crashed into a mountain with everyone killed when the pilot got lost in fog, so I was feeling even more anxious than normal as I began my journey. Nothing, however, was going to deter me. I was determined to see this shaman, praying that what he had achieved for the Australian girl he could also do for me.

I flew from JFK Airport to Caracas, Venezuela, then boarded the 49-seater, which took me without any mishap over the stunning scenery of the Andes to the town of Mérida. The connection to

Mérida at Caracas was tight so I jumped into the first wheelchair I saw at the airport and, after I'd greased an attendant's palm with a little money, he wheeled me past the queues and onto the plane. As I sat there with the little plane's motor thrumming as it taxied down the rugged airstrip I felt exultant: I was in South America, on my own, totally free and loving it. And maybe, I hoped against hope, my MS would soon be a thing of the past.

At Mérida airport I hailed a taxi and took a two-and-a-half-hour ride to where Dr Valentin had arranged to meet me, at the foot of the mountain. That night, when I clambered out of the cab, hot and dusty, he was waiting for me.

The celebrated shaman looked suitably Biblical. He had long, grey, flowing hair, a thick grey beard, and clenched a pipe in his tobacco-stained teeth. Short and slight, he wore a flannel shirt, work trousers, sandals and socks.

Dr Valentin left me in the care of a woman and her daughter, neither of whom spoke English. He told me he would pick me up in the morning and we would take the bus to his farm on the mountaintop for the ceremonies. He then disappeared into the cold and inky Venezuelan night.

The woman cooked me a lovely meal and showed me to my room, a simple space with a mosaic floor made of broken tiles. Eventually the electricity buzzed on. The bathroom was outside. All night the mosquitoes chewed at me and by the next morning, when Dr Valentin came to take me up the mountain, I was a mass of red bites.

As we waited for the bus, the shaman asked me what I did for a living and I replied, 'I'm a rock star.' I said it tongue in cheek, but he obviously thought I was silly. I thought, 'Oh God, I've said the wrong thing, now I'm in for it.'

As we sat together on the grass by the roadside for a bit, he asked me if I'd been sexually abused as a child. I said I hadn't but my father had been a bit of a tyrant. Later, for what reason I still do not know, he told me that Charley did not love me, so I called Charley in New

York and told him what the man had said. I then put Charley and Dr Valentin together on the phone and they spoke. Charley is used to me putting him on the spot! Dr Valentin never said such a thing to me again, although I later learned he and his wife Edna thought it strange that I had ventured to the Andes for treatment all alone.

Eventually the bus came, and took us up into the truly spectacular Andes, winding ever higher through scrub and sky-scraping trees. In due course we were dropped about 800 metres from the top of the mountain. The road had become a rough path and the bus could go no further. At the place where the bus stopped roamed a pack of mangy dogs, some of which were pregnant.

From out of the trees emerged a group of workers from Dr Valentin's farm, with a donkey. For me. I said, 'Gammy foot and bad balance or not, I'm not being carried up the mountain like some kind of princess and, besides, the donkey has no saddle and I'll slide off.' With only my cane and Dr Valentin as support, I climbed, tripped and stumbled the remaining distance up the rough-hewn, circuitous pathway, past the pools of trout and stunning vistas while eagles soared above us in a sky so blue it hurt my eyes. It was magical.

After two and a half hours of plodding, my limbs screaming at every step, Dr Valentin and I arrived at his farm, where the healing ceremonies would take place. I met Edna, a kind and lovely Colombian woman wearing a headband with lots of patterns and colour, who spoke no English. Their home, surrounded by cacti and livestock, was even more rudimentary than the place in which I'd slept the previous night. There was no hot water or electricity, and an outside toilet down the hill was accessible only by a precarious pathway. In the black night when nature called, I stumbled and fell and rolled down the hill to the loo.

Candles and religious icons were the only decorations in the farmhouse. Dr Valentin's office was at the side, with all his herbs and potions. I slept outside in a tent, among the donkeys, roosters and hens. I had to put newspaper under my sleeping bag because the cold seeped up from the ground.

The food was vegetables, vegetables and more vegetables, and some corn meal for variety, all of which I couldn't eat yet as I had to fast before my first ceremony.

When I woke the next morning, Dr Valentin, an Italian student named Mario, and Leonardo, a 15-year-old who worked on the farm, and I climbed to the ceremonial place, another 300 or so metres up the mountain. I could see the village far below and the wheeling, swooping eagles overhead seemed close enough to reach up and touch.

The ceremony began just before nightfall. After placing deities, candles and condor feathers on his altar, Dr Valentin lit the sacred fireplace and we had to walk around it clockwise. Then we sat on benches under a canopy and the stars while he chanted prayers. He prayed to many different angels, and in a variety of languages. I realised in the middle of these prayers that I was totally ignorant of any kind of theology.

Dr Valentin told us that he was making us safe for 150 miles around us. He then produced cigars made of raw tobacco from Ecuador and asked us to smoke them and blow smoke north, south, east and west in the direction of the angels that were protecting us from the four points of the compass. As the night wore on, a thick mist descended on us. By the light of the fire, Dr Valentin produced a liquid which was raw tobacco juice and I had to lie very still while he squirted it, into first my left nostril and then my right—and swallow it. The tobacco juice, the vilest stuff I've ever tasted, coursed down my throat. I vomited and vomited, purging my stomach. The others followed suit. Mario and Leonardo were particularly dramatic at this stage of the ceremony. Dr Valentin also took part.

When I stopped purging, Dr Valentin gave me a peppermint-tasting concoction that took away the foul taste of the juice. This was followed by a shot glass full of ayahuasca beverage made from the vine. I sat on the ground and watched the fire.

As I lay there, waiting for the potion to work its magic and rid me of my MS, Dr Valentin sang songs I had never heard before; some were childlike but they all lifted my spirits. He spoke of angels and prayed and sang in a beautiful voice. My mind roamed free and my multiple sclerosis seemed a bad dream. It was transcendingly beautiful, so beautiful I almost forgot I was literally freezing. I had enjoyed the experience but I was very glad when morning came and brought with it a blazing sun. When the ceremony was over, Dr Valentin told me that 'Mother Ayahuasca has been very gentle with you.'

Edna came with breakfast and then we had a water ceremony to finish. We slowly made our way back to the farm. Crawling into my tent, I slept for 24 hours. I woke up with the sun in my tent and Dr Valentin's grandson exhorting me to come with him to eat his grandfather's rabbit stew. I definitely felt energised. There would be five more ceremonies.

I didn't make it past the third. After I had taken the tobacco juice down my nostrils once more and drunk the plant medicine, I had a vision, and it was vivid and real. I saw Jesus Christ nailed to the cross. I could see and hear the crowd of mourners wailing and I was among them and I could see Christ's terrible wounds. I heard the roar of thousands of locusts. This vision lasted for four hours and it was truly awful. I tried at one point to crack a joke, for some light relief, but even as I was telling it, the joke seemed out of place and insignificant and it was lost on all. I felt very small.

I dug my bare feet into the loose soil and gazed into the fire, my back freezing, pondering the fact that Mother Nature was a woman too. I asked what she would want me to do right now. I then felt calm and relief as the sun rose.

When that ceremony ended at dawn, Edna came up with fresh-cut fruit and wanted to cut my hair off, saying illness was recorded in your hair. I laughed and said I wasn't ready to take that step. Then I saw Luisa, the beautiful Italian criminologist who had joined us for the second ceremony, drinking a glass of her own urine. Even though this is a common practice in Venezuela and some other South American countries, that did it. I laughed. I cried. I knew that I would not be doing any more ceremonies. It was time for me to go back down the mountain and back to civilisation.

Back in my tent, I slept heavily. I dreamed, of Charley, and Mark, and my life and what had become of it. When I woke, cold and covered in mozzie bites, I rose and washed all my dirty clothes then helped Edna with the cleaning. Dr Valentin was listening to music. Children were playing in the dirt in the sunshine. It was so simple and peaceful.

When I informed Dr Valentin that I was returning to New York, he told me I was a baby and asked, 'Don't you want to be a warrior?' His words stung me. I've been many things, but never a quitter.

Dr Valentin helped me down the mountain and then we caught a taxi to the hotel in Mérida where I would stay the night before catching the plane to Caracas, and then on to New York the next day. We parted on good terms with a big hug and I told him the truth: that my two weeks with him and his family had been an amazing adventure and I'd like to have another shot at ayahuasca, but next time I would need to bring a friend who got my jokes, or at least spoke English.

Whatever, trying ayahuasca made me more self-aware and opened my mind to the possibility that maybe there was an alternative medicine treatment that may help me deal with my MS. The Indians had been practising ayahuasca for thousands of years.

My vision of Jesus Christ had made me determined to keep my suffering to myself and not inflict it on others. To be brave and accept my condition, keep moving and live life as best I can.

I caught the elevator up to my hotel room. I hoped with all my heart it would be a clean and happy place, where I could recover from the freezing nights on the mountain. No such luck. It was revolting, scuzzy-dirty and reeking of stale tobacco and indescribably bad food smells. There was no way I was sleeping in the sheets of that bed, so I rolled my sleeping bag out and slept miserably on top of the covers. It was the best hotel in Mérida too!

Morning came at last and I caught a taxi to the airport; six hours later I was in Charley's arms at JFK Airport. Never had I been so happy to see my husband. When I arrived back at my apartment in New York he told me there was a present for me from Keith Richards. It was a beautiful little antique pillowslip and a note: 'Dear Chrissy, put some down in it. Love Keith.' A profound statement after what I'd just been through.

Sadly, no sooner had I settled back into life in Riverdale than I learned that my mother was dying.

MY MOTHER—AND HOPE

At Christmas in 2007, Charley and I had gone to Australia and celebrated with Mum and my sister Leigh at Leigh's home in Apollo Bay, with my nephew Matt and his beautiful wife Chelsea, and my dear old friends Anne and Tom. It was a very different Christmas to the one eleven years earlier. Mum was more frail than I had ever seen her but she was happy.

We were all together.

Andrew McManus kindly loaned us his Bentley car and Charley and I took Mum on trips along the winding country roads. She sat in the backseat wearing a Christmas cowboy hat.

After the festive break I returned to New York, and my Venezuelan adventure followed. Before I left for South America, I called Mum and offered to postpone the trip to be with her, but she insisted, 'Darling, go up the mountain. You've got to climb that mountain.'

By the time my ayahuasca experience was over and I was back home, Mum's health had worsened. Looking back now, I know in my heart that another reason I felt I had to leave Dr Valentin and come home was that my mother was calling to me. She was telling me it was her time to make her transition.

The call revealing to me that Mum's life was drawing to a close came from Pam, the kind lady who lived across the road from her in Geelong. Pam said Mum was in bad shape but refusing to go to hospital. I immediately phoned Mum and told her I was on my way to see her. I asked why she didn't want to go to hospital and she replied, 'Because I'm afraid I'll never come out.' I said she simply had to check herself in, and that I would be there in a day or two. 'I'll come like I always have, and I'll get you out of hospital when you're better.' Very reluctantly, she packed her bag.

When I arrived at the John of God Hospital in Geelong, Mum was lying in her bed in her room. She looked tiny. She recognised me but had trouble speaking because she'd lost her voice yelling at her friend, Barbie, the nurse who was looking in on her at home and trying to persuade her to enter hospital.

I arrived laden with crosses and healing music I'd brought down from the mountain. I placed the crosses around the room and played the music. Even though her voice was only a whisper she burst out laughing. My sister left the room.

Mum's mind was still strong, it was just that her eighty-one-year-old body had given up. She'd had heart disease since she was eighteen, but now, at the end, there was nothing specifically wrong with her, just that once-indomitable body finally breaking down and wearing out. She was beyond having operations. In her final days she had no patience for anything trivial or petty. She was in a wonderful, peaceful state of mind. Sometimes, no doubt dreaming of other times, she played piano in the air.

At the hospital was a thanatologist, an expert in the many issues of those dying. He played calming harp music in the hospital corridors, and in the next days as Mum lapsed into the final stages and her breathing became laboured, he came into the room, sat by her bed, and played his harp in the same rhythm as her breathing.

Mum lingered for three weeks. Leigh and I were with her all the time. Leigh would spend the day in the room and me, ever the night owl, would come at night. I'm sure it was a comfort to my mother knowing her two daughters were there. I talked to her and fussed over her. We read her body language when she couldn't speak. We held her hand and wiped her brow and rubbed her back and moistened her dry lips with Vaseline. I played soothing classical music. Andrew McManus came and sat at her bedside, holding her hand.

Once Mum sat up, pulled me close and whispered in a raspy voice, 'I can't talk to anyone when they come. I just want to die.'

Two days later, on 9 April 2008, she got her wish. Leigh, Barbie and I, the thanatologist, and my old friend Anne, who used to hitchhike to Torquay with me when I was a young girl, were there too.

The church was packed with more than 200 family and friends. Mum was a very popular person. She knew how to work a room. She never admitted to being older than 35 and could always make those lucky enough to be in her company laugh. In the congregation were Mum's dear mate Mary Walker and my ballet teacher Miss Hannah. Charley flew in, and Jerome Smith from the Divinyls. As her coffin was carried out of the church and placed into the hearse, her favourite record was played, Rod Stewart's version of 'Thanks for the Memories'. Mum loved Rod. When the hearse was driven away everyone gave three cheers.

Afterwards, we held Mum's wake in a light, airy reception room by the river. A young man whose family was close friends with Mum played bagpipes in her honour. I remembered how he would play his latest song for her on our front lawn, and how the sound would wake me up when I was staying with Mum.

Charley went around and photographed every single person at the wake for the official record. He was such a support, so thoughtful and sweet. Relatives of mine had been put off by this exotic black man, but when they saw his sweetness at close range, and were the recipients of it themselves, they knew why I loved him and they loved him too.

Typically, Mum had left her affairs in perfect order, but as executor of her will, I still had a lot to do, and it wasn't until I returned to

New York a few weeks later that I was able to grieve. Charley had to go to play in Japan and I was left alone in our apartment.

I thought of Mum and her hard life and how my father, to my knowledge, had never said one kind, let alone loving, word to her and how she deserved so much more. I grieved hard, my feelings of inconsolable sadness no doubt exacerbated by my MS. I had an acute sense of how short life is and in birth and death there are definite bookends with not much in between. I lay on my bed and dealt with my grief. It was as if Mum's passing had left me with a big hole in my stomach. With time the hole filled up. I wasn't so sad. A joyous love for Mum was all that was left.

Today, life goes on. My days and nights are spent managing my illness. I live in hope that a cure will be found. After all, ten years ago immunity balancers like Copaxone were unheard of.

Charley remains my rock, and soulmate. His career is going well: he is in demand from some of the world's top artists to tour with them and play on their records. He played with Simon and Garfunkel on their 2009 tour. When he was with them in Australia, I joined him and it was an experience flying around in a private jet. What a far cry from Divinyls days.

It makes me proud that Charley is held in such high esteem by his peers. His musical knowledge is vast and he can play any style of music. He prepares painstakingly, and by the time he goes into rehearsal he has already done so much work.

He's away a bit, but we're at home together for long stretches too. He is so protective and caring. Not long ago, I was out with friends in Manhattan and time got away from me. When I finally arrived home at 3 a.m., Charley informed me that he'd reported me missing to the police as being out late was so out of character! The last he'd spoken to me was at an ATM around 6 p.m. and he'd thought I'd been abducted. We're a bit like Lucy and Ricky from the old TV show. When I'm late or forgetful or come home with a stray dog he'll put on a Cuban accent and say, 'Chrissy, you got a lot of ess-plainin' to do!'

Ours is a peaceful home, a sanctuary from the harshness of the world outside. We don't argue . . . well, maybe once in a blue moon. We wake up happy to see each other, and Holiday.

I married into a great New York music family. I've already talked of Charley's and his father's and grandfather's musical pedigrees. His dad Bernard walks around the house in a cloud of jazz. He is so knowledgeable about jazz and the blues, as are all his friends.

I'll never forget his 65th birthday party at Charley's parents' brownstone home in Park Slopes, Brooklyn. Isadora, Charley's mother asked me, as a party piece, to sing for all these musical aficionados. Charley said, 'Don't! You *don't* have to do this!' I was terrified at the prospect of laying myself so bare, but by now you'll know I don't back down from a creative challenge. I said to Charley, 'You know what, I *am* going to sing "I Touch Myself".' I composed myself for about an hour, and then I marched into the dining room and sang my song in a soulful, gospel way, a cappella. It brought the house down. The guests were saying, 'Wow!' and 'Mmmm, she's good! Mmmmm, Mmmmmm!' Charley relaxed. Isadora was proud too. Charley's Uncle Peter said to me, 'You're so brave. I have such respect for you.' I'd passed the test. Even Bernard seemed to approve. It only took me ten years!

In December 2008, Charley and I were invited to another 65th birthday party: Keith Richards', and also his and Patti Hansen's 25th wedding anniversary. Keith confided in me he has always really needed to do something new creatively. I could empathise with what he was saying. It is possible to be captive to an era, a set of songs and an image. That's why I had to step out and do *Blood Brothers* and *The Boy From Oz*. I had to go in other directions.

At the party, I wore a beautiful purse over my shoulder. It had a unicorn on it, carved especially for the evening by my friend Joyce Frances. It also had a bright light inside. Charley said it was too bright, and I should turn it down, but it was wonderful. Patti immediately ordered ten from Joyce for her 'girls' Christmas presents. Each one would have a different theme, from wolves to frogs. (Danielle, the French wife of Terry Ellis, who ran Chrysalis Records, once told me that if you were feeling shy, take a great purse to a party and it would be a talking point.)

I love music more and more, and it has become a powerful weapon in my anti-MS armoury. It doesn't matter what kind of music you love, it can transport you and elevate your emotions, your spirit. It can make you happy and turn your mind from pain and sadness. It takes you to another world far away from the mundane everyday existence most of us must live. It can turn a bad day into a good day. It sweetens life. I guess it's part of my purpose.

But sometimes, like now, tonight, I like quiet.

As I sit, finishing this last chapter in my autobiography on the porch of Sandrine and Will's home in Connecticut, it's getting late. I look up and notice the fireflies have departed, gone to wherever fireflies spend the night. A full moon has risen above the trees and is illuminating the grounds like a Klieg light and the warm summer breeze rustles the leaves in trees and the creek tinkles at the bottom of the garden, just as it did when the Mohawk Indians hunted here centuries ago.

Soon I'll take my medication and go to bed, hopefully to sleep soundly and wake refreshed to take on a brand new day.

I will continue to see my neurologist, to take my treatment, and to stay tuned for medical breakthroughs. I seem to have not got worse than that first MS episode when I was diagnosed. Still, every day the sensory symptoms of the nerve pathways are different. I try not to whine and complain. When someone asks me how I am I say, 'Very well, thank you.' Whether I am or not.

Too many people can only see what's wrong. MS has trained me to see what's *right*. Trained me to treasure the little things that make life wonderful. When I was on the mountain I was so grateful for the warmth of the sun when daylight broke, so grateful for a mouthful of clean fresh water. These things I had always taken for granted, but not anymore. Never again.

I try to eat real, not processed, food, to stay hydrated and get lots of sleep, and do what exercise I can. To keep moving.

I have experienced rudeness since I've had MS. Yet I have experienced far more kindness. I had no idea how kind people are. My intuition has developed. My illness has forced me to have empathy for myself, not to blame myself for what has happened to me, and, like the woman in the wheelchair on Madison Avenue, to have empathy for others.

Life is not over for me because I have multiple sclerosis. My last check-up showed no signs that my illness was actively progressing. My arms and legs stiffen some days, some days I am tired, but my heart, as ever, is filled with hope.

ACKNOWLEDGMENTS

Special thanks to Larry Writer—what a huge and thorough job it's been, involving many, many hours of sometimes difficult interviews in Australia, New York and London over the past fourteen months to arrive at the truth of my life and career. It has been a journey for me uncovering the past.

And to Mathew Kelly.

Vanessa Radnidge, Fran Moore, Kylie Kwong, Kurt Baker, Anne and Tom Abrahams, Gail Vogel, Rob Leskovac, Dear Denise, Leigh Moon, Bernard and Isadora Drayton, Holiday, Andy Palmer, Phil Mortlock, Vince Wilburn Jnr, Tracy McArdle and Staff, Tess Streilen.

The following people have generously given their time, memories and cooperation to help tell my story.

Mary Amphlett   Candy Raymond
Patricia Amphlett   Stuart Coupe
Mary Walker   Anthony O'Grady
Janice Smith   Shayna Stewart
Alison Baker   Richard Harvey
Chris Stockley   Vince Lovegrove

Denise Fraser

Rick Grossman

Tony Mott

Phil Stafford

Kate Ceberano

Chris Bastic

Roger Watson

Phil Kaufman

Andrew McManus

Danny Hiller

Wilton Morley

Peter Cousens

Charley Drayton

Charlie Owen

Biccy Henderson

Joe Turtur

Kevin Shirley

Sam Righi

Stephen MacLean

Ben Gannon

Jenni Fairs (who was a researcher in the early months)

Sue Jamieson (who transcribed hours of interviews)

RAM magazine

Rolling Stone

PHOTO ACKNOWLEDGMENTS

All photos courtesy Chrissy Amphlett and the Amphlett family except for those credited below.

Every effort has been made to acknowledge and contact the owners of copyright for permission to reproduce material which falls under the 1968 Copyright Act. Any copyright owners who have inadvertently been omitted from acknowledgments and credits should contact the publisher and omissions will be rectified in subsequent editions.

Picture section one
Page 6: Top left, Vicki Caton
Page 7: *Australasian Post*

Picture section two
Page 3: Tony Mott.
Page 4: All photos by Tony Mott.
Page 5: Top three images courtesy Tony Mott; image of Chrissy pointing by Bob King.

Page 6: Divinyls onstage, Tony Mott.

Page 7: Band photo, Tony Mott.

Page 8: Chrissy ironing by Melanie Nissen.

Picture section three

Page 1: Photo of Mark and Chrissy, Tony Notaberadino.

Page 2: Chrissy sitting, Tony Mott.

Page 3: Both images courtesy Monty Adams.

Page 4: Chrissy and Michael Hutchence, Tony Mott.

Page 5: All images courtesy Monty Adams.

Page 6: Rick and Chrissy, Rick Grossman's collection; about to go onstage, Monty Adams.

Page 7: Chrissy as Judy Garland, courtesy Charley Drayton; leaning against car, Tony Notaberadino; image of Charley Drayton, Hugh Stewart.

Page 8: Chrissy with Charlie Owen, Peter Carrette, www.iconimages.com.au

THE ALBUMS